Teach
— LIKE A —
CHAMPION

FIELD GUIDE
2.0

A PRACTICAL RESOURCE TO
MAKE THE 62 TECHNIQUES YOUR OWN

Doug Lemov, Joaquin Hernandez, Jennifer Kim

JB JOSSEY-BASS™
A Wiley Brand

Uncommon
Schools | Change History.

Published by Jossey-Bass
A Wiley Brand
One Montgomery Street, Suite 1000, San Francisco, CA 94104–4594—www.josseybass.com

Jossey-Bass books and products are available through most bookstores. To contact Jossey-Bass directly call our Customer Care Department within the U.S. at 800–956–7739, outside the U.S. at 317–572–3986, or fax 317–572–4002.

Wiley publishes in a variety of print and electronic formats and by print-on-demand. Some material included with standard print versions of this book may not be included in e-books or in print-on-demand. If this book refers to media such as a CD or DVD that is not included in the version you purchased, you may download this material at http://booksupport.wiley.com. For more information about Wiley products, visit www.wiley.com.

Library of Congress Cataloging-in-Publication Data

Names: Lemov, Doug, 1967- author. | Hernandez, Joaquin, 1985- author. | Kim, Jennifer, 1986 December 30- author.
Title: Teach like a champion 2.0 field guide: a practical resource to make the 62 techniques your own / Doug Lemov, Joaquin Hernandez, Jennifer Kim.
Description: San Francisco, CA: Jossey-Bass, 2016. | Includes bibliographical references and index.
Identifiers: LCCN 2016016202 (print) | LCCN 2016020992 (ebook) | ISBN 9781119254140 (pbk.) | ISBN 9781119254171 (pdf) | ISBN 9781119254157 (epub)
Subjects: LCSH: Effective teaching. | Academic achievement. | College preparation programs.
Classification: LCC LB1025.3 .L486 2016 (print) | LCC LB1025.3 (ebook) | DDC 371.102—dc23
LC record available at https://lccn.loc.gov/2016016202

Cover design: Wiley
Cover images: Provided by Jacob Krupnick and Yuriy Nutsa

Printed in the United States of America
FIRST EDITION

PB Printing   10 9 8 7 6 5

CONTENTS

PART 1   CHECK FOR UNDERSTANDING

CHAPTER 1   GATHERING DATA ON STUDENT MASTERY

Technique 1   REJECT SELF-REPORT   9

Replace functionally rhetorical questions with more objective forms of impromptu assessment.

Technique 2   TARGETED QUESTIONING   17

Ask a quick series of carefully chosen, open-ended questions directed at a strategic sample of the class.

Technique 3   STANDARDIZE THE FORMAT   25

Streamline observations by designing materials and space so that you're looking in a consistent place for the data you need.

Technique 4   TRACKING, NOT WATCHING   53

Be intentional about how you observe. Decide specifically what you're looking for and remain disciplined about it in the face of distractions.

Technique 5   SHOW ME   67

Flip the classroom dynamic. Have students actively show evidence of their understanding.

Use the checkboxes to track your progress through this *Field Guide*.

Making Progress	A Strength
○	○
○	○
○	○
○	○
○	○

	Making Progress	A Strength

	Making Progress	A Strength

		Making Progress	A Strength

DVD CONTENTS

For information on accessing the video clips on the *Teach Like a Champion* website, see How to Access the Video Contents near the end of the book. Please note that some of these clips also appear in *Teach Like a Champion 2.0.* In these cases, to help you easily locate where the clips appear in the main book, we've listed their clip number here.

Clip	Primary Technique(s)	Description	*TLAC 2.0* Clip
1	Standardize the Format	**Front Table:** Nicole Willey enhances her ability to monitor and support students who are struggling academically, by calling them to a separate table while the rest of the class works independently.	
2	Standardize the Format	**10 Minutes to IP:** Ijeoma Duru rolls out a set of codes for common errors to streamline the process of giving feedback to students during independent work.	
3	Tracking, Not Watching	**Yes, You Fixed It:** Megan Broome efficiently gathers mastery data and responds by providing students with feedback as she *Circulates.*	
4	Tracking, Not Watching	**Coefficient:** Taryn Pritchard records data she gathers while *Circulating* and then uses that to drive the whole-class discussion that follows.	
5	Show Me	**Spelling Words:** Amy Youngman collects data on student mastery by quickly scanning each student's answer to see whether it's correct.	Clip 1
6	Show Me	**Rock Paper Scissors:** Bryan Belanger uses tight systems for hand signals to efficiently assess student mastery.	
7	Show Me	**Show Me Montage:** Nicole Willey uses a creative twist on *Show Me* to efficiently gauge her students' comprehension of their shared text.	
8	Affirmative Checking	**Here's the Deal:** Bob Zimmerli sets "checkpoints" where students must check their answers with him before proceeding to more difficult problems.	Clip 5
9	Affirmative Checking	**Green Post-it:** Hilary Lewis uses a "ticket" system to check students' work before they move on to independent practice.	Clip 6

Clip	Primary Technique(s)	Description	TLAC 2.0 Clip
10	Culture of Error	**COE Montage:** Eight teachers use language to build classroom cultures in which students embrace opportunities to learn from their mistakes.	
11	Culture of Error	**Cents:** Janelle Duckett reinforces a culture in which struggling and then succeeding is normal, positive, and universal.	
12	No Opt Out	**Clever Fox:** Shadell Purefoy (Noel) asks a student to repeat a correct answer after she's unable to answer the first time.	Clip 12
13	No Opt Out	**Fifth Root:** Derek Pollak solicits help from the class when a student is very near to a correct answer.	Clip 10
14	No Opt Out	**Cosine:** With his neutral and nonjudgmental tone, Denarius Frazier conveys his confidence in his student's ability to get the right answer.	
15	Right Is Right	**Relentless on Right:** Maggie Johnson pushes students to use precise language to describe a particular scene.	
16	Right Is Right and Format Matters	**Paul's Explanation:** Nicole Willey prompts students to use more specific and technical vocabulary.	
17	Right Is Right	**Until Peaches:** Colleen Driggs persists in requiring a student to answer her original question.	
18	Stretch It	**Well Said:** Art Worrell stretches the original student and then begins stretching other students to build a rigorous classroom culture.	Clip 16
19	Stretch It	**Monster:** MK Pope rewards a student for a right answer with a harder question, and uses directive and nondirective prompting to get her students to the correct answer.	
20	Format Matters	**It Gots to Be:** Darryl Williams actively reinforces the language of opportunity by correcting informal phrases.	Clip 17
21	Format Matters	**Hither:** Beth Verrilli asks a student for more collegiate language.	Clip 18
22	Control the Game	**Two Times:** First-grade teacher Hilary Lewis facilitates *Control the Game* reading to her small group of reading students.	
23	Control the Game	**Grew Serious:** Reading teacher Maggie Johnson facilitates *Control the Game* reading to her eighth-grade students.	

Clip	Primary Technique(s)	Description	*TLAC 2.0* Clip
24	Circulate	**Circulate While Teaching:** Maggie Johnson and Julia Addeo *Circulate* strategically during *Control the Game* reading and teaching.	
25	Circulate	**Circulate during IP Montage:** Rue Ratray and Maura Faulkner *Circulate* strategically during independent work.	
26	Change the Pace	**Talk to Me:** Erin Michels spends a full ten minutes on a "fraction challenge" math problem, but her pacing feels fast.	Clip 22
27	Change the Pace and Everybody Writes	**Listen, Things Have Changed:** Jessica Bracey follows a stretch of reading with *Everybody Writes* to maintain a steady pace and prepare her students for a discussion about *Circle of Gold.*	Clip 23
28	Change the Pace	**Pencils Up:** Ashley Hinton puts together a number of pacing techniques to keep her class moving.	Clip 27
29	Change the Pace	**Who Can Give Me All Four:** Bridget McElduff is changing the format in a lesson about measurement conversions.	
30	Brighten Lines	**Expanded Form:** Sari Fromson *Brightens Lines* in her middle school math class with clean starts, clean finishes, and interactive lines.	
31	All Hands	**Decay:** Bryan uses *All Hands* to maintain strong pacing in his eighth-grade math class.	
32	All Hands	**Essential:** Lauren uses *All Hands* to maintain strong pacing in her first-grade class.	
33	Wait Time	**Focus on Why:** Maggie Johnson gives students think time, encouraging more reluctant scholars to participate.	Clip 29
34	Wait Time	**Wait Time Montage:** Yasmin Vargas and John Ratheram give students *Wait Time* and narrate hands to encourage student participation.	
35	Wait Time	**Wait Time Mini Practice:** Rue Ratray gives students the *Wait Time* they need to think through their answer to a rigorous question.	
36	Cold Call	**In Your Mind:** Jon Bogard makes his *Cold Calls* predictable and positive, including calling on one student whose "hand was up in [her] mind."	Clip 34
37	Cold Call	**Othello:** Beth Verrilli leads a discussion about the text, *Othello,* and builds a culture of engaged accountability through her *Cold Call.*	
38	Call and Response	**Birthdays:** Janelle keeps her students' responses sharp.	Clip 35

Clip	Primary Technique(s)	Description	*TLAC 2.0* Clip
39	Call and Response	**Read to Us:** Jennifer Trapp uses *Call and Response* to reinforce note-taking skills, grammar rules, and difficult pronunciations.	Clip 36
40	Show Call	**Which One Is Right:** Nicole Willey deepens students' grasp of a math problem by asking them to compare two pieces of work side by side and determine which is correct.	
41	Show Call	**Show Call:** Paul Powell normalizes the process of "good to great" and sends a very clear message about accountability for written work by *Show Calling* exemplary work.	Clip 41
42	Show Call	**Out of the Nest:** Sarah Lord responds to a student who seems reluctant about having his work shown, in a way that preserves the positivity and accountability of *Show Call.*	
43	Show Call	**Take and Reveal Montage:** Six teachers demonstrate a range of effective approaches for "taking" and "revealing" student work	
44	Turn and Talk	**Show Not Tell:** Laura Fern uses a number of different techniques to ensure efficiency, consistency, and rigor in her *Turn and Talks.*	Clip 46
45	Turn and Talk	**The Bitterings:** Eric Snider uses a series of efficient prompts and follow-ups to keep *Turn and Talks* accountable and efficient.	Clip 45
46	Turn and Talk	**Roller Coaster:** Ashley Hinton effectively manages what students do before, during, and after the *Turn and Talk* to increase rigor and participation.	
47	Threshold and Strong Start	**Boston Is the Best:** Shadell Purefoy greets each student at the threshold of her classroom.	
48	Threshold, Strong Start, and Strategic Investment	**Thank You for Knowing What to Do:** Stephen Chiger welcomes each student into the classroom, leading them into their entry routine.	Clip 47
49	Strong Start	**Transition to Review Now:** Four teachers use different approaches to seamlessly transition their students to a review of the *Do Now.*	
50	Strong Start	**Complementary Angles:** Katie Bellucci skillfully manages routines for how students enter class, complete the *Do Now,* and transition to a review of the *Do Now.*	
51	STAR/SLANT	**Track Me:** Caitlin Reilly invests students in SLANT by explaining the purpose behind it.	

Clip	Primary Technique(s)	Description	TLAC 2.0 Clip
52	STAR/SLANT	**SLANT Montage:** Four teachers demonstrate various ways to reinforce and remind students to SLANT.	
53	Engineer Efficiency	**Sonnet:** Julia Goldenheim facilitates a series of effective housekeeping routines to ensure that no instructional time goes to waste.	
54	Culture of Error, Turn and Talk, and Strategic Investment	**Closest to the Door:** Erin Krafft effectively installs procedures for agreeing and disagreeing with a partner during *Turn and Talk*.	
55	Strategic Investment	**Stand Up: Group A:** Nikki Bowen works through procedures with her students until they become second nature and support student autonomy.	Clip 49
56	Strategic Investment	**Transfer Ownership:** Sari Fromson effectively transfers ownership of class routines to students over time.	
57	Do It Again	**Do It Again Montage:** This montage shows six different teachers reinforcing their expectations by asking students to *Do It Again*.	
58	Radar/Be Seen Looking	**Pencils Down in Three:** Kerri Rizzolo uses excellent technique to make sure students meet her expectations.	
59	Radar/Be Seen Looking	**Be Seen Looking/Radar Montage:** Patrick Pastore and Rodolpho Loureiro routinely scan from "Pastore's Perch" with a swivel to make sure they are seen looking for follow-through on their directions.	
60	Radar/Be Seen Looking	**Be Seen Looking Dance Moves:** Akilah Bond and Denarius Frazier use a range of *Be Seen Looking* dance moves in different settings to emphasize that they are looking.	
61	Make Compliance Visible	**Show What You Know:** Amy Youngman *Makes Compliance Visible* to her students with visible commands like "pen caps on."	
62	Make Compliance Visible and Firm Calm Finesse	**I Need All Pencils:** Patrick Pastore *Makes Compliance Visible* during a transition, while exuding *Firm Calm Finesse*.	Clip 56
63	Least Invasive Intervention	**Least Invasive Montage:** Six teachers execute different levels of intervention to ensure students remain focused and hard at work.	
64	Art of the Consequence	**Blue Crayons:** Sarah Ott teaches her kindergarteners how to do classroom tasks such as coming together on her signal.	

Clip	Primary Technique(s)	Description	TLAC 2.0 Clip
65	Art of the Consequence and Emotional Constancy	**Examine:** Bridget McElduff demonstrates a number of techniques while giving a productive consequence.	Clip 66
66	Art of the Consequence	**Blow-Up Practice:** Hilary Lewis and Jacobi Clifton practice giving a consequence to a student who then reacts negatively.	
67	Strong Voice	**Good Question:** Ijeoma Duru exudes confidence and poise as she gives directions for independent work.	
68	Strong Voice	**That's One Way:** Laura Fern uses a self-interrupt that illustrates principles of *Strong Voice.*	Clip 46
69	Strong Voice and Emotional Constancy	**Inappropriate Time:** Christy Lundy avoids engaging in a disagreement between two students and calmly shifts their attention back to the lesson.	
70	What to Do	**Prime the Pump:** Art Worrell delivers clear *What to Do* to facilitate a transition between a stretch of whole-class review and his introduction to a unit of study.	
71	Positive Framing	**Positive Framing Montage:** Emily Bisso responds to off-task behavior with language that motivates students and shows she assumes the best.	
72	Precise Praise	**Kudos:** Stephen Chiger doubles back to help a student better see how and why she was successful.	Clip 73
73	Warm/Strict	**Warm Formal:** Kesete Thompkins is both warm and strict as he greets students in the hallway.	
74	Joy Factor	**Who Wants a Word:** Julie Jackson cultivates joy during a vocabulary activity with elements of suspense and surprise.	
75	Joy Factor	**Phantom:** Roberto de Léon makes the act of reading joyful.	Clip 75

ACKNOWLEDGMENTS

Our first debt of gratitude in writing this volume is to teachers—those we've studied and those we've not yet had the chance to meet—for the work they do and for what they've taught us about their craft and profession. You do this work under challenging conditions: one oft-jammed copier for thirty-two people, say, pay and status not always worthy of your role in society and, of course, depending on the grade level you teach, the profession most likely to make you or someone you work with cry during a typical day.

We offer additional thanks to those teachers who we were fortunate enough to observe, either through video or in-person classroom observations. Many shared their lesson plans. Others also passed along student work. Or they answered our questions, our follow-up questions, and then our lingering just-wondering-but-I-promise-this-will-be-the-last-email questions. We've learned so much from them that we had to honor their work by including their materials, ideas, and classroom videos in this book.

Among this crop of generous teachers, some of the most helpful and giving include: Bryan Belanger, Vicki Hernandez, Erica Lim, Kathryn Orfuss, Patrick Pastore, Jen Rugani, Beth Verrilli, and Nicole Willey.

Even with all that great advice, we still had to put this book together. For that, we drafted—it was close to a demand, honestly—the services of the consummately professional Alan Venable, without whose skill and insight we would surely still be slogging away at the first technique. Our editor at Jossey-Bass, Kate Gagnon, has been patient, supportive, and incisive. Our agent Rafe Sagalyn was trusty and wise as ever, prompting us to wonder if we are the first to wonder if sagacious is the root of Sagalyn?

In addition to writing this together we are all three, in our day jobs, members of the Uncommon Schools Teach Like a Champion team. If ever there was a team of all-stars—we mean them, not us—that was also greater than the sum of its parts, ours is that team and the good parts of this book reflect how much we value and learn from the rest of the gang: John Costello, Dan Cotton, Colleen Driggs, Vinnie Hines, Maggie Johnson, Tracey Koren, Hilary Lewis, Rob Richard, and Erica Woolway. The bad parts of the book, by the way, are Doug's fault. Just in case you were keeping track.

The other piece of producing a book like this is the knowledge and perspective gained from working as the part of a larger organization—Uncommon Schools—that runs schools that strive every day to serve the families we care so much about. It's very hard work. It involves making mistakes and learning from them as quickly and as well as possible, and so we are grateful to the students, parents, teachers, and administrators at Uncommon's forty-four schools for their role in making this book possible.

In addition, each of us has some individual thank you's that have come due:

Joaquin: A huge thank you to my family for their unconditional support, patience, and encouragement. And a special thanks to my wife Vicki, who was there for me during my most stressful moments and who did everything she could to allow me the time and space that I needed to finish this project. I wouldn't have been able to do it without her. Also, a final thank you to my colleagues on the Teach Like A Champion Team, who were there at every step to bounce ideas, exchange resources, and share feedback on drafts. If you find the book useful in any way, it's because of them.

Jen: Many thanks to my current and former colleagues who work tirelessly to advocate for and educate all children. I am humbled and honored to share what I've learned from you all. To my mother who empowers with her silent strength, my father whose dreams provided us with seemingly endless opportunities, and my sister Jessica who is my best friend. And, of course, my FABULOUS friends who give endless support and encouragement!

Doug: Thank you most of all to my family. To my wife Lisa for trying all sixty-two techniques and possibly a few more to help bring out my best; and to my three children who, as they have grown up, have taught me much by describing the experience of learning and school from the student's perspective, and who, if I am doing my job, know how much I love them without my saying it. But, heck, I'm gonna say it anyway. Caden, Maia, Willa—I love you. Now go do your homework.

THE AUTHORS

Doug Lemov is a managing director of Uncommon Schools, which runs forty-four high-performing urban charter schools in the Northeast. He focuses his work on teacher training based on the study and analysis of high-performing teachers. In addition to *Teach Like a Champion 2.0*, Doug is co-author of *Practice Perfect* and *Reading Reconsidered*. He has shared the results of his study of high-performing teachers with school leaders and teachers around the world through workshops and speaking as well as his writing. He lives in upstate New York with his wife, Lisa, and their three children. Visit him at http://teachlikeachampion.com/blog/.

Joaquin Hernandez is an associate director of professional development at Uncommon Schools. In this role, he screens footage of classrooms, provides in-depth analysis of great teaching, and designs training for use inside and outside of Uncommon. Prior to this role, Joaquin worked as a high school history teacher in Washington, DC. He also coached and trained teachers as a manager, teacher leadership development for Teach For America. He holds a BA from Stanford University and an MAT from American University.

Jennifer Kim is an associate director of professional development at Uncommon Schools and works on its Teach Like a Champion team. She studies classroom instruction to identify highly effective teachers and instructional coaching practices, designs training for use inside and outside of Uncommon Schools, facilitates professional development, and helps drive special projects on the team. Prior to joining Uncommon, Jennifer taught in Brooklyn, New York, and served as the upper school writing lead. She began her teaching career as a Teach For America corps member in the Bronx, New York. Jennifer holds a BA in philosophy and political science from Baylor University and an MS in teaching from Pace University.

ABOUT UNCOMMON SCHOOLS

At Uncommon Schools, our mission is to start and manage outstanding urban public schools that close the achievement gap and prepare low-income scholars to enter, succeed in, and graduate from college. For the past twenty years, we have learned countless lessons about what works in classrooms. Not surprisingly, we have found that success in the classroom is closely linked to our ability to hire, develop, and retain great teachers and leaders. That has prompted us to invest heavily in training educators and building systems that help leaders to lead, teachers to teach, and students to learn. We are passionate about finding new ways for our scholars to learn more today than they did yesterday, and to do so, we work hard to ensure that every minute matters.

We know that many educators, schools, and school systems are interested in the same things we are interested in: practical solutions for classrooms and schools that work, can be performed at scale, and are accessible to anyone. We are fortunate to have had the opportunity to observe and learn from outstanding educators—both within our schools and from around the world—who help all students achieve at high levels. Watching these educators at work has allowed us to derive, codify, and film a series of concrete and practical findings about what enables great instruction. We have been excited to share these findings in such books as *Teach Like a Champion 2.0* (and now the companion *Field Guide*); *Reading Reconsidered*; *Practice Perfect*; *Driven by Data*; *Leverage Leadership*; *Great Habits, Great Readers*; and *Get Better Faster*.

Doug Lemov has revolutionized teacher training through his work over the past decade to codify the drivers of great teaching. The *Teach Like a Champion 2.0 Field Guide*—co-authored by TLAC team members Joaquin Hernandez and Jennifer Kim—is a great resource for teachers committed to becoming even stronger in the classroom, by providing in-depth practice, reflections, and guidance that are based on the sixty-two techniques covered in *Teach Like a Champion 2.0*. We are confident that the *TLAC 2.0 Field Guide* will be an invaluable resource for ensuring that teachers have the practical resources they need to become more effective teachers.

We are deeply grateful to Doug, Joaquin, Jennifer, and the entire TLAC team at Uncommon Schools for all of their work in supporting teachers. As important, we are excited for the impact this guide will have on teachers and students around the world.

Brett Peiser
Chief Executive Officer
Uncommon Schools

Uncommon Schools is a nonprofit network of forty-nine high-performing urban public charter schools that prepare nearly sixteen thousand low-income K–12 students in New York, New Jersey, and Massachusetts to graduate from college. A 2013 CREDO study found that for low-income students who attend Uncommon Schools, Uncommon "completely cancel[s] out the negative effect associated with being a student in poverty." Uncommon Schools was named the winner of the national 2013 Broad Prize for Public Charter Schools for demonstrating "the most outstanding overall student performance and improvement in the nation in recent years while reducing achievement gaps for low-income students and students of color." To learn more about Uncommon Schools, please visit our website at http://uncommonschools.org. You can also follow us on Facebook at www.facebook.com /uncommonschools, and on Twitter and Instagram at @uncommonschools.

Introduction

Whether you are a teacher in training, a master teacher whose goal is constant improvement, or an educator who simply loves the art of getting better, this *Field Guide* is designed to help you get the most out of the techniques profiled in *Teach Like a Champion 2.0*. Drawing on the experience of top trainers, teachers, and school leaders, the *Field Guide* provides hands-on activities and guidance to master any or all of the sixty-two *Teach Like a Champion* techniques.

We've designed the book to work especially well under what is to us ideal circumstances—small groups of teachers working together as a team to discuss, study, and practice their craft—but we also recognize that many readers, perhaps most, will use it on their own. We've tried to ensure that nearly all the activities and resources can be used solo as well.

But whether you are using this book to support a study group, an *ad hoc* collaboration among colleagues, or as part of your own efforts to improve your teaching, the *Field Guide* is best used as a practical extension of *Teach Like a Champion 2.0*, which discusses the techniques far more deeply than we have attempted to do here. Although we often review key points from it, our assumption is that if you are using this book, you have read *Teach Like a Champion 2.0*.

The 2.0 version of *Teach Like a Champion* was written to replace and improve on the original 2010 book, and this volume updates and aligns the original *Field Guide* as well. That said, the alignment of this book with *Teach Like a Champion 2.0* is, in a few cases, imperfect. Here and there you may notice a component part of a technique that has been added or removed, or that the names or descriptions of elements within some techniques have changed slightly. Those differences are intentional and represent ways in which we have continued to learn about the techniques. We study teachers daily, hone our observations, and refine our understanding of and advice about how each of us can learn to teach "like a champion." We hope the changes improve our advice, and we apologize for any potential confusion.

START WITH THE BIG PICTURE

Most of the techniques in this book work best when you apply them alongside other, complementary techniques; so a good place to begin is to become familiar with the overall structure of the book. You can review it both in the table of contents and in the compact digest that follows this introduction. This will help you to see the relationships among the techniques and how we group them in our own minds. As you use and practice the techniques, expect synergies to emerge among them.

An important step in self-improvement is continued self-assessment. This book is designed to help you reflect on where you stand and what techniques will be most valuable for you. Paradoxically, perhaps, where you find yourself saying "I already do that," you've identified a major reason to *study* the relevant technique. The fact that an idea comes naturally to you and jibes with your overall approach makes it an ideal starting point. A baseball player would never tell his coach, "Oh, I already know how to field ground balls. I don't need to work on that." A musician would know that she should always strive to be as good at her arpeggios as possible. "Knowing how" or using them well already would not keep her from seeking to improve.

We've seen teachers benefit from approaching their craft with a similar mindset. In fact, it's been fascinating to all of us to observe that those teachers who most humble us and take our collective breath away do so not by being without weaknesses but through their excellence with and passion for a handful of skills. These core areas of excellence drive their success. The skills aren't the same ones for every teacher—the combinations are as unique as the applications. But the things they are best at make the biggest difference. The lesson from this is clear: strengthen your strengths, make them exceptional, and use them as a foundation from which to improve what you perceive to be your weaker areas.

As a general principle, then, we urge you to work on strengths as much as weaknesses. Consolidate major skills with which you feel more confident, and use them to build your efficacy, self-assurance, and ability to learn related ones. For example:

Are you strong at planning, but not as strong yet as a classroom performer? Consider starting with one of the planning techniques, and look for ways that further improvements in planning can strengthen your classroom preparedness and confidence.

Are you strong in classroom interaction skills, but not as strong in planning the lesson? Consider beginning by muscling up your classroom skills, and fold in improvements in planning as well.

One other thing we've discovered is that whenever possible, studying classroom technique is best done as a team sport. Try to work with a partner or group—even if it means assembling that group virtually—so that you can discuss what you learn and learn from each other as you explore a given concept.

CHOOSING WHICH TECHNIQUES TO START WITH

You can start wherever you want, and we hope you'll choose what you feel is the right spot for you. But some people, we realize, want suggestions. Part 1, *Check for Understanding*, is a great place to start, especially for an experienced teacher, but if that doesn't look like the best place for you to begin, there are dozens of other good ones. Here are a few.

Starting with *Cold Call* . . . and Staying There Awhile

Of all the sixty-two techniques, *Cold Call* (technique 33) is the one we think might be likely to shift the culture of academic expectations in your classroom the most and quickest. Study it deeply; practice using it slowly and with a smile. Maybe even stay with it when you're tempted to try something new. Use it to backstop writing and pair discussions, and we think you've got a game changer.

Starting from Routines

Some champion teachers argue that great classrooms rest on an everyday culture of strong, apparently (but not really) mundane routines that empower you to teach efficiently and students to excel at academics. Making routine tasks automatic frees more time—often astounding amounts of it—for teaching. You can make almost any routine—from entering the classroom to shifting from one task to another—automatic, efficient, and a source of useful habit. The chapter 10 techniques, 45 through 50, all focus on building strong routines.

Starting from Planning

A third place to begin is at planning. If you feel that your planning is already strong, why not start with *Plan for Error* (technique 7) or *Double Plan* (technique 19)? These two focus on reactive planning—how to plan for the unexpected and change course as your lesson demands it. From there you are halfway to mastery of the Check for Understanding unit.

All about Writing

Writing holds a special place in a high-performing classroom. When all thirty of your students engage in thoughtful writing for a sustained period of time, your levels of rigor and participation are both high. Start with *Front the Writing* (technique 41) or maybe focus on ending every lesson with a short and focused exercise to help students develop and refine their ideas through writing. For that, try *Art of the Sentence* (technique 38) and *Show Call* (technique 39).

Every Teacher Teaches Reading

Control the Game (technique 23) is a mighty sleeper. It allows you to read an immense amount of text engagingly and positively during class—no matter what subject or grade level—and to connect your students to the pleasure of reading. Once you have that, the sky's the limit.

CHART AND NAVIGATE

In the end, your strong opinion about where to start is probably the best choice, but beyond the starting point you choose, we suggest letting your course be a journey, one you need not map entirely in advance. The table of contents is in checklist format so that you can neatly log techniques you've visited and ones to which you'll want to return.

As you work, remember what you probably already know from your experience with students: that deep mastery of a core set of skills trumps partial mastery of a larger number of topics. Rather than starting by touching briefly on all sixty-two techniques, set out to master a handful or so that seem most important for you at this time. With those secured, expand.

Every essential teaching skill develops with repetition and time, and the material for each technique in this book is designed to benefit you every time you visit it again in light of your continuing progress.

RECORD SOME OPTIONS NOW

No matter how you are using the *Field Guide*, take a minute now to reflect on your strengths and weaknesses. Identify one or two broad preliminary goals that address what you want to learn and improve—for example, using questioning to be more rigorous, or remaining calm and poised in the face of nonproductive behavior.

1. _____

2. _____

Now flip through the book and, at closer range, note some specific techniques that could help you address these topics. Your goal is ultimately to master these and a variety of related content, including that related to your strengths.

Technique: _____

Technique: _____

Technique: _____

Next, considering your strengths and weaknesses, your interests and style, the needs of your students, and perhaps your partners in applying this book, consider which techniques in this guide look like the best places for you to start. Choose three or four. Then glance through those techniques, noting one single, focused idea from within each that you're excited to master.

Record the technique names and smaller ideas here:

Technique and idea: _____

_____

Technique and idea: _____

_____

Technique and idea: _____

_____

From among the ones you've listed here, choose your starting point. If you're new to this, starting with one technique (or even part of one!) may be sufficient. Working on it may lead you to start work on one or two other related techniques. But avoid spreading yourself thin; keep the number small. Make progress on techniques that will help you dramatically before you tackle additional techniques.

ACTIVITIES WITHIN EACH TECHNIQUE

For each technique, your hands-on learning is supported by numerous activities, some to do by yourself, others either by yourself or together with a group or partner.

As you will see, the activities constitute a process for assessing outcomes and sharpening your efforts. Nearly all of them are useful to do more than once.

Each technique concludes with an "Action Planning" framework. For this, too, you can print out a generic form in the "Useful Tools" section at my.teachlikeachampion.com.

Use the Online Library of Tools

As we just implied, some of your "Useful Tools" at my.teachlikeachampion.com apply to numerous techniques. Others give you templates and additional information and activities for specific techniques. *Bookmark the site for easy reference.*

Get Full Value from the Video Clips

The idea of watching teachers in action is central to this book—both in our writing it and in your using it. Because studying the videos is a central endeavor, we provide you with dozens to watch and rewatch online, along with other support materials. Be sure to bookmark my.teachlikeachampion.com for easy access to them all—scores of videos of master teachers at work, to which your purchase of this *Field Guide* gives you access. For instructions on how to create an account for this access, please see How to Access the Online Contents located in the back of the book.

You'll be asked to visit and revisit the clips as you read this book under the "Analyze the Champions" heading. Some clips may look familiar with the ones mentioned in *Teach Like a Champion 2.0,* but most are new.

Independent of your work on techniques, we encourage you to watch the clips periodically to absorb more from these champion teachers. Although "Analyze the Champions" is presented for individual work, the clips can be used very effectively by groups working on a specific technique. If you are facilitating the group work, consider having participants also watch clips together to answer the questions in a group setting. You'll notice that we often provide several videos for one technique, so that you can compare different ways of applying the technique and model a version that best matches your own classroom goals, demeanor, and methods.

Mine the Blog Videos and Discussions

Often we'll refer you to a blog entry you'll find at teachlikeachampion.com/blog. This is the primary setting we use to disseminate new ideas that we develop through our observations, so we hope that in addition to reading useful posts we've designated throughout the book, you will visit frequently for ongoing reflections on the craft of teaching. Many of those posts include additional short videos of outstanding teachers.

AUDIO- OR VIDEO-RECORD YOUR TEACHING

We strongly recommend that you videotape yourself in the classroom. You won't necessarily need to rerecord each time. One audio or video recording may suffice to visit and revisit to study your words and behaviors and those of your students.

You can also profit greatly by rerecording and studying more sessions or by being observed by a supportive partner at several points, as the school year and your skills advance.

Please note, though, that we also recommend *lots of practice* in this book. Teaching is a great performance profession. To do it is to "go live" in front of thirty or so 3rd, 7th, or 10th graders several times a day. Preparing for live performance means rehearsal and practice beforehand. That way your skills come out when you perform, whether you are thinking about them or not. We mention that here because one of the fastest developments in performance professions involves videotaping not so much the performance but the practice. Try it, tape it, study the tape, and practice again—a great recipe for rapid improvement.

WORK WITH A GROUP OR PARTNER

If you are starting work on the *Field Guide* alone, begin to look right away *for at least one other teacher with whom you can partner.* You may find someone in your school or district, but you can also work via phone, email, or social media with someone you know and trust, perhaps posting videos and reflections on social media. Both of you can benefit by this in terms of motivation, support, resources, and the power and enjoyment of these activities.

If you can't find a partner, still *begin to talk with at least one other teacher colleague* about matters related to the techniques. What does he or she do to deal with something related to the technique you're on? Share your own ideas as well.

Partners or groups will likely want to arrive at some consensus about where to start among the techniques and periodically where to go next. Often, you may wish to go to a technique that is related to one you've worked on already and that feels within reach.

In a large group, someone may need to be an ongoing facilitator and manager. But ideally group members will take turns as facilitator for each technique or meeting. In most instances, the facilitator also can participate in the activity as everyone else is doing it. The following are basic facilitator tasks:

- Read the technique materials ahead of the rest of the group to notice and call general attention to things that members should do to prepare.
- Lead decision making and communication about what activities the group wants to do.
- Prepare shared materials.
- Lay meeting ground rules.
- Moderate.
- Decide when to switch from one activity to the next.
- Keep track of time or deputize someone else to do it.
- Lead new decision making about what technique(s) the group will do next time.
- Summarize at the end of a meeting.

The group activities often involve brainstorming. If your group does not already have its own effective method, you may want to follow the one presented here from the perspective of the member of the group who is acting as *Facilitator* for a given technique.

1. Set the context by refreshing the group on whatever topic or materials the brainstorming will be about.
2. Appoint a *Timekeeper* and a *Recorder* who will use board, overhead, large paper, or other means to capture all ideas.
3. Go in order around the circle, giving each person a limited number of seconds (thirty to sixty) to contribute one idea. If needed, the *Timekeeper* can call "Time."
4. Allow anyone who has no idea at that moment to say, "Pass."
5. As you go around, no one disrupts by expressing any judgment of or modification to another person's idea.
6. Keep going for an agreed-on time, or call a stop when you've gone around several times and four or five people pass in a row. Invite hands for any last ideas.
7. When the brainstorm is over, keep the recorded results in view of the group. Also, as a group, examine the recorded results to order, cluster, or refine them as needed.

USING A JOURNAL

This guide does not involve keeping an outside journal, but it is compatible with doing so in handwritten or digital form. If you want to make journaling part of your work, be sure to develop a system by which you can easily revisit what you wrote in connection with a given prompt in the book. Design it to help you monitor your progress and benefit more deeply each time you return to a technique. Also index the journal in a way that will let you cull it quickly as you go through the planning, preparation, and follow-up in trying things out in the classroom. You may want to incorporate the digital "Action Planning" framework into your journal.

COACH OR ADMINISTRATOR USE OF THIS GUIDE

We also recognize that some administrators may wish to use this book to assist their teachers in developing the craft, either in groups or on their own. If this is your situation, the following reflections can help support your work.

1. *Success begins with practice.* Especially adults are often reluctant to practice or rehearse, to get in front of a group of four or five peers and, for example, practice *Cold Calling* them in order to get better at the *Cold Call* technique. But practice before the game is the single most reliable driver of success. So strive to build a setting for safe practice where it's OK to experiment, where participants are supported if they fail, and where teachers can practice over and over again to get ready.
2. *Peer-to-peer accountability drives success.* People are at least as motivated by accountability to their peers as they are by their accountability to authority. Although it's important for teachers to be accountable to their organizations, consider letting your teachers form groups (by subject area or grade level or some other common interest) and commit as a group to working on techniques they want to master together—and for which they will hold each other accountable. Giving them vested autonomy is both a gesture of respect and a tool to ensure their success.
3. *Make it safe to fail.* In the classroom, great teachers seek to create a culture where their students comfortably expose their own mistakes and weaknesses. This accelerates the learning process, and what is true for students is equally true for teachers. Thus, good-faith struggle and difficulty are good things, and we urge you not to punish or chastise teachers who try but struggle or even fail. Encourage them and help them improve. If you don't, you risk fostering a culture where people try to hide their weaknesses, and this only causes those weaknesses to fester. Further, if people struggle and know they can safely come to you with challenges and problems, and if you are able to help them find solutions, you will earn their trust and faith.

WHERE THESE IDEAS AND ACTIVITIES CAME FROM

Much of the material here has been developed as part of the workshops and training we've helped run (or observed being run) with and by the incredible and inspiring teachers and leaders at Uncommon Schools. Most of the techniques have gone through various iterations as we've improved and refined them, often based on feedback from the folks who've attended our workshops. The more trainings we do, the more we realize that, as inspiring as the videos are, the work that comes after one watches them is more important. Practice and reflection are what drive results, and that means studying a technique multiple times over the course of a year.

We believe that these tools truly work. We have seen them change teachers' and students' lives—making the former love the work and achieve their goals and helping the latter do something fairly similar. We know this from watching talented peers within and outside our organization put them to the test—in charter schools and district schools; urban, rural, and suburban schools. So we are excited to share this material with you, and wish you the best of success at the most important and most rewarding work in the world.

A Map to the Themes and Techniques

Units	Chapters	Techniques
1. Check for Understanding Differentiating "I taught it" from "They learned it" is the soul of teaching.	1. Gathering Data on Student Mastery	1. Reject Self-Report
		2. Targeted Questioning
		3. Standardize the Format
		4. Tracking, Not Watching
		5. Show Me
		6. Affirmative Checking
	2. Acting on the Data and the Culture of Error	7. Plan for Error
		8. Culture of Error
		9. Excavate Error
		10. Own and Track
2. Academic Ethos Great classrooms are built around academic rigor that engages students in learning.	3. Setting High Academic Expectations	11. No Opt Out
		12. Right Is Right
		13. Stretch It
		14. Format Matters
		15. Without Apology
	4. Planning for Success	16. Begin with the End
		17. 4 Ms
		18. Post It
		19. Double Plan
	5. Lesson Structure	20. Do Now
		21. Name the Steps
		22. Board = Paper
		23. Control the Game
		24. Circulate
		25. At Bats
		26. Exit Ticket
	6. Pacing	27. Change the Pace
		28. Brighten Lines
		29. All Hands
		30. Work the Clock
		31. Every Minute Matters
3. Ratio The goal is for students, rather than teachers, to get the "workout" and for them to do as much of the cognitive work as they can.	7. Building Ratio through Questioning	32. Wait Time
		33. Cold Call
		34. Call and Response
		35. Break It Down
		36. Pepper
	8. Building Ratio through Writing	37. Everybody Writes
		38. Art of the Sentence
		39. Show Call
		40. Build Stamina
		41. Front the Writing
	9. Building Ratio through Discussion	42. Habits of Discussion
		43. Turn and Talk
		44. Batch Process
4. Five Principles of Classroom Culture A strong positive and orderly culture is necessary to achieve the academic goals teachers pursue.	10. Systems and Routines	45. Threshold
		46. Strong Start
		47. STAR/SLANT
		48. Engineer Efficiency
		49. Strategic Investment
		50. Do It Again
	11. High Behavioral Expectations	51. Radar/Be Seen Looking
		52. Make Compliance Visible
		53. Least Invasive Intervention
		54. Firm Calm Finesse
		55. Art of the Consequence
		56. Strong Voice
		57. What to Do
	12. Building Character and Trust	58. Positive Framing
		59. Precise Praise
		60. Warm/Strict
		61. Emotional Constancy
		62. Joy Factor

REJECT SELF-REPORT

OVERVIEW

Teachers frequently use phrases like "Does everyone understand?" or "Everybody got that?" while they are teaching. When they use them, they essentially acknowledge to themselves that they have arrived at a good place to pause and check for understanding. But such phrases usually mean they are doing the opposite—they gloss over struggle and provide false confirmation. Self-report questions, especially those that feel rhetorical, are a very poor source of data on how the class is doing, so it's useful to try to replace such phrases with something more productive.

This is especially true if students are about to embark on independent work. The more time you invest in a task and the more autonomous your students will be in completing it, the more important it is to *Reject Self-Report* and effectively check for understanding—sooner rather than later.

Reflection

What usually happens in your classroom when you ask a student or a group of them, "Got it?" or "Everyone understand?"

Write your own thoughts here before you continue reading our reflections.

_____

_____

_____

_____

Our thoughts (you may have had other thoughts as well): A few students may clearly indicate that they get it, but many may not answer at all, or may simply fall in line with the rest of their peers. As a result, we often come away with little idea of whether or not students understand the material in question. We pause a moment, then take students' silence as implicit permission to go on.

FUNDAMENTALS

You can improve your ability to check for understanding by engineering a short sequence of questions to provide dependable data about what your students know. If these are quick, carefully chosen, precise, and aimed at a strategic sample of the class, they can be useful in demonstrating the extent of understanding very quickly.

Avoiding the Pitfall of "Yes" and "No"

One general problem with yes-or-no questions is that half the time a guess is right, and this results in data of limited accuracy. Additional problems can emerge when you try to use yes-or-no questions to find out whether students understand. Students often think they understand when they don't. For example, a yes may really mean, "Well, I understand *something* about it." In other words, yes-or-no questions do little to call students' attention to specific skills or knowledge they are supposed to understand. This encourages them not to inquire but simply to say yes, and possibly to believe it themselves.

Phrases like "Got it?" and "Understand?"—phrases that ask for a yes-or-no reply where silence appears to be assent—are deeply embedded in most people's natural manner when talking to a group, and there's nothing wrong with that. No doubt we all say them in class, often at a point of transition to reassure ourselves about moving on.

But we can't depend on the answer as *data*. When you really need to understand what your class knows, strive to replace phrases like "Everybody got that?" with a handful of focused questions that help you answer the question objectively: "Why did Keith multiply by *y*?" "Why did France enter the war on our side?" This doesn't have to take long—often less than a minute.

> **blog** Find this blog post at teachlikeachampion.com/blog/coaching-and-practice/especially
> -reject-self-report/.
> To appreciate how valuable and time-saving it is to get beyond self-report, read the entry "When (Especially) to 'Reject Self-Report.'"

Welcoming "No"

When we do ask yes-or-no self-report questions, we often signal that they aren't meant to be answered, by barely pausing before moving on to something else. This can signal that we don't really want an answer, and students learn not to speak up. Sometimes a student really will answer a self-report question with an honest "No" or tell you they "don't really get it." That's a critical moment in the life of a classroom. If we respond with exasperation or by simply repeating an answer for him, he is likely to learn to spare himself embarrassment next time and no longer admit what he doesn't know. If instead, we show that this is a good thing and engage the whole class in any review—"Ah, good. Let me quiz you guys a bit more then . . ."—we show that we welcome rather than punish students for revealing to us when they don't get it.

Draft some phrases you might use when a student responds to a self-report question with a no or a further question. We've started you off with a few examples:

- "Ah, good. Do you understand what's confusing you, or do you want me to ask you questions?"
- "Yes, this is tricky. Let's see if five more minutes can clear it up."

You might ask, is it possible that some students might also sometimes use "I don't get it" to deliberately slow a class? Sure. Take a moment to think through some possible responses. Again, we've started you off.

- "Great. That's good to know, David. Let's go back and have you summarize what you know from the top, and we'll fill in the blanks."
- "Great. That's good to know, David. With the class's help, I'll start a summary, and we can pause and ask you and some others to fill in the blanks."
- "Great. So glad to know that, David. I think we can take care of this during the last few minutes of class when we start independent practice. Let me see the hands of those who'd like a few extra problems."
- "Great. Let me see the hands of those who'd like a few extra problems. [Assume no other hands.] OK, David. Let me get them started, and I'll give you a few to work out on your own."

_____

_____

_____

_____

Improving Requests

Examine each of the statements that follow. If a statement requests self-report, replace it with a question that directs students to demonstrate their understanding in some way. If it's a yes-or-no question that should be changed into a more useful open-ended question, revise it. After you're done, compare your work with that of a colleague.

"You guys already know how to balance this equation, right?"

_____

"Do you follow me on step 2 of this experiment?"

_____

"Class, are we ready?"

_____

"What's the answer? It's a verb."

_____

"Was Virginia Colony formed before or after the one at Plymouth Rock?"

_____

"Thumbs up if you get this; thumbs down if you don't."

_____

"Let me know if I'm going too fast."

_____

"How many of you are getting this logic?"

_____

"Any doubts about why it's spelled with two *t*'s?"

_____

_____

Suppose you want to know whether the class understands what is meant by a "run-on" (or "run-together") sentence. Pose three questions you could ask to quickly test their knowledge:

_____

_____

_____

_____

_____

Heading Off Self-Report

Examine an upcoming lesson plan. Does it include questions you plan to ask to check for understanding? If not, add several at strategic points. Also revise any self-report or rhetorical questions that you find.

THE NEXT LEVEL

As a supplement to (not a substitute for) your own checking for understanding, students can often monitor their own learning and understanding.

Revisit *Teach Like a Champion 2.0*

Under "A Look at Self-Monitoring," Doug cites this example. You may also want to revisit clip 1 from his book.

Unlike self-report . . . , self-monitoring is very useful, so it's worth reviewing the differences between self-report and self-monitoring and exploring how (and maybe when) to encourage the latter.

In a recent review of spelling words, Amy Youngman, of Aspire ERES Academy in Oakland, California, said to her students, "At the end we're going to vote on a scale of one to four about how confident we feel about taking our test tomorrow, so be thinking about that as you practice the words." You might ask, "Isn't this just a fancy version of self-report? One where you ask students to evaluate their own level of understanding?" Not quite. Amy, at the moment she says this, is also gathering objective data, quickly scanning and assessing her students' answers. She asks for their self-reflections not to assess their level of mastery—it's too unreliable for that—but to develop their own self-awareness, their skill, and their desire to think about whether they are approaching mastery. She advises them, "If you gave yourself a three or four, there's a sheet for extra practice you can take home." It's self-monitoring when students reflect intentionally on their own level of mastery. It's a good thing generally, and there are lots of ways to encourage it in the classroom— for example, asking them to reflect as you ask targeted questions, such as, "I'm going to ask you some questions now to get a sense of how ready you are to go on; if you're not getting all of these questions, it's a sign that you may need some extra practice. In that case, please come see me."

Of course, deliberate self-monitoring can be worked into a lesson in other ways, building synergy with effective CFU. You could, for example, take self-report—a yes-or-no question asking students to subjectively evaluate their mastery—and replace it with a session in which you give students time to look back at work they've done and select areas where they have questions. In doing this, you'd probably want to use language that assumes there are questions (for example, "What questions do you have? I'll give you some time to go back and look over the last five problems." You might then even help them reflect by saying, "You should know what I mean by *anaerobic,* and if not, should be ready to ask about it."). You'd probably want to do this activity consistently over time to allow students to build proficiency.

ACTION PLANNING

Use this action planner to continue your work with *Rejecting Self-Report*. (Find a printable version of this form at my.teachlikeachampion.com.) You know you're on the right track when you are . . .

- Weeding out self-report questions about understanding, or at least following quickly with better ones
- Planning questions to ask in class that will give you bits of reliable data about whether students understand

HOW AM I DOING?

_____

_____

Design one or more action steps for improvement. Decide on an interval by which you'll revisit this page to assess your progress.

Action Step 1

By when, with whom, and how you will measure your effort

By _____, I will . . .
   Date

_____

_____

How Did I Do?

Successes: _____

_____

_____

_____

Challenges: _____

_____

_____

_____

Next steps: _____

_____

_____

Action Step 2

By when, with whom, and how you will measure your effort

By _____, I will . . .

Date

_____

_____

_____

How Did I Do?

Successes: _____

_____

_____

_____

Challenges: _____

_____

_____

_____

Next steps: _____

_____

_____

_____

REJECT SELF-REPORT

TARGETED QUESTIONING

OVERVIEW

To gather data efficiently at key points during your lesson, try using a short series of *Targeted Questions*—five or six questions, perhaps asked of a strategic sample of the class, and designed to show whether students grasped the principles of what you just taught or talked about. This can be especially useful as a tool to replace self-report (see technique 1).

Perhaps counterintuitively, the goal of *Targeted Questioning* is to be quick rather than comprehensive, to replace self-report with just enough data to give you a sense of what your students know. If you gather that data quickly enough—in less than a minute, say—you'll be able to do it any time and add checks for understanding throughout your lessons.

Targeted Questioning works best when the questions are drafted beforehand—this lets you concentrate on hearing the answers, not thinking of the best questions to ask—even if they end up getting adapted in the moment of use.

Reflection

Brief, frequent open-ended questions interspersed throughout a lesson are often better for checking for understanding than a longer clump of questions asked at the end. Why, and in what cases?

_____

_____

_____

_____

FUNDAMENTALS

Assess what your students understand while you teach by gathering responses from students who are likely to represent different levels of mastery. Use the data to represent the likely level of mastery across the larger class.

Your *Targeted Questions* don't need to be comprehensive. The goal is to take frequent, small data samples to judge the general level of knowledge in the room.

Speed Matters

Although *Targeted Questioning* adds a little time to the lesson, we think you can often do it in less than a minute or so each time and that, more important, you'll save time in the long run by helping students get things right from the start. The faster you can ask a few questions, the less you break the flow of instruction. To enrich the data you collect, you can also script a very short verbal quiz into the fabric of a lesson. Use a format that lets you tally whom you called on and whether their answers were right or wrong.

Plan in Advance

When consciously checking for understanding, teachers who ask concise, precise, and revealing questions generally plan those questions in advance, along with when to ask them—at a few key points of transition within the lesson. After the lesson, they can look back at what they asked and improve their question-framing skills.

Planning questions with data sets in mind helps you resist the urge to stop checking for understanding as soon as you get a single right response. Asking totally different questions of different students can help you review distinct bits of knowledge with the class, but if you ask the same number of students very similar or parallel questions about one thing, you can get a better feel for what proportion of the class is with you.

Sample Strategically

To check understanding, choose students to answer so that you're hearing from several whose performance is midrange, several who are a little lower, and maybe one whose grasp of the content is typically strong. Call on students (*Cold Call,* technique 33) rather than asking for hands, to ensure that you're able to ask a question of anybody (and everybody). Also *Cold Call* at other times so that students see *Cold Call* as a normal and expected part of your class, not as something you do only when you want to ask *Targeted Questions.* This helps you maintain the ability to *Cold Call* at any time throughout your lesson and increases students' readiness for *Cold Call* when you ask *Targeted Questions.*

Track the Data

Pay attention to what a set of answers tells you, rather than to the idea that the last answer may be entirely right. Perhaps you got that last answer by moving through several that weren't really up to your standard. Does the *data set* show great learning? Be aware of what proportion gave a sufficient answer and of how students may use others' wrong answers to eliminate choices and guess correctly. Notice how these problems creep into this teacher's questions about the first chapter of *Charlotte's Web.* Her class may not be doing quite as well as she thinks:

TEACHER:	So, Peter, what's Mr. Arable about to do as the story starts?
PETER:	Kill the little pig.
TEACHER:	OK, good, but what word does he use for him?
PETER:	Um . . .
TEACHER:	The littlest pig in the litter . . . ?
PETER:	Oh, the runt!
TEACHER:	And why does Fern object? Ronelle? Because of its shape or size or what?
RONELLE:	Because it's just a baby.
TEACHER:	Good, because it's the littlest one, the runt. And Mr. Arable agrees not to kill the piglet, which was surprising, but what was his reason for agreeing? Lacey?
LACEY:	So she could feed it.
TEACHER:	Well, he does say she can feed it, but then what will happen?
LACEY:	But then maybe he thinks she'll learn a lesson.
TEACHER:	Right. Mr. Arable wants Fern to learn a lesson about taking care of things.

Find this blog post at teachlikeachampion.com/blog/replacing-self-report-with-targeted -questioning/.

blog

"Replacing Self-Report with Targeted Questioning" discusses how essentially self-report routines such as "fist-to-five" can be replaced by more reliable, equally fast approaches.

THE NEXT LEVEL: RELIABILITY AND VALIDITY

Reliability and validity are key aspects of effective questions. Although we discuss them in this chapter on *Targeted Questioning,* they are relevant and applicable to any questions you use to assess student mastery.

Reliable data is data that is likely to reoccur. When students give reliable answers, they are likely to get not only your current question right but future questions on the same topic right. Obviously you want to shoot for reliable success rather than lucky guesses. One way to help assess reliability is to use "Why" and "How" questions. If students can explain their thinking process, their answers are less likely to be lucky guesses.

Another way to get at reliability is to vary question types and formats so that you're not always asking similar questions.

A question that is valid actually measures what it is designed to measure. To ensure validity, make sure the difficulty of your questions matches the level of your objective as well as the level at which students must be able to perform by the end of the lesson. For example, if you are teaching students to add fractions and ask them *Targeted Questions* with only unit numerators, you won't really have measured fully.

You'll want to vary the format to be sure that students can answer correctly regardless of format. For example, check for understanding not only with multiple-choice but also with open-ended questions. Or vary formats by first giving students a word and asking them to define it and then giving them a situation and asking what word might apply.

Revisit *Teach Like a Champion 2.0*

Use this passage from "Reliability and Validity" in Doug's treatment of technique 2 as a stimulus for your thinking about ways to vary open-ended question formats:

Consider the following three questions about the Stamp Act of 1765. A teacher might check students' understanding by asking any sequence of these questions:

1. What was the Stamp Act? Why was it important?
2. Here is a line from a history textbook: "If this new tax were allowed to pass without resistance, the colonists reasoned, the door would be open for far more troublesome taxation in the future." What "tax" is it referring to? Was the tax "allowed to pass without resistance"? Explain.
3. What did the Stamp Act propose to do? What governing body passed it? How did the House of Burgesses react? Who led the reaction among the Burgesses? How did the governor of the Virginia Colony react?

TARGETED QUESTIONING

The first question asks for a basic identification of the Stamp Act and a summary of its importance. Pretty good, but the teacher would have no idea how her students would fare if they were asked about the Stamp Act using a different format. The question might allow students to narrate what they know and avoid what they don't know, as some other questions might not. If the SAT asked the question differently, a correct answer to question 1 might not indicate how students were likely to do. Question 2, which asks them to recall the name of the historical event based on a description rather than vice versa, takes a different approach, and combining both in the course of an assessment would give you better validity. Question 3 looks at a broader scope of events and the connections among them. Balancing multiple formats helps you ensure that your students are prepared for uncertainty.

Working with an upcoming lesson plan objective (more about this in the chapter 4 techniques), write several open-ended questions such that if students answered them correctly, you'd feel confident that they'd learned the material. Then, using Doug's examples, the one here, and your own ideas, recast and vary each question in several different contexts or formats that would strengthen validity.

Example
Question: *What are the main parts of an animal cell?*
Variations: *1. Label the main parts of the cell in this drawing. 2. Draw a cell and its parts, labeling each. 3. What's a cell membrane? 4. What in the cell absorbs nutrients? 5. What might happen if a cell had no mitochondria?*

Question: What part of speech is the word *become*?

Variations: _____

_____

_____

_____

Question: _____

_____

Variations: _____

_____

_____

_____

Question: _____

_____

Variations: _____

_____

_____

_____

For mutual learning, compare your variations with those of a partner or group.

ACTION PLANNING

Use this action planner to continue your work with *Targeted Questioning*. (Find a printable version of this form at my.teachlikeachampion.com.) You know you're on the right track when . . .

- You are planning questions with data sets in mind.
- You and your students are able to move through questions quickly at several points in the lesson.
- You are reaping reliable, valid data.

HOW AM I DOING?

_____

_____

Design one or more action steps for improvement. Decide on an interval by which you'll revisit this page to assess your progress.

Action Step 1

By when, with whom, and how you will measure your effort

By _____, I will . . .
        Date

_____

_____

How Did I Do?

Successes: _____

_____

_____

_____

Challenges: _____

_____

_____

_____

Next steps: _____

_____

_____

_____

Action Step 2

By when, with whom, and how you will measure your effort

By _____, I will . . .
<small>Date</small>

_____

_____

_____

How Did I Do?

Successes: _____

_____

_____

_____

Challenges: _____

_____

_____

_____

Next steps: _____

_____

_____

_____

STANDARDIZE THE FORMAT

OVERVIEW

Another way that teachers gather and respond to evidence of student understanding is through observation. For instance, a teacher might *Circulate* (technique 24) during independent work, carefully monitoring what her students write and responding with individual feedback or by discussing common errors with the class. Because gathering data via observation can be so powerful and can usually allow you to assess a much larger proportion of your class than questioning can, you'll want to design student materials and classroom space so that you can easily find the data you need, when you need it.

Reflection

As you move about the classroom observing your students and what they write, consider how easy it is for you to see quickly and simply in each student's work exactly what you need to see to assess their mastery.

ANALYZE THE CHAMPIONS

In a recent lesson with her seventh graders, reading teacher Meghann Fallon asked her students to read Sylvia Plath's complex and challenging poem, "Mirror." She gave students a copy of the poem and asked them to paraphrase it.

Paraphrasing the poem is quite a demanding task—it's full of imagery and allusion and complex syntax. It assumes—without telling readers—that they will know that the narrator is a mirror.

One pitfall of such a task might be that students will choose to paraphrase just parts of the poem—the parts that came easiest to them, perhaps. With that in mind, as you can see in her materials, Meghann has *Standardized the Format*. She gave her students a specific box in which to write their paraphrase. This let her find it quickly and easily as she *Circulated*. Cleverly, she actually gave them two boxes in which to paraphrase—one for the first stanza and one for the second. At a glance, she could now tell how much progress each student had made with both halves of the poem. This simple adjustment meant that students could not just write about the first lines, say, and leave it at that.

Meghann's Handout

STANDARDIZE THE FORMAT

PARAPHRASE A POEM

Uncommon Schools | Change History.

Directions: Actively read the poem below by Sylvia Plath. While reading the poem, paraphrase the meaning of each line or set of lines in the paraphrase box. Then answer the questions on the next page.

"Mirror" by Sylvia Plath

1   I am silver and exact. I have no preconceptions.[1]
2   Whatever I see I swallow immediately
3   Just as it is, unmisted by love or dislike.
4   I am not cruel, only truthful—
5   The eye of a little god, four-cornered.
6   Most of the time I meditate[2] on the opposite wall.
7   It is pink, with speckles. I have looked at it so long
8   I think it is a part of my heart. But it flickers.
9   Faces and darkness separate us over and over.

• • •

10   Now I am a lake. A woman bends over me,
11   Searching my reaches for what she really is.
12   Then she turns to those liars, the candles or the moon.
13   I see her back, and reflect it faithfully.
14   She rewards me with tears and an agitation[3] of hands.
15   I am important to her. She comes and goes.
16   Each morning it is her face that replaces the darkness.
17   In me she has drowned a young girl, and in me an old woman
18   Rises toward her day after day, like a terrible fish.

Paraphrase

Stanza 1

Stanza 2

[1] preconceptions: prejudices, biases
[2] meditate: reflect, think, ponder
[3] agitation: anxiety, worry, nervousness, distress

Meghann's Markup of Her Copy

PARAPHRASE	
Stanza 1	Key Points Line 1: personification—mirror is the speaker. Line 5: "the eye of a little god" showing truth is powerful, like godliness
Stanza 2	Line 10: now it is the reflective surface of a lake that is talking. The connection across both stanzas is that "reflection" is talking. Line 14: "Rewards" is sarcastic, ironic

FUNDAMENTALS

Gathering data via observation shouldn't feel like a scavenger hunt. Teachers who understand this engineer student materials carefully to make it easy to find the information they need. You'll notice in Meghann's materials that she also numbered the lines in the poem so that she could easily reference specific points in the poem with her students. In her own copy of the materials, she also notes the key lines that she wants to check students' paraphrases for, which helps her gather the highest-leverage data as efficiently as possible.

Third-grade teacher Nicole Willey goes a step further by teaching students how to *Standardize the Format* of how they show their work.

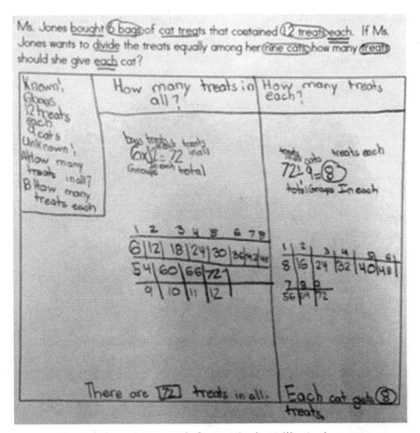

Sample of student work from Nicole Willey's classroom

In a box to the upper left, students include key information from the problem, including "knowns" or important numbers that are given in the problem and the "unknowns" they must solve for. Nicole then has students show in columns the work they use to solve each key question from the story problem. Students then jot their answer to each part of the question as a number sentence at the bottom of their work space and then circle or box the number they solved for. These requirements not only make data gathering easier but also ensure that students develop effective habits for organizing their work whenever they solve word problems.

Brainstorming Ways to *Standardize the Format*

Add to these examples:

Providing a designated space for students to

- Respond in writing to a prompt or to show their work.
- "Redo"/revise/edit their written work.
- Lock in their final answer or a key understanding (for example, a "stamp it" section).
- Take discussion notes.
- Draw a model or illustration (for example, of an atom, to solve a word problem, and so on).

- _____

- _____

- _____

Using consistent headers for different sections of a lesson or levels of work complexity

- "Mild/medium/spicy" problems
- "Before/during/after reading"

- _____

- _____

- _____

Teaching students consistent expectations for taking notes from a text or making notes in the margins while reading independently

- _____

- _____

- _____

MORE CHAMPIONS

▶ **Clip FG1. Nicole Willey, Grade 3**

In clip FG1, what's effective about Nicole's "front table" strategy? How does it support her ability to gather and act on data?

_____

_____

_____

▶ **Clip FG2. Ijeoma Duru, Grade 9**

In clip FG2, how does Ijeoma's approach to _Standardizing the Format_ of her feedback support her ability to check for understanding?

_____

_____

_____

Compare your responses with our notes at the end of this technique.

THE NEXT LEVEL

In great classrooms, the process of gathering and acting on data doesn't stop with student materials. Some teachers are just as intentional about how they arrange their classroom space and the format of their feedback.

Standardize the Field

During the course of a normal school day, a number of factors—both predictable and unforeseen—will inevitably challenge your ability to gather data through observation. Your classroom space shouldn't be one of them. One way that teachers minimize the barriers to gathering data is by arranging students into predictable visual patterns. For instance, during a _Turn and Talk_ (technique 43), you might arrange desks so that it's easy to _Circulate_ to any pair of students and listen in on their conversation. In addition, you might teach students to engage in activities in observable ways, such as turning and making eye contact with each other. This can dramatically simplify the visual field and make it much easier to monitor whether students are engaging productively in the task.

STANDARDIZE THE FORMAT

Another way some teachers we have observed standardize the field is by using a seating chart that facilitates data collection. Recently, our team saw an example of this while watching clip FG1 of Nicole Willey's classroom. Soon after Nicole sends the class off to complete some independent work, she calls three students who struggled to master a key skill up to her front table. Arranging these three students close to each other enables her to efficiently monitor and support their work as needed.

When she first rolled out this "front table" system, she emphasized that being called up was not a negative thing. Students would be called when they needed more help . . . or more challenge. She also made sure to balance the reasons for being called to the front table: both remediation of skills and enrichment. This helped her ensure that everyone was at the front table sometime, which in turn made the reason for students being there less obvious.

Standardize the Feedback

Some teachers, like Ijeoma Duru, who appeared in clip FG2, streamline the process of checking for understanding by *Standardizing the Format* of the feedback they give students. Ijeoma sometimes gives students written feedback using shorthand codes like the ones shown here. With a single stroke of her pen, Ijeoma can provide students with actionable feedback. This leaves her even more time to gather data. See our observations about clip FG2.

Ijeoma's Math Feedback Codes

D = Distribution error
C = Calculation error
I = Incorrect exponent rule
S = Set up (check the operation or order of terms)

Watching footage of Julie Miller's ninth-grade literature class, our team recently stumbled across an example of what Ijeoma's method could look like in a reading context. Here we show some standardized feedback codes that Julie jotted on students' papers while they wrote about Junot Diaz's *The Brief Wondrous Life of Oscar Wao*.

Julie's Feedback Codes for Writing

N = Name the literary technique being used
E = Choose stronger evidence or provide better context for it
Zi = Zoom in closer on language (key words, phrases, or paragraphs)
Zo = Zoom out to connect to broader point/theme
W = Weak or missing analysis
!! = This is a really strong sentence or section of writing

ROLL OUT YOUR SYSTEM FOR STANDARDIZING THE FIELD OR THE FEEDBACK

Whether you're hoping to standardize the field or to standardize your feedback, the success of these systems hinges on the quality of your rollout. In the space provided, plan how you want to roll out these systems. Make sure that you

- Explain the purpose in a way that cultivates student buy-in.
- Clearly model and describe the steps involved with executing the system (if necessary).
- Maintain economy of language.

_____

_____

_____

_____

_____

_____

If you can, practice your rollout with a partner and ask for feedback.

ACTION PLANNING

Use this action planner to continue your work with *Standardizing the Format*. (Find a printable version of this form at my.teachlikeachampion.com.) You know you're headed for success when . . .

- You can reliably find the information you need, when you need it.
- Your format changes enable you to gather data and respond to data more efficiently.

HOW AM I DOING?

Design one or more action steps for improvement. Decide on an interval by which you'll revisit this page to assess your progress.

Action Step 1

By when, with whom, and how you will measure your effort
By _____, I will . . .
_{Date}

How Did I Do?

Successes: _____

_____

_____

_____

Challenges: _____

_____

_____

_____

Next steps: _____

_____

_____

Action Step 2

By when, with whom, and how you will measure your effort

By _____, I will . . .

<small>Date</small>

_____

_____

_____

How Did I Do?

Successes: _____

_____

_____

_____

Challenges: _____

_____

_____

_____

Next steps: _____

_____

_____

_____

OUR OBSERVATIONS ON THE CHAMPIONS

 Clip FG1. Nicole Willey, Grade 3

During a period of independent math work, Nicole calls on three students who struggled to master a skill that the class has begun practicing independently. She sits with them at the front table so that she can more closely monitor their progress and give them additional support.

As these students make their way to the front table, what stands out is, well, almost nothing. As in, almost nothing is what their peers do. We don't hear anyone commenting on or even really noticing this transition. It's a routine part of class, and Nicole has made it clear that everyone will be there at some point. As a result, sitting at the front table carries no stigma.

By seating these students close to one another at the front table, Nicole can more efficiently address their gaps in understanding. She doesn't have to move around the classroom from one to the other to monitor them. This added efficiency gives her even more time to monitor students at the table and address their errors with targeted feedback ("I think that your issue is that you're not labeling your number sentences").

 Clip FG2. Ijeoma Duru, Grade 9

In this math lesson clip, high school teacher Ijeoma *Standardizes the Format* of her feedback by rolling out a set of codes for common errors students typically make during independent work. For instance, she announces that she will mark a "D" on students' papers whenever they make a distribution error or a "C" to denote a calculation error.

After briefly explaining the system, Ijeoma posts a "key" to remind students of what each code represents. This key helps her keep the explanation short and sweet and ensures that students can reliably use her feedback.

This method of *Standardizing the Format* helps Ijeoma streamline the process of giving feedback by

- Minimizing the amount of time she expends describing the same errors to different students
- Keeping her focused on tracking just a handful of errors as opposed to trying to process everything on the page at once
- Putting the onus on students to determine how they will fix their own errors
- Allowing her to give more feedback to more students in less time

STANDARDIZED FORMATS IN LESSON MATERIALS

For more convenient viewing of the following examples, we've reduced some of the blank space allowed for student answers and omitted some decorative graphics and content not relevant to demonstrating standardized format.

LESSON MATERIALS EXCERPT 1: BRYAN BELANGER, GRADE 8 MATH

Uncommon Schools | Change History.

Mr. Belanger asked students to solve the following equation for x:

$2x - 6 = 22$

Solve for x. $2x - 6 = 22$	List the steps you used below.
Solve for x in terms of y and z. $2x - y = z$	List the steps you used below.

☑ STAMP IT:

___

REVIEW

Tom Foolery solved the problem as shown below.

$15 - 3x = -6$
$+15 \quad +15$

$-3x = 9$
$-3 \quad -3$

$x = -3$

YOUR WORK HERE

Did Tom do his first step correctly? Explain.

___

Did Tom do his second step correctly? Explain.

___

Evaluation:

_____

_____

_____

_____

Ideas I could steal from Bryan:

_____

_____

_____

STANDARDIZE THE FORMAT

LESSON MATERIALS EXCERPT 2:
ELLIE STRAND, GRADE 8 READING

Uncommon Schools | Change History.

Everybody Writes #1: Explain how Orwell uses the following line to develop a central idea of the chapter:

> Again the animals seemed to remember a resolution against this had been passed in the early days, and again Squealer was able to convince them this was not the case.

_____

_____

_____

Notes from Discussion

_____

_____

_____

Everybody Rewrites #1

_____

_____

_____

Evaluation:

_____

_____

_____

_____

Ideas I could steal from Ellie:

_____

_____

_____

LESSON MATERIALS EXCERPT 3: ERICA LIM, GRADE 9 WORLD HISTORY

STANDARDIZE THE FORMAT

Main Ideas/Questions	Dates	Notes (Details)
Why was china the only country w/so many discriminations?		c. placed foreign administrar in china *Big charge* d. no more Confucian edu. or examination system e. all cultural & religious traditions 7. Mongols & Buddhism a. Lamaist Buddhism ↳magic & supernatural powers c. Mongols & Eurasian Integration 1. Mongols & Trade
Did mongols trade when they traveled for war?	APR 28	a. merchants travel unmolested through empires b. ↑ long distance trade 2. Diplomatic missions a. negotians/communication btwn kingdoms, states, & regions b. Korea, India, Vietnam, & Western Europe

Terms: ↓Confucianism Lamaist Buddhism Integration diplomatic embassies

Summary: China no longer practiced old traditions b/c of mongol power. Mongols spread Lamaist Buddhism. Mongol merchants traded long distance and communicated w/ everyone w/ diplomatic missions.

Evaluation:

_____

_____

_____

_____

_____

_____

Ideas I could steal from Erica:

_____

_____

_____

_____

_____

_____

STANDARDIZE THE FORMAT

LESSON MATERIALS EXCERPT 4:
VICKI HERNANDEZ, GRADE 8 BIOLOGY

Uncommon Schools | Change History.

Annotation Checklist

☐ Underline only key lines (about 1 per paragraph)

☐ Make a margin note for each key line

☐ Jot a one sentence summary at the end of each page

☐ Underline and define key words/terms in the question stem

Proteins

By Regina Bailey

$$H_2N - \underset{\underset{H}{|}}{\overset{\overset{CH_3}{|}}{C}} - COOH$$

alanine

Proteins are formed from amino acids. This image shows the amino acid alanine. The variable group in alanine is CH3.

Proteins are very important molecules in cells. By weight, proteins are collectively the largest component of the dry weight of cells. They can be used for a variety of functions from cellular support to cellular locomotion, or movement. While proteins have many diverse functions, all are typically constructed from one set of 20 amino acids.

Structure of Proteins
One or more chains of amino acids twisted into a 3D shape forms a protein. The unique shape of the protein determines its function. For instance, structural proteins such as collagen and keratin are fibrous and stringy. Globular proteins like hemoglobin, on the other hand, are folded and compact.

Protein Synthesis
Proteins are synthesized (made) in the body through a process called translation. Translation occurs in the cytoplasm and involves the translation of genetic codes that are assembled during DNA transcription into proteins. Cell structures called ribosomes help translate these genetic codes into amino acid chains that undergo several modifications before becoming fully functioning proteins.

Questions:

1. Which line in the text suggests a reason that proteins have so many diverse roles?
   a. According to their weight, proteins are the largest component of cells.
   b. The specific shape of the protein determines its role.
   c. Proteins are very important molecules in cells.
   d. Proteins are synthesized in the body through translation.

2. Read this sentence from the second paragraph.

   Globular proteins like **hemoglobin**, on the other hand, are folded and compact.

   How does this sentence help develop the ideas in the paragraph?

   a. It explains how the shape of globular proteins is similar to the shape of other proteins.
   b. It shows the similarities between the shape of hemoglobin and the shape of collagen and keratin.

STANDARDIZE THE FORMAT

   c. It shows how the shape of hemoglobin is 3D in structure.

   d. It contrasts the shape of globular proteins with the shape of structural proteins.

3. What is the author's main purpose in this article?

   a. to examine the roles of specific proteins

   b. to explain the process of translation and how proteins are involved

   c. to explain key information about proteins

   d. to explain how the structure of proteins influences their role

4. Describe the structure of structural proteins.

5. Describe the structure of globular proteins.

6. Explain where translation occurs.

Evaluation:

_____

_____

_____

_____

_____

_____

Ideas I could steal from Vicki:

_____

_____

_____

_____

_____

_____

LESSON MATERIALS EXCERPT 5:
ADAM FEILER, GRADE 2 MATH

Uncommon Schools | Change History.

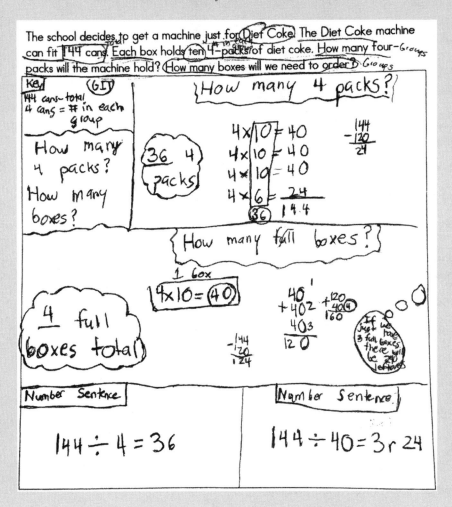

Evaluation:

_____

_____

_____

_____

Ideas I could steal from Adam:

_____

_____

_____

STANDARDIZE THE FORMAT

LESSON MATERIALS EXCERPT 6: BETH VERRILLI, GRADES 11 AND 12 READING

LADY MACBETH   1.5.15-33

believes witches/prophecies will come true

Mb + Lmb
↳ both start by repeating witches' words
↳ potential for evil

15   Glamis thou art, and Cawdor; and shalt be
      King
      What thou art promised   worry abt   Yet do I fear thy nature;

      too kind to kill king
      It is too full o' th' milk of human kindness

      take   shortest route ①   wish to
      To catch the nearest way. Thou wouldst be great,

      Art not without ambition, but without
      ruthlessness
20   The illness should attend it. What thou wouldst
                                    would greatly like
          highly,   wants it alot but he's holy
      would like to do in saintly way
      That wouldst thou holily; wouldst not play false,   ③ cheat

                                            ④ pieces of
      And yet wouldst wrongly win. Thou'd'st have, great ④   evidence

                                            • she is more ruthless
          Glamis,   • she's always been
      Murder   thinking of th.
25   That which cries "Thus thou must do," if thou have   foreshadows
      ·into murder   her taking
          it,   matters into own
      murder   hand
      And that which rather thou dost fear to do,
                                you come here
      Than wishest should be undone. Hie thee hither,
                witches
      That I may pour my spirits in thine ear — say something)   I will talk
      rebuke   — talking   )   him into
30   And chastise with the valor of my tongue   it.
                                crown
      All that impedes thee from the golden round,

      Which fate and metaphysical aid doth seem   push Mb to crown

      To have thee crowned withal.   1) talking
                                                    2) witches
                                                    3) fate

Is she a witch?
    or just capable of
    doing bad things

2

Evaluation:

_____

_____

_____

_____

_____

_____

_____

Ideas I could steal from Beth:

_____

_____

_____

_____

_____

_____

STANDARDIZE THE FORMAT

STANDARDIZE THE FORMAT

LESSON MATERIALS EXCERPT 7: ERIN MICHELS, GRADE 3 MATH

Uncommon Schools | Change History.

1. Ms. Paragas went to the store and bought a carton of 6 eggs.

Write a fraction that represents the whole carton of eggs. _____

She used 4 eggs to make breakfast for her family. Draw a model to represent this thinking.

Is there another fraction that represents the amount of eggs she used to cook breakfast? How do you know?

Circle the numerators in your fractions. Put a box around the denominators of your fractions.

2. Darlene picked 7 apples. Juan picked 4 times as many apples. How many apples did he pick?

Equation _____	
Unknowns	Knowns

Evaluation:

_____

_____

_____

Ideas I could steal from Erin:

_____

_____

LESSON MATERIALS EXCERPT 8: DAVID JAVSICAS, GRADE 7 READING

Uncommon Schools | Change History.

Lord of the Flies

by William Golding

Pre-reading

1. Which <u>best</u> describes the **real cause** of the conflict between Ralph and Jack at the end of yesterday's reading?
   a. Ralph wants to return to the shelters to help Piggy, but Jack wants to find the beast.
   b. Jack mocks Piggy, which angers Ralph because Piggy's intelligence is so valuable to the group.
   c. Ralph wants to continue their search for the beast when there is more daylight, but Jack argues that it will take them hours to go back to the shelters.
   d. Jack challenges Ralph's decisions to make Ralph look weak.
2. Support your answer to #1 with explanation and details. Elaborate!

_____

_____

_____

_____

3. What could you infer about the reason Samneric, Bill, and Robert didn't want to go up the mountain? How was it different from Ralph's reason?

_____

_____

_____

_____

Set the Stage

Vocabulary:

Hierarchy-noun: classification or ____*[ranking]*_____ in a group based on status, ____ *[power]*_____, and ____*[authority]*_____.

- Can be a *formal* hierarchy: In the army, generals are above sergeants.
- Or an *informal* hierarchy: Among the friends, everyone respected and listened to Bob.
  - The wolf pack has a hierarchy in which the alpha male is at the top and everyone else is constantly fighting to move up.
  - The coach doesn't rank the players, but there is a clear hierarchy on the team. Tina is at the top because she is a strong and confident player, and Lisa is at the bottom because she is terrible, and nobody likes her anyway.

Other forms:

Hierarchical-adj: organized by _____[*rank*]_____

1. Do you think the boys in *Lord of the Flies* have a hierarchy? Who is at the top? The bottom?

_____

_____

Active Reading:

By the time you finish reading this portion of the novel, you should be able to . . .

1. Explain Ralph's new understanding of Jack.
2. Describe the events of the expedition and their significance.

Stop, Jot, and Discuss #1

1. **Golden Sentence?** What did Ralph do to make Jack's taunt "powerless"? Start your sentence with "Despite Jack's . . ."

_____

_____

_____

2. Why is it illogical for the boys to go up the mountain right now? (2 reasons)

_____

_____

_____

3. **Challenge:** If it is illogical, why are they going up?

_____

_____

_____

Accountable Independent Reading

1. What did Jack think he saw at the top of the mountain? What do you think he saw?

_____

_____

_____

2. How did Jack feel about what he saw? Explain using evidence from the text.

_____

_____

_____

Challenge: How does Ralph respond? How does this affect the struggle for power between Jack and Ralph?

_____

_____

_____

Evaluation:

_____

_____

_____

_____

_____

_____

Ideas I could steal from Dave:

_____

_____

_____

_____

_____

OUR OBSERVATIONS ON THE EXAMPLES

Example 1. Bryan Belanger, Grade 8 Math

Bryan designates a lined space where students can record the steps they took to solve certain problems. This makes it easy for him to identify precisely where in the problem-solving process students erred if they arrived at the wrong answer, and the most efficient way to address it. He also allocates space for "stamp it," which is where they are expected to lock down into a sentence a key understanding from the lesson. This makes it easy for him to gauge whether students are drawing the right conclusions. Bryan also allocates space for students to "Show Work Here" to distinguish their math from that of the student whose work they're trying to rework. This helps him find what he needs quickly, efficiently, and with clarity. Finally, he frequently requires students to explain their thinking for each answer. This illuminates students' thinking—both correct and incorrect—which in turn helps Bryan more effectively assess and respond to student understanding.

Example 2. Ellie Strand, Grade 8 Reading

Ellie engineers space for students to write about what they just read (a passage from George Orwell's *Animal Farm*), then to record notes from a discussion about their writing, and finally to rewrite their original response in light of the discussion. She also includes the line that she wants students to analyze and write about. This eliminates students' need to flip between the text and their response, which maximizes the time they can spend writing and reflecting. This helps Ellie isolate the markup students do of this key line, which is yet another data point that she can work with. From a *Ratio* standpoint, Ellie builds the read-write-discuss-revise cycle into her students' lesson materials. This requires students to write directly from the text, which is more rigorous than if they'd discussed their ideas beforehand, because it prevents them from being able to piggyback off each other's comments. And the revision that follows holds students accountable for closely tracking the discussion and then using what they learn to refine their ideas.

Example 3. Erica Lim, Grade 9 World History

Students in Erica's class use this template to capture notes during lecture and while reading texts in class. This template helps students organize their thinking while ensuring that Erica can easily monitor the quality of students' note taking, which is a crucial skill for preparing students to succeed in college. It also turns these notes into a useful resource that students can refer back to and study. Specifically, the template allocates space for students to record main ideas and also to document key dates, terms, and a summary of what they've learned. Erica intentionally grafts this template onto what looks like notebook paper, which in turn makes the note taking feel more collegiate. As the year progresses, she gradually removes these structures and transfers ownership of note taking to students, and allows them to take notes on their own paper.

Example 4. Vicki Hernandez, Grade 8 Biology

Vicki embeds the article about protein synthesis that she wants students to read into the handout so that students have everything they need in one place. She also includes an annotation checklist, which standardizes how students will mark it up. Standardizing text markup makes it easier for Vicki to monitor comprehension and identify learning gaps early—*before* students even begin tackling the questions that follow. She also follows multiple-choice questions with a space for students to write their thinking. This helps Vicki balance the need to gather quick data via multiple-choice with the need to study students' thinking more closely in writing so that she can effectively diagnose underlying misunderstandings.

Example 5. Adam Feiler, Grade 2 Math

Adam taught his scholars to *Standardize the Format* of their math work so that he can easily track both their answers and their thought process. As we can see from this photo, Adam's students identify and partition each part of the problem they need to solve for, show the work they used to solve each part, and finally box their answers. They are also expected to report their final answers to the problem as number sentences at the very bottom. This makes it easy for him to isolate and monitor each aspect of the problem-solving process—from the arithmetic to the final answers. He can more efficiently identify errors and retrace the steps students took that may have led them to "wrong." He also teaches students to identify important information they'll need to solve the problem and to box it as a "key." This allows him to track whether students are working with the correct numbers or figures before they even begin tackling the problem. By teaching students to organize their work clearly, he sets them up to succeed not just in his class but in future math classes.

Example 6. Beth Verrilli, Grades 11 and 12 Reading

In this example, we see how a student in Beth's classroom legibly and thoroughly marked up a key speech from Shakespeare's *Macbeth* during a stretch of independent reading. Most notably, we see evidence that the student carefully assembled evidence to support a key argument or interpretation from the lines she arrows out from the text into the margin. The student also numbers the evidence, which makes it easier for her to cite as she formulates her written response. From a design standpoint, we can also see that Beth numbers the lines from the speech to make it even easier for her and students to refer to it for writing and discussion. An added benefit is that it makes it easier for Beth to efficiently monitor the key phrases and lines that students are struggling with or gravitating to, and therefore to gauge comprehension.

Example 7. Erin Michels, Grade 3 Math

Erin provides students with designated spaces to record models that represent their thinking, the equation they've come up with to solve a problem, the figures they'll need to use to solve the problem ("knowns"), the numbers they'll need to solve for ("unknowns"), and ultimately the correct answer to a problem. This enables her to quickly retrace the steps students took to solve the problem, which in turn helps her diagnose and target misconceptions more effectively. The formatting also helps students account for all aspects of the problem. It's harder to skip steps or overlook a part of the problem when the teacher has visibly engineered space for you to do that work.

Example 8. David Javsicas, Grade 7 Reading

Teachers also *Standardize the Format* to make the process of gathering data during writing-intensive lessons as efficient and manageable as possible. David Javsicas, a seventh-grade reading teacher, inserts numbered spaces for students to write responses to various prompts. This helps him avoid having to fumble through sheaves of student writing to locate their responses to specific questions.

TRACKING, NOT WATCHING

OVERVIEW

As we discussed in technique 3, the design of both lesson materials and the classroom itself is critical to maximizing the efficiency with which we can observe our students' level of mastery as they work. But how we approach the task of observing also matters. To gather data most effectively, we must be intentional about observing with diligence and focusing on what is most important, tracking it even, rather than merely watching to see whether students are working. This notion, *Tracking, Not Watching*, might seem obvious, but it presents a constant challenge. As you *Circulate* (technique 24) and observe, there's no shortage of things to see and think about, so it's easy to find your attention sidetracked from the most important thing. Of course there are the mundane distractions: the ringing tardy bell, the need to ask Alberto to move his backpack, Jacinta wearing her glasses for the first time. But there are others. You *Circulate* and think happily, *They are working hard this morning. They are almost done.* This is very different from observing the degree to which each student is factoring correctly, what the most common error is among those who are doing it incorrectly, and that Chris is gamely filling the page with meaningless figures. Your task is to overcome these distractions and focus on the touchpoints of mastery as you observe. To do that, it helps to know specifically what you are looking for. We'll discuss the two things great teachers look for—specific errors and success points—and how to track them to make trends more visible and therefore actionable.

ANALYZE THE CHAMPIONS

 Clip FG3, Megan Broome, Grade 2

Clip FG4, Taryn Pritchard, Grade 6

In these clips, compare what Megan and Taryn do as they collect data while *Circulating* and how they respond to data.

Megan Broome	Taryn Pritchard

Similarities:

_____

_____

_____

When you might try either approach:

Megan's: _____

_____

_____

Taryn's: _____

_____

_____

FUNDAMENTALS

You might divide *Tracking, Not Watching* into two parts. The first is to get as clear as you can on what you're looking for; the second is to use tools that help you collect and track evidence of it.

The legendary basketball coach John Wooden offered this advice to teachers (of basketball and other things): "Never mistake activity for achievement." A busy gym with sneakers squeaking or a classroom full of pencils scratching is evidence of activity. This is often a good thing, but different from and easier to spot than achievement—a gym or a classroom that yields students who pass and move or factor equations impeccably.

It's easier to monitor activity levels than it is to track precisely where and how students' mastery of a skill is starting to break down. When we engage in *watching,* we are often merely observing signs of productivity or completion, and whether students are following our instructions. We are mistaking activity for achievement. Because activity often occurs alongside achievement, it is also the single biggest distraction to observers. When you set out to find evidence of mastery and learning, it's easy to get swept up by all the hard work you see students doing.

Reflection

When do you find yourself drawn to watching for activity when watching for achievement would be better? Why? (Note: this question is asked with complete lack of judgment, considering that we're pretty sure everyone does this at least some of the time.)

_____

_____

_____

_____

Tracking Specific Errors and Success Points

To focus on achievement, we suggest tracking two key indicators of learning: specific errors and success points.

Specific errors are the things students are most likely to struggle with in a given task. These errors complete the phrase, "If they get it wrong, they will probably . . ." We suggest keeping about two specific errors in mind. More than that is too much to focus on with discipline, and watching for too many things isn't always that different from watching for nothing in particular.

Success points are the one or two things that most readily distinguish excellence at the task from mere completion of it. They answer the question, "What would 'great' look like?"

Thinking of specific errors and success points in advance and looking for them as you observe can change the game. It's a simple task, but it helps you see differently.

Here's a thought exercise: Choose a sport or a type of artistic performance that you enjoy watching and know fairly well (modern dance, say, or the saxophone). Jot down two or three success points and try to watch just for those specific things for ten minutes. What do you notice, both about the event and also about your own observation?

_____

_____

_____

_____

A key first step in identifying success points and specific errors can be to draft an ideal answer or target response for the question. This clarifies your sense of what students will likely succeed or struggle with, and lets you more efficiently track for specifics and respond appropriately with reteaching or stretch opportunities that can help students take work from "good" to "great."

Once you know what the success points are in a given activity, *share them with your students*. You could do this by embedding success points directly in students' materials in the form of a "tip box," as self-checks ("You know you're 'showing not telling' if . . ."), or in the form of model student work. You can do the same with specific errors, which we recently saw math teacher Arielle Hoo do. "Make sure that you're careful with your symbols. Think about what kind of line you should have when you're graphing," she said to her students as she sent them off to graph linear equations. She understood what it meant if students lost track of negative and positive when graphing, so she helped them avoid doing so with a helpful reminder.

Try It Out

Jot down a key question that you'll ask students to complete as independent work in an upcoming lesson. Then take a moment to reflect on what you'll look for as you *Circulate* among your students. Draft a target correct response (see technique 2) and use it to generate success points and specific errors.

Key question: _____

_____

Target response: _____

_____

_____

Success points (qualities that distinguish excellence from completion):

- _____

- _____

- _____

Specific errors:

- _____

- _____

How is completing this exercise likely to change this lesson activity and perhaps the overall lesson for you?

_____

_____

Global versus Targeted Tracking

Once you know what you're looking for, a second question to consider is, Am I observing all my students equally on this task, or am I focusing on a subset of the group for some reason?

We refer to the first option—gathering data from every, or nearly every, student within a certain amount of time with the goal of gauging the general trend of the larger group—as *global tracking*. The second option is *targeted tracking*: gathering data on a specific group of students (a group who are ready for more challenge or a group who are struggling) or specifically seeking out student responses that are worthy of study, such as those containing a common error or that demonstrate excellence.

Ordinarily the goal of global tracking is to understand your class by seeing the greatest possible sampling of data. It gives you the most comprehensive (and potentially accurate) snapshot of student learning. You might also use it as an opportunity to give individualized feedback to a large proportion of the class. Global tracking can also build a culture of accountability in which students always do their best work because they know you will check it.

Observing Sari Fromson's classroom, for example, we noticed that students were so accustomed to her looking at their work that they would eagerly flip to the page that Sari intended to examine as she approached them. Scholars welcomed her checking because they knew she would also give them feedback that would help them make it better.

The benefits of targeted tracking are equally rich and varied. When you aren't trying to observe every piece of work, you have more time to thoroughly evaluate the work you do inspect. From there, you can more strategically gather work that is exemplary or that contains a unique strength or common error to learn from.

To mitigate the costs of gathering data from some (but not all) students, many teachers select a strategic subset of students. For instance, Bryan Belanger says that he sometimes prioritizes *Circulating* to a select group of middle- to high-performing students first. They are his proverbial canaries in a coal mine because they're often an indicator of the class's overall mastery. Other teachers strategically observe work done by a student or two from lower-, middle-, and higher-performing subgroups.

Given your class size, grade level, and subjects, when and why might you use each kind of tracking?

	When	Why
Global		
Targeted		

What to Track and Where

As you might already be thinking, a great next step is to record the data as you observe student work. Although there's no one right way, here are some thoughts on how and what to track. *What* teachers write down can include who got a question right or wrong (sometimes expressed as hash marks, dashes, or tallies), whom to call on for a given question and why, and ideas that are worthy of discussion. Some teachers then distill this data into actionable trends and briefly sketch out a response to error. *Where* they record this information can include everything from a copy of student materials with model answers included (Example 1), to a separate planning document (Example 2), or maybe even a class list of some kind (Example 3). There are merits to all of these approaches.

Example 1. Taryn Pritchard

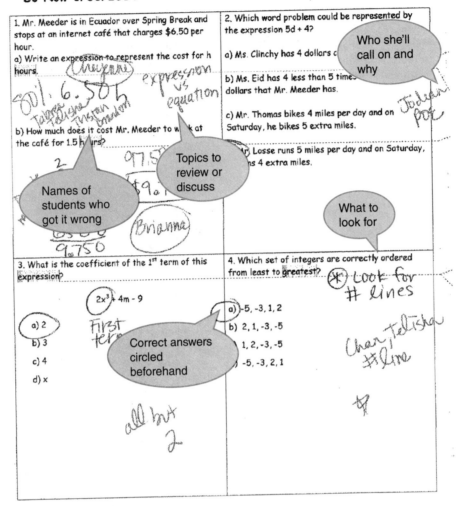

Example 2. Nicole Willey

Point of Error	Number of Students Making the Error
Error 1: Scholars incorrectly multiply 6 × 35.	
Error 2: Scholars incorrectly use the total of 210 beads in the final step of the problem.	
Error 3: Scholars create a bracelet with fewer than 20 beads.	

Example 3. Jen Rugani

Week of:	Question #		Trends
	1	2	
Anndriana			
Jahvon			
Autumn			
Jayden			
Sanoah			
Tarrah			
Jaiden			
Michael			
Joshua			
Tamiyah			
Omrasi			
Kemiyah			
Joshua			Next Steps
Christopher			
Baron			
Kinga			
Christine			
Shayanne			
James			
Adrianalee			
Aiden			
Total %			

To Example 1 we've added comments in labels. Add your own labels to all three. What's effective? What could you use, and how?

_____

_____

_____

We've added more commentary on these examples at the end of this technique.

Individual versus Batched Feedback

As important as gathering data is acting on it. But *when* to provide such feedback, and to whom? It's powerful to provide timely feedback while you *Circulate,* so in some cases you might give immediate and individualized feedback to specific students. This allows you to reinforce positive habits, push advanced students, and address individuals' errors before they snowball into larger misconceptions. It communicates accountability for written work and fosters a sense of productive urgency. Our colleague Paul Bambrick-Santoyo refers to this as "aggressive monitoring."

Another option is to use batched feedback—withholding immediate "real time" feedback as you *Circulate* and spending the time observing and analyzing at a more macro level instead. Then you can give feedback to the class (or a group) at a strategic moment. Batching feedback can allow you more time to observe, analyze, or plan how to reteach to a wider audience. For independent practice, holding off on batching until midstream or the end of the activity can make the practice more truly independent. And batching can allow for more self-checking ("Scholars, make sure you didn't forget to . . .").

Neither method is intrinsically better. Choosing is a matter of when and why. How might these factors matter for you? What are the benefits of each for you?

_____

_____

_____

_____

> **blog** Find this blog post at teachlikeachampion.com/blog/hunting-versus-fishing/.
> "Hunting Versus Fishing" discusses synergies between *Tracking, Not Watching* and several other techniques.

PRACTICE *TRACKING, NOT WATCHING*

This is a great activity to do with a group, with a partner, or by yourself. Print it out to complete on paper. If there are more than one of you, share one "classroom" and one set of examples, but hold and fill out individual copies of the worksheet.

The situation is that a middle school science teacher has asked her class, "In one well-constructed sentence, say what happens to air pressure in a container as volume increases—and why."

Cut the examples apart and, if possible, scatter them on desks or chairs throughout the room. Then *Circulate* (technique 24) about the room, reading and responding to them on the worksheet. ("Success points" on the worksheet refers to good things students did.)

After completing the worksheet, select one example you would use as the basis for a class discussion, and be prepared to tell the group why you chose it.

After everyone has done these things, compare your notes and experience. Go around the group, each identifying a "glow" ("One thing that was effective . . .") and a "grow" in a fellow teacher's work. Look for these success points:

- The teacher effectively records a common, discussion-worthy error that appears in multiple examples of student work.
- The teacher selects a "good" piece of work that also contains this error.

Incorporating the feedback, improve your own worksheet. Also come up with some takeaways about how you might strengthen your own *Tracking, Not Watching.*

WORKSHEET

Question: "In one well-constructed sentence, say what happens to air pressure in a container as volume increases—and why."
Target: "As volume increases, air pressure decreases, because there is more space for the air particles to move, which leads to fewer collisions between air particles."

Student name: _____

Error(s): _____

_____

Success point(s): _____

_____

Student name: _____

Error(s): _____

_____

Success point(s): _____

_____

Student name: _____

Error(s): _____

_____

Success point(s): _____

_____

Student name: _____

Error(s): _____

_____

Success point(s): _____

_____

Student name: _____

Error(s): _____

_____

Success point(s): _____

_____

Common error(s) in these examples: _____

_____

Examples

1. Jimmy

As volume increases, the air pressure decreases because of the space.

2. Martin

As volume increases, It will decrease the air pressure.

3. Lyla

As volume increases, the air pressure decreases because theres more room for the air particles to move around in so they slow down and dont hit each other.

4. Terrance

As volume increases, the air pressure would decrease because there is more space for the molecules to go around and the molecules won't bump into each other as likely as before.

5. Crystal

As volume increases, air pressure decreases because their is more space which decreases the likeability that they will collide.

ACTION PLANNING

Use this action planner to continue your work with *Tracking, Not Watching*. (Find a printable version of this form at my.teachlikeachampion.com.) You'll know you're on the right track when . . .

- You're gathering good data on how well students are doing, rather than just watching to see who is idle, busy, or done.
- You've already strategized a bit about how you will deal with foreseeable errors.

HOW AM I DOING?

_____

_____

_____

Design one or more action steps for improvement. Decide on an interval by which you'll revisit this page to assess your progress.

Action Step 1

By when, with whom, and how you will measure your effort

By _____, I will . . .
    Date

_____

_____

_____

How Did I Do?

Successes: _____

_____

_____

_____

_____

Challenges: _____

_____

_____

_____

Next steps: _____

_____

_____

_____

Action Step 2

By when, with whom, and how you will measure your effort

By _____, I will . . .
_{Date}

_____

_____

_____

How Did I Do?

Successes: _____

_____

_____

_____

Challenges: _____

_____

_____

_____

Next steps: _____

_____

_____

_____

TRACKING, NOT WATCHING

OUR OBSERVATIONS ON THE TRACKING DOCUMENTS

Example 1. Taryn Pritchard

If you look closely at the picture of Taryn's *Do Now* (technique 20) from a recent math lesson, you may notice two layers of notation. The first consists of the notes Taryn made to herself before she observed. They include the target responses to the problems, including the "shown" work for problem 1, and a note to herself to look for the number lines on problem 4. In the picture, we can also see the notes she took as she tracked student data. She noted that 80 percent of students got number 1 right, but four students didn't. She noted a student whom she wanted to call on for each problem, as well as a key issue that emerged unexpectedly—the difference between *expression* and *equation*. Taryn has not only demonstrated fantastic skills in checking for understanding but also prepared herself to review her *Do Now* efficiently and with maximal value in five minutes or less by doing the most important things first.

Example 2. Nicole Willey

In this example, we see how Nicole prepared to gather and organize data on specific errors in response to this story problem:

> Yedidah is making friendship bracelets for her birthday party. At the store, beads are sold in packs of 35. She decides to buy 6 packs. When she gets home, her mother suggests using 20 beads on each of her friends' bracelets. How many complete bracelets can Yedidah make for her friends?

Nicole avoided generalities (for example, "students forget to show work" or "students will multiply incorrectly") and instead planned for highly specific errors students were likely to make. Adjacent to this list of specific errors is a space for Nicole to tally the number of students who made them. In some cases, she may include the names of students on whom she wants to call and bring into the discussion about the common error. The column of tally marks makes it especially easy for her to identify trends so that she knows which errors to prioritize for whole-class discussion and which to address through individual feedback.

Although it's not evident in this planning document, Nicole also planned questions to help herself diagnose the underlying misconception behind each specific error. For example, to diagnose the root cause of error 1, she planned to ask herself the following: "Are scholars struggling to use a tens/ones strategy to find the total? Are scholars in/correctly using partial products to solve?" Attuning herself to errors with this level of detail enabled her to address the error with far greater efficiency than if she had waited to try to diagnose that during the whole-class discussion. Although this level of planning may not be needed for every lesson, it can help if you're already tracking for specific errors and want to take your planning to the next level.

Example 3. Jen Rugani

Jen repurposes her seating chart as a document for tracking data as she *Circulates* during the *Do Now*. If a student gets question 1 correct, she marks that down in the column for that question. As she marks, she identifies trends and briefly jots responses to error. Oftentimes, she'll plan her responses to anticipated trends in error so that she can respond efficiently once she identifies them during her lesson.

SHOW ME

OVERVIEW

In a typical class, a teacher will spend some portion of her instructional time hunting and gathering the data she needs to better understand what her students know about what she is teaching. *Show Me* accelerates this by asking students to actively present their answers—often as data—to the teacher, usually in unison. This can yield a more complete—and possibly more accurate—snapshot of student understanding. In providing that snapshot quickly and efficiently, *Show Me* allows you to start using the data right away. We will discuss two primary forms of *Show Me*: hand signals and slates.

ANALYZE THE CHAMPIONS

Watch the clips in order, answering the questions as you go.

▶ **Clip FG5. Amy Youngman, Grade 5**

In clip FG5, what does Amy do that enables her to efficiently gather accurate data on student understanding? What happens as a result?

_____

_____

_____

▶ **Clip FG6. Bryan Belanger, Grade 8**

In clip FG6, what's effective about Bryan's *Show Me*? Pay particular attention to the system he uses and what he says and does after the *Show Me*.

_____

_____

_____

Compare your observations with ours at the end of this technique.

Reflection

If you're already using *Show Me* or other systematic ways to gather data, what's been your experience so far? If not, what's one idea from the video clips that you could use or adapt when you first try it?

FUNDAMENTALS

As we mentioned, there are two primary types of *Show Me*. The "hand signals" variation involves students simultaneously signaling their answers on their fingers (or with some other simple format). The "slates" variation involves students showing work they've written on individual whiteboards. Both are intended to ensure that students reveal quick, objective data to their teacher, usually at the same time.

Hand Signals

In addition to being useful, hand signals can be fun and energizing for students. As we see in Bryan's classroom in clip FG6, his rock-paper-scissors routine for cueing the activity—quick drumbeats on desks before the crisply synched hand signal—builds momentum. It's fun and rhythmic. His students *want* to reveal their answers, which in turn makes the system more sustainable for him in the long run.

But notice that when teachers like Bryan employ hand signals, they ask their students to present objective rather than subjective data—their *actual* answers rather than their confidence or how much they think they understood. For example, Bryan's students hold up one or more fingers to represent the multiple-choice option they picked (one finger = A, two fingers = B, and so on). This provides him with data he needs to address students' specific misunderstandings. Contrast this with the teacher who asks students to express their comfort level with a topic with a "fist-to-five" or "thumbs up, down, or to the side." Even though hand signals are involved, these approaches yield data that's subjective and less reliable.

Slates

To use slates for *Show Me,* ask students to complete a bit of independent work—on notebook paper or an erasable whiteboard—and then cue them to hold it up to show you what they've done. This allows you to ask students to show you useful data on their understanding in formats other than multiple choice. For example, we recently watched a teacher give his ninth graders an algebraic equation and ask students to show him the *y*-intercept, the slope, or some other key piece of information. You could just as easily ask for the definition of a key term, the property demonstrated by an example, the name of the speaker in a passage from *Animal Farm,* or even an artfully crafted sentence about the Cuban Missile Crisis.

Answers in unison are critical to hand signals but less critical with slates. The method works whether students "show" as they are ready or on your cue—just so long as you ensure that they don't piggyback on their classmates' answers.

CASE STUDIES

Read each case, writing some "glows" and "grows" for each. Then compare your observations with ours.

Case 1. Slates in Grade 8 Science

1. MR. MCCLEARY: On your slates, take forty-five seconds to write down the word equation that represents the process of photosynthesis.
     (Thirty-five seconds later)

Ten more seconds . . . three . . . two . . . one. We need a few sets of eyes . . . now just one more. Thank you. Now show! *(All boards go up. Most are raised high.)*

2. MR. MCCLEARY: *(scans room with a swivel of the head)* Thank you for having those boards nice and high. *(stands on tiptoes to see a few more)* Boards down. Looks like 70 percent of us got it. Jimmy, can you read your answer?

3. JIMMY:

$$\text{carbon dioxide + water} \xrightarrow[\text{chlorophyll}]{\text{light}} \text{oxygen}$$

4. MR. MCCLEARY: What product is he missing, Teresa?
5. TERESA: Oh. Me? Um . . . *(shrugs)*
6. MR. MCCLEARY: Who can help her out? *(Eric raises his hand.)* Eric, give it a shot.
7. ERIC: Jimmy forgot to include glucose as a product.
8. MR. MCCLEARY: Right. And why is that useful for plants, Teresa?
9. TERESA: *(writing on her whiteboard)* Oh sorry, I was adding something to my answer.
10. MR. MCCLEARY: Markers should be capped, Teresa. Listen closely because we're coming back to you. *(Teresa's marker cap snaps along with a few others. More hands go up.)* Why is glucose so important for plants, Gerald?
11. GERALD: Glucose is important for plants because it can be converted into cellulose.
12. MR. MCCLEARY: And how does that help plants, Teresa?
13. TERESA: Cellulose is important to plants because plant cells need it to grow.
14. MR. MCCLEARY: Well done. Erase your boards. Next question.

Glows	Grows
It was effective when Mr. McCleary . . .	Next time, Mr. McCleary could try . . .

SHOW ME

Case 2. Hand Signals in Grade 3 Math

The following is a multiple-choice problem Ms. Martina wants to review from a *Do Now* activity (technique 20) the students completed when they entered the classroom. The hand signals system she uses requires students to raise fingers in the air on cue to reveal the answer choice they selected from the following problem (one finger = A, two fingers = B, three fingers = C, four fingers = D).

Question 4. What fraction of this figure is shaded?

A. **3/8** (one finger)
B. **5/8** (two fingers)
C. **3/5** (three fingers)
D. **1/2** (four fingers)

1. MS. MARTINA: Some of us had some trouble with question four. Let's learn from that. Raise the number of fingers that shows me what choice you picked. Signals in the air on two. One . . . two!
(Nearly all hands shoot up right away. Two more go up a second later.)

2. MS. MARTINA: *(scans room)* Good. I'm seeing mostly ones, but also some twos. Hands down. OK. Jenna, tell me why you chose B?

3. JENNA: The whole was cut into eight pieces, so I knew the eight had to be in the denominator. After that, I kind of guessed.

4. MS. MARTINA: Jenna, you're right. The eight has to be in the denominator. But we need to figure out whether the number three or five goes in the numerator. Tiana, why did you put a five in the numerator?

5. TIANA: It looks like three pieces of the whole were darker, like they were taken out. So there are five left over, which gives us five-eighths.

6. MS. MARTINA: Timothy, you don't seem convinced. Explain why you disagree with Tiana.

7. TIMOTHY: Because the problem asks for which fraction of the figure is *shaded*. Since three parts are shaded, and there are eight parts to the whole, the answer has to be three-eighths.

8. MS. MARTINA: *(subtly nods head)* Class, thumbs up if you agree with Timothy. Thumbs down if you disagree.
(All thumbs go up.)

9. MS. MARTINA: Correct. Your answer should be A. Check or change it.

Glows	Grows
It was effective when Ms. Martina . . .	Next time, Ms. Martina could try . . .

SHOW ME

SOME OBSERVATIONS ON THE CASES

Case 1. Mr. McCleary's Slates

It was effective when Mr. McCleary held out for 100 percent of eyes on him before he moved on with the *Show Me*. This may help account for why *all* students were ready to show him their work on cue. Also, he drew attention to the fact that he was carefully checking students' boards by narrating what he saw ("Thank you for having those boards nice and high") and exaggerating his scan with a swivel or by standing on tiptoes (see technique 51, *Radar/Be Seen Looking*). Twice Teresa opted out of answering his questions, but he continually returned to her with *Cold Call* questions (technique 33) to ensure that she participates.

Next time, Mr. McCleary could hold out for all boards to be up high before moving on with the *Show Me*. If students don't raise their boards as he expects, he could anonymously correct students ("Just need a few in the back to raise theirs even higher") or ask the class to *Do It Again* (technique 50) until everyone gets it right: "Let's try that again with *all* our boards nice and high." Before cueing the *Show Me,* he could scan to see that all whiteboards are down and markers capped. This would help him avoid the pitfall of students' continuing to write on their boards during the discussion. Instead of moving on after Teresa answers one question correctly, he could follow up with *Targeted Questions* (technique 2) to make sure she and others truly understand the topic at hand.

Case 2. Ms. Martina's Hand Signals

Ms. Martina used language that reinforced a culture in which students felt safe exposing and learning from their mistakes ("Some of us had some trouble with question four. Let's learn from that"). She strategically used *Cold Call* on students who selected B (the most common wrong answer) as well as a student who got it right to foster a productive dialogue that ultimately helped clarify the correct answer. Also she held students accountable for recording the correct answer by prompting them to "check" to see whether they got it right and "change" it on their paper if they didn't.

When students don't raise their hands in unison, she could ask them to *Do It Again* (technique 50). After the first two students she called on got it wrong, she finally arrived at a student who got it right and then moved on as if everyone understood. Next time, she might follow up with the students who got it wrong by asking them a few more *Cold Call* questions to test for reliability. Also, without meaning to do so, Ms. Martina subtly hinted at what the correct answer was by nodding in response to Timothy's answer before she announced it. This jeopardized the reliability of the data she received from the class poll she conducted.

Reflection

Using what you've learned, respond to this teacher's concerns about bringing *Show Me* into his classroom. Write your response before you look at ours.

> I'm worried that using a *Show Me* means I have to lower the rigor of my questions and make everything multiple-choice. In my class, students do a lot of reading and writing, and I can't have them *Show Me* that. I'm also just worried about students copying each other's answers. If they're showing me their work, who's not to say they'll see each others' and then change it? I'm sure it works for some, but it seems like a lot more work than it's worth.

Possible responses (we're sure you've thought of others as well): When students "show" their answer to a multiple-choice question, teachers can raise the rigor by asking them to explain their thinking. They can make students' answers the starting point for rich and rigorous discussion, not the end of it. However, multiple-choice questions don't inherently lower rigor. It depends on how they are written. If a question or task demands that students engage in deep and complex thinking, it's probably rigorous, regardless of whether it's multiple choice or free response.

Show Me with slates would allow this teacher to assess students' thinking in multiple formats, including writing. For instance, he could ask students to summarize a complex idea in an artfully written sentence, and then have them show it to him. Other ideas for assessing in different formats: ask students to spell a word, write the definition for a key term, or show their work for a math problem. To prevent students from copying each other's answers, he can teach them to wait to show their answers at his cue ("Three . . . two . . . one . . . show!"). More specifically, for hand signals, he could even ask them to cover their eyes before they reveal their answers (a "blind" *Show Me*) or to hold their signals below their desks before revealing them. For slates, he needs to develop clear expectations for what students will do with their markers or writing utensils before the *Show Me* ("Markers down and capped").

PLANNING FOR AND ROLLING OUT *SHOW ME*

Use these lines and the two frameworks to plan a *Show Me*—either hand signals, slates, or both.

Question students will answer:

_____

_____

_____

Target response:

_____

_____

_____

Likely wrong answer:

_____

_____

_____

SHOW ME HAND SIGNALS FRAMEWORK

How I will cue hand signals (for example, "Rock-paper-scissors your answer on two. One . . . two!")

_____

_____

_____

What I'll say to show I'm looking:

_____

_____

_____

What I'll do to show I'm looking:

_____

_____

_____

My response to low or missing hands:

_____

_____

_____

First question I'll ask of a particular student who got it right:

_____

_____

_____

First question I'll ask of a particular student who got it wrong:

_____

_____

_____

SHOW ME SLATES FRAMEWORK

How I will cue slates (for example, "Markers capped in three . . . two . . . one. Show what you know!"):

_____

_____

What I'll say to show I'm looking:

_____

_____

What I'll do to show I'm looking:

_____

_____

My response to low or missing slates:

_____

_____

What students will do with writing materials (whiteboards, markers, other):

_____

_____

Before: _____

_____

_____

During: _____

_____

_____

After: _____

_____

_____

_____

_____

_____

First question I'll ask of one student who got it right:

_____

_____

_____

_____

_____

First question I'll ask of one student who got it wrong:

_____

_____

_____

_____

_____

SHOW ME

Rolling It Out

In the space here, plan how you want to introduce *Show Me* to your students. Make sure that your rollout

- Establishes clear expectations for what students should do and when
- Clearly and positively communicates the purpose for the *Show Me*
- Is quick and concise (best under two minutes)

_____

_____

_____

_____

_____

_____

If you can, practice your rollout with a partner and ask for feedback.

ANALYZE A CHAMPION

 Clip FG7. Nicole Willey, Grade 3 Reading

How has Nicole effectively adapted *Show Me* for her content area and setting? How could you use her approach—or a variation on it—with a classroom of thirty kids?

SHOW ME PRACTICE WITH TWO OR MORE COLLEAGUES

Select the version of *Show Me* you'll want to practice (hand signals or slates). With two other colleagues, practice the *Show Me* using what you planned earlier.

There are three rotating roles for this activity: *Teacher, Student 1,* and *Student 2.* Here is the basic sequence for each round:

1. *Teacher* poses a question, gives *Students 1* and *2* some wait time, and prompts the *Show Me*.
2. *Students* show their answers (via hand signals or slates). They answer correctly, except during Round 3, when *Student 1* gets it wrong.
3. *Teacher* receives feedback and then practices again to incorporate it.
4. Rotate roles and repeat the practice with a new *Teacher.*

Teacher's added instructions for each round:

Round 1. Both *Students* get it right. *Teacher* scans for data.
Round 2. Both *Students* get it right. Teacher chooses and questions one *Student*.
Round 3. *Student 1* gets it wrong, and *Student 2* gets it right. *Teacher* questions *Student 1*.

ACTION PLANNING

Find a printable version of this form at my.teachlikeachampion.com. Use the following success points to evaluate your progress at mastering *Show Me*:

- You're prepared with follow-up questions for greater rigor or clarifying mistakes.
- The class raises hands or slates in unison.
- No one copies or revises at the wrong time.
- You're getting clear data about the understanding of the class.

SHOW ME

HOW AM I DOING?

_____

_____

Design one or more action steps for improvement. Decide on an interval by which you'll revisit this page to assess your progress.

Action Step 1

By when, with whom, and how you will measure your effort

By _____, I will . . .
    Date

_____

_____

How Did I Do?

Successes: _____

_____

_____

_____

_____

Challenges: _____

_____

_____

_____

_____

Next steps: _____

_____

_____

_____

SHOW ME

Action Step 2

By when, with whom, and how you will measure your effort

By _____, I will . . .

_{Date}

_____

_____

_____

How Did I Do?

Successes: _____

_____

_____

_____

Challenges: _____

_____

_____

Next steps: _____

_____

_____

_____

SHOW ME

OUR OBSERVATIONS ON THE CHAMPIONS

 Clip FG5. Amy Youngman, Grade 5

Amy's routine for slates enables her to see all of her students' answers efficiently and to determine that they struggled most with the word *beautician*. She then combines slates with *Show Call* (technique 39, displaying a student's work to the entire class) to efficiently address errors. To minimize copying and premature revision, she requires students to cap their markers and flip over their boards while they await her cue to raise their boards up in unison.

Amy emphasizes accountability for revealing work by letting students know she's reading their responses ("Eli is holding his board up high . . . so is Natalie."). She also narrates the number of students who she sees revising their mistakes, which reduces the stigma of making errors and makes improving one's work seem normal.

 Clip FG6. Bryan Belanger, Grade 8

On Bryan's "one-two" cue, his students participate in a sort of rock-paper-scissors routine that asks them to hold up fingers to indicate their answers to a multiple-choice math question (one finger = A, two fingers = B, and so on). Because students are advised to raise their hands on cue, students can't delay to see how their peers responded before revealing their answer. This increases the reliability of the data Bryan collects. To draw attention to the fact that he's surveying their answers, he moves to the left-front corner of his classroom ("Pastore's Perch," as we shall call it in technique 51, *Radar/Be Seen Looking*), swivels his head, and narrates back ("That's a great adjustment from yesterday."). Note that he uses a follow-up *Cold Call* (technique 33) of Rayshawn to check the reliability of the data he collected.

 Clip FG7. Nicole Willey, Grade 3

Nicole is teaching a guided reading lesson with her third graders. In this twist on *Show Me,* she asks students to point to the evidence instead of asking them to first write it down and then read it or hold it up on slates. This gives her more time to act on the data and reduces the transaction cost of the *Show Me.* Within seconds of scanning, she's able to strategically call on students who she knows will share strong evidence that will launch the discussion in a productive direction.

If you were using this in a full classroom of students, you might ask them, for instance, to hold up their novels and point to where on a given page the climax or turning point of the story occurs. Or, if you were teaching about the parts of a cell, you might ask students to hold up their cell diagrams and point to the part of the cell that gets rid of wastes (the cell membrane). The key here is that you know exactly *where* students should be pointing.

AFFIRMATIVE CHECKING

OVERVIEW

In *Affirmative Checking,* students take an active role in checking for understanding, confirming (usually with you) that their work is correct, productive, or sufficiently rigorous at key points before they move on to the next stage of a task.

Reflection

What do you currently do to check for understanding during independent work?

ANALYZE THE CHAMPIONS

▶ **Clip FG8. Bob Zimmerli, Grade 7**

Even if you watched these clips while reading *Teach Like a Champion 2.0,* you'll benefit from viewing them now and answering the questions. For convenience, at the end of this technique we've included Doug's comments on them from that text. But answer in writing before you look there.

In Clip FG8, why does Bob give several problems rather than just one before the check?

What does Bob do when he notices several students repeating the same mistake?

Clip FG9. Hilary Lewis, Grade 1

In Clip FG9, you'll hear Hilary refer to STAR. Read technique 47 for more about the attentional and postural ingredients of this invaluable mnemonic cue.

How does Hilary frame the check as a positive and productive experience for her first-grade students?

_____

_____

In this instance, how does she *Standardize the Format* (technique 3)?

_____

Hilary calls students up to check in with her one by one. But Bob has students signal to him when they think they are ready. In what situations would Bob's way work best for you? In what situations would it make sense for you to decide who checks in and when like Hilary?

_____

_____

_____

FUNDAMENTALS

Ensuring Good Effect

One risk to using *Affirmative Checking* is that students who are ready to check in end up waiting for you—wasting time when they could be working, and potentially lessening their concentration. So it's worth thinking through how you can make sure that your students don't end up waiting around. Here are a few ideas; we've also included space to add your own.

Standardize the Format

Design student materials so that you can easily find what you need, when you need it. For instance, you could engineer space on students' handouts where they can write their answers or show their work. This will make you more efficient at finding answers. Or, you can make students responsible for pointing them out: "When I come around to check your work, point to your answer so I can find it quickly."

Use a rubric or answer sheet. This also speeds your checking.

Give several problems. Give students several problems to do. This allows you more time to check and ensures that all your students will finish at once. Bob Zimmerli demonstrates this in his video. Students must complete two problems and then get checked off. But he can start checking students as they finish the first problem. In other words, he's got twice as much time to get to everyone. You could take this up a notch by including "bonus" or "challenge" work.

Have students check. In some situations, you could have students check one another's work, especially if you were to give them a key so that they would be reliably correct in signing off on one another's work. Just remember that there's a strong incentive among kids to give one another positive feedback rather than saying, "No, you aren't getting it yet." Be sure to check on the checkers at some point, and plan lots of time for supporting those who have trouble with checking.

Your ideas:

_____

_____

_____

PLANNING AND ROLLOUT

In an upcoming lesson plan, look for a spot where *Affirmative Checking* would be useful. Make notes in the plan on

- The method of *Affirmative Checking* you'll use
- Which question or activity you'll check and where the sign-off will happen
- How you'll ensure efficiency and accuracy in checking

Because *Affirmative Checking* is a shared process, student buy-in is important. Script a brief rollout explanation you might use to explain to your students how the process works and how it benefits them. Start a draft of that here:

_____

_____

_____

_____

THE NEXT LEVEL

As we mentioned earlier, you don't always need to be the one who checks. When students are self-checking, you could post what to look for, or leave a key at handy places around the room. To yield more data for yourself, you could accompany the key with a check-off sheet on which students mark how well they did. When students are responsible for checking off one another's work, you can assign the job of checking to specific students.

Obviously, you want to be alert to the risk that student checking might dilute the accuracy of the data from *Affirmative Checking,* but it still can be valuable in terms of both efficiency and student ownership.

Perhaps in addition to your earlier lesson plan work, write notes to yourself about how you could distribute *Affirmative Checking* among students.

- Who will check? What work will they check? How and when?
- How will you ensure the efficiency and accuracy of the checking?
- Will you check on the quality of the checkers work at all? If so, how?

ACTION PLANNING

Find a printable version of this form at my.teachlikeachampion.com. Use these success points to assess your *Affirmative Checking*:

- It tells you what you need to know about what your students have learned.
- It leaves no student idle for substantial time.

HOW AM I DOING?

Design one or more action steps for improvement. Decide on an interval by which you'll revisit this page to assess your progress.

Action Step 1

By when, with whom, and how you will measure your effort

By _____, I will . . .
   _{Date}

How Did I Do?

Successes: _____

_____

_____

_____

Challenges: _____

_____

_____

_____

Next steps: _____

_____

_____

Action Step 2

By when, with whom, and how you will measure your effort

By _____, I will . . .
   Date

_____

_____

_____

How Did I Do?

Successes: _____

_____

_____

_____

_____

Challenges: _____

_____

_____

_____

Next steps: _____

_____

_____

_____

Revisit *Teach Like a Champion 2.0*

Doug's comments on the videos:

Clip FG8. Bob Zimmerli: [Bob] asks students to independently solve multistep equations. Because Bob knows that the content can be tricky, he instructs students to check in with him after every two problems. These checkpoints give him a way to collect data from every student, which in turn gives him a richer, more reliable snapshot of student understanding. This system of *Affirmative Checking* also holds students and teacher accountable to each other for achieving the same goal: mastery of the day's objective. By design, the process of spotting and fixing errors becomes a shared endeavor.

Bob circulates and carefully tracks students' papers. Because Bob *Standardized the Format,* carefully engineering the place where students record their work and answers, he's able to spend less time looking all over packets and more time processing and responding to student trends. Practically speaking, saving a few seconds from countless scans every day would enable Bob to add back several days (possibly even weeks) of instructional time to each school year.

After checking in with a few students, Bob begins to notice a trend: students keep forgetting to combine like terms. Initially, he responds by pointing to a poster at the front of the room that outlines the steps students should take to solve each problem. Although the poster helps, Bob soon realizes that it would be far more efficient to reteach everyone the skill of combining like terms. To do this, Bob selects a problem that no one started and begins working through it. This helps him make sure that everyone (including high performers and early finishers) has something to learn from his mini-lesson. . . .

I suspect . . . Bob gave students two problems to do before each check-off . . . so Bob could actually start affirming students as they complete the *first* of two problems. It bought him twice the time to check the room.

Clip FG9. Hilary Lewis: [Hilary] uses *Affirmative Checking* to gauge student mastery before independent work. At the outset, Hilary asks students to complete a math problem on a green sticky note or "ticket" and then to exchange that ticket for the opportunity to start independent practice (IP). She then continues to stoke interest and suspense by comparing this exchange to the experience of "going into a movie." By requiring students to "earn" the privilege of participating in IP, she turns it into a kind of reward. And because students must show correct work in order to move on to IP, they have no incentive to speed through it at the expense of accuracy. This sends an implicit message that Hilary values quality work over speed.

One by one, students complete the problem and patiently await Hilary's signal. She calls them up, and because all students were asked to show their work on a sticky note, Hilary knows immediately where to look. When students hand her work that's correct, she responds with a warm, positive, yet understated tone that seems to suggest: "Good. You got it right, just as I expected." When one student shows her work for the *wrong* problem, she responds with the same warm, supportive tone and comments, "OK. You did your own problem, which is great. I need you to do that problem [as she points to the board]." Her reaction signals to the student that "getting it wrong" is as normal as "getting it right."

PLAN FOR ERROR

OVERVIEW

Every lesson holds the promise of both learning and mistakes. Often they occur in close proximity, with the success of the lesson hinging on the degree to which the latter can be turned into the former. One of the keys to turning error into learning is to plan for it. In the *Plan for Error* technique, you anticipate student misunderstandings and your responses to them. This increases your chances of taking action when you encounter mistakes, and over time develops your ability to accurately predict and address student misunderstandings.

Reflection

As teachers, we know that students will make errors during our lessons, but when we write lessons, we don't always anticipate student errors and plan how we'll address them. Why don't we always do so?

_____

_____

_____

    What are the consequences of not including specifically how we'll address student errors as we create a lesson plan?

_____

_____

_____

    Possible reflections (we're sure you've thought of others!): One reason is the pressure we feel to get through as much material as possible. Then too, we may not be confident about our ability to anticipate errors, and fear that responding to error means we'll have to change our lesson on the fly and compromise its pacing. Besides, *Planning for Error* seems like extra planning that might not pay off.

    One consequence of not planning for error may be that it makes us less inclined to respond to error in the moment and more inclined to ignore data that suggests students aren't "getting it." This in turn can further weaken our confidence about improving our skills at anticipating and responding to error. As a result, performance gaps may widen between those who get it right away and others who struggle more academically. Then frustration grows among the latter group. Meanwhile, we find ourselves with less time overall for covering additional content because we end up spending ever more time reteaching.

FUNDAMENTALS

Plan for Error includes planning both how to handle specific foreseeable errors during the lesson and when and how to reteach.

Planning for Specific Errors

If you can predict what errors students will make, you'll be able to respond more easily on the fly. But even if students *don't* make exactly the errors you expected, the planning still leaves you better prepared—mentally and intellectually—for other, unexpected errors by increasing your attentiveness to the actual errors students make. Also, if you've already allocated time in the lesson for dealing with errors, you won't feel pressured to speed past them in order to get through your plan. Here are three things you can do:

Prioritize. Because your time and energy are limited, save *Plan for Error* for the most important questions in your lesson. One way to determine the importance of a question is to evaluate how closely it aligns to your key objective for the day (see technique 16, *Begin with the End*) or unit you are teaching.

Draft target responses. The best way to start in your planning is often to draft a target response—what a great answer would look like—for the most important questions in your lesson. Through this experience, you'll develop a sharper eye for which aspects of the task students will find most challenging and why. It will also give you a clearer sense of what you're looking for from an answer, which makes you less likely to "round up" student responses and more likely to hold out for all-the-way-right (technique 12, *Right Is Right*). Finally, it will give you a window into what and how you'll need to teach on the front end to set students up to successfully answer this question. In the process, you might actually preempt potential errors instead of having to wait to address them on the back end.

Plan with specific students in mind. Using this approach, middle school math teacher Katie McNickle starts by brainstorming the type of error(s) different students might make. This helps her anticipate the range of errors she might encounter and then prepare her responses accordingly. For instance, in a recent lesson, she anticipated that some students were likelier to make a specific conceptual error, while others, who were comfortable with the topic, would be likelier to make a more minor mistake. As a result, she planned two responses to error for the same question: a series of *Break It Down* questions (technique 35) that would help her excavate the conceptual error for those still struggling with it; and a series of less invasive responses, such as answer rollbacks (repeating an answer back to the student—"Your largest integer is *seven*?") to help more advanced students correct their own mistakes.

Reflection

How would you respond if a colleague of yours said the following?

> In theory, I like the idea of *Planning for Error,* but it's really hard to predict what my students will get and what they won't. Whenever I'm convinced students will struggle with something, they breeze through it, and vice versa. Ultimately, I don't want to invest the time when I'm not even sure it will pay off. I think the best

way to get better at responding to error is by responding to actual student mistakes in the moment. You can't replicate that through planning.

_____

_____

_____

Possible reflections (all right, you've thought of others!): The more you *Plan for Error*, the better you'll get at it. If it's not yet a strength, that's all the more reason to do it. Even if students *don't* make the errors you anticipate, *Planning for Error* is still beneficial because it increases the likelihood that you'll respond to errors in the moment. It also eliminates the "surprise factor": if you're expecting errors, you won't be caught off guard when you encounter them. Then too, it ensures that you've set aside time to respond to errors. This reduces the pressure you may feel to speed past them. *Plan for Error* helps you get better at responding to actual student errors during your lessons.

Planning Time to Reteach or Challenge

Another barrier to taking action in the face of misunderstandings is the pressure you may feel to "cover" everything in your lesson. One way to allay this pressure is to allocate time in your lesson to either reteach or go to more challenging tasks, depending on how your students are doing. A more advanced take on this idea is to embed your lesson materials with supplemental content, some of it aimed at errors.

Bryan Belanger does this by including dozens of questions in his lesson packets—far more than students can complete in a given lesson—and grouping them by topic or complexity. This makes it easy for him to identify where he needs to go to provide remediation or further challenge, and everything he needs in order to do that is ready in advance. Similarly, reading teacher Patrick Pastore's packets contain more than enough content for a lesson. This enables him to make lightning-quick decisions—such as skipping to different questions, giving students more of the same practice, or assigning a more literal or figurative writing prompt—in response to error or success. Through careful planning, such teachers don't just overcome the barrier of time pressure. They turn their lessons into living, breathing documents that help them respond to error by design.

Case Study: Ms. Jacobs, Middle School Math/Science

Read Ms. Jacobs's *Plan for Error* and note some "glows" and "grows." What did she do well? What could still be improved?

Lesson objective: Students will be able to distinguish between shapes that have volume and those that don't.

Key question from lesson: Do both of these shapes have volume? Why or why not?

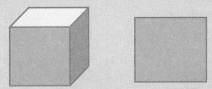

Target response: In order for something to have volume, it has to take up space, and only shapes with three dimensions can do that. The shape on the right doesn't have volume because it has only two dimensions: width and height, but not depth. The shape on the left does have volume and therefore takes up space because it has width, height, *and* depth.

Most likely error(s) or incorrect answers:

- *Error 1:* "Both shapes do because they both have area. (A student who says this is confusing volume and area.)
- *Error 2:* "They both have volume because they both take up space." (A student who says this doesn't understand that a shape must have three dimensions (length, width, *and* depth) to take up space. The shape on the left does, but the shape on the right doesn't.)

My potential response(s):

Error 1:

- To have area, a shape needs two dimensions: length and width.
- How many dimensions does a shape need to have volume? Look back at your notes. [It needs to have three dimensions.]
- Great. So looking at these shapes, do both have three dimensions? [No. The shape on the left does, but not the shape on the right.]
- So which shape has volume? [The shape on the left has volume.]
- Explain why the shape on the right has area but not volume. [The shape on the right has area because it has two dimensions. It doesn't have volume because it has no third dimension.]

Error 2:

- "Let's return to our definition for volume. Can someone repeat it?" [The amount of space that a shape takes up.]
- And in order to take up space, what needs to be true about the shape? [It needs to have three dimensions.]
- Do both shapes have three dimensions? [No, just the one on the left.]
- Why doesn't the shape on the right? [It only has two dimensions.]

Write before you read on.

Glows	Grows
It was effective when Ms. Jacobs . . .	Next time, she could try . . .

Our glows and grows (yours can be different!): Ms. Jacobs wisely prioritizes a key question that aligns to her lesson objective. She plans a thoughtful and complete target response using academic language scholars should use. She plans for errors that seem likely and that are worthy of discussion and excavation instead of simple errors that she could just correct. Her response to error includes more than just general cues. She includes the *Break It Down* (see technique 35) questions and prompts that could guide students' thinking and even students' responses; this is not *necessary* for every *Plan for Error*, but it surely helps.

To arrive at the target response, students must be able to identify the dimensions in each shape and then use that to determine which has volume and why. To make sure students can do this, she could fold questions like these into her plan:

"In order to have volume, what dimensions does a shape need?" (A shape with volume needs three dimensions: length, width, and depth.)

"In that case, do both shapes have volume? Why or why not?" (No. The shape on the right doesn't have volume because it has only two dimensions—length and width. The shape on the left has volume because it has all three dimensions: length, width, *and* depth.)

"Which dimension does the shape on the right need to have volume?" (It needs depth.)

She could plan to *Cold Call* (technique 33) using *Targeted Questioning* (technique 2) to verify understanding:

"So does a cylinder have volume or not? How do you know?"

"How about this tissue box? Why or why not?"

"Or this sheet of paper?"

"Can a shape that has length and width *also* have volume?"

"Can a shape that has volume have two dimensions? Why?"

Evaluate Some Plans

For each of the examples shown of *Plan for Error*, jot some observations on what about it you think is effective. Then compare your observations with ours, following.

EXAMPLE 1. BRYAN BELANGER, GRADE 8 MATH

Key question from lesson:

4. What is the solution set to the inequality $-3q - 42 \geq 18 - 9q$?
   A. $q \geq -5$
   B. $q \geq 10$
   C. $q \leq -5$
   D. $q \leq 10$

Target response: (B) – Requires students to realize that this is an inequality. They should initially try to get variable terms all to left side, since this is where they would need to be in the solution. Otherwise, there is a need to flip the sign when dividing and then again when moving the variable term to the left.

Most likely error(s)/incorrect answer(s):

A. Operation error
C. Operation and sign error
D. Inequality sign error (most common)

The error could come in one of two spots. Initially, students may not get the variable terms to the left side of the equation and as a result may not flip the sign when they divide by -6 or when they switch the order back such that the variable is on the left. There is the off chance that students may wisely start by getting the variable on the left, but flip the sign anyway . . .

My goal is to have students articulate why it is best to get the variable on the left to start and how they would know whether or not the sign should be flipped.

My potential responses:

Me: "There are many possible first steps in solving this equation. Which did you choose, and why?"

Student A: "Add $9q$ to both sides—because we want the variable on the left . . ."

Me: (if Student A struggles to explain) "Why is this a better step than adding $3q$ to both sides?"

(I would then model this step) "Will I need to flip my inequality sign?" "How do you know?"

Student B: "No, because you will not be dividing by a negative and the variable is on the left."

Me: "So what is the correct answer?" (Answer B) "Now, do you think you could still get the same answer by adding $3q$ to both sides?"

(Show a model where this is done correctly to help other students identify their error and revalidate that is it wiser to get variables to the left first, since that is where they need to end up.)

Evaluation:

_____

_____

_____

_____

_____

_____

What I could use:

_____

_____

_____

_____

_____

EXAMPLE 2. ERICA LIM, GRADE 9 PRE-AP WORLD HISTORY

Key question from lesson:

How were the post-classical shifts in Hindu beliefs of caste, duty, and reincarnation a response to competition with Islam?

Target response: Due to its emphasis on spiritual equality before Allah, Islam was attractive to low-class Indians to whom Hinduism offered little to no social mobility through the caste system. Nearly a quarter of Indians converted to Islam in the post-classical era, and the vast majority came from low castes. In order to retain followers and appeal to the lower classes, Hinduism blended in popular Muslim beliefs (such as monotheism and equality of believers) into their religion. Thus post-classical Hinduism de-emphasized the rigidity of the caste system and instead placed an emphasis on worshiping and even achieving salvation through a single god, such as Krishna, within the pantheon of Hindu gods.

Most likely error(s)/ incorrect answer(s):

Students will struggle with the causation between Point A (competition with Islam) and Point B (Hinduism shifts beliefs to appeal to low classes). The key is identifying **lower classes** at the root this analysis. Most students will overlook the two major clues:

1. The vast majority of Muslim converts were low caste.
2. The shifts in Hindu beliefs appealed to and favored low castes.

My potential responses:
Key idea: Islam was attractive to *low-class* Indians to whom Hinduism offered little to no social mobility through the caste system.

- Why might Islam have been attractive to some Hindus? Which Hindus?
- How does one achieve salvation with Islam? *(devotion to Allah, 5 Pillars)*
- Think of the 5 Pillars; what is the very first? *(There is no god but Allah, and Muhammad is his prophet. The Shahabad.)*
- If that is the first and most important requirement, who would be able to achieve salvation with Islam? *(anyone)*
- To whom would this Muslim ideal appeal to most in Indian society? Why? *(low-caste people not given any chance of social mobility in current life according to Hinduism)*
- Go back to our Do Now on page 1. Predict: Who are the 20–25% of the Indian population that are converting to Islam? *(low castes)*

Key idea: In order to retain followers and appeal to the *lower classes,* Hinduism blended in popular Muslim beliefs (such as monotheism and equality of believers) into their religion.

- Why would this be a problem for Hindus? *(They are losing followers to Islam.)*
- So then how did Hinduism respond to this new challenge of losing followers? *(made Hinduism more inclusive by shifting core beliefs on caste system and paths to salvation)*
- Back to our documents—which caste does Lord Krishna highlight in Doc 1? In Doc 2? *(high in Doc 1 vs. low in Doc 2)*
- Why might he be trying to emphasize the low caste in Doc 2? *(giving all an opportunity for enlightenment, to keep them in Hinduism)*

Evaluation:

_____

_____

_____

_____

_____

_____

_____

What I could use:

_____

_____

_____

_____

_____

PLAN FOR ERROR

OUR OBSERVATIONS ON THE EXAMPLES

Example 1

Besides listing the most likely incorrect answers, Bryan identifies the underlying misconception behind each. This makes it easier for him to plan strategically for how he'll address the root causes for each mistake. In addition to identifying the correct answer, he plans out precisely what he wants to hear students say and what he wants them to be able to do ("My goal is to have students articulate why it is best to get the variable on the left to start and how they would know whether or not the sign should be flipped"). He plans out the exact prompts or questions he'll use to respond, and then takes this planning to a new level by anticipating what students will say. In essence, he *Double Plans* his response to error (technique 19), envisioning both what he and his students will do and say.

Example 2

Erica drafts a strong target response using the academic language she wants students to use. Since she is planning for an open-ended response, she's wise not to draft a single "wrong answer." Instead, she identifies two key clues students would most likely overlook and the key understanding they would likely struggle with. This gives her a clear enough picture of what she'll need to plan to address without tying her to a specific response that students may or may not provide. She then drafts a sequence of questions and prompts she could ask to help students uncover those two clues and ultimately arrive at the key understanding.

DRAFT PLANS FOR ERROR

Use the *Plan for Error* Template to plan how you might respond to one or two likely errors or misunderstandings from an upcoming lesson (Your library resources at my.teachlikeachampion.com include a printable version.) If possible, share your completed template with a colleague who's also prepared one, and look for ways to improve them.

PLAN FOR ERROR TEMPLATE

My lesson objective (see technique 17)

_____

_____

Key question from lesson

_____

_____

_____

Target response (ideal or "right" answer)

_____

_____

_____

Likely error or incorrect answer

_____

_____

_____

Underlying gaps or misunderstandings

What might students confuse/forget to do?

_____

_____

_____

My potential responses (See technique 35—cues you will provide or _Break It Down_ questions you could ask.)

Response 1:

_____

_____

_____

_____

_____

_____

Response 2:

_____

_____

_____

_____

_____

_____

PLAN FOR ERROR

blog Find this blog post at teachlikeachampion.com/blog/coaching-and-practice/annals-coaching -planning-error/.
   Doug records some fields notes at "Annals of Coaching: Planning for Error" and shows an example of how he might complete a template very similar to the one you see here.

GROUP OR PARTNER ROLE PLAY: PRACTICE RESPONDING TO ERROR

Bring your *Plan for Error* Template to the meeting. In groups of three (one *Teacher*, one *Student*, one *Coach*) or with your colleague (*Teacher* and *Student*), practice responding to a planned error using the following sequence:

1. *Teacher* asks key question from lesson.
2. *Student* answers incorrectly.
3. *Teacher* responds with a planned response to error.
4. *Student* answers correctly.

After the *Teacher* practices responding to error, the *Coach* then gives a glow ("One thing that was effective . . .") and a grow ("Next time, try . . .") to the *Teacher*. The *Teacher* tries again, implementing the feedback. Look for these success points:

- The *Teacher* responds with language that normalizes error. ("This is a tough one. We'll work together to get it right.")
- The *Teacher* effectively delivers a response to error that gets students to the correct answer.

ACTION PLANNING

Use the aforementioned success points to continue progress with *Plan for Error*. Find a printable version of this form at my.teachlikeachampion.com.

HOW AM I DOING?

_____

_____

Design one or more action steps for improvement. Decide on an interval by which you'll revisit this page to assess your progress.

Action Step 1

By when, with whom, and how you will measure your effort

By _____, I will . . .

Date

_____

_____

How Did I Do?

Successes: _____

_____

_____

_____

_____

Challenges: _____

_____

_____

_____

Next steps: _____

_____

_____

Action Step 2

By when, with whom, and how you will measure your effort

By _____, I will . . .

Date

_____

_____

_____

How Did I Do?

Successes: _____

_____

_____

_____

Challenges: _____

_____

_____

Next steps: _____

_____

_____

CULTURE OF ERROR

One of the most powerful beliefs we can instill in students is the idea that mistakes are a valuable part of learning—an opportunity far better studied than ignored or denied. In classrooms that are alive with what we call a *Culture of Error,* students acknowledge mistakes with comfort. They willingly make them visible to their teachers and classmates. They confidently take risks knowing full well that their efforts may result in failure. Not only does this reinforce the idea that what is worth learning will almost always challenge them, that struggle will almost always precede success, but, more practically, it makes student errors far easier to find and study. And when students respond to mistakes with equanimity rather than defensiveness, unlocking the academic value of studying mistakes becomes easy. Four specific actions can help you build a *Culture of Error*:

- Expect error
- Withhold the answer
- Manage the tell
- Praise risk-taking

Reflection

Few teachers *wouldn't* want students to embrace opportunities to learn from their mistakes. But not every classroom has this culture. What factors prevent it? And how might those factors be overcome?

_____

_____

_____

Possible reflections: Through what they praise, some teachers may indirectly reinforce a fixed mindset—that is, the belief among students that one's innate talent or fixed abilities are what determine outcomes. Sometimes teachers do this by praising students for their talent as opposed to their efforts (for example, "You're so smart!" or "You're a math genius" or "You're a natural at this"). Or they may overpraise outcomes, celebrating high scores and correct answers as opposed to growth and improvement through effort. Others may unintentionally create a culture in which kids are afraid to reveal errors because these teachers respond to them with a tone or body language that conveys annoyance, frustration, or disappointment.

Also, even if a teacher strives to create a culture that values error, if the students in the class do not also, then the culture will not survive.

FUNDAMENTALS

Building a *Culture of Error*

How a teacher responds to error broadcasts a powerful message about how students themselves should interpret or perceive errors. Here we expand on four ways teachers' words and actions can establish a culture in which students view errors—both their own and others'—as valuable sources of academic growth and insight.

Expect Error

Choose your words and actions carefully to show students that making errors is normal and necessary for learning. In other words, teach students that getting it "wrong" is the first step toward getting it "right." We're not saying that you should pretend it's right when it's wrong, just that you show your students that you are fine with that. A great example can be found in Clip FG10, where Bob Zimmerli responds to errors by saying to his class, "I'm actually really glad I saw what I saw. This is going to help me to help you." His remarks remind students that their mistakes are powerful opportunities for growth and learning, both for them and their teacher. They also encourage students to continue revealing their errors willingly rather than trying to hide them.

Withhold the Answer

As teachers, we can often feel compelled to let students know right away that their answer to a question is correct or not. We say "right" or "wrong" and then go back to study the process: "OK, let's think about why and how we got that . . ." However, to build a robust *Culture of Error,* it's often useful to resist this impulse and delay your reveal of the correct answer until after the class has discussed the question and analyzed various answers. Katie Bellucci does this when she says, "I see B, C, and Ds [for answers]." Note that she does not tell students which of those answers is correct yet. That part comes only at the end.

Even if you intend to study the process of getting an answer, hearing that they got it wrong can cause some students to shut down out of frustration, and hearing that they got it right can cause others to tune out the discussion because, well, they know they're already "right." The result? The most important part of learning—your class reflecting on thinking and process—is done with only a handful of students who are fully engaged. Withholding the answer brings more students into the substantive part of the conversation and focuses them on process, not simply whether they got it "right" or "wrong."

Manage the Tell

In poker, players go to great lengths (for example, wearing sunglasses and hoodies) to avoid providing unintentional cues about the strength of the cards they hold. If they have a "tell" that accidentally reveals their thinking to their opponents, they're unlikely to succeed.

Similarly, many teachers also have unintentional tells that reveal more than they intend about the quality of an answer. Often, students can read these tells and conclude, for example, that their comment lacked value. This can cause them to avoid taking risks—or even seeking to participate.

Teachers often have tells for correct answers also. Although unintentionally signaling "Oh, I love that" may not tend to have the same negative emotional effects as unintentionally signaling "Ugh, what an answer," it still gives away critical information. It makes it hard to withhold the answer, for example. And we also need to think about what happens when a constantly positive affect used for most answers is suddenly missing. That lack of positive response can, in and of itself, become a tell for a bad answer.

Common Teacher Tells

For incorrect answers	For correct answers
Gazing skyward as if for divine help in following the thinking of the student answering.	Nodding too eagerly during an answer to affirm it.
Saying "Okaayyy," or "Hmmm . . ."	Subtly making an "mmmmm" sound as if pleased by what you hear.
Writing only correct answers on the board.	"Oooh. Did everyone hear that?"
Pausing for a few long seconds while opening your mouth.	
Responding with, "Does anyone have a different answer?" or "Interesting . . ." or "Are you *sure*?"	

All teachers have tells, and revealing our affective response to an answer isn't *always* problematic, but mastering the art of checking for understanding requires us to mindfully manage and minimize them as appropriate. At the very least try to be aware of them. This can be challenging, as they are often contained in habits that are invisible to us. To manage your tell, it helps to practice responding intentionally to both correct and incorrect answers.

Brainstorming with a colleague if you can, add other tells you think teachers have, including your own, for correct and incorrect answers.

_____

_____

_____

Again with a partner if you can, practice responding to correct and incorrect answers without a tell, while using phrases to create a *Culture of Error.*

Praise Risk-Taking

A fourth way teachers build a *Culture of Error* is by praising students for taking risks and facing down the challenge of a difficult subject. For instance, if students raise their hands to answer a tough question, you might announce that you "love all the brave hands" that you're seeing or thank students "for taking a risk." This reminds students that true scholars offer thoughts when they're not sure, and sometimes *because* they're not sure.

You might also normalize struggle by telling students that "it's a good sign" if they're grappling with the difficult question you just posed and aren't sure what the right answer is. You might even playfully challenge students to attempt a challenging task, as Kiah Hufane does when she tells students, "I *dare* you to use evidence from all three." Such language encourages students to seize opportunities to stretch themselves academically while removing fear of failure or other reasons not to try.

ANALYZE THE CHAMPIONS

Compare your written observations with ours at the end of this technique.

Clip FG10. Katie Bellucci, Bridget McElduff, Jason Armstrong, Erin Michels, Bob Zimmerli, Denarius Frazier, Maggie Johnson, and Kiah Hufane

From the teachers' words in montage Clip FG10, jot down three phrases that you'd like to use or adapt in your classroom to create a *Culture of Error.*

_____

_____

Clip FG54. Erin Krafft, Grade 6

Watch Clip FG54 with *Culture of Error* in mind. What's effective about the procedure Erin Krafft installs for disagreement? What else does she do to reinforce a *Culture of Error*?

_____

_____

_____

Language for *Culture of Error*

In addition to the language you heard teachers use in the *Culture of Error* montage, choose one of these examples of *Culture of Error* language and adapt it for use in your classroom. Then add a few examples of your own.

"Which of these options do you think is my *favorite* wrong answer?"
"I see several students picked answer choice X and that a few picked answer choice Y. How can I defend my answer whether I picked answer choice X or Y?"
"I saw some different answers out there, so let's have a college discussion. Be ready to defend your answer."
"People have debated this question for decades. Who even knows if there *is* a right answer. So let's hear your best thinking."
"This is a tough question. If you're struggling with it, that's a good sign. Now, who will be bold and start us off?"

_____

_____

_____

_____

_____

ANALYZE A CHAMPION

▶ **Clip FG11. Teacher Janelle Duckett, Grade 2**

Watch Clip FG11 and consider what evidence you see that struggling and succeeding in this class is a shared endeavor. What does Janelle Duckett do to reinforce this? What do you think she had to do earlier in the school year to lay the foundation for this?

_____

_____

_____

Considering what you saw in Janelle's classroom, in the space here brainstorm ways you could make *Culture of Error* in your classroom more of a shared endeavor.

Example: During a *Turn and Talk,* I could make it safe for students to disagree with each other by teaching them sentence starters ("Yes, I disagree because . . .")

_____

_____

_____

PRACTICE: ASK BUT DON'T "TELL"

We cast this practice for best use by partners, but if you can't arrange that just now, complete it on your own.

Use the lines here to plan what you will say to create a *Culture of Error* and how you will manage your tells. Then choose a question from your lesson plan and script one correct and two incorrect answers.

With a partner, practice responding to correct and incorrect answers with effective language for *Culture of Error* and without a tell.

Tells You Will Manage
For right answers:
    (Example) *I will try not to raise my eyebrows.*

_____

_____

For wrong answers:
    (Example) *I will try not to look puzzled.*

_____

_____

Culture of Error phrase(s) you will use
    Example: *"I am excited to hear the different thinking in the room."*

_____

_____

    Now choose a question from your lesson plan (or from materials provided for you). Script two incorrect answers and one correct answer. With a partner or two, use your entries to practice responding to correct and incorrect answers without a tell while using phrases to create a *Culture of Error.*

Question:

_____

_____

Correct response:

_____

_____

Incorrect response 1:

_____

_____

Incorrect response 2:

_____

_____

_____

blog Find these blog posts at teachlikeachampion.com/blog/clip-day-katie-bellucci-checks-understanding/ and http://teachlikeachampion.com/blog/worked-emilie-tarrafs-culture-error-video/.

Both of these posts include commentary and outstanding video of classroom *Culture of Error:* "Katie Bellucci Checks for Understanding" and "'He Worked It Out!' Emilie Tarraf's Culture of Error."

Reflection

Imagine you woke up tomorrow morning and your classroom had transformed into a learning environment with exemplary *Culture of Error.* What would you see and hear? How would you know this transformation occurred?

_____

_____

_____

ACTION PLANNING

Use this action planner to continue your work with *Culture of Error.* (Find a printable version of this form at my.teachlikeachampion.com.) You're on the right track when you are . . .

- Withholding answers and managing tells
- Creating a climate in which error is considered normal and worthy of discussion
- Students feel safe and willing to take risks

HOW AM I DOING?

Design one or more action steps for improvement. Decide on an interval by which you'll revisit this page to assess your progress.

Action Step 1

By when, with whom, and how you will measure your effort

By _____, I will . . .
Date

How Did I Do?

Successes:

Challenges:

Next steps:

CULTURE OF ERROR

Action Step 2

By when, with whom, and how you will measure your effort

By _____, I will . . .

Date

_____

_____

_____

How Did I Do?

Successes: _____

_____

_____

_____

Challenges: _____

_____

_____

Next steps: _____

_____

_____

OUR OBSERVATIONS ON THE CHAMPIONS

 Clip FG10. Katie Bellucci, Bridget McElduff, Jason Armstrong, Erin Michels, Bob Zimmerli, Denarius Frazier, Maggie Johnson, and Kiah Hufane

Here's language these teachers use to reinforce a *Culture of Error.*
Withhold the answer:

Katie Bellucci (grade 7 math): "We have some different answers out here. I see 2s, 3s, and 4s . . . B, C, and D." (We still don't know which one was right.)
Bridget McElduff (grade 5 math): "I have a feeling we're going to have a few different options here, so let's make a list, and then we can discuss it. Give me your answers."
Jason Armstrong (grade 6 math): "For the four answers we have here, I don't want to start with which one you think is right. I want to focus on the explanations we have."

Expect error:

Erin Michels (grade 3 math): "We have a *lot* of disagreement on this one."
Bob Zimmerli (grade 7 math): "I'm seeing so much of a common mistake I need to address it. I'm actually really glad I saw what I saw. . . . This is going to help me to help you."

Praise risk-taking:

Denarius Frazier (grade 10 math): Looking out at the raised hands of volunteers: "Ooh. I like this bravery. Thank you for that."
Maggie Johnson (grade 6 reading): "Mel has been so gracious as to offer his answer to revise so we can make it even stronger. So give him two claps on two. One, two! Build that confidence."
Kiah Hufane (grade 6 history): "I *dare* you to use evidence from all three."

 Clip FG54. Erin Krafft, Grade 6

Erin installs a system that students will use to express agreement or disagreement with their partner during the *Turn and Talk* (technique 43). Notably, she teaches them sentence starters they can use to respond to their partner's answer to keep the pair discussions productive whether or not the partners share the same opinion ("Yes, I agree" or "No, I disagree"). This shows students that Erin expects some students to arrive at different answers—both correct and incorrect—and to disagree over which one is ultimately right. After she asks students to turn and talk, she polls the class to see how many partners disagreed with one another, then warmly points out that most of them did. By incorporating this procedure into a staple system like *Turn and Talk,* she sows the seeds for daily reinforcement of her *Culture of Error.*

 Clip FG11. Janelle Duckett, Grade 2

There's no implicit pressure from the rest of the class as a student struggles to answer Janelle's question. No one calls out the answer, announces that they know, or smirks at her. Students quietly and respectfully track their peer while she works it out. Janelle continues to reinforce this supportive culture when she prompts students to "Help [her] make it better." This normalizes the process of improving one's work and reinforces the norm that checking for understanding is a shared endeavor. She then punctuates the sequence with the celebratory prop, "We got this!" This emphasizes that struggling through work is normal, positive, and universal.

To help build and reinforce this *Culture of Error,* Janelle routinized the following expectations: looking at whoever is speaking; offering to answer a question by raising a "vertical hand"; keeping hands down and voices off when a peer speaks; and celebrating peers' progress with props like "We got this!"

EXCAVATE ERROR

OVERVIEW

Both teacher and student can learn from the mistakes students make. This is because such mistakes are rarely random but rather are characterized by "logical mistakes" and thus reveal the thinking behind them. To fully reveal what errors can teach, however, teachers must *Excavate Error.* By that we mean analyzing errors with the class to discover and address underlying misconceptions. As you can imagine, the depth or breadth of a teacher's response to error can vary dramatically depending on the situation. A teacher might choose to engage the class in a deep, more extended discussion about an error at one point, and bypass discussion in favor of one-on-one reteaching at another. To better describe the range of approaches (and the decision making that drives them), we'll look at three of them and the factors that might influence a teacher's decision to use a particular one. The options are

- Assess and move on
- Light excavation
- Deep excavation

These approaches form a continuum of sorts and remind us that we can study mistakes in a variety of ways and settings. Sometimes the simplest option works best; other times a more in-depth approach is in order. Great teachers seek to strike the most productive balance between these three.

Reflection

What factors are most important for you in deciding how much time to spend discussing students' responses to a question?

FUNDAMENTALS: THREE OPTIONS

Assess and Move On

In some cases, you may want to make the strategic decision *not* to study an error at a given time and to instead push forward with your lesson. For instance, you might opt to check in individually with a student when he or she struggles with a question that everyone else has answered correctly. Or, during a lesson you might take a page from Nicole Willey's playbook by calling up the two or three students who continue to struggle to a separate table for more individualized feedback, monitoring, and support. These and other forms of *assess and move on* are best used when only a few students made the error or the error itself is minor (like a simple miscalculation) or unimportant (not closely related to your lesson objective). To clarify, this form of excavation should not be confused with inaction. The question isn't whether or not you will respond to error. It's a matter of *when* and in *which setting.*

Light Excavation

Many errors a teacher encounters surface unexpectedly and require a relatively quick study. If several students make a certain error or if the error merits a bit of discussion, consider responding with *light excavation* by having students analyze the positives implicit in a wrong answer ("There's a lot of good thinking here") and what's wrong or missing ("but there's one especially important line right at the end that some of us could have read—or even reread—more closely").

Here are some forms of light excavation that we've seen teachers implement:

- **Ask for an alternative response.** After calling on a student to share his or her answer and discussing it, you could, with or without revealing whether that response was correct, ask for an alternative: "Who can share another interpretation of what the passage is telling us Jonas can see?"
- **Compare responses.** Instead of looking at alternative responses in sequence, you could compare them side by side. "So let's look at these two responses. Which one is stronger?" Although it's not necessary, you might consider *Show Calling* two pieces of student work and placing them alongside each other to spur this type of analysis.
- **Analyze wrong choices.** Ask students to evaluate incorrect responses by explaining why they're wrong or stating the plausible yet faulty reasoning behind them. "A lot of people said the answer was 36. Let's try to figure out their mistake."
- **Ask for a proposed response.** Instead of proposing a "common error" yourself, you might ask a student to do so: "Let's say I found this passage really difficult. What's something I might have guessed Jonas could see that I would have had a good reason for guessing, even if it was wrong?"

Deep Excavation

Some errors are so fundamental to students' mastery of a lesson or unit that they warrant deeper excavation. In some situations, the teacher might survey a wide variety of possible responses and dig into the various errors. Other times, she might study one incorrect response with unusual depth and thoroughness, asking students to evaluate strengths and areas that need revision (you'll see this in Case 1, following). Such approaches require considerable time, so you'll need to reserve deep excavation for the most important questions.

Reflection

Besides limited time, why else might it be important for you to vary your choice among the options?

_____

_____

_____

CASE STUDIES

For each case, record your "glows" and "grows." Then compare your comments with our observations, which follow Case 2.

Case 1. Algebra, Mr. Jordan

Mr. Jordan had asked the class to simplify the following expression as part of a *Do Now* task (technique 20) at the start of class:

$$4x(2x-9)-2(5x-6)$$

He decided to project one student's response so that the class could learn from it. Here's the way one student solved it:

$$4x(2x-9)-2(5x-6)$$
$$8x-36x-10x+12$$
$$-38x+12$$

1.	MR. JORDAN:	This answer isn't correct, but it shows some good math, so I think there's a lot we can learn from it. What am I happy to see in this scholar's work?
2.	JESSICA:	The student distributed the $4x$ and the -2.
3.	MR. JORDAN:	What lets you know the scholar distributed?
4.	TERRANCE:	There are no more parentheses.
5.	MR. JORDAN:	Did this student distribute -2 correctly? How do you know?
6.	MIGUEL:	Yes. I know this because he multiplied what was inside the parentheses by -2. Multiplying -2 and $5x$ gave him $-10x$, and multiplying -2 by -6 gave him 12.
7.	MR. JORDAN:	And what did he remember to distribute?
8.	MIGUEL:	The negative sign.
9.	MR. JORDAN:	Correct. Let's jump to steps two and three. What did this scholar do here that I like?
10.	JOHN:	He added and subtracted like terms.
11.	MR. JORDAN:	So where did he make his mistake?
12.	JOHN:	The scholar got $8x$, which is incorrect. It should say $8x$-squared.
13.	MR. JORDAN:	That's right, he got $8x$ and it should be $8x$-squared. So if we plug in $8x$-squared in place of the $8x$, what answer does that give us?
14.	ERIN:	$8x$-squared minus $46x$ plus 12.
15.	MR. JORDAN:	That's exactly right. Make sure you've got the answer. On to question three.

Glows	Grows
It was effective when Mr. Jordan . . .	Next time, he could try . . .

Case 2. Biology, Ms. Hernandez

Certain poisons are toxic to organisms because they interfere with the <u>function</u> of enzymes in the <u>mitochondria</u>. This results directly in the inability of the cell to . . .

A) Store information
B) Build proteins
C) Release energy from nutrients
D) Dispose of metabolic wastes

1.	MS. HERNANDEZ:	Let's start with A. What function is A referring to?
2.	MCKAYLA:	It's talking about storing information.
3.	MS. HERNANDEZ:	Do the mitochondria store information?
4.	MCKAYLA:	No, the DNA do that. So A can't be right.
5.	MS. HERNANDEZ:	Great. B said "build proteins." Jimmy, you didn't select B. Why?
6.	JIMMY:	I didn't select it because mitochondria create energy. And proteins aren't energy.
7.	MS. HERNANDEZ:	So which organelle does serve this function?
8.	JIMMY:	Ribosomes.
9.	MS. HERNANDEZ:	Dayquan. You picked D. Explain your thinking.
10.	DAYQUAN:	Well, the question said something about poisons and toxins. And so, that's a type of waste. So I picked D because it said something about metabolic wastes.
11.	MS. HERNANDEZ:	What are the poisons in the question doing?
12.	DAYQUAN:	They are affecting the function of the mitochondria.
13.	MS. HERNANDEZ:	So does the question say anything about getting rid of wastes?
14.	DAYQUAN:	No.
15.	MS. HERNANDEZ:	So, which organelle *does* dispose of metabolic waste?
16.	DAYQUAN:	The cell membrane. So D can't be correct.
17.	MS. HERNANDEZ:	Good. Let's cross that one out. So, we're left with C. Why is that right?
18.	GERALD:	Because the question is asking us about which function of the mitochondria is being affected. And the mitochondria's function is to give the cell energy.
19.	MS. HERNANDEZ:	Good. Circle C if you got that correct.

Glows	Grows
It was effective when Ms. Hernandez . . .	Next time, she could try . . .

Case 3. English Language Arts, Ms. McCarthy

First stanza of "Mirror" by Sylvia Plath

I am silver and exact. I have no preconceptions.
Whatever I see I swallow immediately
Just as it is, unmisted by love or dislike.
I am not cruel, only truthful—
The eye of a little god, four-cornered.
Most of the time I meditate on the opposite wall.
It is pink, with speckles. I have looked at it so long
I think it is a part of my heart. But it flickers.
Faces and darkness separate us over and over.

1. MS. MCCARTHY: So we know that the speaker is a mirror. What language does Plath use to convey that? Take three minutes to read this stanza on your own and jot down every relevant piece of evidence in the box below.
   (Students complete task.)
   Great. So what did you all find?
2. GERALD: "Silver and exact."
3. MS. MCCARTHY: How might that describe a mirror?
4. GERALD: Because mirrors can often be silver.
5. MS. MCCARTHY: What about "exact"?
6. GERALD: A mirror shows things exactly as they are. It just reflects what it sees.
7. MS. MCCARTHY: Good. Place a check next to that piece of evidence if you had it. Jot it down if you didn't. What other evidence shows this is a mirror?
8. JEN: It calls itself "four-cornered."
9. MS. MCCARTHY: Elaborate.
10. JEN: Mirrors have four corners because they often come in the shape of squares or rectangles.
11. MS. MCCARTHY: Great. Check if you had that. Add it if you didn't. Anything else?

12.	MICHAEL:	"It is pink, with speckles."
13.	MS. MCCARTHY:	OK. Let's jot that down. Now, what is "it" referring to?
14.	MICHAEL:	The mirror?
15.	MS. MCCARTHY:	Well, let's jump back to the previous line: "I meditate on the opposite wall." What's the subject of that line?
16.	MICHAEL:	The mirror.
17.	MS. MCCARTHY:	Let's step back for a second. Underline "meditate." Jot this in the margin: *meditate* means "to think about (something) carefully, often in a quiet space." What is the mirror *meditating* on?
18.	MICHAEL:	The mirror is meditating on the opposite wall.
19.	MS. MCCARTHY:	So returning to the next line, what is "it" referring to?
20.	MICHAEL:	The wall. The mirror is talking about the wall. So this evidence can't work.
21.	MS. MCCARTHY:	Great. So if you had that on your paper, go ahead and cross that out. Other evidence we haven't discussed? *(no response from students)* OK, let's look at one of the trickier ones in line 2: "Whatever I see I swallow immediately." How might a mirror do this, Hector?
22.	HECTOR:	Because it sees things right away.
23.	MS. MCCARTHY:	Explain more. Make "swallow" a part of your answer.
24.	HECTOR:	When you look at a mirror, it looks like everything that's in front of it is being taken in . . . like it's being swallowed.
25.	MS. MCCARTHY:	Right. Go ahead and add that. It's an important one.

Glows	Grows
It was effective when Ms. McCarthy . . .	Next time, she could try . . .

Some Observations on Case 1

Mr. Jordan effectively facilitates deep excavation of this error by prompting students to evaluate what's right and wrong about it. He also reinforces a *Culture of Error* by emphasizing the value of studying and learning from mistakes ("I think there's a lot we can learn from it."). To improve, Mr. Jordan could have pressed John to explain *why* $8x$ was incorrect. This would've helped clarify the student's key mistakes for the class, which was that he forgot to distribute both the term and the variable and that an x multiplied by itself makes x^2. In addition, he doesn't explicitly hold students accountable for *Owning and Tracking* (see technique 10). Specifically, he could ask students to correct their work if it was wrong, and make notes to themselves about what aspects were right and wrong about their original response.

Some Observations on Case 2

Ms. Hernandez helps systematically guide students through a close study of all four answer choices. This deep excavation addresses students' confusing the functions of mitochondria with the functions of other organelles (ribosomes, cell membrane, and so on). She is also diligent about asking students to cross out incorrect answer choices so that they don't confuse them with the right answer. Finally, when students reveal incorrect answers or correct answers, she manages the tell by withholding any commentary. Instead, she responds with "Why" or "How" questions that put the onus on students to explain their thinking, without signaling whether their answer is right or wrong.

To improve this example, Ms. Hernandez could then ask students to lock down "right" by asking them to explain in writing (see technique 10, *Own and Track*) why C is correct. She could also boost participation by prompting students to evaluate their peers' responses instead of responding immediately herself ("What do you think about [peer's] response? Thumbs up or down? [Student], explain why you showed a thumbs-up."). This would hold students accountable for closely attending to and building on their peers' contributions during the discussion.

Some Observations on Case 3

Ms. McCarthy starts with a challenging poem, Sylvia Plath's "Mirror," and surfaces the various evidence students cited to support the conclusion that the speaker is a mirror. She then asks students to cross out incorrect evidence and to add or place a check mark next to the correct evidence. This helps students prioritize and organize the evidence they've assembled. Finally, she makes it safe for students to struggle with a part of the analysis when she announces that a piece of evidence in line 2 was "one of the trickier ones."

One point of growth relates to the fact that Ms. McCarthy accepts Michael's response and moves ahead without asking students to do something in writing with all of the evidence they've assembled. This would have enabled her to lock in students' understanding of what they discussed and set them up to more deeply comprehend the rest of the poem. An example: "Now, I want you to go back. I want you to summarize in one paragraph how the mirror characterizes itself, using all four pieces of evidence that we discussed."

PLANNING TO GO DEEP

Techniques 16 and 17 say more about defining an objective for every lesson. From a lesson plan you're creating, identify the most important question students will need to answer. Draft your target response and anticipate the most likely error. Plan a series of *Cold Call* questions (technique 33) you could ask to deeply excavate that error. If possible, exchange your plan with a partner, receive feedback, and incorporate that into your planning.

Key question:

_____

_____

Target response:

_____

_____

EXCAVATE ERROR

Most likely error:

_____

_____

_____

My plan to excavate deeply:

_____

_____

_____

_____

GROUP ROLE PLAY: *EXCAVATE ERROR*

Prepare by first completing "Planning to Go Deep." Then gather ideally in groups of four to rotate through four roles: *Teacher, Coach,* and two *Students*. Each *Teacher* will get three rounds of practice.

In each round as *Teacher,* imagine that you just finished *Circulating* (technique 24) during independent work in which your *Students* answered your key question. Now you decide to call the class back together to address an error you noticed. Fortunately, you have time right now to script your responses for each round.

Round 1. In this round, you'll *assess and move on* because both *Students* got the answer right.
Round 2. Lightly excavate because one *Student* got close to your target answer, but the other did not.
Round 3. Excavate deeply because neither *Student* got close to your target answer.

Here, script what you'll say and do as *Teacher* for rounds 1 and 2. For round 3, you will use the script you created in "Planning to Go Deep."
Round 1 script:

_____

_____

Round 2 script (consider asking for an alternative response, comparing responses, analyzing wrong choices, or asking for a proposed response):

_____

_____

_____

Play out each round by its script with the *Coach* observing and the *Students* responding as indicated. Conclude each round with feedback from the *Coach*: one glow ("It was effective when . . .") and one grow ("Next time, try . . .") based on success points like these:

- Using supportive language that makes it safe to make and reveal errors ("That error is going to help me to help you." "A lot of us struggled with this one.").
- Managing the tell by responding to error with a neutral tone or expression.
- Posing questions or prompts that help efficiently and effectively address the misconception.

Record here what you learned from the role play:

_____

_____

_____

_____

_____

_____

blog

Find these blog posts at teachlikeachampion.com/blog/derek-pollak-excavates-error/ and http://teachlikeachampion.com/blog/tales-positive-outlier-part-3-nicole-willeys-show-call-video/.
Study this video and extensive comments on how one teacher excavates deeply: "Maggie Johnson: How Derek Pollak Excavates Error."
Then see and read how Nicole Willey matches Derek's skills as she takes her young students from a *Show Call* (technique 39) to champion *Excavate Error*: "Tales of a Positive Outlier, Part 3: Nicole Willey's Show Call."

ACTION PLANNING

Use the success points listed in "Group Role Play" to track your progress at *Excavating Error*. (Find a printable version of this form at my.teachlikeachampion.com.)

HOW AM I DOING?

_____

_____

Design one or more action steps for improvement. Decide on an interval by which you'll revisit this page to assess your progress.

Action Step 1

By when, with whom, and how you will measure your effort

By _____, I will . . .
     Date

_____

_____

How Did I Do?

Successes: _____

_____

_____

_____

Challenges: _____

_____

_____

_____

Next steps: _____

_____

_____

Action Step 2

By when, with whom, and how you will measure your effort

By _____, I will . . .

_{Date}

_____

_____

_____

How Did I Do?

Successes: _____

_____

_____

_____

Challenges: _____

_____

_____

_____

Next steps: _____

_____

_____

_____

OWN AND TRACK

OVERVIEW

If we do our jobs right, as teachers, we will probably invest a tremendous amount of time and energy studying mistakes and helping students convert their misconceptions into mastery, their "wrong" answers into "right."

But if our goal is to help students learn from their mistakes and improve their work, then having students fix their mistakes gets them only halfway. The real measure of whether students process and internalize key ideas is whether they can use them to improve their future work. This requires reflecting on what they learned and why their initial answers were wrong. Students must *Own and Track*: learn from and reflect on what they have learned in the process of getting from incorrect to correct. This means attending to and even making notes on how they got there.

We will distill this *Own and Track* process down to four steps that teachers can train students to follow:

1. Lock in the "right" answer in writing.
2. Improve the work.
3. Get "meta" (metacognitive) about wrong answers.
4. Get "meta" about right answers, too.

We'll also explore how teachers can balance directive prompts with less directive ones.

Reflection

What's lost if students don't *Own and Track* a correct answer? What's lost if we don't get students to reflect on why one answer is correct while a different one is wrong? Write before you read on.

_____

_____

_____

Possible reflections (we're sure you've thought of others!): Even having given a correct answer, students may still be mixed up about how another answer would be wrong. Or students whose grasp of the content wasn't as strong may remain unclear about what the correct answer actually was and what was right about it.

From a teacher's point of view, not having students *Own and Track* what's "right" makes it more difficult to verify whether they can truly apply what they learned from discussion. It also means that students won't have the opportunity to improve their work.

When students refer back to their work, they may not remember the thought process that led to the right answer, or the process that led to the wrong one. Consequently, they won't be able to learn much from it, let alone apply it to future work. Not knowing what they did wrong, they may become discouraged by errors and see errors as random and therefore not worth learning from.

FUNDAMENTALS

As we said, *Own and Track* entails a variety of types of tracking that students can do to get more learning out of error analysis: differentiating and explaining a right answer, making notes about what made a wrong one incorrect, and by labeling their errors so that they do not overlook them.

1. Lock Down the "Right" Answer

Research suggests that students are, under some conditions, as likely to remember what they did wrong when solving a problem as what they did right. If you don't help them distinguish clearly between the two, you run the risk that students will come away fuzzy about what the correct answer was. Even more important, research suggests that weaker students are the ones most likely to confuse correct answers with incorrect ones. Even if you believe you've been clear that a + b is correct and a − b is wrong, there is the constant risk that students will come away thinking that there was something important to remember about a − b. What was it?

So after you've spent time analyzing errors and right answers, it can be useful to make sure that students have marked the correct answer and distinguished it from the alternatives. For example, you might ask students to label answers as "correct" or "not correct," have them cross out wrong responses and circle correct ones, star correct answers or mark them up in some other way. It's especially important to clearly communicate what the notation or labeling should look like so that, as you *Circulate,* you can easily monitor whether students have followed through.

Perhaps most important, having students legibly differentiate wrong from right answers—or mere completion from excellence—transforms their written work from a potential source of confusion and misconceptions into a useful and accurate tool for review. When they return to it later, it will be clear what they learned.

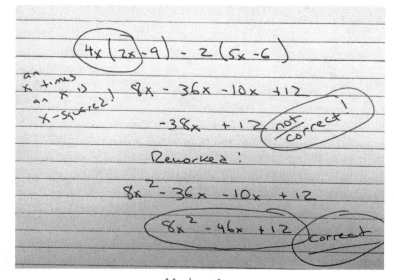

Markup 1

2. Improve the Work

After a thorough discussion of right and wrong answers, it's often beneficial to ask students to use what they learned to revise and improve their work. This holds them accountable for tracking the discussion through a constructive lens. It's also a useful way to gauge how well you've addressed misconceptions. If students can readily apply what they learned to improve their work, it's an indication that they are on the path to mastery. If they struggle, it suggests that you should resume the discussion or gather more data to diagnose the cause of the struggle. If a full revision of the original task isn't necessary, you might ask them to mark up or rework a specific step, sentence, or phrase.

3. Think Metacognitively about Wrong Answers

The more you invest in the process of studying or improving on mistakes, the more important it is for students to reflect on how these revisions enhanced their work. Thus they create a written record of the technical process and the thinking that led them to "right." From there, they can study and apply what they learned to similar work again and again. For example, in Markup 1, the student circles the precise location of his error. He then tags his correction with a clear label that captures in specific terms what he should have done differently (an x times an x is x-squared!). Instead of dwelling on what was incorrect ("I forgot your exponent rules!"), this note describes the fix, which the student can apply to future work. From a cultural standpoint, this exercise also helps students experience the value of reflecting critically on their mistakes. It testifies visually to all they learned by doing so.

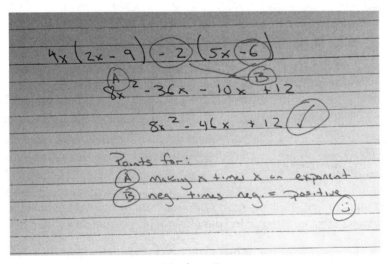

Markup 2

4. Do Meta-Work for Right Answers, Too

Letting students know what parts of a solution they got right can be just as useful as showing them what they got wrong. It can remind them of what they should keep doing, as opposed to what they should do differently. And it can provide them with a crucial study guide later on. Helping students see what's correct about imperfect work can also show them how close they are to success—closer than they initially thought, perhaps. In one of our favorite *Culture of Error* clips, one produced by the Teaching Channel (https://www.teachingchannel.org/videos/class-warm-up-routine), you can observe Leah Alcala systematically reinforce this mindset with an exercise she calls "My Favorite No." In this activity, she selects her "favorite wrong answer" from a *Do Now* (technique 20) and asks students to discuss its merits in addition to ways they can make it better. Of her rationale for this activity she says, "I call this 'My Favorite No' because I want students to recognize that what they're seeing is wrong. And I want them to recognize that there's something good about the work because it showed some good math." This helps students see the value in learning from what *is* positive about an ultimately incorrect answer. More fundamentally, it signals to students that regardless of whether or not they answered correctly, the discussion they're about to have will be valuable to them and that they'll be accountable for tracking what they learned from it.

In many ways, how students mark up and reflect on successes should and often does resemble what they do to reflect on their mistakes. As we see in Markup 2, it can help to have students identify precisely *where* they did correct work and what made it correct. In this instance, the teacher asked a student to circle key points that led to the right answer. Then he pushed students further by asking them to "footnote" those points with explanations of the thinking. This system for notation provides students with sufficient space to fully articulate *why* the work was correct without crowding out the work itself.

For an example of what student work could look like when you ask them to *Own and Track,* refer to Markup 3.

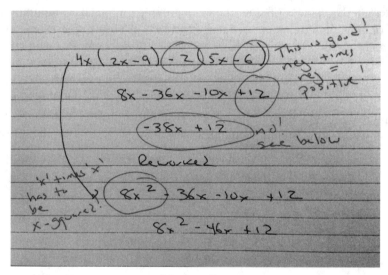

Markup 3

PROMPTING FOR *OWN AND TRACK*

From this list of prompts to help students *Own and Track,* mark two that appeal most strongly to you. Following the list, adapt at least one for use in your classroom and come up with a few more of your own.

1. "Give yourself a check for every one of these steps that you got correct. If you're missing one, add it and then make a note to yourself."
2. "Cross out answer choice B and write a margin note that explains how it uses the wrong operation."
3. "Draw a line through the [insert grammar mistake] and rewrite it correctly in the space above/in the margin."
4. "Cross out the word 'dissatisfied' from your response. In the margin, replace it with a word that has a more negative tone and captures just how strongly the character feels."
5. "Circle the negative sign outside the parentheses. Draw a line to the margin and make the note: 'distribute the negative → negative × negative = positive.'"
6. "Reread your response. Add at least one piece of evidence from our discussion to better support your answer. Be sure to note in the margin why you added it."
7. "Cross out the phrase 'become equal,' and directly above it, write 'reach equilibrium.'"

8. _____

9. _____

10. _____

THE NEXT LEVEL

Fewer Scaffolds

Once students grow familiar with the processes of *Own and Track*, you may decide to use less directive prompts. By "less directive," we mean giving students greater decisional power (and broader accountability) in *how* they *Own and Track*. For instance, after discussing some common mistakes in a lab write-up, you could ask students to "make some notes on what you've learned from studying this write-up." This approach lets students begin to internalize their own best system for tracking their learning.

Revisit the prompts you chose, created, or recreated earlier. Or write three new ones you can envision yourself using frequently in your class. Here, rewrite them to be more or less directive than before. We give two examples.

More Directive	Less Directive
Revised: Circle the negative sign outside the parentheses in step one. Draw a line to the margin and make the note: "Distribute the negative → negative × negative = positive."	*Original: Circle the error you made and make a note to yourself about it.*
1.	1.
2.	2.
3.	3.

Variations on *Own and Track*

Here are two examples of what *Own and Track* could look like across different types of questions and content areas. Record your observations about each and note what you might borrow or adapt.

Example 1

Suppose a teacher is conferring with a student in his English class who is reading Jane Austen's *Pride and Prejudice.* He has asked her to paraphrase the italicized lines from this excerpt in chapter 5:

> Within a short walk of Longbourn lived a family with whom the Bennets were particularly intimate. Sir William Lucas had been formerly in trade in Meryton, where he had made a tolerable fortune, and risen to the honour of knighthood by an address to the King, during his mayoralty. *The distinction had perhaps been felt too strongly. It had given him a disgust to his business, and to his residence in a small market town; and, quitting them both, he had removed with his family to an house about a mile from Meryton, denominated from that period Lucas Lodge,* where he could think with pleasure of his own importance, and, unshackled by business, occupy himself solely in being civil to all the world.

Her paraphrase is this:

> Sir William Lucas made too much of a big deal about the distinction between himself and the townspeople. He began to hate his business and the idea of living in a small market town and so had quit his job and moved his family a mile outside of town to a house he called, from then on, "Lucas Lodge."

The teacher sees that the student's paraphrase is quite good, actually, but that she missed a few subtle things. "The distinction" that Sir William feels too strongly is not the difference between himself and the townspeople per se, though he clearly feels that. Here it specifically refers to the "distinction" of being knighted and made a "sir" by the king. That is, once the king knighted him, he started to put on airs. Also the word "quitting" refers to leaving them (work and town) behind. It's a subtle difference, but he didn't "quit" his job. Stopped working and left town would be a better paraphrase than "quit his job."

The teacher brings these points out in conference and says, "Good work. Now just go back and mark up your paraphrase to make it fully correct and mark up the changes." The student then made the following markings:

being made a knight
Distinction = becoming sir Wm

Sir William Lucas made too much of a big deal about ~~the distinction between himself and the townspeople.~~ He began to hate his business and the idea of living in a small market town and so had ~~quit his job~~ and moved his family a mile outside of town to a house he called, from then on, "Lucas Lodge."

stopped working

She has now not only refined her paraphrase but noted the reasons why she made the changes she did.

My observations:

_____

_____

_____

What I could use:

_____

_____

_____

Example 2

During a recent lesson, Vicki Hernandez, an eighth-grade biology teacher, asked her students to answer this question about cell respiration:

Certain poisons are toxic to organisms because they interfere with the <u>function</u> of enzymes in the <u>mitochondria</u>. This results directly in the inability of the cell to . . .

A) Store information
B) Build proteins
C) Release energy from nutrients
D) Dispose of metabolic wastes

Students struggled to answer it correctly, their answers ranging from A to D. The correct answer was C. Because this question was so crucial to students' understanding of the lesson and unit, she decided to deeply excavate it (technique 9) and then have her students *Own and Track*.

Here is one student's *Own and Track*:

My observations:

_____

_____

_____

What I could use:

_____

_____

_____

_____

PLANNING FOR *OWN AND TRACK*

Select a question from an upcoming lesson plan that's important to the main objective of the lesson (see *4 Ms*, technique 17). Anticipate two erroneous answers that you might receive from students. Script an *Own and Track* prompt for each. If possible, exchange your prompts with a partner for feedback and then revise one.

Your question:

_____

Target answer:

_____

Likely incorrect answer or error 1:

_____

Your *Own and Track* prompt:

_____

Likely incorrect answer or error 2:

_____

Your *Own and Track* prompt:

_____

ROLE-PLAY PRACTICE WITH A GROUP OR COLLEAGUE

Revisit one of the *Own and Track* statements that you drafted. If you have three participants, the roles are *Teacher*, *Student*, and *Coach*. Practice delivering your *Own and Track* prompts. Here is the general sequence of actions for practice:

1. *Teacher* asks question.
2. *Student* provides anticipated wrong answer.

3. *Teacher* analyzes the error with the help of the *Student*.
4. *Teacher* has *Student Own and Track* the answer (including the right and wrong answers, as well as why they are right and wrong).

   After the *Teacher* practices an *Own and Track* moment, the *Coach* (or partner) gives one glow ("It was effective when . . .") and one grow ("Next time, try . . ."). Using that feedback, the *Teacher* tries again. In the feedback, address whether the *Teacher*

- Gave the students clear, explicit directions for how to mark up correct and incorrect answer(s)
- Managed the tell (see technique 8, *Culture of Error*) by maintaining a neutral expression and tone in response to a wrong answer

ACTION PLANNING

Use this action planner to continue your work with *Own and Track*. (Find a printable version of this form at my.teachlikeachampion.com.) You're on the right track when all your students are progressing at

- Locking in the "right" answer
- Improving their work
- Thinking and writing metacognitive notes about both wrong and right answers

HOW AM I DOING?

_____

_____

_____

Design one or more action steps for improvement. Decide on an interval by which you'll revisit this page to assess your progress.

Action Step 1

By when, with whom, and how you will measure your effort

By _____, I will . . .
    Date

_____

_____

How Did I Do?

Successes: _____

_____

_____

_____

_____

Challenges: _____

_____

_____

_____

Next steps: _____

_____

_____

_____

OWN AND TRACK

Action Step 2

By when, with whom, and how you will measure your effort

By _____, I will . . .
<u>Date</u>

_____

_____

_____

How Did I Do?

Successes: _____

_____

_____

_____

_____

Challenges: _____

_____

_____

_____

Next steps: _____

_____

_____

_____

NO OPT OUT

OVERVIEW

What you do when a student doesn't answer a question you've asked plays a major part in shaping academic expectations in your classroom. Many successful teachers use *No Opt Out* to ensure that when a student is unable (or unwilling) to answer a question, the sequence ends as often as possible with that student answering correctly.

This technique raises academic expectations in the classroom by

- Building a culture of individual accountability, in which there's no reward for not trying
- Causing students to rehearse success, hearing themselves getting the answers right when they initially could not

Once a student answers the question correctly, you can ratchet up the positivity and rigor by adding challenge, such as asking students to explain "why" or to apply what they know in new ways.

Reflection: When You Don't Get an Answer

There are many potential reasons why a student might not answer your question. It's worth considering them. List as many reasons as you can for why students might not answer your question.

_____

_____

_____

_____

What happens if you allow students not to answer the questions you ask them?

_____

_____

_____

Possible reflections (we're sure you've thought of others as well): Students might not answer because they legitimately don't know the answer, feel afraid to try to show what they know due to social pressure, aren't motivated to try, want to show you that *they* decide when they will work, or perceive the question as too easy and unworthy of their effort.

The consequences of teachers' allowing students not to answer include erosion of their authority in the eyes of students, normalization of a pattern of opting out and not participating, fewer opportunities for students to experience success, and a conviction among students who opt out that you're not invested in their success.

ANALYZE THE CHAMPIONS

View both video clips and answer the following question. We've also included a transcript of each clip for your reference.

Compare what's effective about Shadell's and Derek's use of *No Opt Out*. Compare your written observations with ours at the end of this technique.

Shadell Purefoy	Derek Pollak

Commonalities between them:

_____

_____

_____

_____

▶ **Clip FG12 Transcript: Shadell Purefoy, *No Opt Out***

1.	SHADELL:	OK scholars. So, today we're going to read a book called *Clever Fox*. The title of our book is *Clever Fox*. The title of our book is *Clever Fox*. Does anyone know what *clever* means? What does *clever* mean? What does *clever* mean? Kayla, do you know what *clever* means?
2.	KAYLA:	No.
3.	SHADELL:	No. OK, Azaiah?
4.	AZAIAH:	Clever means smart.
5.	SHADELL:	Clever means that you're really smart. Kayla, what does clever mean?
6.	KAYLA:	Clever means smart.
7.	SHADELL:	Clever means that you're smart. So looking at the front cover, looking at the front cover, what do you notice? What do you notice?

▶ **Clip FG13 Transcript: Derek Pollak *No Opt Out***

1.	STUDENT:	Negative one-third.
2.	DEREK:	Good. Last one. LN [natural log] of one over the fifth root of E squared. LN of one over the fifth root of E squared. Think . . . [inaudible]
3.	STUDENT 1:	Negative five halves.
4.	DEREK:	Try again. It was the fifth root.
5.	STUDENT 1:	So it's one-fifth and then squared.
6.	DEREK:	You said negative five halves.
7.	STUDENT 1:	So, then . . . five halves?
8.	DEREK:	Someone explain what her mistake is and then she'll be able to correct it; don't give her the answer, though. Simmerson?
9.	SIMMERSON:	So when you get the cubed root, or a fifth root, or anything, that's the denominator of the fraction. So you have five halves, but the five is supposed to be in the denominator.
10.	DEREK:	That's good enough. So [Student 1], what's the answer?
11.	STUDENT 1:	So it's two-fifths.
12.	DEREK:	Ah.
13.	STUDENT 1:	Negative two-fifths.
14.	DEREK:	Good, you guys can sit.

FUNDAMENTALS

Skilled teachers rely on four basic formats of *No Opt Out* to help students get to "right." Although each sequence looks a little different, they all end with the student answering the question correctly:

Format 1. You provide the answer; the student repeats it.
Format 2. Another student (or the entire class) provides the answer; the initial student repeats it.
Format 3. You provide a cue; the student uses it to find the answer.
Format 4. Another student provides a cue; the initial student uses it to find the answer.

> ### Revisit *Teach Like a Champion 2.0*
>
> In addition to the examples of *No Opt Out* in these pages, you also may want to look back at Doug's examples under this technique at "Four Basic Formats of *No Opt Out.*"

NO OPT OUT

Analyzing *No Opt Out* Moments

Classify these *No Opt Out* moments from Shadell's and Derek's clips according to the four format types. Explain why each is effective.

 Excerpt of Clip FG12

SHADELL:	Kayla, do you know what *clever* means?
KAYLA:	No.
SHADELL:	No. OK, Azaiah?
AZAIAH:	Clever means smart.
SHADELL:	Clever means that you're really smart. Kayla, what does clever mean?

Format type(s):

_____

Why it's effective:

_____

_____

 Excerpt of Clip FG13

DEREK:	Someone explain what [Student 1's] mistake is and then she'll be able to correct it; don't give her the answer, though. Simmerson?
STUDENT 2:	So when you get the cubed root, or a fifth root, or anything, that's the denominator of the fraction. So you have five halves, but the five is supposed to be in the denominator.
DEREK:	That's good enough. So [Student 1], what's the answer?

Format type(s):

_____

Why it's effective:

_____

_____

Planning *No Opt Out* in Multiple Formats

Read the example. Then complete two versions of a *No Opt Out* sequence for one of the subject areas that follow. Use a different format for each version. Choose formats that will challenge you.

NO OPT OUT

No Opt Out Sequence Example

NOO Sequence (Version 1)	*NOO* Sequence (Version 2)
Teacher: In the heliocentric model, what celestial body lies at the center of the solar system? **Student:** I don't know. *Teacher: OK, class. On two, tell me what lies at the center of the heliocentric model. One . . . two!* *Class: The sun!* *Teacher: Correct. So, what lies at the center of the solar system?* *Student: The sun lies at the center of the solar system.*	**Teacher:** In the heliocentric model, what celestial body lies at the center of the solar system? **Student 1:** I don't know. *Teacher: OK. Student 2, can you give Student 1 a hint?* *Student 2: Yesterday, we talked about Helios, who was the Greek sun god.* *Teacher: Correct. So if Helios was the sun god, what lies at the center of the heliocentric model, Student 1?* *Student 1: In the heliocentric model, the sun lies at the center of the solar system.*

Math

NOO Sequence (Version 1)	*NOO* Sequence (Version 2)
Teacher: Which fraction is bigger: 1/2 or 1/3? **Student:** I don't know.	**Teacher:** Which fraction is bigger: 1/2 or 1/3? **Student:** I don't know.

Reading

NOO Sequence (Version 1)	*NOO* Sequence (Version 2)
Teacher: What does *hurl* mean? [Answer: to forcefully throw something—usually something offensive—away from yourself] **Student:** I don't know.	**Teacher:** What does *hurl* mean? [Answer: to forcefully throw something—usually something offensive—away from yourself] **Student:** I don't know.

Science

NOO Sequence (Version 1)	*NOO* Sequence (Version 2)
Teacher: What are the products of photosynthesis? [Answer: oxygen and glucose] **Student 1:** I don't know.	**Teacher:** What are the products of photosynthesis? [Answer: oxygen and glucose] **Student 1:** I don't know.

History

NOO Sequence (Version 1)	*NOO* Sequence (Version 2)
Teacher: What contributed to the rise of totalitarianism in 20th-century Europe? [Possible answers: Great Depression; nationalism; new systems of communication, like the radio] **Student:** I don't know.	**Teacher:** What contributed to the rise of totalitarianism in 20th-century Europe? [Possible answers: Great Depression; nationalism; new systems of communication, like the radio] **Student:** I don't know.

Cues

> ### Revisit *Teach Like a Champion 2.0*
>
> In the section "On Cues, Hints, and Questions," Doug distinguishes between cues and hints. By "cue" he means
>
> > a prompt that offers additional useful information to the student in a way that pushes him or her to follow the correct thinking process. A hint, by contrast, could offer any related information. If I ask, "Can anyone give James a hint to help him find the subject?" a student might say, "It starts with the letter *m.*" This would surely help James guess the answer, but it doesn't teach him anything that will help him next time.
> >
> > Four cues are particularly useful for cueing students in a *No Opt Out*:
>
> 1. The place where the answer can be found.
>
> "Who can tell James where he could find the answer?"
>
> 2. The next step in the process that's required at the moment.
>
> "Who can tell James what the first thing he should do is?"
>
> 3. Another name for a term that's a problem.
>
> "Who can tell James what denominator means?"
>
> 4. An identification of the mistake.
>
> "Who can explain what James might have done wrong here?"

NO OPT OUT

Teaching Students to Ask for Help

An alternative method for getting students to "right" involves teaching them to ask clarifying questions to help themselves when they feel stuck.

As Fishman Prize–winning science teacher Michael Towne told Doug, "If I ask them, 'What's the speed of the magnetic flux here?' I want them to be able to say, 'I'm actually not that clear on what you mean by magnetic flux.'"

In teaching students to do this, he empowers students to replace "I don't know" with productive, self-advocating behavior. To set this up, Michael gives his students examples of clarifying questions. An added benefit of this approach is that it makes it easier for you to discern whether a student is *unable to answer* or *choosing not to*.

Star two of the following examples that appeal most strongly to you. Adapt at least one example to improve it. Then come up with a few more examples.

1. Can you explain what "_____" means?
2. Can I take a second to look back at my notes?
3. Can I call on a friend for help?
4. Who is . . . ?/What is . . . ?
5. Can you repeat/clarify the second part of your question?
6. To check my understanding, are you asking [paraphrase of question]?

7. _____
8. _____
9. _____
10. _____

Facing Resistance

As every teacher who has used *No Opt Out* knows, it doesn't always go smoothly, and sometimes you will encounter a bit of resistance. This can manifest itself as anything ranging from a passive shrug to a sarcastic "I don't know" to willful defiance. In spite of this pushback, it's critical that the sequence end with the student answering correctly. Allowing a student to opt out not only erodes your authority but also teaches the class that opting out is a viable option.

Preparing for Pushback

Following this example, plan for how you would respond to moments of resistance.

If a student says . . .	I will respond . . .	Other things I could do
Nothing, but shrugs apathetically	*"OK, listen to what [insert peer's name] says because we'll be coming back to you for the answer."*	*Look calm and assured*

If a student says . . .	I will respond . . .	Other things I could do
"I don't know." [with sarcasm]		

If a student says . . .	I will respond . . .	Other things I could do
"I already told you. I don't know." [with hint of frustration]		
"Are you asking *me*? I wasn't raising my hand."		
"I didn't get that far." [when you know he or she did]		
"Why are you always calling on *me*?"		

THE NEXT LEVEL

Good teachers frequently push students beyond the threshold of "right" by following a successful *No Opt Out* with a question that adds rigor or provides extra practice. Here are four methods we've seen teachers use to do it:

Technique 25, At Bats. Follow up by asking the student to answer a similar question. Alternatively, ask a series of *Targeted Questions* (technique 2) to make sure the student has truly mastered the skill or topic.

Technique 13, Stretch It. Reward a correct answer to your original question with more challenging ones (for example, asking why or how, asking for evidence, asking a question that combines this recently mastered skill with another one, and so on).

Error analysis. See chapter 2. Ask students to analyze their initial error. "And what did you do incorrectly the first time?" This ensures that the student who got it wrong internalizes and learns from the error alongside the rest of the class.

A "star." Publicly celebrate the student's persistence, a specific action ("I see you used your notes"), or ultimate success by capping the sequence with motivating language. "Yes! *That's* the kind of work I want to see from you." To keep them potent, reserve stars for responses that truly merit public recognition.

ANALYZE A CHAMPION

 Clip FG14. Denarius Frazier, Grade 9

Answer this question after viewing the video clip. Compare your written answer with our observations at the end of this technique.

How does Denarius add rigor to his *No Opt Out* while also keeping the culture around it positive and supportive?

_____

_____

_____

_____

CASE STUDIES

Read these cases with *No Opt Out* in mind. Consider what each teacher does that's effective and what could be improved. Compare your written comments with ours.

Case 1. Mr. Walker, ELA

1. MR. WALKER: What's the definition of *insidious*? Chantal.
2. CHANTAL: *Insidious*? *(shrugs)*
3. MR. WALKER: Javon, help her out.
4. JAVON: Gradually causing serious harm (and it often goes unnoticed until it's too late).
5. MR. WALKER: Thanks, Javon. So what's *insidious*, Chantal?
6. CHANTAL: *Insidious* means gradually causing serious harm *(next words seem not to be heard)* that goes unnoticed until it's too late.
7. MR. WALKER: Yeah, and can you add a bit more detail?
8. CHANTAL: It goes unnoticed.
9. MR. WALKER: So can you name a character who has an *insidious* influence on Othello.
10. CHANTAL: Iago.
11. MR. WALKER: Why do you say that?
12. CHANTAL: Iago makes Othello really jealous by falsely suggesting that Desdemona and Cassio were having an affair.
13. MR. WALKER: Yes, That was indeed very insidious! Nice work.

Glows	Grows
It was effective when Mr. Walker . . .	Next time, he could try . . .

Case 2. Ms. Nelson, Algebra

1.	MS. NELSON:	Use the distributive property to simplify this expression: $-5(x + 2)$
2.	JEREMY:	$-5x + 10$.
3.	MS. NELSON:	Now tell me how you got that.
4.	JEREMY:	I multiplied everything in the parentheses by -5.
5.	MS. NELSON:	OK, you multiplied x by -5 and the product was $-5x$. What happens when you multiply 2 by -5?
6.	JEREMY:	The product would be a *negative* 10.
7.	MS. NELSON:	Good. So what did you forget to do the first time?
8.	JEREMY:	I forgot to distribute the negative from *negative* 5.
9.	MS. NELSON:	That's right. And when we distribute the *negative* 5, we multiply a *positive* number (2) by a *negative* number (-5), which means we must get a *negative* product (-10). So what do you get if you simplify $-5(x + 2)$?
10.	JEREMY:	$-5x - 10$.
11.	MS. NELSON:	*That's* the way to stick with it. Nicely done.

Glows	Grows
It was effective when Ms. Nelson . . .	Next time, she could try . . .

Observations on Case 1

Mr. Walker effectively adds *Stretch It*: "Name a character who has an insidious influence on Othello." Also, he makes an attempt to celebrate the student's effort at the end. Next time he could provide more *At Bats* (technique 25):

MR. WALKER:	Name a character who has an insidious influence on Othello.
CHANTAL:	Iago.
MR. WALKER:	What famous lines from act III foreshadow this?
CHANTAL:	When Iago says, "O, beware, my lord, of jealousy;/ It is the green-ey'd monster, which doth mock/ The meat it feeds on."
MR. WALKER:	Why does this foreshadow Iago's *insidious* influence on Othello?
CHANTAL:	It foreshadows how the lie Iago tells Othello about Desdemona will consume him with jealousy.
MR. WALKER:	Well, now you're just showing off!

Observations on Case 2

Ms. Nelson was effective in adding a "star": *"That's* the way to stick with it. Nicely done." Also, she *Excavated Error* (technique 9), revisiting Jeremy's error for the class to learn from it: "So what did you forget to do the first time?" Like Mr. Walker, she too could have added more *At Bats.* For example:

MS. NELSON:	Now, what if I asked you to simplify $-5(x-2)$?
JEREMY:	You would multiply x by -5 and -2 by -5. That would give you $-5x + 10$.
MS. NELSON:	And why did you get *negative* 10 instead of *positive* 10?
JEREMY:	Because when you distribute the negative (-5), you multiply a negative (-5) by a negative (-2), which gives you a positive (10).
MS. NELSON:	*That's* the way to stick with it. Nicely done.

In *Excavating Error,* she could have pushed Jeremy to explain his own error instead of doing that thinking for him:

MS. NELSON:	Good. So explain what your mistake was the first time.
JEREMY:	I forgot to distribute the negative from *negative* five, and when you multiply a *positive* by a *negative* you get a *negative* product ($-5 \times 2 = -10$). So the *positive* 10 should have been a *negative* 10.

ROLE-PLAY PRACTICE WITH COLLEAGUES

This role play will help you improve your execution of *No Opt Out* by giving you multiple opportunities to practice it. For best results, practice with two other people.

Start simply. Rotate roles before moving on to the two variations here.

There are three roles: *Teacher, Student 1,* and *Student 2.* Here is the basic sequence:

1. *Teacher* asks *Student 1* a simple question. ("What's 3 plus 5?")
2. *Student 1* responds with "I don't know."
3. *Teacher* asks *Student 2* to provide a correct answer.
4. *Student 2* answers directly and correctly.
5. *Teacher* returns to *Student 1* for repetition of correct answer.
6. *Student 1* answers correctly.
7. *Teacher* acknowledges correct answer.

During your partner's practice, focus on his or her mastering these success points first:

- Responds consistently and neutrally to both correct and incorrect answers
- Responds to incorrect answers with a cue, an answer, or by calling on another student
- Quickly and efficiently acknowledges when the student finally gets it right, either verbally or nonverbally

ACTION PLANNING

Find a printable version of this form at my.teachlikeachampion.com. Using the success points just listed, evaluate where you are now at implementing *No Opt Out.*

HOW AM I DOING?

_____

_____

Design one or more action steps for improvement. Decide on an interval by which you'll revisit this page to assess your progress.

Action Step 1

By when, with whom, and how you will measure your effort
By _____, I will . . .
<small>Date</small>

_____

_____

How Did I Do?

Successes: _____

_____

_____

_____

Challenges: _____

_____

_____

_____

Next steps: _____

_____

_____

_____

Action Step 2

By when, with whom, and how you will measure your effort

By _____, I will . . .
     Date

How Did I Do?

Successes: _____

_____

_____

_____

Challenges: _____

_____

_____

Next steps: _____

_____

_____

NO OPT OUT

OUR OBSERVATIONS ON THE CHAMPIONS

 Clip FG12, Shadell Purefoy, and Clip FG13, Derek Pollak

Shadell strategically *Cold Calls* (technique 33) the only student whose hand isn't up. At this moment, this student is arguably the most important one to call on in the room. Shadell uses a combination of formats 1 and 2: she goes to another student for the definition of *clever,* which she then reiterates before returning to Kayla (who repeats the definition).

Derek repeats the question and rolls back a student's answer to give her a chance to self-correct (format 1). When that doesn't work, he calls on another student for a cue (format 4). Unlike Shadell, who asks for the answer, Derek explicitly asks the second student *not to provide the answer.* This makes the *No Opt Out* more rigorous and "high school." When the student forgets the negative sign, Derek combines *No Opt Out* with *Right Is Right* (technique 12) to ensure that the student truly rehearses success by providing an answer that is fully correct.

The teachers are similar in that both begin with a *Cold Call.* This enables them to minimize the risk of getting false positives and enables them to help the students who need it the most (as demonstrated by the *No Opt Out* that follows). Also, both execute *No Opt Out* quickly and efficiently, and then get *right back* to teaching. This efficiency helps them preserve the thread of instruction and maintain effective pacing.

 Clip FG14, Denarius Frazier

When Denarius asks an important question from his lesson and his student gets it wrong, Denarius repeats his answer back to him while adding emphasis to it (*"Reverses?"*). This gives the student the opportunity to hear his response and possibly fix it himself without further support from Denarius. When the student offers another wrong answer, Denarius rolls it back again ("secant?") and then gives the student a heads-up that he will come back to him about this question. He then calls on another student for the correct answer. As promised, Denarius then returns to the original student. But instead of asking the student to merely repeat the correct answer, he builds rigor by asking him to explain the correct thinking behind his peer's right answer ("Why would we have to do the inverse cosine, Michael?"). The original student then provides a correct explanation, and in doing so shows Denarius that he knows not only the right answer but also the *why* behind it. This gives Denarius the data he needs to feel confident enough to end the discussion and transition students to the *Exit Ticket* (technique 26).

Denarius consistently responds to this student's errors with a neutral and nonjudgmental tone which suggests that making mistakes is normal and expected. His calm demeanor and *Emotional Constancy* (technique 61) convey his confidence in the student's ability to ultimately get it right. When the student succeeds, Denarius subtly honors this by repeating his right answer to the class so that everyone can hear and learn from it.

RIGHT IS RIGHT

OVERVIEW

In an ideal world, teachers would react to almost-right answers by *holding out for all-the-way right* and causing students to do the work necessary to upgrade their answers. They would avoid confusing "almost" with "all-the-way" and be careful not to do the work of completing the last step or two for students, a process we call "rounding up."

While it may not be possible to achieve the ideal and always push students to get to a perfect answer every time, teachers should strive to get there as much as they can, setting and upholding a high standard for correctness in their classrooms and pushing students to make their answers as thorough and accurate as possible. In other words, they should strive for answers that meet an academically rigorous standard for excellence. Maintaining a high standard for "right" can help you establish a culture of precision and excellence that motivates students to do their best work. More important, it can help you prepare students to meet and even surpass the academic expectations they'll face throughout their educations.

Reflection: Temptations to "Round Up"

By "rounding up" we mean the habit of improving on a student's almost-right answer to make it fully correct:

TEACHER: What's the relationship like between the Montagues and Capulets at the start of *Romeo and Juliet*?
STUDENT: They don't like each other.
TEACHER: Right. They don't like each other, and they've been feuding for generations.

Here the teacher rounds up a thin or partially correct answer by adding important context ("they've been feuding for generations") that enhances the quality of the student's response. By saying "Right," she suggests that the student must have had the additional information in mind but simply hadn't mentioned it. In other words, she gives him credit for knowledge he may not have had.

Once you've written, compare your thoughts with ours.

In what situations are you or other teachers likely to be tempted to round up like this? What factors might draw you in?

What are some likely bad results of rounding up?

_____

_____

Possible reflections (we're sure you've thought of others as well): We can be at risk of rounding up when we're not certain what a fully correct answer is or when we ask an especially rigorous question. We may round up when we want to encourage effort and participation by affirming students' answers, want certain students to publicly experience success, or want to have faith that our students are "getting it" (especially if we're evaluating our effectiveness in light of how students are doing). Sometimes we round up in order to move things along quickly.

Consequences of rounding up may be that students won't learn what you're trying to teach or, even worse, will learn inaccurate information; at the same time, they may overestimate how well they know and understand the material. Rounding up can also lower students' expectations for themselves and weaken their confidence in your subject-matter expertise (especially if you're saying answers are fully "right" when they're not).

ANALYZE A CHAMPION

 Clip FG15. Maggie Johnson, Grade 8

We've also included a transcript of this video for your reference. View the clip and respond to the following questions. Then compare your responses with our observations at the end of this technique.

How does Maggie hold out for all-the-way right?

_____

_____

_____

What differences do you hear between the student's first and second answers? What impact has Maggie had?

_____

_____

_____

 Clip FG15. Transcript: Maggie Johnson, Grade 8

1. MAGGIE: You should box it up if you haven't already. This describes Aunt Alexander. Frost?
2. FROST: I agree with Damani that Aunt Alexander is preoccupied with heredity because her family . . . Simon, well, the dad he was really rich so back then he's like—

3.	MAGGIE:	He owned a what?
4.	FROST:	He owned a farm.
5.	MAGGIE:	Not just any kind of farm.
6.	FROST:	Not a farm, it was Finch's Landing.
7.	MAGGIE:	Which was a . . . ?
8.	FROST:	Ah, I forgot.
9.	MAGGIE:	Monique?
10.	MONIQUE:	It was a birch.
11.	MAGGIE:	Nope. Diane?
12.	DIANE:	A plantation.
13.	MAGGIE:	It was. Which means he had?
14.	FROST:	He had a lot of money.
15.	MAGGIE:	And? Keara?
16.	KEARA:	Slaves.
17.	MAGGIE:	Correct. He had what?
18.	FROST:	Slaves.
19.	MAGGIE:	Continue your thought.
20.	FROST:	I think that she's like—trying to look back on that, and she's still preoccupied on it, so she's like trying to act like that while the other family is not.
21.	MAGGIE:	Act like what?
22.	FROST:	Like act rich—that's what I don't know.
23.	MAGGIE:	Tell me more; you're right. Continue.
24.	FROST:	She's like trying to act rich because like she was—wasn't she wearing like, the way she was like wearing things, like she's trying to present herself, like she's like superior to like the rest of the family.
25.	MAGGIE:	*(to the class)* Thoughts?

FUNDAMENTALS

"Kitchen Sink" Responses

In some cases, the shortcoming in a student's answer isn't that it *lacks* detail, but that it contains an *overabundance* of it. A student gives you "everything but the kitchen sink," saying every true thing that he knows about the topic at hand. Students might do this for a variety of reasons, but an important and common one is this: they know a lot about a topic, but *not* the answer to your specific question. They suspect that if they start rattling off facts and information, you will stop them when they mention the crucial detail and then they will have said the right answer. But this, we note, is very different from knowing an answer.

In the following transcript, notice how fifth-grade teacher Kathryn Orfuss responds to a kitchen-sink answer.

KATHRYN:	What happens to Hercules at the very end, after killing his children?
STUDENT:	After Hercules killed his children, he regained his senses and since he was horrified by what he had done, he went to the Oracle of Delphi and he asked the Oracle to tell him his crime, and he had to serve ten years as a slave for his cousin, Eurystheus.
KATHRYN:	Great, you're giving us a lot of information. Put it into one crisp sentence we can add to our summary. What happens to Hercules? *(to another student)* Track, Amber.
STUDENT:	After Hercules killed his children, he regained his senses, and he served ten years as a slave for Eurystheus.

Be sure to write before you read on. What's effective about how Kathryn Orfuss holds out for all-the-way right? What's the result?

_____

_____

_____

_____

Possible answers: Kathryn doesn't accept the student's original answer, even though it contains the correct information. Instead, she asks for precision with these words: "Put it into one crisp sentence we can add to our summary. What happens to Hercules?" In so doing, she makes sure that her student can separate wheat from chaff.

At the same time, Kathryn also acknowledges the hard work and thinking her student has done. She's careful not to say that the student's answer is wrong, because, strictly speaking, it's not. It's just not precise enough yet.

By eliciting a crisp, one-sentence *Right Is Right* response, Kathryn helps her students understand the value of precision. If some students try to couch misunderstandings in long-winded kitchen-sink responses, they will find themselves unable to. More important, she is teaching all of her students the importance of excluding redundant and extraneous information and prioritizing key details.

Supportive "Back-Pocket" Phrases

One of the biggest challenges in implementing *Right Is Right* is striking the right balance in tone. On the one hand, we want to encourage and openly appreciate the work students put into developing their almost-there answers. On the other, we want to be honest about the fact that more work is needed. The best way to satisfy both needs is to draft some back-pocket phrases ahead of time that accomplish both.

Star two of the following examples that appeal most strongly to you. Adapt at least one of them for use in your classroom. Then come up with a few more examples.

1. I like *most* of that . . .
2. You're *almost* there . . ./That's getting us get *closer* . . .
3. I like where you're going with that. Say a little more about . . .
4. I see that you [completed all of the steps; nailed the first two parts of the question; used that scientific language, and so on], but can you tell me what final piece is missing?
5. Good. We're 80 percent of the way there . . .
6. That sets us up nicely to solve this. How do we?

7. _____

8. _____

9. _____

10. _____

Planning to Hold Out for All-the-Way Right

Use this framework to plan your responses for a crucial question you'll be asking in a lesson. Draft your target response and two anticipated almost-right answers. Then script two prompts with which you could respond to hold out for all-the-way right.

Your question:

_____

Your *Right Is Right* target answer:

_____

One anticipated almost-right answer:

_____

Another anticipated almost-right answer:

_____

A prompt for *Right Is Right*:

_____

Another prompt for *Right Is Right*:

_____

Other Aspects of *Right Is Right*

Besides complete and focused answers, careful teachers maintain a high bar for correctness in terms of

Answering the question. Keep students disciplined about answering your original question, not the question they think (or hope) you'd asked.

Right answer, right time. Resist giving students credit when they skip ahead and try to answer a question that the class hasn't covered yet.

Specific vocabulary. Ensure that students lock down their answers in precise words and technical terminology.

ANALYZE THE CHAMPIONS

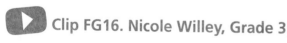 Clip FG16. Nicole Willey, Grade 3

 Clip FG17. Colleen Driggs, Grade 5

View both videos before you write. Then compare your answers with our observations at the end. Which types of *Right Is Right* do Nicole and Colleen use in these clips? What happens as a result?

Nicole's *Right Is Right:*

_____

_____

_____

Colleen's *Right Is Right:*

_____

_____

_____

Similarities between the two:

_____

_____

_____

Right Is Right Sequences

Read the example, then complete two versions of a *Right Is Right* sequence for one of the subject areas that follow. Use a different type for each version.

Example

Right Is Right Sequence (Version 1)	*Right Is Right* Sequence (Version 2)
Teacher: What does volume measure? [Answer: Volume measures the amount of space that an object occupies.] **Student:** Volume is equal to length times width times height. **Teacher:** You're telling me how to solve for volume, but I'm asking for what volume measures. **Student:** Volume measures the amount of space an object occupies.	**Teacher:** What does volume measure? [Answer: Volume measures the amount of space that an object occupies.] **Student:** It measures the amount of space that an object takes up. **Teacher:** What's our technical term for "takes up"? **Student:** Occupies. **Teacher:** Great, so tell me again, what does volume measure? **Student:** Volume measures the amount of space that an object occupies.

Math

Right is Right Sequence (Version 1)	*Right is Right* Sequence (Version 2)
Teacher: Find the area of the triangle below. (Answer: ½ × b × h = <u>6 m²</u>) *[triangle diagram: sides labeled 5m, 4m, 3m]* **Student:** To find that, you have to multiply ½ (b × h).	**Teacher:** Find the area of the triangle below. (Answer: ½ × b × h = <u>6 m²</u>) *[triangle diagram: sides labeled 5m, 4m, 3m]* **Student:** The area of the triangle is 6m.

Science

Right Is Right Sequence (Version 1)	*Right Is Right* Sequence (Version 2)
Teacher: Explain what happens to air pressure as volume increases. [Answer: As volume increases, air pressure decreases, because there is more space for the air particles to move.] **Student:** It goes down.	**Teacher:** Explain what happens to air pressure as volume increases. [Answer: As volume increases, air pressure decreases, because there is more space for the air particles to move.] **Student:** We know it will change because of Boyle's Law.

Two *Right Is Right* Case Studies

Read these cases with *Right Is Right* in mind. Note what each teacher does that's effective ("glows") and what could be improved ("grows"). Include what different aspects of *Right Is Right* the teacher does or does not address.

Case 1. Science

TEACHER: During diffusion, how do molecules move in terms of concentration? [Answer: Molecules move from a high concentration of molecules to a low concentration.]

STUDENT 1: Molecules move without the use of energy.

TEACHER: That's true, but what I was asking was how molecules move during diffusion.

STUDENT 1: They move from high to low.

TEACHER: Be more specific. High to low what?

STUDENT 1: Diffusion moves from high concentration to low concentration.

TEACHER: Right. The molecules move from high concentration to low concentration. *(to Student 2)* And when will the molecules stop moving? [Answer: When the molecules reach equilibrium.]

STUDENT 2: When they're equal.

TEACHER: Right. Well done.

Glows	Grows
It was effective when the teacher . . .	Next time, the teacher could try . . .

Compare your responses with our thoughts following the cases.

Case 2. History

The students have just written a response to the following prompt. The teacher asked them to reread this line from Lincoln's Gettysburg Address and describe what Lincoln is saying is at stake in the ongoing Civil War.

> Now we are engaged in a great civil war, testing whether that nation, or any nation, so conceived and so dedicated, can long endure.

The teacher picks up a piece of student work and puts it under a document camera to reveal it to the class.

TEACHER: Take a look at what John wrote. *(reading John's writing aloud to the class)* "What's at stake is the survival of this nation and its government, which is ruled by the people and for the people." How does John's response set us up really nicely to answer this prompt?

STUDENT 1: He points out that this nation is run by a government ruled by the people and for the people. And he talks about how we don't want to lose that.

TEACHER: Right. He clearly outlines that what's at stake here is America's democratic system of government. What else is at stake here that we could add to this response?

STUDENT 2: Democracy around the world.

TEACHER: I like where you're going with that. Say more.

STUDENT 2: He's saying that what's at stake is an opportunity to show the world that democratic governments like ours can survive big "tests" like this war.

TEACHER: You got it. Let's add that to John's response now . . .

Glows	Grows
It was effective when the teacher . . .	Next time, the teacher could try . . .

Some Observations on Case 1

The teacher effectively holds out for all-the-way right with "Be more specific. High to low what?" She also requires the student to *answer her actual question*. Some possible grows: The student says, "Diffusion moves from high concentration to low concentration." This answer isn't fully correct because it's not diffusion that moves but the molecules. Instead of holding out, the teacher rounds up the answer. Also, the teacher could have prompted for specific vocabulary when the student says, "when they're equal." The more scientifically technical way to say this is "when the molecules *reach equilibrium.*"

Some Observations on Case 2

The teacher is good at back-pocket phrases: "How does John's response set us up really nicely to answer the prompt?" "I like where you're going with that. Say more." She also holds out for all-the-way right at two moments. At one, "What else is at stake here that we could add to this response?" even though Student 1's analysis of John's answer is technically right, it doesn't add anything to fully answer the question. So the teacher probes deeper to make sure students understand what *else* is at stake. The teacher could have held out better for all-the-way right, pushing both John and Student 1 to replace the vague noun "this nation" with the more specific noun "America." Doing so would make their answers more comprehensible to an outside reader. Regarding specific vocabulary, when both John and Student 1 describe our government as being "ruled by the people, for the people," the teacher rounds up by assuming that they're referring to a *democratic system of government.*

ROLE-PLAY HOLDING OUT FOR ALL-THE-WAY RIGHT

With a partner, as *Teacher* practice holding out for all-the-way right in response to partially correct responses from a colleague who plays the role of *Student*.

1. *Teacher* asks the *Student* a simple question. ("If I have three dollars and spend two, how much money do I have left?"). *Student* responds with an answer that's only partially correct. ("You'll have one left.")

2. *Teacher* responds with a *Right Is Right* prompt. ("So close. One *what*?") *Student* answers directly and correctly. ("One dollar!")
3. Switch roles until each of you has played the role of *Teacher* twice. Then each revisit your work at "Planning to Hold Out for All-the-Way Right." Make at least one revision to it based on what you learned from practicing with your colleague.

You're on the path to success when you . . .

- Have a clear sense of what a fully correct answer should be
- Consistently and effectively respond to almost-right answers with a *Right Is Right* prompt
- Use language that affirms effort while communicating that there's more to be done

ACTION PLANNING

Use the aforementioned success points to evaluate where you are now with *Right Is Right*. (Find a printable version of this form at my.teachlikeachampion.com.)

HOW AM I DOING?

_____

_____

Design one or more action steps for improvement. Decide on an interval by which you'll revisit this page to assess your progress.

Action Step 1

By when, with whom, and how you will measure your effort

By _____, I will . . .
   <small>Date</small>

_____

_____

How Did I Do?

Successes: _____

_____

_____

_____

Challenges: _____

_____

_____

Next steps: _____

_____

_____

Action Step 2

By when, with whom, and how you will measure your effort

By _____, I will . . .

Date

_____

_____

_____

How Did I Do?

Successes: _____

_____

_____

_____

Challenges: _____

_____

_____

_____

Next steps: _____

_____

_____

OUR OBSERVATIONS ON THE CHAMPIONS

 Clip FG15. Maggie Johnson

Maggie's student has a lot of insight about the sentence and generally about Aunt Alexandra's personality, but he doesn't quite grasp the significance of the (slave-holding) family history Aunt Alexandra is referring to. There's a big difference between bragging about your agrarian lineage and bragging about your plantation-running lineage. In short, he's very observant and insightful and is "right" about a lot in the passage, but has missed an important detail. Rather than simply praise him, Maggie warmly and relentlessly pushes him to grasp the final critical detail. Notice her subtle smile (and occasional nods) while she repeatedly prompts him with follow-up questions such as "He owned a *what*?" "Which was a . . . ?" "And?" "Act like *what*? Tell me more . . ."

She punctuates this sequence of relentless questioning with finger snaps (a form of praise) and a warm smile to celebrate the student's arrival at a thoughtful, complete, and accurate answer to her question.

 Clip FG16. Nicole Willey

Nicole effectively uses specific-vocabulary *Right Is Right* when she delivers these prompts: "Talk about our skills." "What do you mean 'our world' and 'this world'?" "And who is 'they'?" "And specifically, Paul was talking about which immigrants?" As a result, Nicole helps take the student's answer from "Paul's explanation shows an understanding of our world and what they thought about this world," to "Paul's explanation helped us understand the perspectives of Chinese immigrants and what they thought of America."

By pushing students to use more specific and technical vocabulary, she builds a culture of precision in which they speak with specific, academic language. This makes it easier for other students to follow and learn from the discussion.

 Clip FG17. Colleen Driggs

Colleen asks students to interpret the following key line from *Esperanza Rising*: "If she kept working until peaches, she would have enough for Abuelita's travel." When Colleen asks, the student explains, among other things, why Esperanza wants to make the trip with Abuelita. Then she goes on to share more details about Abuelita. She's saying everything she knows, but isn't actually interpreting the line as Colleen has asked her to. It's a classic kitchen-sink moment wherein a student says every true thing she can think of, possibly because she doesn't understand the line in question.

Still, many teachers might accept the student's summary because, after all, so much of it is true and correct. But Colleen persists in requiring an answer to *her* question. Her persistence ultimately causes the student to correctly answer the original question. She did know the answer after all! In the short term, this helps students better comprehend the text; in the long term, it reinforces a culture of precision and high standards.

STRETCH IT

OVERVIEW

When students get an answer right, there's a temptation to feel as though we—or they—are done with something. But when we respond to "right" answers with more questions—the idea we call *Stretch It*—we do at least three important things:

- We make a habit of pushing students to think more deeply.
- We signal that we are "never done" with learning.
- We help build a growth mindset by constantly "rewarding" success with challenge.

Reflection: "Good Job"?

Many teachers respond to right answers with an affirmation like "Good" or "Nice job." How would responding to right answers with questions instead change your classroom culture and benefit your students? Write your reflection before you read on.

_____

_____

_____

    Here are some things we've noticed (you might have seen others): Asking follow-up questions in response to right answers engages students constantly. It lets us differentiate for those who require challenge. Asking these questions provides students exciting ways to push ahead, apply their knowledge in new settings, think on their feet, and tackle harder questions, thus create a culture of learning. *Stretch It* also allows you to avoid false positives (moments of luck, coincidence, or partial mastery that lead you to believe that students have achieved fuller mastery than they really have), and gives you a more accurate benchmark of where students' understanding is.

ANALYZE A CHAMPION

 Clip FG18. Art Worrell, Grade 12

View the video with the following questions in mind. Compare your answer with our observations at the end of this technique.

What's effective about Art's use of *Stretch It*? What impact does it have on the quality of the discussion that follows?

FUNDAMENTALS

There are various types of *Stretch It* questions. While you shouldn't get too hung up on the categories, it's worth thinking intentionally about different ways to stretch students with a broad variety of question types and thus reinforce more types of thinking.

Directive Prompts or Questions

Questions and prompts can be directive—worded to push and guide students along specific lines about something they have shown they've mastered. These provide students a verbal template to help them structure their response. Other questions can be less directive or nondirective—merely urging the student to think further. The "Revisit" box distills Doug's examples of directive questions.

Revisit *Teach Like a Champion 2.0*

Ask How or Why

The best test of whether students can get questions right consistently on a given topic is whether they can explain how they arrived at the answer.

"How far is it from Durango to Pueblo?"

"Six hundred miles."

"How'd you get that?"

"By measuring three inches on the map and adding two hundred plus two hundred plus two hundred."

Ask for Another Way to Answer

When students solve it one way, it's a great opportunity to make sure they can use all available methods.

"How'd you get that?"

"By adding two hundred plus two hundred plus two hundred."

"Is there a simpler way than adding three times?"

Ask for a Better Word or More Precise Expression

Students often begin framing concepts in the simplest possible language. Offering them opportunities to use more specific words, as well as new words with which they are gaining familiarity, reinforces the crucial literacy goal of developing vocabulary.

"Why did Sophie gasp, Janice?"

"She gasped because the water was cold when she jumped in."

"Can you use a word that shows *how cold* it was?"

"Sophie gasped because the water was freezing."

"OK, how about using one of our vocabulary words?"

"Sophie gasped because the water was frigid."

Ask for Evidence

By asking students to describe evidence that supports their conclusion, you emphasize the process of building and supporting sound arguments. . . . You don't have to say that an argument is poor; just ask for the proof.

"How would you describe Dr. Jones's personality? What traits is he showing?"

"He's spiteful."

"And *spiteful* means?"

"*Spiteful* means that he's bitter and wants to make other people unhappy."

"OK, so read me two sentences from the story that show us that Dr. Jones is spiteful."

Ask Students to Integrate a Related Skill

In the real world, questions rarely isolate a skill precisely. Try responding to mastery of one skill by asking students to integrate the skill with others recently mastered.

"Who can use the word *stride* in a sentence?"

"I stride down the street."

"Can you add some detail to show more about what stride means?"

"I stride down the street to buy some candy at the store."

"Can you add an adjective to modify *street*?"

"I stride down the wide street to buy some candy at the store."

"And can you put that in the past tense?"

Ask Students to Apply the Same Skill in a New Setting

Once students have mastered it, consider asking them to apply it in a new or more challenging setting.

"So what's the setting of our story?"

"The setting is in a town called Sangerville in the recent past."

"Good. I notice that you remembered both parts of setting. Can you remember the setting of *Fantastic Mr. Fox* then? Do movies have a setting?"

Later we'll say more about less directive and nondirective prompts like "Go on."

Scripting Your *Stretch It*
Pick three or four of the following questions to practice scripting different types of directive *Stretch It* questions. For each question, draft at least two questions of different types.

1. *Question:* "Use the word *wonderful* in a sentence."
    Student response: "My mother told me that I was wonderful after I had completed my homework."
    Your Stretch It *prompts:*

    _____

    _____

    _____

2. *Question:* "What are the properties of a quadrilateral?"
    Response: "A quadrilateral is any four-sided figure whose sum of the interior angles equals 360 degrees."
    Your Stretch It *prompts:*

    _____

    _____

    _____

3. *Question:* "What are the three branches of the US government?"
    Response: "The three branches of government are the executive, legislative, and judicial branches."
    Your Stretch It *prompts:*

    _____

    _____

    _____

4. *Question:* "What is the fraction equivalent of 80 percent in its simplest form?"
    Response: "Four-fifths."
    Your Stretch It *prompts:*

    _____

    _____

    _____

STRETCH IT

5. *Question:* "What are the four main stages in the water cycle?"
    Response: "The four main stages are evaporation, condensation, precipitation, and collection."
    Your Stretch It *prompts:*

_____

_____

_____

6. *Question:* "What do you think is the lesson of the story 'The Boy Who Cried Wolf'?"
    Response: "The lesson in the story is that you shouldn't cry for help unless you really need it."
    Your Stretch It *prompts:*

_____

_____

_____

Choose a few of the questions you've written and draft a target answer you'd hope students would give.

What observations do you have about the types of *Stretch It* questions you asked?

_____

_____

_____

What observations do you have about the types of thinking your questions required of students?

_____

_____

_____

Stretch Your Partner

You'll both be on the right track when you . . .

- Ask a diversity of types of questions.
- Ask the questions in a way that builds a positive culture of *Stretch It* in your classroom.

With your partner, practice planning and asking *Stretch It* questions you might use in your classroom. Before you meet, draft questions and *Stretch Its,* along with your target (exemplary) student response or responses. (See technique 2, *Targeted Questioning.*) As you choose among the types, consider what target response you want.

1. *Question:*

_____

Target response(s) to question:

_____

_____

Stretch Its:

_____

_____

_____

Target response(s) to Stretch Its:

_____

_____

_____

2. *Question:*

_____

Target response(s) to question:

_____

_____

Stretch Its:

_____

Target response(s) to Stretch Its:

3. _Question:_

Target response(s) to question:

Stretch Its:

Target response(s) to Stretch Its:

4. _Question:_

Target response(s) to question:

_____

_____

Stretch Its:

_____

_____

_____

Target response(s) to Stretch Its:

_____

_____

_____

5. *Question:*

_____

Target response(s) to question:

_____

_____

Stretch Its:

_____

_____

_____

Target response(s) to Stretch Its:

_____

With your partner, alternate roles in these steps:

1. One question at a time, the *Teacher* asks the *Student/Coach* a scripted question. Once the *Student* has answered, ask the *Stretch It* question.
2. As *Student/Coach*, as you answer each question, also think about feedback to give to the *Teacher*.
3. As *Student/Coach,* give feedback to the *Teacher* (one glow, one grow) in this general form, based on the success points listed earlier: "One thing I liked about your *Stretch It* was . . ." "Next time, try . . ."
4. The *Teacher* tries again, based on the feedback.

What did you notice about how different *Stretch It* question types affect your student answers?

When might you want to use different types?

Less Directive Prompts

Nondirective questions or prompts use simple phrases such as "Tell me more" or "Develop that."

Partially directive prompts:
"Say more. How do we know that this connects to that idea?"
"Develop that last argument about the role of gender in *Henry IV* further."
"Keep going. What are the next steps to solve the problem?"

Nondirective prompts:
"Say more."
"Keep going."

Directive prompts push and guide students to think in a specific way, providing students a verbal template to help them structure their response, whereas a nondirective prompt doesn't tell a student how to think, merely to think further. Being nondirective gives students more autonomy. However, autonomy is not necessarily the same thing as rigor. Sometimes a specific probing question is just as demanding or more so. The idea is to strike a balance between directive and nondirective prompts.

The range from directive and to nondirective is a continuum. Partially directive prompts are in between. For example, in response to what a student has just said, you might combine the nondirectiveness of "Say more" with an identification of a part of the previous answer that is particularly useful to expand on: "Say more about that last point."

As you make prompting a habit, you can begin to remove the verbal portion of the prompt and replace it with a nonverbal prompt. Effective nonverbal prompts include the following:

- Rolling gesture with your hands—like the "traveling" signal in basketball
- Head nod
- Raised eyebrow or other distinctive facial gestures

As you're probably starting to recognize, you could put a variety of *Stretch It* prompts on a spectrum like this:

Nonverbal →	Nondirective →	Partially directive →	Directive follow-up
"Traveling" gesture	"and?"	"Tell me more about the first part specifically."	"What evidence tells you that?"

When might you want to use more nondirective prompts or more directive prompts? How might you balance using *Stretch It* questions with different levels of directiveness?

_____

_____

_____

_____

ANALYZE A CHAMPION

▶ **Clip FG19. MK Pope, Grade 7**

What does MK accomplish by asking her initial *Stretch It* question, "What is the monster?"

_____

_____

What do you notice about MK's prompting?

_____

_____

See our observations at the end of this technique.

STRETCH IT

THE NEXT LEVEL

Keep Stretching Your Partner

This continues the earlier "Stretch Your Partner" practice. These success points mark the right track:

- Your prompt is clear.
- Your prompt causes students to push their thinking in a productive way.

Under "Question" in the following Partner Prompting Table, insert two of the questions you scripted in "Stretch Your Partner." You already know the exemplar responses. Plan how you would try asking those questions using less directive prompting. Then continue with the steps that follow the table.

Partner Prompting Table

Question	Nondirective Prompt	Partially Directive Prompt	Nonverbal

STRETCH IT

1. One question at a time, the *Teacher* asks the *Student/Coach* the original question. Once the *Student* has answered, continue with the prompts.
2. As *Student/Coach,* as you answer each question, also think about feedback to give to the *Teacher.*
3. As *Student/Coach,* give one glow and one glow feedback response, based on the success points listed earlier: "One thing I liked about your *Stretch It* was . . ." "Next time, try . . ."
4. The *Teacher* tries again, using the feedback.

ROLLING OUT A *STRETCH IT* CULTURE

Stretch It works best when practiced frequently. Here are some tips to build a culture of *Stretch It* in your classroom.

Explain Stretch It. Explain to your students that you will reward correct responses with more questions. Teach your students how to respond when they do and don't understand the question.

Make Stretch It *fun and transparent.* Celebrate your students' success and continue to empower your students to embrace a "growth mindset."

Get students to stretch each other. True cultures are built collectively. Find opportunities for your students to ask each other *Stretch It* questions or prompts.

Consider what you want the culture of your classroom to look like, and all the steps you need to get there. In a separate space, script how you want to roll out the concept of *Stretch It* to your students, and incorporate your rollout into an upcoming lesson.

For feedback, consider practicing your rollout with a partner.

ACTION PLANNING

Consider some aspects of *Stretch It* you want to work on, perhaps first simply increasing how often you use it, then perhaps increasing your comfort with various types. Use that thinking to create a purpose for each action step you undertake. In a few weeks, revisit the step to reflect on progress and ways to improve further. (Find a printable version of this form at my.teachlikeachampion.com.) Use these success points to see where you are:

*   I'm being intentional about basing the type of *Stretch It* questions I ask on the student outcome I want.
*   I'm rewarding right answers with more questions.
*   I'm using directive, nondirective, and nonverbal prompts strategically.
*   My students are "stretching" each other.

HOW AM I DOING?

_____

_____

Design one or more action steps for improvement. Decide on an interval by which you'll revisit this page to assess your progress.

Action Step 1

By when, with whom, and how you will measure your effort

By _____, I will . . .
　　Date

_____

_____

How Did I Do?

Successes: _____

_____

_____

_____

Challenges: _____

_____

_____

Next steps: _____

_____

_____

STRETCH IT

Action Step 2

By when, with whom, and how you will measure your effort

By _____, I will . . .

Date

_____

_____

_____

How Did I Do?

Successes: _____

_____

_____

_____

Challenges: _____

_____

_____

Next steps: _____

_____

_____

OUR OBSERVATIONS ON THE CHAMPIONS

 Clip FG18. Art Worrell

Note that this sequence of questioning follows a period of independent work in which kids wrote out their responses to some questions. After Art solicits a quick response to his first question, he then delivers a follow-on to another student: "What line or piece from that clued you in to Washington?" In doing so, he holds students accountable for staying engaged and tracking their peers' responses to his questions.

When Art moves on to Kamari, he gets a great answer from him. But Art doesn't stop there. Instead, he rewards Kamari with an even more rigorous follow-up question: "Why'd you pull that out?" In doing so, he verifies that Kamari didn't just get lucky by randomly pulling the correct quote from the text, but that he had a clear rationale for his answer.

Note that Art strikes a muted, largely neutral tone in response to Kamari's strong answer as opposed to fawning over it with excessive praise. In doing so, he signals that he's *not* surprised by it—he expects great things from Kamari. He punctuates this sequence with a calm but still positive "Well said." Art then uses Kamari's answer as the foundation for students to take the discussion even further (for example, "Yemi, you want to add?"). In doing so, he uses *Stretch It* not only to communicate high expectations for Kamari but also to signal his same high expectations for the entire class.

 Clip FG19. MK Pope

MK relishes constant challenge in her classroom. The reward she gives the student for a right answer is a harder question. MK is also able to determine whether the student's answer is a false positive or not. The first student MK calls on gets the answer correct. However, when MK asks the *Stretch It* question "What is the monster?" the student's response to that follow-up reveals that the student's knowledge was not in fact as reliable as it appeared. Awareness of this enables MK to continue prompting her students to get to the correct answer.

You may have noticed that her next question is a prompt: "Can somebody build on that, please?" This spreads the culture of *Stretch It* by holding students accountable to listening to their peers.

The next student replies, "This builds on the idea of institutional racism." That's the right idea, but again MK decides to stretch a good answer rather than praise, confirm, or restate it: "Good; say more. How do we know that this connects to that idea?"

MK's questions straddle partially directive ("How do we know that this connects to that idea?") and nondirective ("Say more."). She seems to be preparing her students to be familiar with what will ultimately be completely nondirective prompts like "Say more."

FORMAT MATTERS

OVERVIEW

In school and in life, how students say something matters sometimes almost as much as what they say. To be able to write a scientific paper or run a board meeting in the future, students must be able to write or participate in a discussion employing the language used in academic and professional settings. In a way, this manner of communicating is the language of opportunity. It involves not only mastery of the complete sentence but also mastery of a variety of unspoken rules. *Format Matters* describes how teachers can help students make a habit of communicating—while in school—in a format that matches the worthiness of their ideas and ensures them constant opportunities to express them.

Reflection

Why is it important to encourage students to communicate their ideas in the language of opportunity? Finish writing before you move on to our reflections.

Our reflections (we're sure you've thought of others as well): It's important to teach students to communicate their ideas clearly and persuasively. Setting high expectations for how and when they do so instills in them the belief that they're headed for academic and professional success and a familiarity with its expectations when they get there. This is a form of cultural capital that will help them knock down barriers to opportunity.

Proper format also elevates the expectations others have of your students, allowing students to overcome others' hasty perceptions of who they are. It signals preparedness and proficiency to the broadest possible audience in schools as well as professional settings.

ANALYZE THE CHAMPIONS

View each video and respond to the following questions. Refer to the end of the technique to read our observations.

▶ Clip FG20. Darryl Williams, Grade 3

What's effective about Darryl's *Format Matters* correction?

_____

_____

What does he do to make his tone nonjudgmental?

_____

_____

▶ Clip FG21. Beth Verrilli, Grades 11 and 12

What is effective about Beth's correction?

_____

_____

Overall, what do Darryl's and Beth's clips illustrate about *Format Matters*?

_____

_____

_____

_____

FUNDAMENTALS

Format Matters helps teachers establish and uphold the expectation that students should consistently communicate in a format that is clear and complete when in school. To reinforce this standard of discourse, they respond to lapses quickly and in a tone that's supportive and nonjudgmental. In the simplest form of *Format Matters,* teachers require students to format their responses in complete sentences that are grammatical and audible.

Complete Sentence Format

The complete sentence is the battering ram that knocks down the door to college. Push students to express their ideas in complete sentences as often as possible to ensure that they get plenty of practice with this crucial skill. We've seen great teachers respond to incomplete sentences with the following methods:

- Reminding students before they start to answer ("Who can tell me in a complete sentence what the setting of the story is?")

- Providing the first words of a complete sentence ("The setting is . . .")
- Reminding students with a quick and simple prompt after they answer ("Complete sentence.")

Grammatical Format

Ensure that students communicate with correct syntax, grammar, and usage. The following are two methods that may be especially helpful:

- *Identify the error.* Repeat the error back to the student as if you're asking a question. ("We *was* walking down the street?")
- *Begin the correction.* Begin repeating the answer back as if it were grammatically correct and ask the student to complete it. ("We *were* . . .")

Audible Format

Expect students to express their ideas loudly enough so that everyone in the class can hear and learn from them, especially when their comments are part of a discussion. One of the fastest ways to undercut the value of participation is to allow it to be inaudible to other students. This suggests to students that the ideas weren't important for classmates to listen to anyway.

The *Format Matters* Sequence

Following these examples, complete the four *Format Matters* exercise sequences.

Example 1 (from a vocabulary lesson):
Teacher: Can you find "solitude" at amusement parks?
Student: No.
Teacher: No, you cannot . . .
Student: No, you cannot find solitude at an amusement park.
Teacher: Because . . .
Student: Because they are too crowded.
Teacher: Good. Can you put that all together?
Student: No, you cannot find solitude at an amusement park because they are too crowded.

Example 2 (same lesson):
Teacher: Can you find "solitude" at amusement parks?
Student: You can't find solitude at amusement parks because they usually crowded with so many people.
Teacher: They usually crowded . . . ?
Student: You can't find solitude at amusement parks because they are usually crowded with so many people.

Sequence 1
Teacher: When Abuelita teaches Esperanza how to crochet, she tells her, "Don't be afraid to start over." Is Abuelita just talking about crocheting?
Student: No. When her grandma and her talk, the grandma is also using crocheting as a metaphor for how to deal with life's challenges.
Teacher:

Student:

Sequence 2
Teacher: What is one product of photosynthesis?
Student: Oxygen.
Teacher:

Student:

Sequence 3
Teacher: In what year did Johannes Gutenberg invent the printing press?
Student: *(barely audible)* Gutenberg invented the printing press in 1440.
Teacher:

Student:

Sequence 4
Teacher: How did we know those two angles were complementary?
Student: We knew they was complementary because they added up to 90 degrees.
Teacher:

Student:

_____

_____

Planning to Uphold Format Expectations

Select a crucial question from an upcoming lesson. Anticipate two incorrectly formatted answers that you might receive from students. Then script two corrections you might give to ensure that students provide answers in the correct format.

Your question:

_____

Target answer (in correct format):

_____

An incorrectly formatted answer:

_____

A *Format Matters* correction:

_____

Another incorrectly formatted answer:

_____

A *Format Matters* correction:

_____

THE NEXT LEVEL: COLLEGIATE FORMAT

The next level of *Format Matters* involves helping students make their clear, complete, and grammatically correct responses even stronger via more explicit use of the language code employed in college and professional settings.

Starting with Basil Bernstein in 1971, sociologists have documented how the speech patterns and habits a person uses, their "speech code," expresses their social identity. This usually happens without their realizing it, but this is not to say that others do not notice. There is a hidden code that uses more complex syntax and distinct academic vocabulary in certain settings. It is one of the benefits of privilege to speak this hidden code, and conversely, to speak it is to become more likely to be included. Fortunately, many of its habits aren't just useful for inclusion in the institutions of meritocracy; they also reward technical vocabulary and greater specificity: replacing references to "him" or "her" with "the author" or specifying the title of a work instead of referring vaguely to "the story," say.

In the table, you can track the evolution of a sentence as it becomes more collegiate in format.

Evolution of a Sentence

Question: Why does Orwell name the pigs as he does? Original sentence: "He's giving them roles like the people in Russia."	
Specific references in place of pronouns and vague nouns	"<u>Orwell</u> is giving <u>the pigs</u> roles like <u>the leaders </u>in the <u>Russian Revolution.</u>"
Complex syntax	"Orwell gives the pigs roles like those of the leaders of the Russian Revolution."
Details and evidence	"Orwell gives the pigs roles like those of <u>Lenin, Trotsky, and other</u> leaders of the Russian Revolution."
Precise academic vocabulary	"Orwell uses pigs to <u>personify</u> Lenin, Trotsky, and other leaders of the Russian Revolution."
Collegiate format sentence: "Orwell uses pigs to personify Lenin, Trotsky, and other leaders of the Russian Revolution."	

Watch Beth Verrilli again in Clip FG21 with collegiate format in mind.

Planning the Path to a Collegiate Answer

For one of the subject areas here, draft example prompts you could use to help a student make a response more collegiate.

History question

"Explain why Gandhi's use of civil disobedience and nonviolent resistance was so effective in helping India gain its independence from Great Britain."

A target (collegiate format) response: "Mahatma Gandhi's use of civil disobedience was effective because it captured the attention of the international community, which then pressured Great Britain to cede control of India to its people."

Student's actual first response: "His peaceful protest worked because it made Great Britain look really bad in the eyes of the world."

To get the student closer to the target response, I could use the following prompt(s):

_____

_____

_____

_____

_____

Science question
"Explain what happens to air pressure as volume increases."
A target (collegiate format) response: "As volume increases, air pressure decreases, because there is more space for the air particles to move without colliding into one another."
Student's actual first response: "As it goes up, air pressure goes down, because there is more space for the particles."
To get the student closer to the target response, I could use the following prompt(s):

_____

_____

_____

_____

_____

Math question
"What does volume measure?"
A target (collegiate format) response: "It measures the number of cubic units that an object occupies."
Student's actual first response: "It measures the amount of space something takes up."
To get the student closer to the target response, I could use the following prompt(s):

_____

_____

_____

_____

_____

Brainstorming Collegiate Format Prompts

Star two of the following examples that appeal most strongly to you. Adapt at least one of them for use in your classroom. Then come up with a few more collegiate format prompts of your own.

"Try that again in a sentence that starts with [insert starter phrase]."
"Use that mathematical/scientific/technical language."
"What's a more sophisticated way to say [insert phrase]?"

"Tell me who 'she'/'he'/'it' is."
"Once more, with evidence from the text."
"Make it sound like college."

"_____"

"_____"

"_____"

"_____"

ANALYZE A CHAMPION

 Clip FG16. Nicole Willey, Grade 3

View this clip with an eye toward *Format Matters*. Then compare your responses with our observations at the end of this technique. We've also included a transcript.

What about the student's response is Nicole trying to correct?

_____

_____

_____

What impact do Nicole's corrections have on the student's answer?

_____

_____

_____

Transcript: Nicole Willey, Grade 3

1. NICOLE: So what does Paul's explanation show an understanding of?
2. STUDENT: Paul's explanation shows an understanding of how immigrants . . .
3. NICOLE: Use our . . . talk about our skills.
4. STUDENT: Helped us understand the perspectives of our world and what they thought about this world.
5. NICOLE: What do you mean "our world" and "this world"?
6. STUDENT: I mean America.
7. NICOLE: Oh, OK!
8. STUDENT: Because . . .
9. NICOLE: And who is "they"?

FORMAT MATTERS

10. STUDENT: The immigrants.
11. NICOLE: And specifically, Paul was talking about which immigrants?
12. STUDENT: The Chinese immigrants.

ROLL IT OUT

Revisit *Teach Like a Champion 2.0*

Remember how great teachers explain *Format Matters* to students:

Many teachers worry that their [format] corrections implicitly say, "You can't use that language because it's not good enough." They don't want to engage in such a conversation, nor appear negative or disparaging. You could address this concern by initiating a preliminary conversation that explains your intention, pointing out that everybody switches codes—most of us speak differently in different settings. You might say, "If you think that the way I speak in the classroom is the same as the way I speak when I'm out with friends, you're wrong. We all speak differently in different settings, but when we're in class, we'll all speak the language of college." Once that rationale is established, champion teachers reinforce the fact that *Format Matters*.

In the space here, plan how you want to roll out *Format Matters* to your students. Make sure that your rollout

- Establishes clear expectations for the format of answers in your class
- Cultivates student buy-in
- Maintains economy of language

_____

_____

_____

_____

_____

_____

If you can, practice your rollout with a partner and ask for feedback.

FORMAT MATTERS

ROLE-PLAY PRACTICE WITH A COLLEAGUE

Revisit your earlier work at "Planning to Uphold Format Expectations." Taking turns in the roles of *Teacher* and *Student/Coach*, practice responding to the incorrectly formatted student answers using the corrections that you drafted.

PARTNER ROLE PLAY

Here's a simple but effective way to practice. Partners each bring several questions they plan to ask in an upcoming lesson.

1. *Teacher* asks a question.
2. *Student* responds with an incorrectly formatted answer.
3. *Teacher* poses a *Format Matters* correction.
4. *Student* responds with the correctly formatted answer.
5. *Student* then gives feedback to the *Teacher* based mainly on the first two success points shown later in "Action Planning"—one glow ("One thing that made your *Format Matters* correction effective was . . ." and one grow ("Next time, try . . .").
6. *Teacher* tries again, implementing the feedback.
7. Switch roles.

ACTION PLANNING

Evaluate where you are in your implementation of *Format Matters*. (Find a printable version of this form at my.teachlikeachampion.com.) You know you're on the right track when you . . .

- Respond to format errors with a tone that's both supportive and unapologetic.
- Correct students efficiently and concisely.

HOW AM I DOING?

_____

_____

Design one or more action steps for improvement. Decide on an interval by which you'll revisit this page to assess your progress.

Action Step 1

By when, with whom, and how you will measure your effort

By _____, I will . . .

_{Date}

_____

_____

How Did I Do?

Successes: _____

_____

_____

_____

Challenges: _____

_____

_____

_____

Next steps: _____

_____

_____

_____

Action Step 2

By when, with whom, and how you will measure your effort

By _____, I will . . .
    Date

_____

_____

_____

How Did I Do?

Successes: _____

_____

_____

_____

Challenges: _____

_____

_____

Next steps: _____

_____

_____

OUR OBSERVATIONS ON THE CHAMPIONS

 Clip FG20. Darryl Williams

In this clip, Darryl keeps his *Format Matters* corrections for grammar fast and efficient. During the first one, he repeats the student's answer as a question; during the second, he repeats the student's response back in corrected format. These methods enable Darryl to address these format errors briefly so that he can quickly resume instruction.

When students fall short of Darryl's format expectations, he is supportive and encouraging, but still clear and honest about what they need to fix. Instead of chastising or dismissing their ideas, he helps students reformat and refine them. Once students get it right, he warmly acknowledges their progress to ensure that they leave the exchange feeling successful.

 Clip FG21. Beth Verrilli

Beth's *Format Matters* correction is effective because it's especially clear and concise. To make it as clear as possible, Beth explicitly taught students about what answers "in AP language" sound like. Now all she has to do is say that prompt aloud, and Ashanti knows to switch codes and reformat her answer more collegiately (from "She gonna talk all this evil stuff in his ear" to "She's going to try to impose her negative beliefs onto Macbeth").

By punctuating Ashanti's response with the statement "*Now* you're ready for college," Beth turns a potentially embarrassing moment into an opportunity for this student to shine in front of her peers. It also reminds the rest of the class of where they're headed and that mastering the language of opportunity is essential to getting there.

Overall, Beth's clip reminds us of what students are capable of when they get plenty of practice using academic language and speaking in a clear, complete, and grammatical style. What we see in her class is the culmination of hundreds of microteaching moments—like the kind we see in Darryl's classroom. Through such small exchanges between teacher and student, one can build the foundation for collegiate discourse.

 Clip FG16. Nicole Willey

Nicole uses *Format Matters* to encourage a student to upgrade the format of her response by using more technical vocabulary: "Talk about our skills . . ."

Nicole also wants her to replace vague pronouns like "they" with clearer forms of reference:

- "What do you mean 'our world' and 'this world'?"
- "And who is 'they'?"
- "And specifically, Paul was talking about which immigrants?"

Nicole's corrections help the student express her ideas in greater detail and with more specific, academic language. Ultimately, the result is a response that isn't just complete and grammatically correct but also more collegiate. It's the kind of answer that tells the world, "I'm headed for college."

WITHOUT APOLOGY

OVERVIEW

Effective teachers should always seek to find a way to make the material students need to know meaningful and engaging. This means they avoid labeling what students need to study as uninteresting, too hard for them to master, or beyond their frame of reference. These teachers are careful to avoid such "apologies"—that is, excuses for watering down the content and rigor of what they teach.

Teachers "apologize"—at times unconsciously—by

- Telling students that something will probably be boring
- Blaming some outside entity for the fact that they are teaching certain material
- Diluting material under the rationale of making it "accessible"
- Presuming that students will be unable to master the most challenging material

We are all at risk of apologizing at times. In fact, let's assume that we've all allowed apologies to change our teaching at least once. Becoming aware of this risk enables you to stay vigilant and find alternatives, so that your students embrace challenging, rigorous content and the hard work of scholarship.

Reflection

Have you ever been tempted to think—or articulate—something like the apologies we described? Why? Are there other thoughts or actions that might signal to students that certain material is not really for them?

Write your response before you see what we say.

Possible thoughts (you may have more useful ones for your purposes): You might be worried about student engagement or enjoyment in your class. Doing what's hard can seem like a big risk. Or perhaps the material isn't that interesting to you (which is different, we note, from whether others will love it). Or you may not yet be confident that you've found a way to teach it effectively, because students have struggled with it in the past. Students themselves might tell you at first that they can't or don't want to do it. Their own beliefs might waver or be influenced by low expectations. Or you may not feel that you have sufficient time left in the school year to cover or teach the content in the way that you'd ideally like to.

WITHOUT APOLOGY

FUNDAMENTALS

Become conscious of your potential to apologize and any patterns you need to escape. Rehearse motivational replacements for apologetic language.

Sound Familiar?

"Guys, I know this is dull. Let's just do our best to get through it."
"You need to know this for the test."
"This isn't my favorite story, but I don't decide what we read."
"This probably seems irrelevant to some of you, but . . ."
"Spelling time. Oh, well, let's do it."
"This may be a little beyond some of you, but . . ."

Try framing the following in a positive way for students. Not only write what you could say but also try saying it out loud.

- An article on tundra ecosystems that is very important but that you secretly think is a little boring
- A chapter that discusses ancient Greece . . . and a cynic might suggest your kids won't care about ancient Greece
- A math concept that's highly abstract

Is there anything you've said in class that apologized for the material that your students needed to learn? (All of us, or at least every teacher we've met, has done this. The goal here is to recognize, not judge.) Jot down your best recollection of what you've said (or might be inclined to say). Why do you think you said it? Can you think of any alternatives or solutions right away? If you can't recall apologizing, imagine that you said things similar to the lines we quoted earlier.

1. What you said: _____

_____

_____

Why you think you said it: _____

_____

_____

Alternatives? _____

_____

_____

2. What you said: _____

_____

Why you think you said it: _____

_____

_____

Alternatives? _____

_____

_____

Nothing That Matters Is Boring

1. Think through the material you are teaching this year. Identify two or three parts of that material that you or someone else might be inclined to regard as boring for students.

_____

_____

2. Why is that material important on the path to college? (Sometimes framing this for students can be a way in.)

_____

_____

3. Cite any evidence you have that students are bored by it.

_____

_____

4. How reliable is your evidence? Does it apply to all students? What, other than the topic itself, could account for the evidence you perceive?

_____

_____

5. What signs of interest do you also notice?

_____

_____

6. How might you stoke those flickers of interest?

_____

_____

7. Put yourself in the shoes of people who are fascinated by this material—people who spend their lives studying it or who use it every day or who find it gratifying. There are such people for every topic. Why do you think it interests them? How would they introduce it?

_____

_____

_____

_____

Expanded Horizons

1. What do you think are the main interests of your students?

_____

_____

_____

2. Do those interests apply to all of your students? For your most engaged students, the ones you wish all your students could be like, what experiences or interactions (and with whom) made them that way?

_____

_____

_____

3. What do you think your students aren't interested in?

_____

_____

4.   How might you probe further for possible evidence to the contrary?

_____

_____

5.   All of us have developed a love for things that did not interest us at first. This might include our college major or even our decision to teach! Think of something in which you developed a strong interest over time. What changed that got you fascinated? Something you read or heard? Someone you met? How can you bring that kind of experience to your students?

_____

_____

_____

_____

Roots of Retreat

Try to identify how and why you sometimes apologize for what is really worthy content.

Blaming Outside Forces
1.   Name something large or small that you include in a lesson mainly to satisfy some outside authority or standardized test.

_____

_____

2.   What about the material feels unworthy to you? Push yourself to be specific and demanding here. Try to put your concerns into writing.

_____

_____

3.   What's the academic reason for its being there? Why might an authority decide that it was critical for students to learn this material? How can you communicate that to students?

_____

_____

4. Is there a different place for the material, serving some other learning objectives than where it is now?

_____

_____

Dilutions and Substitutions

1. Write down one way a teacher might dilute material in order to make the lesson more "accessible."

_____

_____

2. What more might you yourself be able to learn about the original material that might lead you to an effective "hook" into it?

_____

_____

3. The fact that material is challenging is a good thing. Can you use the challenge as part of a hook? Take a shot at drafting a hook here—one that draws on the fact that achieving what's hard will set your students apart and that the ability to rise to a challenge is both rewarding and another word for excellence.

_____

_____

Apologizing for Students

1. In the material you teach, what do you worry your students may not be able to "handle"?

_____

_____

2. What skills or background knowledge do you think they lack that prevents them from successfully working through the material?

_____

_____

3.   Do you have hard evidence that they can't successfully work through the material? If so, what activities could help them overcome that? If not, what could you ask them to do to show you they had the wherewithal to do it?

_____

_____

> ### Revisit *Teach Like a Champion 2.0*
>
> In his discussion of technique 15, Doug models what a teacher might say instead of apologizing for content:
>
> - "This material is great because it's really challenging!"
> - "Lots of people don't understand this until they get to college, but you'll know it now. Cool."
> - "This can really help you succeed."
> - "This gets more and more exciting as you come to understand it better."
> - "We're going to have some fun as we do it."
> - "A lot of people are afraid of this stuff, so after you've mastered it, you'll know more than most adults."
> - "There's a great story behind this!"
>
> And these rather than apologies for students:
>
> - "This is one of the things you're going to take real pride in knowing."
> - "When you're in college, you can show off how much you know about . . ."
> - "Don't be rattled by this. There are a few fancy words, but once you know them, you'll have this down."
> - "This is really tricky. But I haven't seen much you couldn't do if you put your minds to it."
> - "I know you can do this. So I'm going to stick with you on this question."
> - "It's OK to be confused the first time through this, but we're going to get it, so let's take another try."

Try putting some of Doug's alternatives into your own words. And what other alternative language can you add to your repertoire when . . .

You anticipate boredom?

"_____"

"_____"

You sense low confidence among the students?

"_____"

"_____"

You want to blame?

"_____"

"_____"

You're deliberately not diluting?

"_____"

"_____"

Your students might not appear up to the challenge?

"_____"

"_____"

THE NEXT LEVEL

When Students Apologize

Do your students make apologies for themselves—for example, assuming they will not be able to do something yet or excusing themselves from trying? Come up with three good responses, verbal or otherwise.

1. He says:

"_____"

"_____"

You respond:

"_____"

"_____"

2. She says:

"_____"

"_____"

You respond:

"_____"

"_____"

3. He says:

"_____"

"_____"

You respond:

"_____"

"_____"

Script Ahead

1. Where in your next lesson plan might you be at risk of apologizing for or diluting content? Why might you be tempted? In the plan, script a phrase or two to use in that moment to keep your expectations at their highest.
2. Deliberately remove anything from the plan that you worry might be diluted or that might distract students from reaching the objective. Replace it with full-strength material. Consider any scaffolding you may need to add to reach that material.
3. Script a great opening for the lesson. Even if you end up not using it, it can help by exciting you about the lesson!

PRACTICE

Compare Your Responses

Revisit the individual work you did in the previous section to share and compare your responses with a partner or group. Listen for options you hadn't considered.

Compare perspectives on material mandated by tests that you are inclined to dodge or apologize for. Give another teacher your best devil's-advocate reaction to any negative thoughts he has about specific content in his curriculum or on standardized tests. Also get that teacher's perspective on your inclinations.

What insights do you glean from those conversations?

_____

_____

Take turns again, and for each apology, one at a time brainstorm alternative, unapologetic things to say instead. Then share some of your reactions with the group.

How did it feel different to be sitting in the circle the second time around? Other insights?

_____

_____

WITHOUT APOLOGY

ACTION PLANNING

Use this action planner to continue your work with *Without Apology*. (Find a printable version of this form at my.teachlikeachampion.com.) Refer to these success points to see where you stand:

- You've identified content for which you tend to apologize and have addressed that in a lesson plan.
- You can give your students more than one genuine reason for why you look forward to teaching this content.
- Your students know that you teach in a way that nothing is beyond their reach.

HOW AM I DOING?

Technique 16, *Begin with the End,* will strengthen your hand at planning lessons free of apology. Whether or not you've already covered that technique, start with and finish Round 1 here. Come back for more rounds as needed.

Action Step(s)	For Later: How Am I Doing?
Round 1	
I need to embrace rather than apologize for teaching this: In the lesson plan, I will: Here's the essence of my script: I'll define measurable success as:	What's worked that I should *keep doing*? Ongoing challenge: How I plan to overcome that challenge:

Action Step(s)	For Later: How Am I Doing?

Round 2

I need to embrace rather than apologize for teaching this: In the lesson plan, I will: Here's the essence of my script: I'll define measurable success as:	What's worked that I should *keep doing*? Ongoing challenge: How I plan to overcome that challenge:

Round 3

I need to embrace rather than apologize for teaching this: In the lesson plan, I will: Here's the essence of my script: I'll define measurable success as:	What's worked that I should *keep doing*? Ongoing challenge: How I plan to overcome that challenge:

BEGIN WITH THE END

OVERVIEW

Successful planning usually begins with a larger goal—something important you want your students to achieve or master in a unit that stretches over days or even weeks. Once you've identified that larger goal, the next step is to break it down into a sequence of smaller, daily *objectives*. Once you've done that, you design the lessons and activities your students will do to achieve those daily objectives.

This sequence order is essential:

1. *Define the major goal or topic for a unit.* It could be the water cycle, adding and subtracting fractions, or understanding *Lord of the Flies* as literature.
2. *Break the unit goal down into daily lesson objectives.* One goal might be to understand how condensation works in the water cycle or to analyze the symbolism in chapter 3 of *Lord of the Flies*.
3. *Determine how you'll assess your effectiveness in meeting each daily objective.* You might come up with, "Students will describe the process of condensation and differentiate it from precipitation by comparing and contrasting," or "Students will identify and explain the symbolism in a given passage from the chapter, comparing it to other symbols in book."
4. *Choose lesson activities that work toward the objective and that will result in mastery on your assessment.*

Reflection: How Close Are You Now?

Write your thoughts before you consider ours.

Most likely you've tried something like this process before and found that simple ideas can often be challenging to execute. What aspects of *Begin with the End* have proven most challenging for you in the past? That said, why is this approach important to use?

_____

_____

_____

Our thoughts: Teachers may not always have a clear vision of what they want students to learn by the end of a unit or a lesson. Some concepts are hard to break apart without missing something. It's hard to determine which objectives deserve more time, energy, and focus than others. Also, sometimes it's hard to focus on just one thing per day, and hard to project how much content you can cover per day.

When students' progress toward mastery comes faster or slower than you imagined, it's a challenge to adjust the unit. It's also hard to structure and build in time for important review of content from previous days' objectives. And, sadly, sometimes a fun activity we'd envisioned doesn't align with our daily lesson objective. With some content—reading works of literature, say—it may be more difficult to identify a particular outcome.

Still, this ordered approach of breaking apart large, broad topics and concepts is important for helping us see what's implicit in understanding them and for helping us make complex ideas accessible to students. It can also help us chart our progress.

FUNDAMENTALS

Here are some key steps to follow in *Beginning with the End.*

1. Define the Major Goals for a Unit

To begin, list *as concretely as possible the three to five most important things* students will have to master to be successful in this unit. Even if you see more than five, distill them down to this few to ensure that, when in doubt, you know what you most want to spend your time on. As you work, you might also consider why the topic is important and how it will be assessed, both explicitly (on a yearly assessment or final exam) and implicitly (by what students will need to be able to do at the next grade level and perhaps once they arrive at college).

2. Break the Unit Goal Down into Daily Objectives

Consider roughly the number of sessions or classroom weeks you have and *draft a sequence of objectives,* one for each day in the unit. Each objective should cover a slightly different aspect of the larger skill or content. Even if objectives vary only slightly, each day should be different. For example, a first day's objective is to introduce common denominators, the second day's is for students to be able to find them independently, the third day's is to find them with automaticity. If you are unable to cover everything you intended in the time allowable, you have two relatively obvious choices: increase the time you allocate or reduce the scope of the unit. As you work you might also *reserve a few lessons (or parts of lessons) for going back* and reteaching the things your students struggle with. A decent rule of thumb is to reserve 10 to 20 percent of instructional time.

Use *4 Ms* (technique 17) to evaluate and possibly improve the precision of the objective: ask whether it is **m**easurable, **m**anageable, **m**ade first (determined before any activity is chosen), and **m**ost important.

3. Decide How You'll Assess How Well You Met Each Daily Objective

Under each objective, make some notes about how you might assess your students both at the end of that day (say, via an *Exit Ticket*) and at the end of the unit.

At this point you may want to digest this information in a form like Unit, Objectives, Assessments, shown here.

Unit, Objectives, Assessments

Unit goal:
Objective 1:
Assessment notes:
Objective 2:
Assessment notes:
Objective 3: (and so forth)

4. Choose and Design Activities That Work toward the Objective

For two or three of your objectives, plan lesson activities that will ensure that students meet those objectives. Think about how the activities will build on what students can already do, and particularly about what students will do during the activity that will cause them to master the objective.

Before you settle on an activity, come up with at least two other activities you could consider using in its place. Can strong aspects of alternative activities be combined into one new, more effective one?

Consider whether the activity could be tightened in some way to use the time more efficiently and maintain pacing. There are no throwaway two minutes at the end of class. Throwaways like that add up over the course of the year to more than six hours of instruction—a whole school day.

Now *Double Plan* (technique 19): go through your lesson and write out what students should be doing at each point. Challenge yourself to make their task always something active, rigorous, and aligned to your daily objective or broader unit goals.

Making Knowledge Durable

As teachers we are sometimes quick to overlook the need for students to continue practicing skills they have mastered to keep those skills fresh or even extend students' facility in using them. Use a template like the one we show here to plan for places in future lessons where you can later reinforce and extend content that students have mastered. (It's also printable in larger, "landscape" format at my.teachlikeachampion.com.)

Template for Weekly Reinforcing and Extending

Date:					
Do Now Periodically use your 3- to 5-minute class introduction to review mastered skills.					
Integrate review into core lesson Find meaningful opportunities to incorporate some extra practice into the core parts of a lesson that focuses on other topics. Planning intentionally can help make sure you do so.					
Mini-review Spend 5 minutes in class on high-energy spiraled review using *Pepper* (36) or *Everybody Writes* (37): "OK guys. Bringing back some of your old favorites today. We're gonna make sure everyone is still solid on condensation" or ". . . the symbolism we saw in chapter 3."					
Homework Review not only the day's lesson but, occasionally, important content from previous lessons.					

Format Your Plan for Classroom Use

Depending on your experience and other factors, you may need to have your lesson plan in front of you more or less frequently during the lesson and in more or less detail. Prepare it in a format or medium that will work for you in class. Consider having two versions—a detailed one that you can refer to if necessary, and a more skeletal one on a card or half-sheet of paper that you can glance at quickly.

THE NEXT LEVEL

Economizing Planning Time

Good planning does take time, and it's important to be realistic about how much time you need given your level of experience, the number of classes you teach, and their content. However, being consistent in your process can help make you more efficient. You'll need less time if you always plan from objectives and continually use the techniques in part 1, Check for Understanding.

You can also reduce planning time by developing standard "events"—recurring activities that you frequently use. This enables you to insert your content into a trustworthy framework rather than having to design every lesson from scratch. Following are some examples of "recyclable" events.

English, Humanities

Passage analysis: the teacher gives students a short passage from a book and asks them to "analyze it" in writing (or alternatively with a partner in discussion). The steps involved in "analysis" are always the same and established in advance. For example, Doug proposes a version of this activity in his book *Reading Reconsidered* with these four questions:

- Identify the characters in the passage—those who speak and those who play a significant role.
- Identify where in the plot of the book the scene takes place (that is, before or after what? And if relevant, foreshadowing, alluding to or referring back to what?).
- Explain how the scene discusses or reflects on theme(s) or idea(s) that are important to the larger text.
- Compare the scene in the passage to at least one other scene in this novel/story or in something else the class has read, explaining how the themes, ideas, and motifs are portrayed.

One of the many benefits of this activity is that you can use it to ask students to analyze any passage from any text. The planning and execution are simple, and you would match them to your objective by choosing your passage accordingly.

Math

You could make a habit of a "challenge problem"/*Show Call* (technique 39). Essentially, you could include a tricky problem in every lesson, give students a few minutes to try to solve it on their own, then *Show Call* two students' answers and ask them to analyze and compare the answers. Again, the planning is simple and merely requires matching the problem to the objective.

Lesson Plans for Teaching Reading Skills

When a great lesson in reading and English classes involves working with a segment of a book or other extended piece of literature, an effective plan and its objective may look different than in other content areas.

Most of a reading lesson is spent in the activity of reading and/or discussing or writing about what has been read. Although most champion reading teachers include other activities (vocabulary building, some writing or grammar exercises, and so on) as part of their lesson, the most important part of planning a reading lesson is thinking about what students will be doing during reading. Ask yourself:

- How much reading will students do independently and together by reading aloud?
- Are my students ready to do some portions of the reading on their own?
- What questions can I ask or tasks can I give to make sure that students understand the reading they've done on their own?
- Are there key moments when reading aloud with students can unlock some of the depth or pleasure of a particular passage?

Then plan the questions you will ask of the students during reading in order to

- Provide students with plenty of practice applying the most important skills.
- Balance the need to check for basic understanding of the details and language within the story (sentence level, paragraph level) with the need to check for understanding about big ideas.
- Ensure that students can express their understanding in both written and spoken language.

Reading teachers (and history teachers and others) often find it useful to write their questions and stopping points directly into the text the class is reading and use this marked-up text while they read aloud with students. It's more efficient than typing their questions into a separate lesson plan because the questions (and answers) are directly based on the content of the text, and they don't have to flip back and forth between the text the class is reading and their lesson plan as they ask a question.

Reflection

For some subjects and units, might you benefit from organizing a series of lessons around one object of study (a literary work, a project, a place or culture), rather than around a sequence of skills? If so, what specific objectives might you need to weave in throughout the course of studying it?

_____

_____

_____

What does what you've written suggest about how to choose the best object of study?

_____

_____

_____

_____

PRACTICE PLANNING WITH A GROUP OR PARTNER

Revisit the individual work you've done. Share and compare your responses to see other options.

Bring copies to share of two lesson plans you've used in the past: one that went relatively well and another that you'd like to improve for future use. Also bring at least one copy of the unit overview materials from which you derived your basic breakdown of lessons.

Evaluate Past Lesson Plans

1. Exchange copies of the plans that went well. Take a few minutes to look at them. Then talk about how the plan reflects any or all of the four steps of _Begin with the End._
2. Next, take turns sharing comments about what you liked and possibly found useful about another person's plan. Then discuss any ways in which you feel you might further improve your plan. Invite input from the rest of the group about it.
3. Do steps 1 and 2 again with the plan that did not work as well.
4. Write down and share observations of what you learned in this group work.
5. Revise one or both of your plans for possible future reference.

Share and Evaluate Upcoming Plans

Using a lesson plan you haven't tried yet, follow the same general process you followed in steps 1 through 4 for past lesson plans. After you have taught the lesson, report back to the group (in a meeting or by message) about how it went and what you learned.

ACTION PLANNING

Periodically after lessons, revisit *Begin with the End* to reflect on progress and how you can continue to improve. (Find a printable version of this form at my.teachlikeachampion.com.) Use these success points to see where you stand:

- I'm planning from the unit level down to lesson objectives.
- I plan opportunities for students to review and get additional practice with important skills from the unit.

HOW AM I DOING?

_____

_____

Design one or more action steps for improvement. Decide on an interval by which you'll revisit this page to assess your progress.

Action Step 1

By when, with whom, and how you will measure your effort

By _____, I will . . .

Date

_____

_____

How Did I Do?

Successes: _____

_____

_____

_____

_____

Challenges: _____

_____

_____

_____

Next steps: _____

_____

_____

_____

Action Step 2

By when, with whom, and how you will measure your effort

By _____, I will . . .

Date

_____

_____

_____

How Did I Do?

Successes: _____

_____

_____

_____

_____

Challenges: _____

_____

_____

_____

Next steps: _____

_____

_____

_____

4 Ms

OVERVIEW

Begin with the End is based on the idea that starting with objectives gives lesson planning meaning, discipline, and direction. The *4 Ms* technique focuses on crafting objectives for maximum impact. Each *M* represents one criterion for an effective lesson objective.

Manageable. The objective can be reached within the time of the lesson. (Of course there are some learning goals that cannot be taught within a single lesson, but as we discuss later, focusing on some aspect of that goal can help you gauge the rate of your students' progress.)

Measurable. It's possible to assess to some plausible degree how fully the objective has been realized, ideally by the time the lesson is over.

Made first. The objective was chosen first and determines what activities the lesson plan includes, rather than, say, being chosen to explain the benefits of a favorite activity that may or may not be in sync with the larger unit goal or not the best tool for achieving that goal.

Most important. The objective focuses on what's most important for the class right now on its path to maximum achievement and learning. It describes the next step straight up the mountain to college.

Reflection

Which of the *4 Ms* stand out as most challenging or most important for you to work on? Why?

_____

_____

_____

FUNDAMENTALS

Manageable

Can the objective be taught in a single lesson? Is there a good activity that will fit within the time frame, including time for independent practice—plenty of it, possibly? Does some means of assessment also fit within the time? By the time the lesson has ended, it's best for you to know whether or not your students have reached the objective—and they should want to know that, too.

What about "big goal" things that can't be accomplished in forty-eight minutes? Deep understanding often takes students numerous sessions, days, or even weeks to reach; but it's still useful to determine what you can accomplish *today* to move students toward mastery. By doing so, you can make sure they are progressing steadily and meaningfully. This enables you to diagnose and address pitfalls promptly.

Of course, you should let your students know the larger goal and how what they do today will help them get there. Posting both the larger goal and the more immediate one can help. Intentional learners learn faster, and there's no reason they can't be aware of both the big and the slightly smaller purposes for their work.

Consider a recent lesson in which you ran out of time or might have tried to do too much. Write down the original objective for that day, then tweak it to make it more precise and manageable. Could you have narrowed it a bit? How? Could you have split it in two?

_____

_____

_____

When you ran out of time during this lesson, what got cut? Why do you suspect you ran short?

_____

_____

_____

Measurable

Understanding how well you implemented an objective makes every lesson a learning opportunity for you, rather than a vague experiment.

"Measured" doesn't necessarily mean a "test" or a result you can quantify in a rigorous way. It could mean the careful use of any technique of part 1, Check for Understanding. Not all students in the class will reach the same level of success in a given session, so you need some idea beforehand about how you will define success.

We encourage you strongly to include an *Exit Ticket* (technique 26) to assess student progress toward the objective for the day. If you have been using them, make a stack of your *Exit Ticket* forms from ten recent lessons. Make another stack of the ten lesson plans; then shuffle each stack. Can you match them? Can a partner teacher do it? How well do you (or your partner) think the *Exit Tickets* match the objectives you've written?

If you sometimes hold off "assessment" until tomorrow or the end of the week, in what ways can you be sure to measure progress today on today's objective?

_____

_____

_____

Made First

"Made first" means the objective comes first, shaping the activities within it. Starting with the goal helps you think about the content and design of the activity *and* how you might adapt it. Even an activity you've used ten times can be tweaked to align more effectively to a specific objective.

Think of an activity you use frequently in class. Then choose two similar but different learning objectives and map out the changes you would make to the activity in view of the differing objectives.

Activity:

_____

Objective 1:

_____

Modified activity:

_____

_____

Objective 2:

_____

Modified activity:

_____

_____

Most Important

An effective objective focuses on what's most important at this point on your students' path to higher education. That will most likely align to established curriculum and/or standards, but it's a great habit to practice making the case—at least in your own mind—for an objective's importance anyway. In other words, as part of your planning, explain to yourself why the objective is important to teach today.

Reflection

Do you wonder whether the outcomes of some of your lessons meet the criteria of the *4 Ms*? Consult a colleague. Give her an objective or even a learning goal you are struggling with and ask for her best shot at turning it into one—or several—*4 Ms* objectives. Any useful new ideas?

_____

_____

_____

Critique Some Statements of Objectives

Each of these objectives fails to meet at least one *4 Ms* criterion. Decide what's missing and rewrite each so that it meets all the criteria. Then compare your thinking with our comments that follow.

1. Students will see why Shakespeare is the greatest author in the English language, and possibly in all languages.

Rewrite:

_____

_____

2. Students will develop a four-point list of criteria for whether a group of words is a complete sentence.
    Rewrite:

_____

_____

3. Students will be able to name the parts of a cell and describe their functions.
    Rewrite:

_____

_____

4. Students will discuss chapter 2 of *To Kill a Mockingbird.*
    Rewrite:

_____

_____

4 Ms

Are your responses similar to these?

1. *Students will see why Shakespeare is the greatest author in the English language.* Verbs in objectives are very important; they describe the action students will take. "Seeing" is vague and not *measurable.* Using verbs like *describe, explain, argue for, summarize,* or *determine the justness of Shakespeare's reputation* makes for a more measurable objective. And they cause you to ask yourself, How *will* I know they "see" it? By the way, this objective probably isn't *manageable* either. It's a lot to do in a single lesson—and to do it well, students would need to have first read and discussed a lot of Shakespeare's writing and the writing about him. Thus a better objective might be, "Students will source and describe examples of the sorts of plot elements from *Romeo and Juliet* that characterize Shakespeare's greatness."

2. *Students will develop a four-point list of criteria for whether a group of words is a complete sentence.* This statement mixes objective and activity (writing a list). Perhaps the objective is, more briefly, "Identify the difference between complete and incomplete sentences." A more rigorous version might be "Identify the difference between complete and incomplete sentences and successfully correct incomplete sentences to make them complete." Notice how measurable the second part of the objective is.

3. *Students will be able to name the parts of plant and animal cells and describe their functions.* This objective isn't *manageable.* Realistically, this goal would most likely span multiple lessons within a unit.

4. *Students will discuss chapter 2 of* To Kill a Mockingbird. This is an activity, not an objective. Therefore, it's not *made first.* The objective might ask students to characterize the relationship between Jem and Dill or to identify a key theme that is developed in the chapter and compare it with a similar theme in another novel.

THE NEXT LEVEL

Write a Week's Worth of Objectives

Not quite fulfilling one day's objective can require you to revise your objective for the next day, and so on; but for the purposes of this exercise, working with a unit you are teaching or are likely to teach, create the objectives for a sequence of five related lessons. Apply the *4 Ms* to each. Write your finished objectives here:

Day 1:

_____

_____

Day 2:

_____

_____

Day 3:

_____

_____

Day 4:

_____

_____

Day 5:

_____

_____

Ever More Manageable

Can you be stricter with yourself about how much you can realistically expect to achieve? To be so, try inserting more intentional internal timings in the lesson plan—for example, that you should be at point 1 at twenty minutes and point 2 at thirty-five minutes. In case you miss these timings, plan a "first drop" activity that you'll shorten or exclude if you're running behind. (Plan a back-pocket activity, too, that you can include in case you come up short.)

Ask a colleague to listen to you for about five minutes as you describe the lesson. Then ask for his analysis of it in terms of *4 Ms*.

Imparting Love

> **Revisit *Teach Like a Champion 2.0***
>
> In this technique at "Measurable," reread Doug's revealing confession.

Even if you plan to make students *love* something in your field, your *objective* should still be skill or knowledge based. This doesn't rule out also attempting to inspire your students to share your passion. Excluding that consideration from your guiding lesson objective, what are some ways you could still inspire your students that respect their differences in taste?

_____

_____

_____

MORE PRACTICE WITH COLLEAGUES

1. For the partner or group, bring enough copies of your answers to "Critique Some Statements of Objectives" and "Write a Week's Worth of Objectives" to share and discuss with the partner or group. Also bring the written objective for a lesson you will be teaching soon, along with notes about how you will measure progress or success.
2. Compare your rewrites for "Critique Some Statements of Objectives." Apply the *4 Ms* criteria to all of them. What gray areas might there be with respect to any of the *Ms*? Make and share any useful changes.
3. Also compare your sets of five objectives from "Write a Week's Worth of Objectives." Describe how they relate to the larger unit and to each other. Again apply the *4 Ms* criteria. What improvements can you make?
4. Take turns reading the objectives of a lesson each of you will be teaching soon. Field questions about how each of the *Ms* applies or other issues or opportunities.

ACTION PLANNING

Use this action planner to continue your work with *4 Ms*. (Find a printable version of this form at my.teachlikeachampion.com.) Have a look at some of your recent lessons or assess each new lesson as you write it. Are your objectives . . .

- Manageable?
- Measurable?
- Made first?
- Most important?

HOW AM I DOING?

_____

_____

If you are already doing well at some the *Ms*, set them aside and focus on your weakest one for now. Pick one of the *Ms* to improve. After the session, record how you did.

Action Step 1

By when, with whom, and how you will measure your effort
By _____, I will . . .
    Date

_____

_____

How Did I Do?

Successes: _____

_____

_____

_____

_____

Challenges: _____

_____

_____

_____

Next steps: _____

_____

_____

_____

4 Ms

Action Step 2

By when, with whom, and how you will measure your effort

By _____, I will . . .
<u>Date</u>

_____

_____

_____

How Did I Do?

Successes: _____

_____

_____

_____

_____

Challenges: _____

_____

_____

_____

Next steps: _____

_____

_____

_____

For each lesson objective you create, it's a champion idea to post the objective for everyone to see. We call this technique *Post It*. It's useful because research suggests that intentional learners learn more quickly and because it helps other people in the room—observers, a co-teacher, a push-in special education teacher—know what you are trying to accomplish and help you get there.

When posting, strive for consistency: try to use the same location every day. Where and how to post the objective are naturally affected by the way you've arranged your classroom in general, including the seating pattern you choose, so we'll discuss those factors, too.

Reflection

Explore and record your own thoughts, then compare them with ours.

What might be some other advantages of posting the lesson objective where everyone can see it?

_____

_____

_____

Are you already composing an objective for each lesson you teach? Do you already use *Post It* and/or other methods to keep students focused on the objective throughout the session? How well does this currently work for you?

_____

_____

_____

Our thoughts (likely you have others): An objective that is easy to see and read can be a touchstone for you and for students throughout the session. When a visitor enters the room, you can also inform her of what's going on by pointing, rather than interrupting the lesson to explain. It can take some discipline on everyone's part to stay in touch with a basic objective. If you or your students rarely look at it or drift away, is it posted in the best spot? Is its language plain, specific, and readily understandable to the students? Do you check to be sure they understand it and keep it in mind?

FUNDAMENTALS

Post It is straightforward:

Draft the objective in as brief and plain language as possible, before you arrive in class. Some teachers write state learning standards on the board as objectives—for example, "3.7.6 Students will read for understanding." We recommend instead that what you write is a daily objective as *you* define it in your lesson plan and in a way that's plain and comprehensible for students. (By the way, if you are working on a daily objective that is part of a larger learning goal, consider posting both the short- and longer-term objectives. This would help students see and reflect on how what they are doing on the given day relates to the bigger picture.)

Post the objective in the same location every day. Everyone will know where to find it, and students will get in the habit of looking for it. Looking at it is important because students need to know what they're trying to do, which will help them work more intentionally toward the goal.

Writing on "the board" may be simplest and best. However, a presentation-size piece of newsprint or a sticky note can also be effective, especially if your board handwriting is not a strong suit or if you transition quickly into space you share with other teachers and want to have certain key tasks done in advance. You can also put the objective on student handouts and on your lesson plans, leaving a copy by the door for observers.

Make it part of the dialogue. Call attention to your *Post It* and check that students understand it. Occasionally ask students to reflect on or review it at the outset or at the conclusion of the lesson. You might even occasionally ask your students to put the objective in context, to say why it matters, to connect it to what happened yesterday, and so on. For what it's worth, however, we are not big fans of having students copy objectives in writing. It tends to consume time with little benefit, and over time, students tend to do it less and less intentionally.

During class, occasionally refer to the objective verbally and by gesture. At the end you might refer back to it as well: "We set out to do X and Y. How'd we do?"

After class, reflect on your posted objective. Was any substantial part of the session taken up by something else? Could and should that have been avoided? How?

Be sure that visitors to class are aware of the objective. Afterward, encourage them to give you feedback about how well you helped your students master it, rather than about other, less relevant criteria.

GROUP OR PARTNER WORK

Try *Post It* in the classroom for at least a week before you meet to discuss it. Then share examples of objectives you have posted, and talk about the following:

- Practicalities of simple or "high-tech" ways to *Post It*
- Wording the objective briefly but unmistakably
- Ensuring that all members of the class notice it, can read it from their seats, and understand it

Share your current ways to use *Post It,* brainstorm new ways, and discuss ways to reinforce the posting. During or shortly after the meeting, write your next five objectives and plan how you will post and reinforce them.

ACTION PLANNING

Use this action planner to continue your work with *Post It.* (Find a printable version of this form at my.teachlikeachampion.com.) Refer to these success points to assess how you're doing:

- Your students understand the objective and consult it periodically.
- At the end of a class, students can express in their own words what the objective was and how well they achieved it.

HOW AM I DOING?

_____

_____

Design one or more action steps for improvement. Decide on an interval by which you'll revisit this page to assess your progress.

Action Step 1

By when, with whom, and how you will measure your effort

By _____, I will . . .
   Date

_____

_____

How Did I Do?

Successes: _____

_____

_____

_____

_____

Challenges: _____

_____

_____

_____

Next steps: _____

_____

_____

_____

Action Step 2

By when, with whom, and how you will measure your effort

By _____, I will . . .

Date

_____

_____

_____

How Did I Do?

Successes: _____

_____

_____

_____

_____

Challenges: _____

_____

_____

_____

Next steps: _____

_____

_____

_____

DOUBLE PLAN

OVERVIEW

Double Plan refers to the process of planning what both you *and your students* will do at each step of the lesson. This planning causes you to see the lesson through your students' eyes and to ensure engagement and a balance of meaningful activities. Your *Double Plan* might resemble a simple T-chart, with your actions listed on the left and what your students should be doing during each step on the right. Alternatively, you can go further and *Double Plan* by engineering lesson materials such as handouts, note-taking templates, assigned readings, lesson packets, and more.

Reflection

It's natural for teachers to plan out what *they* will do during a lesson. What's the benefit of also planning for what *students* should be doing at every step? After you write, compare your observations with ours.

_____

_____

_____

Our observations (we're sure you have others!): Planning what students should be doing helps ensure that students have something productive to do from start to finish and aids us in spotting moments when students won't have a task in front of them; it can also help us push rigor, streamline pacing, or collect data on what students know. It helps us more accurately estimate how long specific tasks will take. Then, too, it gives us a clear picture of what excellence looks like so that we can reinforce it when we see it and correct for it when we don't.

FUNDAMENTALS

Effective *Double Plans* come in all shapes, sizes, and forms. But they should all achieve the following goals:

1. Everything in one place
2. Synergy with pacing (chapter 6)
3. Engineering for accountability
4. Synergy with checking for understanding (chapters 1 and 2)
5. Orientation toward success
6. Embedded adaptability

Goal 1. Everything in One Place

Let's say you've planned a lesson where students will read a chapter but pause periodically to write a short response, comparing developments now to what they observed in the previous chapter. It's a good lesson plan. But for a student, it looks like this: Read, then every few minutes put down your book and open your binder. Write a response. But also have out your notes from yesterday. Flip back and forth between them and the book as you write your thoughts. Then find where in your book you left off and continue reading. It's a strong lesson, and the logistics are doable—but they are also complex. They require a lot of time spent flipping from place to place among three materials that are on the student's desk. It's inefficient, and potentially distracts students from thinking about the book.

A well-designed lesson packet or handout can put everything students need at their fingertips could help. So, what if you copied the day's reading and inserted spaces where students could write and even revise after each few paragraphs? What if the class summarized key points from yesterday and wrote them at the top of the first page? Then everything they needed would be right in the same place. Less flipping. Less thinking about flipping and checking whether they have enough loose-leaf paper and other materials they might need.

Embedding all required materials in one place—graphs, tables, novel excerpts, places to write and show work, and more—can be one useful *Double Planning* tool. For instance, biology teacher Vicki Hernandez embeds excerpts from scientific articles, illustrations of key processes like cell reproduction, and choice excerpts from her students' textbook in a single working document for some classes. Others, like history teacher Emily Bisso, integrate primary source documents and key maps so that students have everything they need on hand.

Are there some *supplementary* resources that you regularly ask students to refer to—novel excerpts, primary source documents, graphs, periodic table, or articles? Brainstorm ways that you can combine or incorporate them into your core lesson packets or handouts so that everything is in one place. List a few conclusions here:

_____

_____

_____

Goal 2. Synergy with Pacing

Another advantage of designing all-in-one-place lesson materials—often referred to as "packets"—for students is that you can use a copy too, marking it up with reminders to yourself that make it easier for you to run the lesson smoothly and seamlessly.

For example, Colleen Driggs used the margins of her lesson packets to document everything, from the length of her *Do Now* (technique 20) to the amount of time she would give students to read and then write for each independent practice question. Some teachers go even further by detailing the different formats students will interact with during a given task. In one lesson, Bryan Belanger made the following margin note to himself:

> Spend four minutes reviewing work. Use Call and Response to orally review the fractions, take hands for questions about reducing coefficients, and Cold Call on students to identify how they reduced like base fractions.

Notes like these remind him to switch the format of his questions to keep students engaged throughout his lessons while staying within an ambitious yet feasible time frame.

Goal 3. Engineered for Accountability

Another advantage of *Double Planning* is that it helps you hold students accountable for producing written work of quality throughout the lesson. For example, as shown in the excerpt from lesson materials here, eighth-grade teacher Maggie Johnson provides space for her students to write in response to the text or to take notes on a discussion or a *Show Call* (technique 39) discussion. She even notes where students should "leave this space blank" for them to go back and revise and improve their response.

Since there's a clear place for everything, such *Double Planned* materials let you tell at a glance whether everyone has done each activity, and students usually sense this. There's an incentive to complete each task. It also helps you hold yourself accountable for doing all the things you set out to do in the lesson.

EXCERPT FROM MAGGIE JOHNSON'S LESSON MATERIALS

Uncommon Schools | Change History.

1. Which of the following details explains why Scout compares Atticus to Ike Finch?
   A. Cousin Ike Finch was Maycomb County's sole surviving Confederate veteran.
   B. "I'd walk every step of the way there an' every step of the way back, just like I did before . . ."
   C. "Old Blue Light was in heaven then, God rest his saintly brow . . ."
   D. "This time we aren't fighting Yankees, we're fighting our friends."

   What does Atticus mean when he says, "we're fighting our friends"?

   [After students answered this prompt in writing, Maggie *Show Called* a student response that she thinks the class could take from "good" to "great" (technique 39). That is, she projected this work to the class using a document camera.]

   [During the *Show Call*, students took notes on what they gleaned from the discussion about how to take their classmate's work from "good" to "great."]

   Show Call Notes:

   [Maggie then asked students to rewrite their original response to the question above ("What does Atticus mean when he says, 'we're fighting our friends'?") using what they learned from the *Show Call* discussion.]

   Leave this space blank (for revision):

DOUBLE PLAN

Note something you find useful about Maggie's lesson materials that you could use or adapt in a lesson of your own:

_____

_____

Goal 4. Synergy with Checking for Understanding

Double Planning with handouts and packets also inherently *Standardizes the Format* (technique 3), enabling teachers to gather data through observation quickly and efficiently. Occasionally, they might stop to compare students' written work with the target responses that they've scripted in the margins of their copy of the lesson materials.

Some teachers also use their lesson materials to *Plan for Error* (technique 7). For instance, we've seen some teachers list anticipated misunderstandings and their responses to them in the margins, which may include a few *Break It Down* questions (technique 35) or a quick prompt or two to *Excavate Error* (technique 9). Others allocate time in their lessons to respond to errors ("Spend four minutes discussing option D"), which makes them likelier to do so.

Once teachers gather data during the lesson, they find different ways to record and organize it in their lesson handouts or packets. For instance, teacher Taryn Pritchard uses the margins to keep track of common student errors and those producing standout work. Later, she intentionally *Cold Calls* (technique 33) these students to address their misunderstandings in front of the class or have students with great work share out their unique approaches or insights.

Goal 5. Success Oriented

Some *Double Planners* wire their packets to help as many students as possible meet or exceed a high standard of excellence. To do this, they view the lesson from the student's perspective and then systematically add supports or remove obstacles to success, without diluting rigor.

Some teachers add such supports as a "tip box," examples of correct work, signs of success ("You know you're 'showing not telling' if you can act it out"), standard-setting directions ("Remember to include at least *three* pieces of evidence"), and reminders about the resources students should refer to when tackling a question ("Use your notes from yesterday's lesson about civil disobedience during the Indian independence movement"). Such additions can set up students to practice success while also preparing them to self-monitor the quality of their work. Obviously, there are lessons where you wouldn't provide such scaffolds. But when you need them, embedding them is a great way to make them handy.

Double Plan Success

Select two specific activities from an upcoming lesson. Plan the features you will include in student materials to support success. For example:

- A useful "tip box"
- Examples of correct or exemplary work
- Reminders about resources students should use ("Refer to your notes from yesterday's lecture about cellular respiration.")
- Success points ("You know you're 'showing not telling' if you can act it out.")
- Standard-setting directions ("Include *more than four* sentences," "Solve the problem using *two* different strategies.")
- Rubrics against which students can readily score their work

Name of activity 1:

_____

Brief description:

_____

Success-oriented feature to include (choose one):

☐ A "tip box"
☐ Correct/exemplary work
☐ Reminders about resources
☐ Success points
☐ Standard-setting directions
☐ Rubrics

Draft or mock-up of success-oriented feature:

_____

_____

_____

_____

Goal 6. Embedded Adaptability

Strong *Double Plan* teachers recognize that their lesson packets are living, breathing documents that should help them respond to the evolving needs of their students. Bryan Belanger regularly includes more questions in his packets than his students need so that he can strategically speed ahead or double back, depending on student mastery.

Taryn Pritchard applies similar thinking to independent practice by dividing it into sections by order of "mild," "medium," and "spicy" difficulty. Taryn asks all students to complete the "mild" independent practice first and then to get as far as they can without rushing. This allows students to speed ahead without having to continually ask the teacher for permission before moving on. Other teachers have taken a slightly more binary approach by embedding their handouts with "challenge" or "deep thinking" questions. Whatever your strategy, strive to design independent practice so that all students can challenge themselves at their own pace.

EVALUATE SOME *DOUBLE PLANNED* LESSON MATERIALS

Visit the "Useful Tools" section of my.teachlikeachampion.com and download lesson materials that exemplify *Double Plan*. Evaluate what makes these materials effective and jot down your observations in the space provided. Then compare your remarks with ours at the end of the technique.

1. Bryan Belanger evaluation:

_____

_____

    Ideas I could steal from Bryan:

_____

2. Ryan Miller evaluation:

_____

_____

    Steals:

_____

3. Taryn Pritchard evaluation:

_____

_____

    Steals:

_____

4. Maggie Johnson evaluation:

_____

_____

    Steals:

_____

DOUBLE PLAN A LESSON ACTIVITY

Use the *Double Plan* Template (or something like it) to plan for precisely what you and your students will do during a specific activity from an upcoming lesson. If possible, share your template with a colleague who has also prepared one, and look for ways to improve them.

   Here are some ideas. Feel free to plan for them or some other activity.

Writing. Stop and jot, single-paragraph journal entry, one polished sentence (see technique 38, *Art of the Sentence*), mini-essay, multi-paragraph response.

Discussion. Turn and Talk (technique 43), small-group discussion, teacher-led whole-group discussion, mainly student-led whole-group discussion.

Revision. Peer reads work aloud, teacher *Show Calls* work (technique 39) or models and self-evaluates.

Note taking. Cornell notes or similar graphic organizer (T-chart, Venn diagram), jotting key takeaways (for example, in bullet format).

Reading. Student oral reading (technique 23, *Control the Game*); teacher reads while students annotate; students independently read, annotate, and respond to a writing prompt—an exercise we call *accountable independent reading* (AIR). (For more on AIR, see pages 182 and 183 in *Teach Like a Champion 2.0.*)

Double Plan Template Example

Activity: *Accountable independent reading*	
I Will . . .	**Students Will . . .**
1. Tell students to box the section of the text they will read or mark their stopping point with an "X."	Mark up their texts per my directions
2. Give an annotation task and a reading focus question.	Make a 1–2 word margin note about what they're annotating for.
3. Tell how long they have to read and write. Start timer and circulate to monitor annotations.	Read and annotate text.
4. Give 30 seconds to finish reading and begin answering focus question.	At my signal, switch from reading/annotating to answering focus question.

Double Plan Template

Activity: _____	
I Will . . .	**Students Will . . .**

ACTION PLANNING

Find a printable version of this form at my.teachlikeachampion.com. You'll know that your *Double Planning* is on the right track when it . . .

- Keeps students actively engaged throughout the lesson
- Helps you not overlook what you meant to do
- Makes it easier for students to find what they need

HOW AM I DOING?

_____

_____

Design one or more action steps for improvement. Decide on an interval by which you'll revisit this page to assess your progress.

Action Step 1

By when, with whom, and how you will measure your effort

By _____, I will . . .
  Date

_____

_____

How Did I Do?

Successes: _____

_____

_____

_____

_____

Challenges: _____

_____

_____

_____

Next steps: _____

_____

_____

_____

DOUBLE PLAN

Action Step 2

By when, with whom, and how you will measure your effort

By _____, I will . . .
_{Date}

_____

_____

_____

How Did I Do?

Successes: _____

_____

_____

_____

Challenges: _____

_____

_____

_____

Next steps: _____

_____

_____

OUR OBSERVATIONS ON THE *DOUBLE PLANNED* MATERIALS

Example 1. Bryan Belanger

As mentioned earlier, Bryan regularly includes extra questions in his packets so that he can push forward when students are ready and circle back to reteach or give students additional practice problems when they struggle (embedded adaptability). He also includes target responses for many of his questions, especially the most crucial. This helps him minimize the risk of "rounding up" and makes it likelier that he'll hold out for all-the-way right. To support his response to error, he identifies the misconception behind incorrect choices so that he doesn't have to do that on the fly (synergy with checking for understanding). In some cases, he includes time stamps to help him maintain effective pacing so that direct instruction doesn't run too long at the expense of independent practice (synergy with pacing). Finally, for question 29, he plans a sequence of targeted questions that he can use to verify understanding once he has responded to error (synergy with checking for understanding).

Example 2. Ryan Miller

In the margins, Ryan makes a note to himself to check in with students who struggled with the *Exit Ticket.* This visible reminder increases the likelihood that Ryan will take action in response to this data (synergy with checking for understanding). Although it's not visible on this packet, he also prints different sections of his packets on different colored paper (lecture notes on red paper, readings on yellow, and so forth) so that he can more efficiently deliver directions. All Ryan has to say is "Flip to your notes on Social Security," or "Make sure your one-pager is in your portfolio." This helps him shave several seconds off each transition and makes it easier for him to ensure that all students are on the same page. Like Bryan, he also notes how long he should take with each portion of his lesson ("Leave 3 minutes for student discussion and 1 minute for revision before Exit Ticket"). Moreover, Ryan includes stage directions for himself while also outlining what students should be doing at key points (for example, "Use *CTG* [*Control the Game*] to start document, students answer 1 and 2" or "Students do independently. Wait for a check from me on 1 & 2 and then receive Reflection and ET [*Exit Ticket*]"). This frees him from having to refer to any other documents to keep track of what he and his students should be doing at each step. Everything he needs is in one place.

Example 3. Taryn Pritchard

Taryn uses lesson materials as a tool for documenting and organizing student data that she gathers through observation and then planning for how she'll take action (synergy with checking for understanding). She documents everything from the names of students who got certain problems wrong to whom she'll call on and why, as well as key misunderstandings that unexpectedly surface while she *Circulates* during independent work. This ensures that her response to the data she gathers is as efficient and effective as possible. She also scripts in concrete actions she'll take at key moments as well as important questions and prompts she intends to ask students. Finally, she divides her packet up into discrete sections by order of difficulty: "mild," "medium," and "spicy." Taryn asks all students to complete the "mild" independent practice first and then to get as far as they can through the final two sections for additional enrichment. This ensures that all students—from the early finishers to the students who work more slowly and methodically—have useful tasks to complete at the level of rigor that they're ready for (embedded adaptability).

Example 4. Maggie Johnson

Our observations are embedded within the downloadable version of the packet located under this technique at my.teachlikeachampion.com.

DO NOW

OVERVIEW

The *Do Now* is the first academic task of a great lesson. Upon entering class, students can begin working right away. Short in length but long on value, a *Do Now* is a powerful tool for both assessing understanding and ensuring that students engage with important academic content right from the opening bell. Effective *Do Nows* tend to be

- Same place every day
- Self-managed
- Short and sweet
- Review or preview

Reflection

If you don't already use a *Do Now*, jot down what typically occurs at the start of the lesson. What impact does this start have on students and the rest of the lesson?

_____

_____

_____

    If you use *Do Now*, reflect on a recent one that wasn't as effective as you had hoped. Was the problem with one of the aforementioned criteria or something else? Explain.

_____

_____

_____

FUNDAMENTALS

Hallmarks of a Strong *Do Now*

As many experienced teachers know, not all *Do Nows* are created equal. Let's expand on what makes them most effective.

Same place every day. Be consistent. Each day, students should find their *Do Now* in the same location—on the board, printed on a half-sheet of paper, or even on the first page of the packet for today's lesson—so that finding and starting it right away becomes habit.

Self-managed. Students should have everything they need to start the *Do Now* right away. If you have to assist in any way, be it to clarify directions or distribute materials, students will lose precious time they could otherwise spend working. They'll also miss an opportunity to practice managing their own work process.

Short and sweet. A quality *Do Now* typically lasts three to five minutes and causes students to produce some written work. Requiring a written product makes the task more rigorous and enables you to more effectively gather and respond to evidence of student understanding.

Review or preview. The *Do Now* either previews the content you're about to cover or reinforces students' mastery of previously covered content, especially if it's relevant to this lesson.

Evaluate Some *Do Nows*

Here are *Do Nows* from four classroom teachers. Evaluate each by the hallmarks and other qualities, jotting down your observations. Then compare your remarks with ours, which follow.

Example 1. Maggie Johnson, Grade 6 Reading

This *Do Now* was created partly to check whether students completed an assigned reading from Elie Wiesel's *Night*:

Complete the following questions based on your knowledge from pages 1 and 2 of "Perils of Indifference." You may not use your novel or notes. Fill in your answers on the Cumulatest bubble sheet and put it face down on your desk. Then turn to page 2 in your packet and begin your prereading.

1. Elie illustrates how he was "grateful for rage" by
   a. Explaining how indifference is a weapon of the enemy.
   b. Describing how the "Muselmanner" felt and feared nothing.
   c. Explaining his resentfulness to the American people for not liberating concentration camps sooner.
   d. Remembering the day he was liberated from Auschwitz by American soldiers.
2. Elie argues that indifference can be tempting because
   a. It is easier to ignore victims than be involved in another person's pain.
   b. Indifference etymologically means "no difference."
   c. Neighbors often view one another's lives as meaningless.
3. **Challenge:** Explain the meaning of the following line from "Perils of Indifference."

   Indifference reduces the other to an abstraction.

Evaluation:

_____

_____

_____

_____

_____

Ideas I could steal from Maggie:

_____

_____

_____

_____

_____

Example 2. Bryan Belanger, Grade 8 Math

This one assesses a wide array of skills that were covered during the school year.

1. One of the oldest living species on Earth is a fish known as the Coelacanth at 3×10^6 years old. If the Earth itself is 4.5×10^6 years old, how many times older is the Earth than the Coelacanth?
   a. 0.125 times older
   b. 1.25 times older
   c. 12.5 times older
   d. 125 times older

2. Which of the following must be true about the diagram to the right?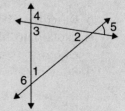
   a. $m\angle 4 = m\angle 2 + m\angle 3$
   b. $m\angle 5 = m\angle 1 + m\angle 2$
   c. $m\angle 5 = m\angle 1 + m\angle 3$
   d. $m\angle 6 = m\angle 2 + m\angle 3$

3. Which of the following is equivalent to the expression
   a. $\dfrac{4w^?}{3x^?}$ c. $\dfrac{4}{3x^?}$

   b. $\dfrac{4w^?}{3x^?}$ d. $\dfrac{4w^?}{3}$

4. What is the first step in solving a problem like the one above?

_____

_____

_____

Evaluation:

_____

_____

_____

_____

Ideas I could steal from Bryan:

_____

_____

DO NOW

Example 3. Ryan Miller, Grade 8 History

This one introduces some content that students will be exploring in more depth during the lesson.

Directions: Analyze and read the article below. Answer the contextualization questions that follow.

The Crisis says, first your Country, then your Rights!

Certain honest thinkers among us hesitate at that last sentence. They say it is all well to be idealistic, but is it not true that while we have fought our country's battles for one hundred and fifty years, we have not gained our rights? No, we have gained them rapidly and effectively by our loyalty in time of trial.

Five thousand Negroes fought in the Revolution; the result was the emancipation of slaves in the North and abolition of the African slave trade. At least three thousand Negro soldiers and sailors fought in the War of 1812; the result was the enfranchisement of the Negro in many Northern states and the beginning of a strong movement for general emancipation. Two hundred thousand Negroes enlisted in the Civil War, and the result was the emancipation of four million slaves, and the enfranchisement of the black man. Some ten thousand Negroes fought in the Spanish-American War, and in the twenty years ensuing since that war, despite many setbacks, we have doubled or quadrupled our accumulated wealth.

Source: The Crisis was a leading black-owned and -published magazine in the early 1900s. W.E.B. DuBois wrote this article in the September 1918 issue of *The Crisis*.

1. *Context:* When was this article written? Of the following events/topics, which two provide the best context for understanding the document?
   a. Jim Crow Era
   b. Women's Suffrage Movement
   c. Trench Warfare
   d. U.S. entry into World War II
2. Explain why you chose the answer you did.
3. *Summative:* Why does DuBois think African Americans should fight in the war?

Evaluation:

_____

_____

_____

_____

Ideas I could steal from Ryan:

_____

_____

_____

DO NOW

Example 4. Taryn Pritchard, Grade 6 Math

This one assesses previously covered skills.

1. A widget is 3 gizmos, and a gizmo is worth 5 gadgets. How many widgets is 45 gadgets worth?	2. Chris thinks that $2x$ and x^2 are the same expression, while Cliff argues that they are completely different. What two (and only two!) positive values of x make Chris think that $2x$ and x^2 are the equivalent expressions?
3. Write a simplified expression for the perimeter of the regular pentagon below. 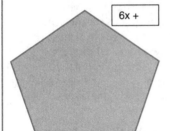 6x +	4. Mark comes to the farmer's market, where the trade values for several items are as follows: 1 cow = 10 bales of hay 1 bale of hay = 5 ears of corn 1 turkey = 4 pumpkins 1 cow = 40 ears of corn If Mark comes to the market with 2 cows, what is the maximum amount of ears of corn he can receive?

Evaluation:

_____

_____

_____

_____

_____

Ideas I could steal from Taryn:

_____

_____

_____

_____

OUR OBSERVATIONS ON THE EXAMPLES

Example 1. Maggie Johnson

Maggie begins the *Do Now* with clear directions about exactly what to do. She also uses the *Do Now* as a "reading check" to verify whether students did the assigned reading and to assess their readiness for discussion about it. She adds a challenge problem so that students can stretch their thinking even further. Finally, she includes a task for students to complete once they finish, ensuring that everyone has meaningful work to do from beginning to end.

Example 2. Bryan Belanger

Using data from a recent unit assessment, Bryan designed this *Do Now* to reinforce skills that students need to practice. The inclusion of multiple-choice questions streamlines his ability to identify trends in student understanding. His more open-ended prompt requires students to reflect on their problem-solving approach, which will enable him to identify precisely where student understanding breaks down. He also provides students with plenty of space to show their work, which they're expected to do.

Example 3. Ryan Miller

Ryan's inclusion of a primary source document sets the stage for rich analysis and discussion. It also prepares students for the kind of task they'll be expected to tackle in an *Exit Ticket* (technique 26). Ryan also mixes multiple-choice and open-ended questions, enabling him to check for student understanding in different formats. This mix of question types is also likely to yield more useful and reliable data.

Example 4. Taryn Pritchard

Taryn's *Do Now* pushes her students on critical thinking skills. The open-ended prompts also require students to do even more writing than we often see in a math *Do Now*. The page leaves students plenty of space to write and to show their work.

Design a *Do Now*

To plan a *Do Now,* use the *Do Now* Design Template as a model. Then exchange your planned *Do Now* with a colleague's for feedback. Make revisions as needed. The template refers to an *Exit Ticket* (technique 26), meaning brief written problems or questions for students to give evidence of understanding at the end of the lesson.

DO NOW DESIGN TEMPLATE

Lesson objective:

_____

_____

Sample *Exit Ticket* question:

_____

_____

My *Do Now*:

Directions to students:

_____

_____

Questions for students:

_____

_____

_____

_____

_____

_____

_____

☐ Same place? ☐ Self-managed? ☐ Short and sweet? ☐ Review or preview?

Reflection

Following are some brief statements from a teacher about the biggest challenges she faces when implementing *Do Now*. Given what you've learned, what advice might you give her to help her overcome them? If you haven't done so already, how could you apply that advice to your classroom?

> Sometimes, my *Do Nows* go for too long. A task I thought would take five minutes actually takes students fifteen. This causes students to get frustrated because they're not able to finish, or, if I give them the extra time they need, half of my lesson is suddenly gone. When my *Do Nows* have been too short, early finishers get restless, which can lead to misbehavior, and I don't have enough time to circulate to gather sufficient data. But the biggest challenge of all has probably been that my review of a *Do Now* tends to go for much longer than I intend for it to, often because I have to spend time addressing errors that I hadn't predicted or lose track of time while discussing a good problem or question. This results in my having to cut independent work time short.

_____

_____

_____

_____

_____

_____

DO NOW

DO NOW

THE NEXT LEVEL

Another champion move is to use the *Do Now* as a tool for anticipating, documenting, and responding to student error (per chapter 2). For example see how sixth-grade math teacher Taryn Pritchard marked up a *Do Now*.

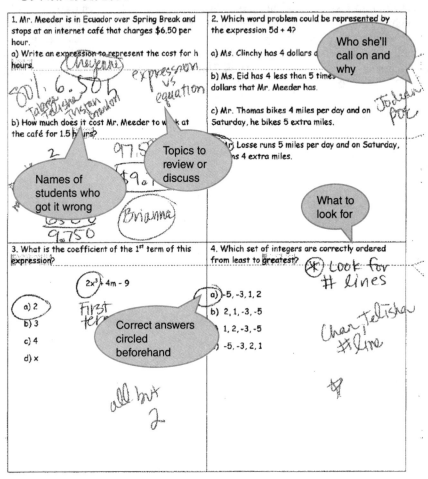

Taryn Pritchard's Markup

Prior to the lesson and in darker ink, she prepared for student error by scripting her target response for each question, flagging what to look for in responses to problem 4, and sketching out the work she wants students to show for problem 1—which she identified as a bellwether of student performance on the rest of the *Do Now*.

To prepare her response to data she gathered while *Circulating,* she recorded (in lighter ink) the names of the four students who got problem 1 wrong when 80 percent of students got it right. She also identified a student whom she wanted to call on for each problem; for example Brianna for 1.b, Jordan for 2. She also tracked unanticipated issues that she might want to review or discuss, including the difference between *expression* and *equation*.

ACTION PLANNING

Same place? Self-managed? Short and sweet? Review or preview? Evaluate where you are in using *Do Nows*. Find a printable version of this form at my.teachlikeachampion.com.

HOW AM I DOING?

_____

_____

Design one or more action steps for improvement. Decide on an interval by which you'll revisit this page to assess your progress.

Action Step 1

By when, with whom, and how you will measure your effort
By _____, I will . . .
     Date

_____

_____

How Did I Do?

Successes: _____

_____

_____

_____

Challenges: _____

_____

_____

_____

Next steps: _____

_____

_____

_____

DO NOW

Action Step 2

By when, with whom, and how you will measure your effort

By _____, I will . . .
  _{Date}

_____

_____

_____

How Did I Do?

Successes: _____

_____

_____

_____

Challenges: _____

_____

_____

Next steps: _____

_____

_____

DO NOW

NAME THE STEPS

OVERVIEW

Skills that seem easy and intuitive to those who have already learned them can nonetheless be complex and difficult to those who have not, and this discrepancy is compounded if the person with mastery has strong intuition and affinity for a topic. The fact that you learned something quickly and easily only puts you at greater risk for not understanding how much some students may struggle. To overcome this, consider breaking complex tasks down into simplified steps. We call this *Name the Steps*. It offers more than a simple scaffold; it can also lead to a surprising amount of metacognition: What am I doing now? Why? What am I doing next? In other words, What's my process?

Name the Steps can be divided into three activities:

1. Identify the steps.
2. Make steps "sticky" (memorable) by naming them and by other means.
3. Switch back and forth between how students are solving the immediate challenge or problem and reflections on the process they are using to solve it. We call this "using two stairways." The goal is for students to be attentive to both product and process.

Reflection

Take a moment to reflect in writing. Then feel free to compare your answer with some of our thoughts.

In your experience, when following steps in a recipe or other set of instructions, what makes them easier or harder to follow and apply, especially from memory?

_____

_____

_____

Our thoughts (yours might be different): At the outset, a good recipe lists every ingredient we'll need. Some bad instructions abbreviate the names of parts too much. We sometimes want more advice about how long a procedure will take. We rarely actually remember all steps. We need them to be written down. Good street directions name the streets and tell us which direction (right or left) and how far to go on each.

NAME THE STEPS

FUNDAMENTALS

1. Identify the Steps

> #### Revisit *Teach Like a Champion 2.0*
>
> Doug gave an interesting example to convey the value of identifying steps:
>
> One of my soccer coaches had been an all-world superstar as a player. As coach, he'd stand on the sidelines and shout, "Defense, you guys! Defense!!" We were pretty aware that we were on defense, though, and also pretty aware that we weren't playing it especially well. He coached by offering pointers like "Don't tackle there, Doug!"
>
> When I started to play for another coach, I realized how a coach might also be a teacher. The second coach broke down defense into a series of steps: First, position yourself increasingly closer to your man as he gets closer to the player with the ball. Second, deny the ball [meaning reposition yourself from between the offensive player and the goal to between the ball and the offensive player] if and only if you are certain you can intercept. Third, prevent your man from turning if he is facing away from the goal. Fourth, steer your man toward the sidelines if he has the ball and has turned. Fifth, tackle if you must. Sixth, otherwise keep position between him and the goal.
>
> He focused his coaching (before the game, rather than during!) on reminding us what step came next. If my man got the ball, he would gently remind me, "Don't let him turn." If I let him turn (I usually did), he would say, "Take him wide." If, as was often the case, I found myself unsuccessful, he would say, "If you must . . . ," a reminder that keeping my position between the player and the goal was more important than winning the ball. For years after I stopped playing for him, I'd recall his steps ("If you must . . .") while I played. Once I asked the second coach how he thought to teach the way he did. His reply was revealing: "That was the only way I could learn it."

One objective of a great science teacher might be for students to learn how to study a specimen of an animal in order to determine what species it belongs to. This might involve posing an initial question or step and then, depending on the answer, posing a certain second question or step, and so forth. The exercise might lead to learning a broader process of steps for assessing other animal specimens.

Suppose you're introducing your students to the craft of writing a chapter summary, either fiction or nonfiction, depending on your subject area. Take several minutes now to write a list of up to seven steps that the students can follow:

Steps of Summarizing

1. _____

2. _____

3. _____

4. _____

5. _____

6. _____

7. _____

Once you've written the list, go back to make sure that you haven't included too many steps. Limit the number by making sure that you've included only steps that are absolutely essential, eliminating those that are not.

It's always wise to test a list of steps on a variety of examples before you teach it to students. Are there cases to which the steps won't apply? For example, some chapters have headings, while others don't. Adapt the steps or plan how you'll explain limitations to students.

2. Make Steps "Sticky"

> ### Revisit *Teach Like a Champion 2.0*
>
> You may recall Doug's technique 21 discussion of the sticky acronym for the five story elements: *STORY.*
>
> S—The setting is where and when the story takes place.
> T—Talking characters are who the story revolves around.
> O—*Oops,* there's a problem. A problem is what a character wants but cannot have.
> R—The attempts to resolve are when characters try to fix the problem and they fail.
> Y—*Yes!* A solution!! A solution is when a problem is solved.
>
>   . . . There are lots of elements here to make the mnemonic memorable—the acronym isn't a straight transliteration of the five story elements (setting, characters, problem, attempts to solve, solution) . . . [and] the addition of "Oops" and "Yes!" helps students connect to the story on an emotional level. . . .
>   As students get older, they learn to diverge from the STORY template, but for a young scholar, the road map to summarizing a piece of fiction is certainly helpful—both in understanding it and in attending to important pieces—the first couple dozen times through.

A Stickier Summary

Use the following lines to make your chapter summary steps stickier—for example, by making them briefer and giving each one a short, memorable name that is likely to stick in your students' minds. Also try creating a story or mnemonic device around the names for your steps.

Name of list of steps: _____

1. [_____] _____

   _____

2. [_____] _____

   _____

3. [_____] _____

   _____

4. [_____] _____

   _____

5. [————————————————————]————————————————————

——

6. [————————————————————]————————————————————

——

7. [————————————————————]————————————————————

——

A Stickier *Field Guide*

This *Field Guide* contains various lists of steps for you, the reader, or for students to follow. Browse through them (and other lists of component ideas, such as "What's Pepper Made Of?" in *Pepper,* technique 36) for any you could make stickier by naming the steps, rephrasing the wording of the steps or their names to create a useful acronym, creating a mnemonic device, or by other means. Apply those methods to at least one of the lists. Write down your results:

——

——

——

——

Again, share your insights with a partner—and with us if you think we could use them!

3. Use Two Stairways

Once students know the steps, classrooms can have two parallel conversations going at once, narrating both substance and progress through the steps. A great teacher switches back and forth. For example:

TEACHER:	So tell me about the setting, Paul.
PAUL:	The setting is in England.
TEACHER:	And what else do we need to know for step 1? David.
DAVID:	When!
TEACHER:	Where *and* when. OK. Matleena, when?
MATLEENA:	When Queen Victoria was living.
TEACHER:	We call that "The Victorian . . ."
MATLEENA:	Victorian times. The Victorian era!
TEACHER:	What would that be in years, dates? Luke?
LUKE:	The story is set sometime in the middle of the 1800s.
TEACHER:	Good, that pins it down. After step 1, *S* for setting, what comes next? Morgan?
MORGAN:	*T.*

TEACHER:	Which stands for?
MORGAN:	Talking. The characters, the main ones.
TEACHER:	What about them, Carlotta?
CARLOTTA:	That's *O,* the next step, Ooops!
TEACHER:	I mean who are they?
CARLOTTA:	Well, there's Scrooge like always . . .

Remember that you can ask a student to

- Explain the process while you complete or perform each step.
- Complete the steps while you explain the process.
- Both do the steps and explain the process.

You can also

- Ask one student to concentrate on the problem while another student concentrates on the process.
- Make mistakes and ask students where you went wrong or might have used a better step.

Plan *Name the Steps*

1. Consult your next few lesson plans and find one whose objective can be served in part by an activity that involves breaking down some task into steps.
2. Identify the steps as they would apply to a single instance or problem, and plan how you will present them or how you will help the class build them.
3. Possibly identify each step with an underlying process that generalizes to similar problems.
4. Script some pairs of questions to ask that will move students back and forth between steps to solve the immediate problem and the steps as a general process.
5. If appropriate, ahead of time or as part of class activity, create a poster of process steps as a tool that students can consult in future sessions.

THE NEXT LEVEL

Have your students reached a point at which they've learned a certain set of steps so well that they might try the whole task without such deliberate "stepping-stones"?

As the "thinking ratio" techniques of chapters 7 through 9 suggest, you can increase your students' critical thinking by making them more accountable for their own efficient use of steps.

- Could a whole-task activity help students see which, if any, steps they might need to shore up?
- Students can be asked to identify steps behind solving a hitherto "stepless" challenge they've had trouble overcoming. Together, they and you can go beyond the steps you may have been handed in a commercial curriculum package.
- Consider an activity that involves the students taking notes on steps. Consider the notes as a resource they can look back to when they get stuck in another problem for which they might need to retrace their steps to see where they strayed. Students can also use the notes as a tool for working out the underlying, more generalized pattern of steps in a process, possibly to consult during homework.

PRACTICE WITH A GROUP OR COLLEAGUE

Share your earlier work on the steps for summarizing a chapter. Compare your experiences as you worked on the problem. Also compare your actual lists of steps. Do any lists stand out for

- Including steps other lists missed?
- A good level of ease and precision in each step?
- A good sequence of steps?
- Stickiness of steps?
- Other reasons?

Overall, which lists seem likely to work best for the students? Why?

Last, if you have time, as a group, share what you've done individually in "A Stickier *Field Guide*." Possibly select and work together on a different list in the *Field Guide*.

ACTION PLANNING

Find a printable version of this form at my.teachlikeachampion.com. Use these success points to assess how you're doing with *Name the Steps*:

- Students are doing better at complex tasks because we're *Naming the Steps*.
- Students are increasingly able to move their attention back and forth between the "stairways" of immediate problems and underlying process.

HOW AM I DOING?

_____

_____

Design one or more action steps for improvement. Decide on an interval by which you'll revisit this page to assess your progress.

Action Step 1

By when, with whom, and how you will measure your effort

By _____, I will . . .
   <small>Date</small>

_____

_____

How Did I Do?

Successes: _____

_____

_____

_____

_____

Challenges: _____

_____

_____

_____

Next steps: _____

_____

_____

_____

Action Step 2

By when, with whom, and how you will measure your effort

By _____, I will . . .
<small>Date</small>

How Did I Do?

Successes: _____

Challenges: _____

Next steps: _____

NAME THE STEPS

BOARD = PAPER

OVERVIEW

Board = Paper is a technique for modeling the habit of taking classroom notes that capture information you present (or the class itself discovers). Ultimately the notes may also record the student's own perspective on that knowledge.

In their written notes, younger students generally should start by replicating exactly what their teacher writes on the board (or shows on an overhead). The teacher makes that expectation explicit at first by using an overhead projector (or other device) to display a copy of a partially completed sheet on which students are taking their own notes.

Over time, students learn to take notes on their own, gradually earning more autonomy as they learn to apply and adapt the note-taking structures you've modeled.

Revisit *Teach Like a Champion 2.0*

In the opening of this technique, reread Doug's confession of his own "enduring weakness" at note taking.

Reflection

How's your note-taking skill?

_____

_____

Why do you think so many students fail to master this critical skill, and what's the cost of a weakness at it later in life? How would students benefit by being diligent, proficient note-takers?

_____

_____

_____

FUNDAMENTALS

Students need to learn how to take effective notes. Even late into high school (and after), many have not acquired the skills to make sense of an instruction like "Take careful notes" or to know what to do when no one's told them what to do.

Board = Paper involves modeling and scaffolding. It starts with your modeling exactly what the notes should be and enables you to gradually shift more and more actual note-taking thought and work onto the students themselves. It starts with students filling in the blanks in a graphic organizer. Over time, the blanks get larger. The *Board = Paper* overhead is an example of basic scaffolding.

A *Board = Paper* Overhead for Literary Setting

SETTING

The Basics

The basic definition of the setting of a story is its (*time*) and (*place*).

Taking Setting to the Collegiate Level

This year, we are going to consider the (*five*) facets of setting.

1. (*Place*): (*geographic*) location. (*Where*) is the action of the story (*taking*) place?
2. (*Time*): (*When*) is the story taking place?
   (*historical*) period, time of (*year*)
3. (*Weather*) conditions: Is it (*rainy, stormy*), sunny, etc.?
4. (*Social*) conditions: What is the (*daily*) life of the (*characters*)?
5. Mood or (*atmosphere*): What (*feeling*) is created in the story?
   Is it bright and (*cheerful*) or (*dark*) and frightening?

Marking Up the Text

When you see any of these facets in the text, mark it up as follows in the margin . . .

1. P = (*place*)
2. T = (*time*)
3. WC = (*weather*) conditions
4. SC = (*social*) conditions
5. MOA = mood or (*atmosphere*)

Gradually, students should progress in the amount of the note taking over which they exercise discretion, filling out longer and longer passages of their graphic organizers on their own and finally taking notes on a separate sheet of paper as you write terms and definitions on the board exactly as you wish students to copy them down. In the long run, the exercise can shift to students' helping determine what the stems should be and eventually taking notes from the board or other sources on their own.

In the course of scaffolding, tell students what to title their notes, when to skip a line, and how to make subheadings and headings. When they can reliably do this, you can also begin to divest yourself gradually of responsibility for exact phrasing and let students own that, too. Remember that it takes years before most students are ready to own full responsibility for such a critical process as taking notes.

THE NEXT LEVEL

Don't let yourself or your students slip into thinking of *Board = Paper* as filling out "worksheets." Keep *Board = Paper* explicitly tied to the broader goal of learning to take one's own effective notes.

Students may work at vastly different paces when filling in notes. If you find that numerous students are finished and simply waiting for their classmates to finish taking notes, provide a copy of the filled-in notes for the slower note-takers to fill in after class. Or have challenge problems prepared for "faster" note-taking students to work on while they wait for classmates to complete notes.

ROLL IT OUT

Using *Begin with the End* to create your lesson plans, notice one in which the objective warrants an activity involving *Board = Paper*.

In the lesson plan, consider when you will *Circulate* (technique 24) to check for understanding several times before you and the class have completed the page. Decide whether you will have your copy of the notes filled in ahead of time or will fill in the notes during class, or some combination of the two. Also plan how students will save their notes over the course of the year.

A GROUP PRACTICE ROLE PLAY FOR *BOARD = PAPER*

If possible, work with other teachers who teach at grade levels close to your own, but not all at exactly your level. The group's *Facilitator* may need to arrange equipment in advance.

1. Before the meeting, *Teachers* each create a *Board = Paper* organizer that they might use in a future lesson. If you don't yet have such a plan, create the organizer based on notes you wrote on the board in a previous lesson. Make copies for everyone in the group.
2. Depending on the size of your group, availability of an overhead, and so on, take turns as *Teacher* and actually do *Board = Paper* with the rest of the group as *Students*. Then discuss the experience from both perspectives.
3. Share copies and discuss:
   What challenges arose as you created your organizer?
   Did creating the page cause you to alter your plans for what notes to present to the class? How so?
   What previous *Board = Paper* work prepared your class for this current level of note-taking challenge?

What might be the next small step?
What might be the next fairly large step?

Reflection: Plans for Teaching Note-Taking Skills

What have you learned from the group that will improve your short- and longer-term plans for teaching note-taking skills?

_____

_____

_____

ACTION PLANNING

Using feedback from your study group or other peers, and reviewing on your own lesson notes and observations, monitor your progress on *Board = Paper*. (Find a generic printable version of this form at my.teachlikeachampion.com.) Consider these success points:

- My students understand the point of *Board = Paper* activities as developing their independent note-taking skills.
- With each *Board = Paper* task, I'm aware of how it advances my students toward better note taking.
- I'm providing for situations in which some students finish much faster than others.

HOW AM I DOING?

_____

_____

Action Step 1

In my lesson planning for _____, I will . . .

_____

_____

_____

How Did I Do?

Successes: _____

_____

_____

_____

Challenges: _____

_____

_____

_____

Next steps: _____

_____

_____

_____

Action Step 2

In my lesson planning for _____ , I will . . .

_____

_____

_____

How Did I Do?

Successes: _____

_____

_____

_____

Challenges: _____

_____

_____

_____

Next steps: _____

_____

_____

_____

CONTROL THE GAME

OVERVIEW

Control the Game is a system for engineering student oral reading in the classroom. It makes oral reading a productive, accountable, and efficient activity. This, in turn, makes it easy to read a lot—and to instill a culture of joyful reading.

Control the Game relies on the idea of "leveraging" one student's reading aloud by having everyone else reading along silently. In this way, you have thirty readers instead of just one. *Control the Game* does this in part by modeling the pleasure of reading and in part by making the shifts in who reads constant and unpredictable, so our discussion here focuses on building high leverage and building a positive culture around oral reading.

Reflection

What are some reasons teachers are often given for not having students read aloud in class?

_____

_____

_____

What might be the benefits of having students read aloud?

_____

_____

_____

Write your thoughts before you read on.

Possible arguments against and for having students read aloud (you may have heard others): Against: only one student is reading, and the others are passive. But if one student is reading actively and twenty-seven students are reading along with her, as actively engaged in the text as if they were reading independently, then no student is reading "alone." Against: it seems like a waste of time. But reading aloud helps you observe and gather data on how your students are reading. Against: students might struggle, and they may be shamed and/or hate reading in the future. But we believe that great classroom cultures make it safe to struggle and take risks. Skilled teachers manage the experience so that students gradually get better as their fear of reading yields to the normality of it.

ANALYZE A CHAMPION

 Find this blog post at teachlikeachampion.com/blog/teaching-and-schools/jessica-bracey -control-the-game-and-fluency/.

It's called "Jessica Bracey: Control the Game and Fluency." View it and read the commentary about this fifth-grade lesson. Then also respond to the question here.

How much reading is getting done by how many students in Jessica's class? How do you know? What can you conclude about the quality of the students' reading experience?

_____

_____

_____

FUNDAMENTALS

Control the Game is a great way to pass your own love of reading on to your students and nurture them to love it, too, and to share that love among themselves. In this and other respects, *Control the Game* will work best if you:

Keep durations unpredictable. To increase students' engagement with the text, don't specify how long you want your primary reader to read in class. Moving quickly among primary readers and keeping the durations of reading unpredictable can make the lesson feel energetic and engaging to students because they will focus more closely on the text in order to follow along. As your students get more comfortable with *Control the Game* reading, you may want to increase the lengths that they read.

Keep the choice of reader unpredictable. Be unpredictable about whom you'll call on next to be primary reader. Calling in a predictable pattern makes students more likely to tune out. Switching durations and readers will help you gather data about your leverage. If you ask a student to pick up reading and the student is with you immediately, you know that the student is following along closely.

Cut down the transaction costs of cueing. Have a consistent, simple method to cue the next reader. Verbose phrasing can sap momentum. Simple prompting such as "Pick up, Jessica" or "Read next, Perry" are much more efficient than "Thank you, Alan; would you pick up reading, Kianti?"

Bridge. Another way for you to switch between primary readers is to read a short segment of the text as a bridge. By reading a sentence or two, you can quickly model great reading (fluency, expressive reading, love for the story). Bridging is especially good when

You want to model how to read complex sections of text with precision.

The pace of the reading might slow down because of the complexity of the text, and you want to move the reading forward. Conversely, you may want to bridge when you want to speed up through a passage.

You want to model how to read fluently and expressively.

Be sure to alert your students to the start of a *Control the Game,* so that it doesn't come across as a "gotcha!" You might want to remind them to follow along because they don't know who might be called on next and, of course, don't want to miss out. You can also invite them to alert you if they get lost or need other help.

Control the Game is a great setting for making reading joyful. Celebrate expressive, engaged reading by modeling it yourself; then reinforce it in your students. Over time in great classrooms, reading becomes one of students' favored activities. It's a reward! And kids compete to read expressively. Now that's a victory.

Write down some phrases you could use to build excitement and student investment in *Control the Game,* such as "Love that beautiful reading!" or "I could really hear Jonas's voice there, Rashad. Beautiful!"

_____

_____

_____

Videotape yourself to see how you're doing!

ANALYZE MORE CHAMPIONS

▶ **Clip FG22. Hilary Lewis, Grade 1**

▶ **Clip FG23. Maggie Johnson, Grade 8**

First-grade teacher Hilary Lewis applies *Control the Game* when the class reads from a reading mastery text. Eighth-grade reading teacher Maggie Johnson facilitates a session of *Control the Game* during a lesson on Harper Lee's *To Kill a Mockingbird.* How does each teacher effectively apply *Control the Game*?

_____

_____

_____

_____

Compare your notes with ours at the end of this technique.

PRACTICING ALONE OR WITH A PARTNER

Choose a text excerpt that you plan to read aloud with your students. Practice the following rounds, ideally with a partner. (*Note:* The two final rounds are more advanced and recommended for teachers with at least some experience with *Control the Game*.)

We suggest marking up your text based on each round and incorporating what you learn into upcoming lesson plans.

Round 1. Practice Your Prompt to Switch between Primary Readers

In your lesson plan or spare notebook/piece of paper, script one or two prompts that you'll use consistently in your classroom. Mark up the text you'll be reading to show when you want to switch between readers. You may also want to plan which students you want to call on.

Practice the prompts by yourself; better yet, have a partner play the part of the students, reading a few lines aloud before each time you call on the "next" primary reader. Then give the partner a turn at being teacher.

For this round and for your performance as you conduct these problems in class, score yourselves positively for fulfilling the following success points:

- Using fewer words to cue the next reader
- Eliminating words or addressing fewer words to a reader who's just finished (for example, try "Thank you" instead of "Thank you. That was great reading.")
- Calling on a student whom you've already asked to read to keep kids on their toes
- Calling on readers without making eye contact with them (what we refer to as the "No-Look" call)

Round 2. Practice Using Bridging

Mark up your text and indicate where you want your students reading and when you want to read a few sentences. Again you can practice alone or with a partner.

Success points for this round in practice and in class:

- Bridging for longer or shorter segments of text to model fluent reading and keep your *Control the Game* less predictable
- Being more expressive while bridging
- Being more intentional about the spot that you choose to bridge (in other words, consider bridging difficult sections to support comprehension or sections that you want to model reading with strong expression)

Round 3 (Advanced). Placeholders and Questions

This round is about having your students pause and use placeholders as you ask them questions about the text—for example, "Place your finger on the word *ambiguous*. How does the author use the word 'ambiguous'?"

Plan your placeholder and your text-based questions. Remember, you're not limited to having students keep their fingers on the words. Annotation or an *Everybody Writes* (technique 37) would work well here.

Success points for this round in practice and in class:

- You've given your students adequate *Wait Time* (technique 32) or provided them with an *Everybody Writes* to process their answers.
- You minimize transaction costs and pick up reading seamlessly.

Round 4 (Advanced). Responding to a Student Who's Not Ready to Read

Plan how you'll respond to your student who's not ready to read. Make sure you keep this response standard and consistent so that students are clear as to what the consequences are if they're not ready to read (see techniques 53, *Least Invasive Intervention,* and 55, *Art of the Consequence*).

Success points for this round in practice and in class:

- Giving a small consequence to the student who is not ready to read (for example, "Aaron, that's two scholar dollars. You need to be with us. We're at the top of page 3.")
- Returning to the student who is not ready to read after another student has read (to emphasize accountability)
- Using a quick private individual correction (per *Least Invasive Intervention*) with the student who isn't ready to read

ACTION PLANNING

Use this action planner to continue your work with *Control the Game.* (Find a printable version of this form at my.teachlikeachampion.com.) You know you're on the right track when both primary and secondary readers are attentively engaged.

CONTROL THE GAME

HOW AM I DOING?

_____

_____

Design one or more action steps for improvement. Decide on an interval by which you'll revisit this page to assess your progress.

Action Step 1

By when, with whom, and how you will measure your effort

By _____, I will . . .
   Date

_____

_____

How Did I Do?

Successes: _____

_____

_____

_____

_____

Challenges: _____

_____

_____

_____

_____

Next steps: _____

_____

_____

_____

Action Step 2

By when, with whom, and how you will measure your effort

By _____, I will . . .
     <small>Date</small>

_____

_____

_____

How Did I Do?

Successes: _____

_____

_____

_____

_____

Challenges: _____

_____

_____

_____

Next steps: _____

_____

_____

_____

OUR OBSERVATIONS ON THE CHAMPIONS

 Clip FG22. Hilary Lewis, and FG23. Maggie Johnson

What makes their *Control the Game* effective? First-grade teacher Hilary Lewis wisely begins *Control the Game* by setting clear expectations for oral reading. She keeps the length of reading and the choice of next reader unpredictable, which encourages students to follow along carefully in their texts. She maximizes reading time and the flow of the story's narrative by reducing her transaction cost in selecting students to read.

The speed and pacing with which she switches between readers also keeps students on their toes. Her cue is quick and clear: she calls out each student reader's name.

Since her cue is so short, she is able to transition without a break between readers at any point within the passage. Students know they have to be ready to read at a moment's notice. Hilary's *Control the Game* achieves high leverage. We can tell that *all* of her students are following along with the text because all of her students turn the page exactly on cue with the reader and visibly track their pages.

In her skillful *Control the Game* with Harper Lee's *To Kill a Mockingbird,* Maggie starts by showing some spunk, modeling how to read slowly, carefully, and with the kind of fluency and expression that conveys (and even enhances) meaning. Quickly and efficiently, she prompts students by name to pick up and continue the primary reading, switching smoothly between them. Every student is ready to pick up and read at her cue—strong evidence for Maggie that her secondary readers are closely following along in the text.

When she calls on Arshe and he reads without much expression, she asks him for some drama with a hint of challenge in her tone. Arshe rereads with a lot more spunk, and Maggie and her students laugh appreciatively. Even though they're knee-deep in a challenging text, students don't forget to enjoy reading with fluency and expression.

When Maggie calls on the second student, a struggling reader, she offers some reassuring hums each time the student successfully pronounces tricky words. This boosts the student's confidence and also helps Maggie maintain the pace of the oral reading. When the student makes a decoding mistake, Maggie corrects the error and then asks the student to reread that sentence. Thus Maggie gives the student an opportunity to practice being successful.

After the weaker reader finishes her turn, Maggie picks up with some expressive, fluent reading to rebuild any lost momentum and reengage the rest of the class.

She then positively frames her request (technique 58, *Positive Framing*) for fluent reading by saying, "I need an irritated Atticus. Who wants it?" In doing so, she clarifies what she's looking for in a reader (as opposed to waiting to correct him or her after the fact) and turns the act of reading fluently into a reward. We then see Ronnie rise to the occasion when he reads the line "Stop that noise!" with convincing expression.

CIRCULATE

OVERVIEW

A skilled teacher uses proximity, positioning, and movement throughout the classroom to gather data, understand what's happening in the room, and build a culture of positive accountability and engagement among students. We call this set of skills *Circulate* and often notice that top teachers execute it with chess-like strategy.

For many teachers, the first step is moving past the imaginary wall or "plane" that separates a corridor of "their" space about six feet deep at the front of the room from "student" space that essentially takes up the rest of the room. "Breaking the plane" means getting out into that space, moving at will and with comfort around the classroom during all parts of the lesson to maximize engagement, achievement, and opportunities to build relationships with students.

Reflection

How widely and intentionally do you move while you're actively teaching? What about while your students are working?

_____

_____

_____

ANALYZE THE CHAMPIONS

▶ **Clip FG24. Julia Addeo and Maggie Johnson**

▶ **Clip FG25. Maura Faulkner and Rue Ratray**

Watch both clips, taking notes on the following questions:

What do/did the teachers have to do to be able to move freely throughout the room as they do?

_____

_____

What do you notice about the teachers' general manner as they move throughout the room? What are some themes you see among all four and some variations you see in just one or two that appeal to you most?

_____

_____

How does *Circulating* appear in the videos to affect students and classroom culture?

_____

_____

Makes some specific observations about their *Circulating* during teaching.

_____

_____

Make some additional observations about *Circulating* during independent work.

_____

_____

Compare your observations with ours at the end of this technique.

FUNDAMENTALS

Start with the Basics

Break the Plane

Don't hesitate to pass through that imaginary wall. Breaking the plane adds energy to your teaching and sets you up to better see what your students are doing. It also sends the message that it is normal for you to go anywhere you want in the classroom at any time.

Secure Full Access

Make sure you can access all parts of your classroom so that you can move without interrupting the flow of your lesson. You should be able to get anywhere quickly without moving furniture or student belongings. If you're already *Circulating,* and if teaching from various points in the classroom is the norm in your classroom, you can easily walk to any student to have private conversations, to praise him or her, or to make a correction. This will increase the privacy of your interaction with individual students while keeping the rest of the class focused on the content of your lesson.

In order to have full access to your classroom, get rid of any "no-fly zones"—places where any physical or mental obstruction prevents you from going. This could be as simple as a backpack on the floor or as irksome as that crate of books you've been meaning to take to the supply room for weeks. The barrier might also be some reluctance you have to venture toward the back where a student or two use posture or other signs to cordon off some "private" space.

Reflection: No-Fly Zones

Are there no-fly zones in your classroom? What are they? What sort of action is required to get rid of them?

_____

_____

_____

Engage While You *Circulate*

When *Circulating,* you can both monitor work students might be doing at their desks and interact with them to maximize their engagement with you and the learning. Keep two goals in mind:

Affirmation. Use *Circulate* to build relationships and reinforce behavioral and academic expectations. *Expectations* are yours; *engagement* is what you want from your kids. Reinforce your students' engagement positively by showing appreciation for it and engaging them in the ideas they develop.

Accountability. By *Circulating,* you show that you see everything. Ensure that your students remain meaningfully engaged and on task throughout the lesson; take steps to underscore that you are interested in and looking at what students do at their seats. Just pausing, looking, and nodding can often have a significant effect.

The table here lists some tools for engagement. Underline ones you are currently using for affirmation or accountability.

Circulate Tools for Engagement

	Nonverbal	Verbal
Affirmation	Gestures Smiling/nodding Positive touch (e.g., light hand on shoulder) Pointing out work that is on the right track	Acknowledgment *Precise Praise*—public voice or private voice Expressing appreciation for student ideas
Accountability	Gestures Nonverbal corrections Consistent phrases Reading off a student's document Pointing to a student's notes	*Precise Praise*—public or private Whispering corrections Expressing appreciation for student ideas

Consider rewatching Clip FG24, Julia Addeo and Maggie Johnson, and Clip FG25, Maura Faulkner and Rue Ratray, and note which tools the teachers use.

Are there certain situations or student behaviors for which you wish you had greater power to affirm or to promote accountability? Envision one or two of them. From all the tools, which ones might serve you best? Record several situations and potential tools here:

Situation:

_____

_____

Tool and how to use:

_____

_____

_____

Situation:

_____

_____

Tool and how to use:

_____

_____

_____

CIRCULATE

Be Systematic . . . and in Control

As you _Circulate_, your goal is to cover all parts of the room, to be aware of what's happening everywhere, and to show that your movements and any interactions when you _Circulate_ are natural and normal.

Frantic or overly quick walking can distract your students and suggest that you are nervous. This in turn implies that you are in "their" space. Strive to move at a steady, even stately pace.

As you _Circulate_, generally position yourself to see as much as possible of what is happening in the room. Face the class as often as possible, and _Be Seen Looking_ (technique 51). Contrive ways to subtly (or not so subtly) remind students that you see.

ROLL IT OUT WITH YOUR MAP, AND PRACTICE

Use a large part of a sheet of paper to sketch your classroom as it is set up. Outside the sketch, write these reminders:

Cover all parts
Stately pace
See the room

Then draw a route on the sketch and annotate it according to what you might do at various points along the way.

- Trace multiple routes that you'd like to try while teaching your next lesson.
- With a star, mark strategic points in your room where you'd like to pause and teach.
- Inside or outside the square, write down specific tools for engagement you'd like to employ.

In the empty classroom before the lesson, practice *Circulating* according to your plan. Get a feel for what it's like and for whether the seating layout of the room allows you to *Circulate* close to each student without inconveniencing others. As you see fit, make changes to the classroom and your plan.

WORKING WITH A GROUP OR COLLEAGUE

1. Compare past experiences with *Circulating* freely and any challenges it has involved.
2. Troubleshoot your classroom. With a partner, either observe your classroom or a photo or video of it and identify your no-fly zones. Commit to taking time with your partner to immediately get rid of your no-fly zones!
3. Compare and discuss your rollout maps, routes, and your current *Circulate* tools.
4. Try *Circulating* and using your tools for engagement. Pick a couple that you're working on in your classroom and solicit the thoughts of your peers.

ACTION PLANNING

Use this action planner to continue your work with *Circulate*. (Find a printable version of this form at my.teachlikeachampion.com.) You know you're on the right track when you . . .

- Cover all parts of your room.
- Engage with your students as you *Circulate* (for affirmation and accountability).
- Position yourself to see the room.

CIRCULATE

HOW AM I DOING?

_____

_____

Design one or more action steps for improvement. Decide on an interval by which you'll revisit this page to assess your progress.

Action Step 1

By when, with whom, and how you will measure your effort

By _____, I will . . .
    _{Date}

_____

_____

How Did I Do?

Successes: _____

_____

_____

_____

_____

Challenges: _____

_____

_____

_____

Next steps: _____

_____

_____

_____

CIRCULATE

Action Step 2

By when, with whom, and how you will measure your effort

By _____, I will . . .
　　Date

_____

_____

_____

How Did I Do?

Successes: _____

_____

_____

_____

Challenges: _____

_____

_____

Next steps: _____

_____

_____

CIRCULATE

CIRCULATE

OUR OBSERVATIONS ON THE CHAMPIONS

 Clips FG24. Julia Addeo and Maggie Johnson, and FG25. Maura Faulkner and Rue Ratray

All four teachers in these clips have set up their classrooms with wide-open travel lanes so that they can move freely throughout the room. They have eliminated any no-fly zones and are able to teach from any place in the room as they wish. The teachers have also normalized *Circulate* by walking around all parts of their classrooms and pausing occasionally not just to pass through but to teach from different spots.

In general manner, all of the teachers move at a slow and stately pace, which conveys comfort. The teachers use their movement as a tool, and it never distracts from the content that the teacher is delivering or the feedback that they are giving their students.

They are also intentional in their movement. The teachers are diligent about breaking the plane before they need to. They systematically walk down rows or aisles, and engage their students to emphasize both affirmation and accountability.

Their *Circulating* certainly affects the students and the classroom culture. Because the teachers are moving at a pace that is easy and natural to them, you see that there is an ease and comfort about the teaching. Students feel comfortable, and the teachers are increasing their efficiency in delivering feedback to students.

During her teaching of math, Julia comfortably *Circulates* throughout her classroom. She easily, quickly walks to her whiteboard if she needs to point out anything for her students to read, and she's also able to use her proximity to check in with students if she needs to. Her ability to make interactions feel normal in her classroom further enables her to make a correction or give praise if she needs to, and because it's so normal, it becomes private.

Maggie *Circulates* as she's leading *Control the Game* reading. You can see that she leverages her proximity and is able to give very private nonverbal corrections to her students. She communicates that her presence in the classroom is comfortable, and you can tell that the students are comfortable having her walk everywhere. Because she is always moving throughout her room, she is able to do small, subtle things that build a special culture in which students are eager to learn.

During independent work, Maura *Circulates* intentionally. She offers affirmation and builds accountability depending on what she observes, and this balance makes the mood feel fair but rigorous. She is systematic in her movement, and her gentle check-ins with her students enable them to stay focused on the task rather than being distracted.

Rue *Circulates* for accountability while not saying a single word. His movement is quiet. With a simple lean and a touch of the desk, he communicates that he is intently looking at student work.

AT BATS

OVERVIEW

No one masters a new skill of any substance on the first go-round or the second. Or possibly even the tenth. And when you get a skill right once or twice, you are not finished. Getting it right is often the mid-point of mastery. Only ten, twenty, thirty iterations will let you own it.

Repeated opportunities to try a key skill—*At Bats*—ingrain skills deeply in long-term memory. They expose learners to lots of variations in how a skill might be applied later on, and, in building familiarity, they free up "working memory" to focus on other, more complex tasks or questions that may need attention at the same time that the skill is being executed. Only when you know the math cold can you start to think of whether there is a simpler way to solve for x. Even in a busy lesson, remember repetition.

Reflection

How many *At Bats* did you need to master the techniques you like best as a teacher? Did you get to proficiency the first time you tried *Cold Call* or *Stretch It*? What kind of mistakes and adaptations did you have to make before you settled into a reliable swing? How long did it take?

_____

_____

_____

_____

What can you take about *At Bats* from your own learning process during the study of this book that can help you get your students to mastery?

_____

_____

_____

Possible reflections (you've likely had others): Most likely you had to try using a technique many times before you were able to make it work and to use the range of possible formats. On some *At Bats*, you missed, but you were able to look back on them later and see where things went wrong. Other tries went better. Almost every time, though, your degree of success or failure gave you a better sense of how to think on your feet and use the technique in a more comfortable and effective way next time. When learning something is a challenge for your class, your knowing how you yourself can need many *At Bats* can help you see more readily where your class and individual students need you to give them chances to practice.

FUNDAMENTALS

Batters learn the most when pitchers serve up different types of pitches. Use multiple variations and formats so that students can handle changing contexts and variables and look forward to each pitch. Among the ways to keep things fresh are three of the techniques found in chapter 7, Building Ratio through Questioning: 33, *Cold Call*; 34, *Call and Response*; and 36, *Pepper*.

Mixing Pitches

Consider a math teacher teaching students how to determine the slope of a line in the x/y coordinate plane, given two points on the line. How many different ways could she pitch the problem? Students could be asked to find the slope where

The coordinates are all positive numbers.
The coordinates include negative numbers.
The slope is a fraction, a whole number, positive, or negative.
The slope will be zero or undefined.
One value in one of the points is a variable.
All four points are variables.

We call this a set of permutations: systematic variations on the core skill to address key variations in context.

Now try to work out a set of viable permutations for a skill you will be teaching in the coming weeks. *The skill:*

_____

_____

Variations:

_____

_____

_____

_____

Scripting *At Bats*

As you begin to integrate *At Bats* into your lesson plans, keep track of your stats. Make a note of roughly how many *At Bats* you gave in a given class session. At what moments in the lesson did you give them? Should you up the numbers?

Working with previous lesson results, script at least ten pitches into an upcoming lesson plan. Consider the following:

- Do the students need more *At Bats* from the previous lesson? Should you begin with a few as cumulative review? How will those *At Bats* pick up from or differ from the ones you pitched last time?
- What's the objective in the new lesson plan? What *At Bats* will you pitch directly at it?
- What related skills can be learned and strengthened with *At Bats*?
- At what points in the lesson will students be primed to step up to the plate? Script pitches for each point.
- Consider ending the class with more *At Bats*, getting everyone off the bench and scoring.
- An *Exit Ticket* (technique 26) is a great last *At Bat.*

Written *At Bats*

Written *At Bats* are good in that they tie in with the techniques of chapter 8, Building Ratio through Writing, and cause every student to have to answer each question. Plus, they are the most independent form of work. Giving students sufficient *At Bats* for writing may result in your being very quiet and merely *Circulating* (technique 24) and checking for understanding (part 1).

THE NEXT LEVEL

Emerging Challenges and Solutions

Watch for inevitable challenges. Anticipate possibilities here.

Possible Challenges	Possible Solutions
1. Students lose interest in the work.	*Up the rigor! Increase variations slightly; fold in more challenge. Or:*
2. Too many strikes.	*If kids aren't answering with success, it's a good thing. Use the techniques of part 1, Check for Understanding, to home in on what you need to reteach. Or:*
3.	
4.	

Can Homework Tasks Be More *At Bats*?

Homework is usually not an effective way to introduce new material. And it should not be "busy work." For the most part, it should offer steadily increasing challenge as students seek to execute their skills or apply knowledge in increasingly complex contexts. At the same time, it should be as efficient as possible at reinforcing and stretching students' skills and knowledge base.

How might you adapt your use of homework to emphasize *At Bats*?

_____

_____

DISCUSSION WITH COLLEAGUES

With *At Bats* in mind, compare lessons that group members are planning, or discuss what generally happens in your class:

1. How many *At Bats* do students get in your lessons for a given skill?
2. How do you plan where to start pitching?
3. How do you decide when to stop?
4. How might you give students more *At Bats*?

From this discussion, come up with some objectives for action steps, which you can elaborate on here.

1. _____

2. _____

3. _____

ACTION PLANNING

Plan one or two action steps for making your *At Bats* more effective. In a few weeks, revisit each step to reflect on progress and how you can continue to improve. (Find a printable version of this form at my.teachlikeachampion.com.) Use these success points to assess how you're doing:

- You continue giving students *At Bats* until they are able to continue practicing on their own.
- You vary the type of pitch in terms of format, range, and context in which students must demonstrate the skill.
- You give more challenging, bonus *At Bats* to students who've mastered the basic material.

HOW AM I DOING?

_____

_____

Design one or more action steps for improvement. Decide on an interval by which you'll revisit this page to assess your progress.

Action Step 1

By when, with whom, and how you will measure your effort
By _____, I will . . .
      Date

_____

_____

How Did I Do?

Successes: _____

_____

_____

_____

Challenges: _____

_____

_____

_____

Next steps: _____

_____

_____

_____

Action Step 2

By when, with whom, and how you will measure your effort

By _____, I will . . .

Date

_____

_____

_____

How Did I Do?

Successes: _____

_____

_____

_____

Challenges: _____

_____

_____

_____

Next steps: _____

_____

_____

_____

EXIT TICKET

OVERVIEW

End each class with an *Exit Ticket*—a written assessment of your objective that you can use to evaluate your (and your students') success. Just three or four questions in various formats can provide valuable data on who learned what and who needs more help. This information can help you respond to individual students, decide what to focus on in the next lesson plan, and even reflect more broadly on what works and what doesn't in your classroom.

Reflection

Have you tried using an *Exit Ticket*? If so, what's one benefit and one challenge?
    If not, what stands in the way of your trying it?

_____

_____

_____

FUNDAMENTALS

When you begin to use *Exit Tickets*, inform your class about their purpose—what they and you will do with them.

Creating Strong Tickets

You needn't call it an Exit Ticket if some other label is more appealing. As we suggested in technique 17, plan *Exit Tickets* as part of the *4 Ms* process for creating your objective. The following are qualities of any great *Exit Ticket*:

- It asks just a few questions, numbered. Each is slightly different.
- All questions focus on the same important aspect of the lesson objective.
- The same basic challenge is posed in more than one way (for example, one multiple choice, another more open ended).
- The answers can be analyzed quickly.
- The layout lets you see easily whether each answer is right or wrong.
- You can process the lot in ten minutes or less.

Find this blog post at teachlikeachampion.com/blog/even-analyzing-exit-tickets/.

At "(Even) More on Analyzing Exit Tickets," John Costello explains why he combines multiple-choice and open-ended questions on one *Exit Ticket*.

blog

My thinking is that a good Exit Ticket has both a multiple choice question (with a right answer, 2–3 well-crafted distractors, and a wrong-is-wrong choice) and an open-ended response where students explain their rationale. To get "my students understand A but they don't understand B," I think multiple choice questions (with specific concept-based distractors) are sufficient, but what an Exit Ticket gives you . . . is the time to carefully read through each student's rationale and pinpoint where the comprehension breakdowns occur.

Basically, I couldn't assume I understood why a student was missing a concept until they explained to me the thinking that led them to the wrong answer—and reading the Exit Tickets each night was my opportunity to get that detailed information before I got to teach the next day.

Exit Tickets for reading sessions or English lessons may need to be a bit longer than tickets for other subjects. At least one question should probe the student's understanding of the reading, while another tests some more specific analytical skill.

Examples

Rate the example of an *Exit Ticket* here according to the criteria listed earlier and others you choose to apply.

GRADE 8 MATH

Exit Ticket

Name _____   Date _____

1. Simplify: $\dfrac{m^7}{m^3}$
2. Simplify: $6^5 \times 6^{10}$
3. New York City covers an area of x^7 miles. Minneapolis, Minnesota, covers an area of x^4 miles. How many times greater is the area of NYC than the area of Minneapolis?
4. Simplify: $4x \times 7x^3$
5. Simplify: $\dfrac{9c^2}{3c^2}$

Your critique:

_____

_____

_____

_____

MIDDLE SCHOOL GRADE READING

1. Which of the following best describes how the meetings have changed since the beginning of the story?
   A. In the beginning, only Piggy took the meetings seriously; now everyone realizes their importance.
   B. In the beginning, they boys loved meetings; now everyone refuses to attend.
   C. In the beginning, the boys left the meetings and completed their assigned task; now they fail to follow through.
   D. In the beginning, the boys were quiet and attentive at meetings; now no one obeys the rules of the conch.
2. What does your response above show about Ralph's position as chief?

_____

_____

_____

3. What does the change in meetings show about what the littluns value most? Why?

_____

_____

_____

Your critique:

_____

_____

_____

_____

_____

_____

_____

_____

_____

LOWER ELEMENTARY MATH

Name: Date: Monday, ___/___/____
Question: How would you find the number 278 on the 1,000 Chart?

1. Answer this question in one sentence.
2. Use this sentence frame to start your sentence: Even though there are 1,000 numbers on the chart, . . .

_____

_____

_____

Your critique:

_____

_____

_____

blog   Find this blog post at teachlikeachampion.com/blog/exit-tickets-encourage-self-reflection/.
In his field notes post "Exit Tickets That Encourage Self-Reflection," Doug passes on some clever ideas from teacher Leanne Riordan about enabling student self-monitoring and self-reflection through *Exit Tickets.*

Following Through

Exit Tickets ensure solid, classwide data you can use to check for understanding and determine what needs reteaching:

• What percentage of the class got it right?
• What mistakes were made?
• What does written commentary tell you about where students went astray?
• How could today's lesson plan be improved?
• In tomorrow's lesson plan, does something need to be retaught or practiced more?

Return *Exit Tickets* to students the next day and follow up as needed. You can take students aside for individual work. You can also use the return of the ticket and your analysis (perhaps on the board) as the start of a classwide *Do Now*. If a lot of students give incorrect answers, don't single anyone out, but let the class know aggregate results. Involve them in spotting possible sources of error.

Fourth-grade teacher Alexa Miller leaves *Exit Tickets* in student mailboxes to be corrected the next morning. Her students can fix mistakes during breakfast while she *Circulates* to assist and recheck.

Make It Easier on Yourself

Think about ways to simplify your task of analyzing the data. For example, right after the lesson, if you can, sort the exit tickets into three piles that represent different levels of success in students' answers. Make notes right on them about what your may have missed or failed to grasp. Then decide whom you might want to see in small groups the next day.

Or let students place their exit tickets in different bins according to how confident they feel about their answers or what level of help they think they need. This will strengthen habits of self-monitoring.

ALONE OR WITH A GROUP OR A COLLEAGUE

Share and compare your critiques from the earlier examples you rated. Or share and compare a lesson plan and a corresponding *Exit Ticket* you want to use in class. Critique the tickets and discuss how

- The *Exit Ticket* is related to the lesson objective.
- You might follow up if a number of students answer incorrectly.

Then improve your plan and ticket.

Revisit *Teach Like a Champion 2.0*

In the conclusion of chapter 5, Doug suggests the following practice for structuring a lesson that ends with an *Exit Ticket*. Consider taking your results before a group or colleague to show, discuss, or even try out:

1. Choose one of the following deliberately informal topics and sketch out a lesson plan that follows an I/We/You structure. In fact, you can go one step further by planning a five-step process: I do; I do, you help; you do, I help; you do; and you do and do and do. You don't have to assume you'll be teaching your actual students.
    - Students will be able to shoot an accurate foul shot.
    - Students will be able to write the name of their school in cursive.
    - Students will be able to make a peanut-butter-and-jelly sandwich.
    - Students will understand and apply the correct procedure for doing laundry in your household.
    - Students will be able to change a tire.
2. Now take your lesson and design a three- to five-minute hook that engages students and sets up the lesson.
3. Be sure to *Name the Steps* in the "I" portion of your lesson. Review them and find four or five ways to make them stickier.
4. Design an *Exit Ticket* that will allow you to accurately assess student knowledge at the end of the lesson.

ACTION PLANNING

Use this action planner to continue your work with *Name the Steps*. (Find a printable version of this form at my.teachlikeachampion.com.) You know you're on the right track when . . .

* You're conducting and analyzing your *Exit Tickets* in not a lot of time.
* You're gaining data by which to plan what to do in the next lesson and onward.
* Your students experience the benefit, too.

HOW AM I DOING?

_____

_____

Design one or more action steps for improvement. Decide on an interval by which you'll revisit this page to assess your progress.

Action Step 1

By when, with whom, and how you will measure your effort
By _____, I will . . .
<small>Date</small>

_____

_____

How Did I Do?

Successes: _____

_____

_____

_____

Challenges: _____

_____

_____

_____

Next steps: _____

_____

_____

_____

Action Step 2

By when, with whom, and how you will measure your effort

By _____, I will . . .
_{Date}

_____

_____

_____

How Did I Do?

Successes: _____

_____

_____

_____

Challenges: _____

_____

_____

Next steps: _____

_____

_____

CHANGE THE PACE

OVERVIEW

Change the Pace is a technique that allows you to manage your students' perception of their own forward progress. It allows you to create the "illusion of speed," the feeling that the class is moving quickly, or bring a more reflective tone to class—to slow things down, as it were.

Primarily, *Change the Pace* involves managing the changes you make to what students are doing during the lesson. These changes can be of two varieties: changes in activity type and changes in format. Executed well, the technique results not only in the maximization of participation but also, in many cases, just the right type of participation.

Reflection

When do you try to speed up or slow down in instruction? Why?

_____

_____

_____

Generally, does your class tend to respond positively to classes that feel faster or slower?

_____

_____

ANALYZE A CHAMPION

 Clip FG26. Erin Michels, Grade 4

Working on fractions, Erin spends a full ten minutes on a single "challenge" problem, but her pacing still feels fast. Describe what you see in this clip that creates the feeling of speed. Compare your written comments with our observations at the end of the technique.

_____

_____

_____

_____

FUNDAMENTALS: SWITCHABLE TYPES OF ACTIVITY

There are generally five types of activities (we sometimes call them "muscle groups") to use and switch among in the classroom. Each requires students to think and engage in a different way. It's important to note that you won't always be able to draw perfect distinctions between types; some activities will combine them.

Knowledge Assimilation

During knowledge assimilation, students are presented with new information while they listen, take notes, and ask or answer basic questions about the content. This could involve a teacher lecturing, modeling a problem and how to solve it, or sharing PowerPoint slides. Reading is also a form of knowledge assimilation.

Guided Practice/Guided Questioning

Guided practice/guided questioning activities involve task-oriented back-and-forth between teacher and students, such as

- Questioning a group of students to see how well they understood the presentation on daily life in America in the eighteenth century
- Telling students, "Let's examine some passages from the novel and see if we can find examples of juxtaposition together"
- Solving a system of equations as a class with the teacher asking various students to explain the steps or share an answer for each step

Frequently, guided practice or questioning comes after knowledge assimilation. Or it might require students to report and assess the answers they got during a problem set after they have worked on it independently.

Independent Practice

Independent practice involves students completing work solo and usually silently on their own. It involves executing a skill or application of a knowledge base, which differentiates it from the next type. Independent student practice could be

- Summarizing key points from the recent unit on daily life in eighteenth-century America
- Examining additional sections of the novel on one's own to find and analyze further examples of juxtaposition
- Solving a problem set with various problems involving systems of equations

Do Nows and _Exit Tickets_ are also usually independent practice.

Reflection and Idea Generation

Reflection is usually solo work—student time to try to make sense of things they are in the midst of learning or questions for which there is no clear answer. Reflection is usually silent and most often involves writing. It is the process of working through answers on one's own. For example, students might be asked to

- Reflect (in writing or in thirty seconds of silent *Wait Time*) on how the role of family in the eighteenth century might have differed from its role today.
- Reflect on examples of juxtaposition that students could use in their autobiographies and what purpose it might serve.
- Think about how they might be more successful during hard steps in solving systems of equations.

Discussion

Discussions require students to develop ideas as a group. Whether these groups comprise the whole class or a few students, they imply direct interaction between and among peers about content. See techniques 42, *Habits of Discussion*; 43, *Turn and Talk*; and 44, *Batch Process*.

MORE CHAMPIONS

▶ Clip FG27. Jessica Bracey, Grade 5

▶ Clip FG28. Ashley Hinton, Grade 4

Watch these two clips and identify which activity types (muscle groups) Jessica and Ashley use, when, and how they use them to make their classrooms both rigorous and energetic.

_____

_____

_____

Reflection

Look back on the last two or three lessons you taught. How many of the five activity types did you use? For what percentage of the lesson did you use them? In terms of pacing, how satisfied were you with each type?

_____

_____

_____

_____

_____

CHANGE THE PACE

Are there other types you could use more often and strategically to increase engagement by *Changing the Pace*?

_____

_____

_____

THE NEXT LEVEL

Change the Pace in an Upcoming Lesson

These directions lead you through analyzing the sequence of activities in a lesson plan and adding or revising three activities to deliberately *Change the Pace*.

Go through the following steps using an upcoming lesson plan you want to work on:

1. Analyze the sequence of activities in your lesson plan, annotating when you'll be exercising each muscle group:
   Knowledge assimilation (KA)
   Guided practice/Guided questioning (GP/Q)
   Independent practice (IP)
   Reflection and idea generation (RIG)
   Discussion (D)
   In the margin, write "FP" for the activities that are fast paced and "SR" for the activities that are slower and more reflective.
2. Reviewing your annotation, identify three activities that you would add or modify to *Change the Pace* more effectively. If you're *adding* an activity, mark its type in the margin and describe it briefly. If you're *revising* an existing activity, note how you'd modify it to *Change the Pace*.
3. Where could you insert more changes in activity type or employ a wider range of activity types to increase the illusion of speed?
4. Looking at your lesson plan, which muscle groups do you use the most? Just as important, how often do you switch among muscle groups?

Reflection

When would you want to add more activity types to increase reflectivity among your students?

_____

_____

Change the Format

In addition to switching among activity types, you can also *Change the Pace* by changing formats within an activity type. This is particularly helpful when you are spending a longer time than usual on one type.

YET ANOTHER CHAMPION

 Clip FG29. Bridget McElduff, Grade 5

This clip shows Bridget using Change the Format to enliven what for some might be a dreaded lesson topic: measurement conversions. Moving back and forth between metric and standard, cups and gallons, can be tedious, but must be done. As you watch, how does Bridget change formats effectively while keeping her students engaged?

ACTION PLANNING

Find a printable version of this form at my.teachlikeachampion.com. Look at an upcoming lesson plan in which you're teaching a long stretch of a specific action type. How are you going to *Change the Pace* during the lesson? Mark up your lesson plan. You'll know you're on track when . . .

- Your range of activity types *Changes the Pace*.
- You see the benefit of those changes in the energy and focus of the class.

HOW AM I DOING?

_____

_____

Design one or more action steps for improvement. Decide on an interval by which you'll revisit this page to assess your progress.

Action Step 1

By when, with whom, and how you will measure your effort
By _____, I will . . .
   Date

_____

_____

How Did I Do?

Successes: _____

_____

_____

_____

Challenges: _____

_____

_____

_____

Next steps: _____

_____

_____

Action Step 2

By when, with whom, and how you will measure your effort

By _____, I will . . .
<small>Date</small>

_____

_____

_____

How Did I Do?

Successes: _____

_____

_____

_____

Challenges: _____

_____

_____

Next steps: _____

_____

_____

OUR OBSERVATIONS ON THE CHAMPIONS

 Clip FG26. Erin Michels

Erin manages to shift deftly among different types of activities to quicken the pace while staying laser-focused on the objective. In ten minutes of instruction about a single problem, 2/5 + 3/8, she shifts students between three activities:

Independent practice. Erin asks students to solve the problem on their own, working independently on small whiteboards. As they finish, Erin asks them to show their answers to her.

Discussion. She then holds up one student's whiteboard, asking the class to reflect on their peer's thinking. "Talk to me," she says, and students raise their hands. When it becomes clear that some see errors in the model, she says she's "seeing people disagree. Turn and talk [technique 43] to your partner and explain why you disagree."

Guided practice/guided questioning. After a minute's discussion, she reconvenes the group and asks one student to begin analyzing the problem. Quickly, she engages others with rapid guided follow-up questions.

By shifting frequently between activity types (some up-tempo, others slower and more reflective), she adds mileposts to her lesson that contribute to an illusion of speed.

 Clip FG27. Jessica Bracey, Grade 5

Jessica creates the illusion of speed by moving between various muscle groups during a ten-minute stretch of instruction on *Circle of Gold.* The objective for the lesson is for students to make inferences about characters' motivations. Here is an outline of the activities Jessica shifts between and the amount of time she allots for each:

- Review where class left off in the novel—guided practice and interchange (1 min, 20 sec)
- *Control the Game* reading—knowledge assimilation (2 min, 30 sec)
- *Everybody Writes*—independent practice (3 min, 55 sec)
- Whole-class discussion—guided practice and interchange (5 min, 30 sec)
- *Control the Game* reading—knowledge assimilation (9 min, 20 sec)

Each shift between activities adds new mileposts, which creates the illusion of speed. It also gives Jessica a chance to engage and assess student understanding of the content through a variety of formats.

 Clip FG28. Ashley Hinton

Ashley works multiple muscle groups during a writing lesson to establish a sense of change while engaging students in rigorous content. Throughout this clip, students prepare for an independent writing task: a "show not tell" description of a person riding a roller coaster. Within just three to four minutes, Ashley moves them through discussion, reflection and idea generation, guided practice and interchange, and independent practice. Each shift adds a milepost that intensifies the illusion of speed. Ashley does this all without diluting the rigor of the content or distracting kids from the task. Incidentally, Ashley's effective pacing is also supported by tactics based on other pacing techniques (30, *Work the Clock,* and "clean start" from 28, *Brighten Lines*) and by pre-calling selected students to share especially juicy ideas; each new student share-out adds a milepost to the discussion.

Clip FG29. Bridget McElduff

Bridget shifts formats at various times while using guided practice/guided questioning to keep kids engaged during a lesson on measurement conversions. She divides up an oral review of the answers and shifts between the following three formats: First, she calls on a single student to report in rapid-fire fashion his answers to several problems. Next, she *Cold Calls* (technique 33) a wide range of students about other problems, asking them to share their answers, one per student, while moving around the room widely and quickly, narrating the sense of urgency she sees among them. When the timer goes off, she quickens the speed of her *Cold Calls* and raises the pitch of her voice in order to add to the sense of urgency and anticipation and keep the lesson "feeling fast." For yet another section, with momentum and energy high, she allows students to begin raising their hands to volunteer answers, which seems like a whole different activity. All this in what students might have experienced as a deadly dry lesson!

BRIGHTEN LINES

OVERVIEW

Brighten Lines works in concert with technique 27, *Change the Pace*. It ensures that students clearly perceive changes in activities or formats as well as the passing of other "mileposts," reference points within a lesson that mark the completion of a task or progress toward a goal. When students are more aware that activities and other events within a lesson have begun and ended, they perceive more to be happening, and a lesson can feel "fast"—even if it isn't.

To accomplish this sleight of hand, make beginnings and endings of activities visible and crisp via the "clean start" and the "clean finish." Some of our favorite teachers also add student interaction to these moments. We call these "interactive lines."

Reflection

How often do you notice signs among your students that they're not sensing forward progress in a lesson? What causes this? What tells you that students are feeling this way?

FUNDAMENTALS

Here's a brief expansion on the three key ideas:

Clean start. Shift from one activity to another with a simple, clear signal. Starting everyone on cue ("Go!") makes an activity seem like a special event or a race. In addition, you (and they) can see everyone else snap into action. This makes it more likely that they will too.

Clean finish. End a task in a similar way: crisply and cleanly to establish a clear and discernible transition point from one activity to the next. Make endings pop by counting down to the end, for example: "OK, I can't wait to hear about what you wrote in three-two-one and hands!"

Interactive lines. When the class passes a milepost—the beginning or end of an activity—you can build energy by letting the class take part in marking the event. You can do this verbally in set patterns of

Call and Response (technique 34). For example, the teacher counts down, "Three, two, one . . ." and the students respond in unison, "Done!" Or you can have students slap down their pencils energetically and on cue.

In line with building momentum through your pacing, the phrases you use to *Brighten Lines* will often focus on getting things moving and building a sense of urgency ("Let's take a minute to discuss in pairs. Ready? Go!"). Other times, by contrast, you may wish to signal the need to be more reflective. ("Three minutes to sort this out in your journals. [pause, then whispered] Begin.") Keep both uses— *urgency* and *reflection*—in mind as you apply the three key ideas.

Take a moment here to create some interactive lines you could use in the classroom. Think also about how you could introduce them to your students:

_____

_____

_____

ANALYZE A CHAMPION

▶ **Clip FG30. Sari Fromson, Grade 5**

How does Sari *Brighten Lines* during her lesson?

_____

_____

_____

_____

Compare your written insights with our observations at the end of this technique.

THE NEXT LEVEL

If you haven't already done so, try completing the "Pacing Case Studies," which you'll find in your library at my.teachlikeachampion.com. Or you could check them out as you work on technique 30 or 31.

Go through a lesson plan you're likely to use in the next week. Find several key activities during the lesson, and write a short script for beginning and ending the task in which you *Brighten Lines* at both beginning and end.

PRACTICE ALONE OR WITH COLLEAGUES

Brainstorm a list of phrases that you could use to establish clean starts and clean finishes that emphasize reflection and urgency. Record in the chart a few you personally favor. You'll know you're headed toward success when . . .

- Students find your cues for clean start and clean finish transitions clear, visible, and crisp.
- Your phrases emphasize reflection or urgency, according to the situation.

Line Brighteners

	Clean Start	Clean Finish
Phrases to emphasize urgency		
Phrases to emphasize reflection		

Practice at least one brightener of each kind alone or with a partner. Then imagine that your students started too fast on a certain *Brighten Lines* moment. Consulting technique 50, *Do It Again,* plan here how you would practice it again with the students.

_____

_____

_____

_____

With your partner, practice the *Do It Again.*

Reflection

For the class or classes and content you teach, when would you choose to deliver your clean start or finish phrases quickly versus slowly? Slowly versus quickly? Why?

_____

_____

_____

_____

_____

_____

_____

_____

ACTION PLANNING

Use this action planner to continue your work with *Brighten Lines*. (Find a printable version of this form at my.teachlikeachampion.com.) You'll know you're on track when your students join you in clean starts and finishes.

HOW AM I DOING?

_____

_____

Design one or more action steps for improvement. Decide on an interval by which you'll revisit this page to assess your progress.

Action Step 1

By when, with whom, and how you will measure your effort

By _____, I will . . .
   Date

_____

_____

How Did I Do?

Successes: _____

_____

_____

_____

Challenges: _____

_____

_____

_____

Next steps: _____

_____

_____

Action Step 2

By when, with whom, and how you will measure your effort

By _____, I will . . .

Date

_____

_____

_____

How Did I Do?

Successes: _____

_____

_____

_____

Challenges: _____

_____

_____

_____

Next steps: _____

_____

_____

_____

OUR OBSERVATIONS ON THE CHAMPION

 Clip FG30. Sari Fromson

The clip begins with Sari preparing her students for independent work time. Sari reinforces her expectations and engages her students with a *Call and Response* sequence to set her students up for success. To *Brighten Lines,* she sets a clean start when she whispers to her students, "Silently go to work." The whisper signals to the students that it is time to work quietly and that they should shift their energy down from their energetic *Call and Response.*

After four minutes, in which Sari has *Circulated* to track what her students are working on, she notices that her students have finished early, so she cuts the time short with a crisp, clean finish and a positive moment in which the students congratulate themselves with three "stadium claps" for their hard work. The stadium clap is an example of interactive lines because the clap signals that students are now transitioning to a new activity.

With the review process, Sari changes formats (technique 27, *Change the Pace*) by asking her students in a whisper to *Turn and Talk* on cue—another clean start. She then uses *Call and Response* interactive lines as a clean finish.

ALL HANDS

OVERVIEW

How and when students raise their hands is one of the most mundane and familiar aspects of teaching, and thus something we don't think about as deeply as we could. *All Hands* is the concept of managing how and when you ask your students to raise or refrain from raising their hands. It helps fulfill two purposes: *Changing the Pace* (technique 27) and increasing student focus.

Reflection

Consider a student who raises his (or her) hand to answer a question, and keeps it up throughout the duration of the discussion. What's on his mind? Why does he do it? And what does the behavior communicate to the rest of the class?

What would you prefer he be thinking about instead?

Write your answer before you read on.

Our thoughts about the student: We suspect she (or he) is thinking about the initial question for which she raised her hand. She's wondering when she will be called on, not about what peers are saying. She does it because she does not yet fully understand how collective an endeavor a discussion should be. Her behavior communicates boredom. We'd rather she were thinking about the ongoing discussion—what her peers are saying and how she'll develop her ideas.

FUNDAMENTALS

For Pacing and Focus

As a tool of *Change the Pace,* having students lower their hands after a question and raise them again for a new question creates mileposts, distinguishing between each question you ask, boosting energy, and increasing engagement.

All Hands can also increase *student focus.* When students have their hands raised while peers are talking, it's unlikely that they're listening to what those peers are saying. Asking students to put their hands down when others are speaking helps build listening habits that enable productive discussion.

Managing Participation to Include All Students and Maximize Mileposts

Mix modes. Encourage students to raise their hands—frequently. But balance taking hands with a bit of *Cold Call* and *Call and Response* (techniques 33 and 34) to make the process a bit unpredictable. Or vary the amount of *Wait Time* (technique 32) you allow, using long and short waits to make the process a little different each time.

Bright hands. Ensure that hands go down while someone is answering and back up at a new question. This will keep students focused, engaged, and listening more carefully to your questions and their peers' answers. It will also cause them to differentiate in their own minds each new question as a separate event, as opposed to a long blur of indistinguishable prompts for which their hand is permanently raised. Since this is a system you want to operate in your class all the time, make sure you explicitly introduce and explain your expectations, model and practice what you want it to look like, and reinforce constantly.

Unbundle and scatter. Break your questions up into smaller parts when you can (that is, "unbundle" them) and parcel out your questions to multiple students. This makes the pace feel quicker and increases the number of participants. Hint: frame this expectation in how you ask your question: "Who can tell me one cause of the Civil War?" or "What caused the Civil War? Tell me one reason," rather than "What caused the Civil War?"

Follow-on. To keep ideas alive, make your questions refer to or be contingent on a previous answer—for example, "Can you add to that, Katie?" "Develop Jasmine's idea, please . . . Jabari." Follow-ons cause students to listen carefully to their peers because they know they are as accountable for what their classmates have said as for what the teacher has said.

Cut off rally killers. Your lesson's pacing can be unintentionally sabotaged by a long-winded, meandering comment from a student at the wrong time. Using a stock phrase such as "Pause" or "Hold that thought" can help. You can tell students they've given the class some good ideas already that you're eager to talk about, and still keep it positive. "Ooh. Pause there. I want to give people a chance to respond to your use of the word 'anaerobic.'" Note how you can use this approach to also refocus the class on the most productive part of an answer: "Pause. Go back to that phrase, 'Maycomb's usual disease.' Let's focus on that."

ANALYZE THE CHAMPIONS

 Clip FG31. Bryan Belanger, Grade 8

 Clip FG32. Lauren Moyle, Grade 1

Using terms and ideas we discussed so far in the chapter, what are some similarities between Bryan's and Lauren's use of *All Hands*?

Some differences?

Bryan:

Lauren:

SCRIPTING AND PRACTICE ALONE OR WITH COLLEAGUES

Unbundle, Scatter, and Follow-On

Do this yourself first whether or not you'll be practicing with others. Prepare script questions using the chart here, thinking about how you would want to unbundle, scatter, and add follow-on questions for the next few rounds of practice. Use our questions or, on a blank sheet, substitute questions that you'll use in an upcoming lesson. Label them as unbundle, scatter, or follow-on.

Sample Questions	Your Script
Q: What are the three branches of federal government in the United States? A: Executive, judicial, and legislative	Example *(scatter/unbundle):* What is one branch of government? Example *(follow-on):* Tell me another, [student name].
What are the roles of the executive branch?	Example *(unbundle):* Tell me one role of the legislative branch. Example *(follow-on):* Tell me another. Example *(follow-on):* Give me an example of a specific action the president might take as part of that role.

Sample Questions	Your Script
Who holds office in the executive branch?	
What about the judicial branch?	

Planning Bright Hands

If you can, do this with a partner or group that responds in the role of *Students*. In the space here, plan how you're going to indicate hands up/hands down to your students. You can use verbal or nonverbal cues. Then practice using both, using questions that you scripted. The point is to practice switching seamlessly between taking hands and taking no hands. Consistency is key.

Success points:

- Clear, crisp cueing
- Speed, minimizing transaction costs

Verbal	Nonverbal
Example: *"Hands" or "Hands down."*	Example: *If I want hands, I raise my hand. If I don't, I gesture that I want hands down.*

Plan how you're going to roll out bright hands to your students. Students keep their hands up in nonproductive ways because we haven't thought to explain how and why they should do something different. Script how you want to describe it to them, explaining how and why.

Combine Questions and Hands

In another round of practice, parse out your questions into more bite-sized pieces and add follow-ons to create the illusion of speed. Also incorporate your bright-hands cues. As signs of success, shoot for

- Well-planned and scaffolded questions (starting very simply, adding complexity)
- Smoothly asking questions while managing hands

Prepare for Rally Killers

Script several things you could say to your students who provide long-winded answers that slow down pacing in your class. For example: "Pause. Let's focus on the first part of your answer." Then practice your questions, this time with the intent to cut off the rally killers.

Success points:

- Your phrase shows civility and positivity. The student is focused on content.
- Economy of language—you don't want to be a rally killer with your attempt to cut off a rally killer.

ACTION PLANNING

Use this action planner to continue your work with *All Hands*. (Find a printable version of this form at my.teachlikeachampion.com.) You know you're on the right track when . . .

- Your students are following your cues about raising or not raising hands.
- You're managing hands for pacing and mileposts.
- Hands don't linger in the air.
- Your "handiwork" and questioning mesh.

ALL HANDS

HOW AM I DOING?

_____

_____

Design one or more action steps for improvement. Decide on an interval by which you'll revisit this page to assess your progress.

Action Step 1

By when, with whom, and how you will measure your effort

By _____, I will . . .
<small>Date</small>

_____

_____

How Did I Do?

Successes: _____

_____

_____

_____

Challenges: _____

_____

_____

_____

Next steps: _____

_____

_____

_____

ALL HANDS

Action Step 2

By when, with whom, and how you will measure your effort

By _____, I will . . .
_{Date}

_____

_____

_____

How Did I Do?

Successes: _____

_____

_____

_____

Challenges: _____

_____

_____

Next steps: _____

_____

_____

OUR OBSERVATIONS ON THE CHAMPIONS

 Clip FG31. Bryan Belanger, and Clip FG32. Lauren Moyle

Bryan and Lauren both use the following *All Hands* techniques to maintain strong pacing:

Follow-on. Both frequently *Cold Call* students (technique 33) to respond to or build off points that are made during the discussion. This socializes students to closely track class discussions and, in doing so, draws their attention to mileposts.

Unbundle and scatter. Both break their questions into smaller parts and then scatter them across the room. This drives up participation ratio (see the part 3 techniques) and enables these teachers to quickly assess a wide sampling of students at different skill levels.

Mix modes. Both use a mix of taking hands, *Call and Response*, and *Cold Call* (techniques 33 and 34) to keep the energy level high and students engaged. They also provide students with a bit of *Wait Time* (technique 32) whenever necessary, which keeps the pace from becoming frenetic.

Lauren uses two *All Hands* methods that Bryan does not:

Cut off rally killers. More than once when she gets the answer she is looking for, she interrupts students rather than letting them continue on with information that is not crucial at that moment, which would slow the pace and could distract them from key points.

Bright hands. She alternates between *Call and Response* (repeating information and giving "props") and calling on individual students to keep all students participating frequently. She uses finger snaps and half-statements to cue students for a *Call and Response,* which minimizes the transaction costs of switching back and forth between individual and whole-group responses.

WORK THE CLOCK

OVERVIEW

Time is our greatest classroom resource. Given its scarcity, it's wise to manage it intentionally and to maximize learning and engagement in the classroom. Squandering minutes and seconds not only wastes the time currently at hand but signals more broadly that time just doesn't matter that much.

Reflection

How do you communicate the importance of time in the classroom? What are your best classroom moves or habits to preserve and protect time?

_____

_____

_____

    Are there times when you don't, but might? Where are your weak spots? Are there pitfalls to overdoing time management?

_____

_____

_____

    Possible thoughts (we're sure you've thought of others!): Setting time constraints not only helps students learn how to manage how much time to spend on certain activities but also disciplines you as a teacher to stay on track. Being transparent with how you allocate time can help students understand that you value it and will instill in them the importance of being attentive to time. Of course you can overdo it. One risk is not distinguishing valuing time from creating a classroom that feels rushed.

FUNDAMENTALS

Four Main Ideas

Show the clock. Make time visible to your students. Help them learn how to manage their time as well. There are many ways to do this: an online countdown timer, a kitchen timer projected on your document camera, or simply a large countdown digital timer are all ways to "show the clock." The ticking clock doesn't have to be present every second of the day, but the more your students know time matters and learn to manage it, the easier for you and the better for them.

Use specific, odd increments. Be specific about how long students have for an activity, and vary your time allocations. The variation (different times allocated to different activities) communicates your intentionality about time. It shows that you have chosen carefully just the right amount of time. Odd increments make this point implicitly. We often find at workshops that giving adults an eleven-minute break is more efficient than a ten-minute break because the latter sounds like an estimate, and people treat it accordingly.

Set goals. When you set time goals in your classroom, you can communicate a variety of messages to your students: that you want your students to accomplish things efficiently or, if you set a longer goal, that they should spend time thinking deeply and reflectively about content.

Use countdowns. Counting down is a great way to have a clean finish to an activity and *Brighten Lines.* Beware of excessively short or excessively long countdowns. Also beware of stretching the countdown and slowing it down when students are not successfully completing a task. Better to finish your countdown and say, "We didn't make it. Let's make sure to do that a little faster next time" than to stretch the countdown and make students think they did fine.

Audit and Plan

Right now, which of the four ideas are you using? Include notes about more you could do to *Work the Clock.* Use these responses in your action planning later.

To show the clock, what device are you currently using? Would some other device be more effective?

_____

_____

Are you specific about how long students have for an activity?

_____

Do you show precision by varying even short amounts of time you stipulate (not always five minutes—sometimes four or six)?

_____

Read each series of activities. Then decide if each activity deserves more than two minutes or less. Explain why and how much time each activity deserves.

1. *Turn and Talk* (technique 43) to a neighbor about what the conflict is in this passage.

_____

2. "Go back to the text. Reread the last two paragraphs and answer the following question: How does the author use symbolism to illustrate the theme of the text?"

_____

3. "Solve for the following: The division of a whole number N by 13 gives a quotient of 15 and a remainder of 2. Find N."

_____

4. "Simplify the fraction 8/100."

_____

Does your *Working the Clock* entail goals and specific tasks students should complete?

_____

Do you encourage your students to learn to manage time by setting up opportunities for them to complete multiple tasks during a block of independent time? For example, you might say, "I'm putting twenty minutes on the clock. In that time you need to edit your paragraph and complete your self-assessment."

_____

PRACTICE WITH A COLLEAGUE OR ALONE

Script solutions to the countdown challenges in the table, and practice alone or with a partner.

Countdown Challenges

Challenge	Solutions
Feeling you must stretch out the last number of your countdown: "Books away in four, three, two, and one . . ." (stretching "one" out over three seconds)	

WORK THE CLOCK

Challenge	Solutions
Counting down from too high a number: "Pencils down and eyes on me in ten, nine . . ."	
Counting down too slowly: "Three [hold], two-and-a-half [hold], two [hold], one-and-a-half [hold] . . ."	

In several upcoming lesson plans, note points at which you can *Work the Clock*.

MORE WITH A GROUP OR COLLEAGUE

Remember "Giving Feedback in Group Practice Activities" among the "Useful Tools" at my.teachlikeachampion.com.

Compare your current practices. Share knowledge of devices for timing and showing the time. Discuss changes you intend to make or hesitations you have about *Working the Clock*.

ACTION PLANNING

Use this action planner to continue your work with *Work the Clock*. (Find a printable version of this form at my.teachlikeachampion.com.) You know you're on the right track when . . .

- You show the clock and set specific increments of time in which students should complete a task.
- Your *Working the Clock* helps students become more efficient.
- Your *Working the Clock* adds energy to the lesson.

HOW AM I DOING?

Design one or more action steps for improvement. Decide on an interval by which you'll revisit this page to assess your progress.

Action Step 1

By when, with whom, and how you will measure your effort
By _____, I will . . .
_{Date}

How Did I Do?

Successes: _____

_____

_____

_____

Challenges: _____

_____

_____

_____

Next steps: _____

_____

_____

WORK THE CLOCK

Action Step 2

By when, with whom, and how you will measure your effort

By _____, I will . . .

Date

_____

_____

_____

How Did I Do?

Successes: _____

_____

_____

_____

Challenges: _____

_____

_____

Next steps: _____

_____

_____

EVERY MINUTE MATTERS

OVERVIEW

Spend each minute with your students as productively as possible.

Reflection

In your most recent week of classes, how many moments can you remember when you were with your students and they were academically idle? How much time would that likely add up to per year?

FUNDAMENTALS

Every Minute Matters means spending time with the greatest possible productivity. A good place to start is to attend to those everyday moments when time is squandered. Next, try to seize small intervals of time and put them to better use. Have thirty seconds when you are standing idly somewhere with your students—outside the art room, say? It's actually kind of fun to think of all the ways you could use those thirty seconds productively and how much your students could learn.

Revisit *Teach Like a Champion 2.0*

Doug's technique 31 discussion includes some thoughts on where those moments lie:

> at the end of class, when you're stuck in a hallway, while children are waiting for buses. Time spent waiting outside the cafeteria or by the flagpole during a fire drill is a perfect time for a vocabulary review. Packing up backpacks at the end of the day is a great opportunity for reading aloud from an inspiring novel. There's no better way to keep kids engaged while lining up for the next class than by peppering them with multiplication problems and mental math. You can, in short, always be teaching. . . .
>
> Waiting with a group of his students outside his classroom for the rest of the class to arrive, [history teacher Jamey Verrilli] begins quizzing students on their vocabulary:
>
> - "What does it mean to be 'bound' to do something?"
> - "Can you use it in a sentence, John?"
> - "Who would have been bound to the land in a Middle Ages town?"
> - "What are you bound to be doing right now?"
>
> The students are standing in a line in the hallway just outside his classroom. Class has not even started yet. Not in the classroom, not during class time, and Jamey doesn't care: there's learning to be done. Meanwhile, his students are excited, smiling, happy to be engaged, and showing off their knowledge.

Revisit the book for more rich examples.

Even though downtime is often unpredictable, a bit of planning can help you keep productive ideas at the ready . . . in your "back pocket," you might say:

Back-pocket questions. Have a set of back-pocket questions ready to go. They can live on real note cards in a pocket or as mental ones. Create the questions periodically in advance, aligned with key objectives for your current units. These questions are perfect to reinforce previously taught content that you can strategically spiral-review throughout your day.

Back-pocket activities. Also plan high-value activities that students can complete autonomously—for example, *Control the Game* (technique 23) or written responses to planned back-pocket questions.

Look forward. Set your students up for success by hinting at the task that is to come. Mild suspense and anticipation can create positive tension and excitement while providing time for students to prepare for the activity.

> **blog**
>
> Find this blog post at teachlikeachampion.com/blog/clip-week-megan-broome-makes -routines-academic/.
>
> It's called "Clip of the Week: Megan Broome Makes Her Routines Academic." See how deliberately champion teacher Megan plans her day so that *Every Minute Matters.*

Reflection

Outside actual classroom teaching time, at what other times are you in contact with your students and could have some academically related interaction?

_____

_____

THE NEXT LEVEL

For the next few days, keep track of the idle moments in your students' day. Write them down as they happen and try to estimate their length. Then think about the three most productive academic topics your students could work on. Plan three minutes' worth of back-pocket questions and activities for them.

Modify these back-pocket questions and activities to fit the different time increments and settings you observed

Share your ideas with a partner and then evaluate again after you've tried some of them out in the classroom.

ACTION PLANNING

Use this action planner to continue your work with *Every Minute Matters.* (Find a printable version of this form at my.teachlikeachampion.com.) You know you're on the right track when you're keeping students actively learning throughout more and more of their time with you.

HOW AM I DOING?

_____

_____

Design one or more action steps for improvement. Decide on an interval by which you'll revisit this page to assess your progress.

Action Step 1

By when, with whom, and how you will measure your effort
By _____, I will . . .
Date

_____

_____

How Did I Do?

Successes: _____

_____

_____

_____

Challenges: _____

_____

_____

_____

Next steps: _____

_____

_____

_____

Action Step 2

By when, with whom, and how you will measure your effort

By _____, I will . . .
<small>Date</small>

_____

_____

_____

How Did I Do?

Successes: _____

_____

_____

_____

_____

Challenges: _____

_____

_____

_____

Next steps: _____

_____

_____

WAIT TIME

OVERVIEW

After asking a question, the average teacher waits about a second before taking an answer. While there will be times in which a quick response is most appropriate, for the most part, these answers are unlikely to bring out the best in your students. Using more *Wait Time* allows students time to think before answering a question and creates conditions in which all students can participate.

Reflection

How's your *Wait Time*? How do you know? What challenges do you notice when trying to use more *Wait Time* in the classroom?

_____

_____

_____

FUNDAMENTALS

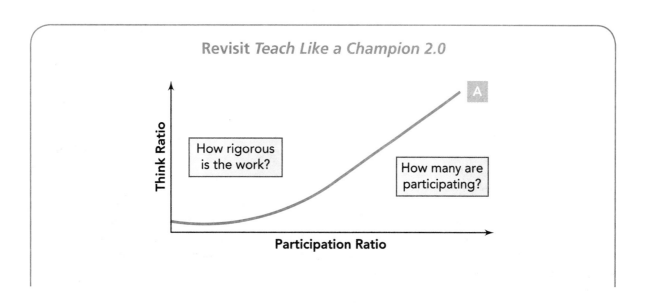

Revisit *Teach Like a Champion 2.0*

> The main aim of *Wait Time* (and the other techniques in this chapter) is to build two kinds of ratio. Look again at this figure from Doug's introduction to chapter 7, Building Ratio through Questioning. About it, he writes:
>
> > We've all seen the lesson where the teacher gets a keen workout at the front of the room. She explains why the chapter is so critical to the novel, and some ways you might interpret it. . . . Meanwhile, students' primary activity is to "listen"—something they're not very active in doing and not very accountable for. By contrast, in a lesson with *ratio,* the workout belongs to students: they are constantly on their toes answering questions, drawing on their knowledge base, reflecting, and refining their ideas.
> >
> > Ideally, every time you ask a question, every student tries to answer, and you ask a lot of questions. Still, it's important to recognize that you could have a lesson with lots of engaged and active student participation, but not much rigor. Your lesson could have fifty interactions that engage students actively but superficially. . . . Although participation is necessary, it is insufficient by itself. Participation must be rigorous, too. . . .
> >
> > [Suppose I had] a deep and demanding discussion of the role of class and caste in *To Kill a Mockingbird* with a handful of engaged, insightful students, while the rest of the class essentially watched passively. My lesson would have a very high think ratio, but not much participation ratio. Of course, you need both: full and energetic participation from everyone, and work that is rigorous and demanding. . . . When you seek ratio, . . . seek to be high on both axes [of the figure]— somewhere like point A.

Effective *Wait Time* relies, in many ways, on an effective culture in your classroom—one where students want to answer questions, expect to share their ideas when they have them, and know what to do during silence to develop and refine ideas. Here are four ways you can build a culture that makes *Wait Time* work:

1. *Narrate hands.* If students expect to participate after being given *Wait Time,* they will use that time far more actively. You can help make participation the expectation by "narrating hands," encouraging and reinforcing hand raising when you see it start. You might simply count the raised hands aloud: "Three, four, five hands. Now I've got eight . . ." Or you might offer more praise: "I'm starting to see those hands. Some brave folks who might not be sure they have it but aren't afraid to try." Sometimes you can even tell students to put their hands down at first—"No hands right now. I want you to take all fifteen seconds to find the answer in the text." And then say, "OK, now hands!"

2. *Prompt thinking skills.* Just because you give *Wait Time* does not necessarily mean students will know how to use it! Teach students how to use *Wait Time* by providing guidance about how to maximize the time you give them. You can really shape the culture of how your students view their work with the way you prompt their thinking skills, so think carefully about what you want to say. Some prompts you might give:

   "I'm seeing people thinking deeply and jotting down thoughts. I'll give everyone a few more seconds to do that."

   "If you're not sure, flip back to your notes from yesterday."

   "I'm going to give everyone a bit more time to think deeply about this question. Your initial answer may not be the best answer."

   "I'm waiting in case someone can connect this scene to another play. *Macbeth*?"

3. *Make* Wait Time *transparent.* Let's say you decided that a tough question you were asking warranted twenty to thirty seconds of *Wait Time.* If your students didn't know you were going to give them that much time, they might finish their thinking in four or five seconds and merely wait out the last twenty-five expecting you to call time. It can help, then, to let students know when you intend to give them more than a handful of seconds of *Wait Time* so that they can learn to manage their time accordingly. Examples:

   "This is a hard question. I'll give you twenty to thirty seconds to reflect."

"You're thinking about this for ten seconds before you write down your answer."

"This question is difficult. Take some time . . . think *before* you raise your hand."

4. *Give real think time.* This last step is simple: make sure to provide real sequences of silence. This is critical because the three other actions described here require you to interrupt student thinking. It's important to balance that with *real uninterrupted think time.* This can be difficult, but it's important to build your self-discipline. Count to yourself or walk around your classroom or simply use a timer. It's also important to note that more rigorous questions with complex answers will require more think time than simpler questions.

"I'll start taking answers in ten seconds."

"Hands down. We're thinking."

"You can use this time to think in writing."

". . ." (silence)

ANALYZE THE CHAMPIONS

▶ Clip FG33. Maggie Johnson, Grade 8

▶ Clip FG34. Yasmin Vargas, Grade 1, and Jon Ratheram, Grade 10

View the clips, answer the following questions, and compare your observations with ours at the end of this technique.

In clip FG33, what's effective about Maggie's use of *Wait Time*? How does she give her students real think time?

_____

_____

_____

Compare Yasmin's and Jon's *Wait Times.* In particular, what do you notice about how each teacher narrates hands?

_____

_____

_____

_____

THE NEXT LEVEL

Even though *Wait Time* is a simple idea, it's hard to do in a busy classroom. When the clock is ticking away on your forty-five precious minutes, it may seem counterintuitive to discipline yourself to wait. However, ensuring self-discipline for you and your students is a key challenge that will ultimately benefit your students immensely. We think of disciplining yourself to use *Wait Time* in three categories:

Teacher self-discipline. We often intend to wait. We even think we've waited when in fact we are rushing ahead. Making yourself slow down when you need to is a key part of this technique. In a moment, we'll ask you to brainstorm some ways you could do that.

Student self-discipline. Your students too want to race ahead sometimes. During your six seconds of precious *Wait Time,* they might call out an answer, preventing their peers from thinking. (We'll also ask you to brainstorm solutions for getting students to slow down.)

Student diligence. Students should be thinking deeply rather than peripherally. They need to be using all of the time available rather than deciding on an answer and spending the remaining time looking out the window. That too will require some solutions.

Here, supplement our examples with your own solutions to three common obstacles teachers face when using *Wait Time.*

Challenge to *Wait Time*	Solutions
Teacher self-discipline: the need to slow *yourself* down.	Example: *Count in your head or out loud.*
Student discipline: the need to slow students down (vs. raising their hands when they don't really even know what they want to say)	Example: *Avoid consistently taking the first hand; ask students to put their hands back down until ...*
Wait Time diligence: the need to maximize the quality of the *Wait Time* by teaching students to use it well.	Example: *Maintain a list of things you want to socialize during Wait Time: "Checking your notes," say, or "Challenging yourself to take a risk."*

Find this blog post at teachlikeachampion.com/blog/implementing-wait-time-guest-post-charlie-friedman/.

For more insights, go to "Implementing *Wait Time*: Guest Post by Charlie Friedman."

WAIT TIME

ANALYZE A CHAMPION

 Clip FG35. Rue Ratray, Grade 6

To prepare for the next activity, watch this clip with a colleague. What do you notice about Rue's tone and delivery? How might it impact his use of *Wait Time*? Compare your notes with ours at the end.

WITH A COLLEAGUE, WATCH AND PRACTICE

With a colleague, build on what you just observed in clip FG35. Focus on slowing down your delivery of questions in order to start to build muscle memory for *Wait Time*.

1. In "Questions for *Wait Time* Practice," script two questions that you might ask in an upcoming lesson. Also plan *how* you'll ask them.
2. In three rounds in the presence of a partner, ask the questions, emphasizing a slow and reflective tone in each round:
   Round 1. Teach from the front of the class.
   Round 2. Circulate at a slow, stately pace.
   Round 3. Call your shot. What do you want to focus on in this round of practice?

   Success points:

   - Your students know how to spend their *Wait Time*.
   - Your *Wait Time* is proportional to the rigor of your question.
   - You've allowed your students adequate think time by disciplining your teacher actions.

Questions for *Wait Time* Practice

(Example) *Question you will ask*: **How does Scout's internal monologue show her innocence?**
How you'll keep self-discipline to slow down and maximize reflection:
I will slow my pace and take ten steps before calling on a student.
Your first question:

To slow down and maximize reflection:

Your second question:

_____

To slow down and maximize reflection?

_____

_____

ACTION PLANNING

Use this action planner to continue your work with *Wait Time.* (Find a printable version of this form at my.teachlikeachampion.com.) You know you're on the right track when you . . .

- Delay at least three or four seconds before taking an answer much of the time.
- Make *Wait Time* explicit.
- Stop your own talk to give students real think time.
- Narrate hands as they go up.
- Remember to teach students how to use *Wait Time* productively.

HOW AM I DOING?

Design one or more action steps for improvement. Decide on an interval by which you'll revisit this page to assess your progress.

Action Step 1

By when, with whom, and how you will measure your effort
By _____ , I will . . .
Date

How Did I Do?

Successes: _____

Challenges: _____

Next steps: _____

Action Step 2

By when, with whom, and how you will measure your effort

By _____, I will . . .

<small>Date</small>

_____

_____

_____

How Did I Do?

Successes: _____

_____

_____

_____

Challenges: _____

_____

_____

_____

Next steps: _____

_____

_____

OUR OBSERVATIONS ON THE CHAMPIONS

 Clip FG33. Maggie Johnson

Maggie facilitates a discussion about a section of text from the novel the class is reading: *To Kill a Mockingbird*. She uses *Wait Time* to give students time to process her question and to foster motivation and enthusiasm to participate. It also encourages students to engage in deep thinking during a discussion.

In the first cut, she waits about five seconds between asking her question and taking a hand. Soon after she asks the question, she scans the room and raises her eyebrows and smiles. This bit of inviting warmth motivates even more students to participate. The result: within four seconds, we see eight students' hands go up

In the second cut, she uses even longer *Wait Time* (twelve seconds) before taking a hand. Note her strategic movement to the right-hand corner of the room (we call it "Pastore's Perch" in technique 51, *Radar/Be Seen Looking*). This makes it easier for her to see students whose hands go up and for those students to see her looking for their hands as well. She then uses an obvious scan to draw attention to the fact that she's looking, which enhances the accountability.

Note also her use of *Wait Time* as an opportunity to reinforce academic skills: "Great. And if you're looking in your book, make sure you pause and track Arshe." In doing so, she reinforces the expectation that students should track peers during discussion and encourages more students to revisit the text. The result: several students eagerly raise their hands to participate.

In the third cut, Maggie waits eight seconds before taking a hand. During her *Wait Time,* she again moves to Pastore's Perch and uses what we call a "swivel" (a left-to-right turn of her head) to ensure that she is *Seen Looking* for raised hands. Again, she warmly invites students into the discussion by smiling and raising her eyebrows as she looks around. The result: nine students' hands shoot up.

 Clip FG34. Yasmin Vargas and Jon Ratheram

Both teachers narrate hands to encourage participation after *Wait Time* during a lesson. After Yasmin asks her question ("How can we use compromise to think about what happened in this part of the story?"), notice that she pauses and takes a couple of steps to wait for her students. She then narrates hands, "One, two, three people are thinking . . . more . . . ooh, almost half the class is thinking." She pauses again, then calls on a student.

After Jon poses a question to check for understanding, he uses motivational *Wait Time* to boost the participation in his classroom. ("You've spotted it . . . you've spotted it. More. Good. Nice!") In pointing out that some have "spotted it" and narrating the hands that go up, he builds momentum and motivates kids to try to figure out what "it" is. With each second that ticks by, more and more hands go up. He then positively yet subtly acknowledges the up-tick in participation by adding, "Nice." He doesn't flatter or gush, but merely tips his hat. After giving students *Wait Time,* Jon *Cold Calls* one of the few students who doesn't have her hand up. In doing so, he maximizes the value of his check, exposing a misunderstanding.

 Clip FG35. Rue Ratray

In this reading lesson, Rue leads students in a literary discussion about *The Giver.* After posing a rigorous question ("What can we infer about how Jonas's father feels about what he did?"), he pauses for several seconds. Instead of taking a hand, he then sends students off into a *Turn and Talk* so that they can continue to refine their thinking.

Rue speaks with a soft, barely audible tone of voice and with a slow, deliberate cadence that encourages students to carefully consider his question. He then keeps think ratio high by quietly reminding students to "think" as he slowly scans the room.

After posing the question, Rue pauses his movement and gestures, as if to signal to students that nothing is more important than the question he just asked. His use of quiet power (see *Strong Voice,* technique 56) ensures that students get real think time and that he doesn't interrupt the thread of students' thought processes. Rue is so effective at socializing students to use *Wait Time* to truly think that we don't see a single hand go up prematurely.

Rather than take hands after the *Wait Time,* Rue capitalizes on students' eagerness to answer this critical question by sending them into a *Turn and Talk* (technique 43), during which he moves into Pastore's Perch and slowly swivels his head to *Be Seen Looking* for follow-through.

COLD CALL

OVERVIEW

Cold Call means calling on students regardless of whether they have raised their hands or not. Among all of the techniques in this book, it is perhaps the one that can most help you achieve rapid changes in the rigor, ratio, and level of expectations in your classroom.

Here are four things *Cold Call* can help you do:

Check for understanding. It is difficult to know whether your students have learned what you've taught. When gathering data on what students have learned, you will get a more accurate assessment when you call on all students in your classroom rather than only those who raise their hands.

Maintain the expectation that everyone participates and is engaged. Normalizing *Cold Call* in your classroom creates a culture of engaged accountability. The expectation becomes that any student might be called on at any moment to share his or her answer or opinion. This means that raising your hand signals a desire to add to the conversation; it no longer controls whether or not you will participate in a lesson.

Manage pacing. Cold Calls can increase efficiency and build momentum when you question students. You can avoid wasting time, no longer waiting for sufficient numbers of students to offer to answer, and this can bring energy and a quick pace to a class. Interestingly, though, *Cold Calling* can then help you slow things down as well—for example, "Hands down for now. I'll call on a few of you in a minute. For now I want you to think and reflect."

Increase think ratio and participation ratio. See technique 32 about this concept. You can ensure that all students are engaged and ready to answer. And you can ensure their engagement in your most reflective, deep thinking activities if you "backstop" them with *Cold Call,* letting students know, for example, that you plan to *Cold Call* after a *Turn and Talk* (technique 43) or a bit of writing or other independent work.

Reflection

Do you *Cold Call* in your classroom? How do you approach it? When has it been successful, and when has it been a challenge? Why?

_____

_____

_____

_____

FOUR FUNDAMENTALS

Keep It Positive

Cold Call with a smile. Express sincere interest in the answers you get. Clearly convey to your students that you want them to be successful when you *Cold Call* them. Praise them when they crush it. Remember that it is an academic technique that engages all students in the discourse of your classroom. Ask them rigorous and worthy questions. Through *Cold Calling,* you may even benefit students who know the answer but for social reasons are hesitant to volunteer. A couple of ways to do that:

- Make sure that you never use it as a "gotcha" moment or to chasten a student. You don't want to confuse an invitation to participate with a correction or a consequence.
- Use an upbeat tone, and ask your question suggesting that you couldn't imagine a world in which a student would not want to participate. If you're worried that a student might be anxious, then start with a simpler question as an entry point to establish comfort before following on with a more substantive question.
- As you can imagine, you have a lot to think about when *Cold Calling*; set yourself and your students up for success by planning your exact questions verbatim in your lesson planning process, knowing what an exemplary response would be. That will make it easier for you to tweak the question as necessary depending on the student.
- Praise success—it's a challenge to respond when you hadn't prepared to. An important one to master, but a tricky one nonetheless. So let the positive feedback flow.
- Let students reinforce each other. In some classrooms, students snap to show approval of a good answer when a classmate is *Cold Called.* This can make students feel really good when they succeed. Alternatively in those same rooms, students "send magic" (via a nonverbal gesture) to support students while they think. Smirking or scoffing at a student who has been *Cold Called* would never, ever be countenanced.

Keep It Predictable

Keep *Cold Call* predictable by using it reliably, and often early in a class. The more accustomed students are to being *Cold Called,* the more they see it coming, the more they will anticipate it and be engaged in the class even before you start to use it. So be up front: don't use *Cold Call* to surprise your students, as this can leave them feeling caught off guard and ambushed. Students will be left wondering why the teacher did that, rather than focusing on the actual question.

Make It Systematic

Intentionally include all students in your *Cold Calls.* Keeping *Cold Calling* universal sets the expectation that it isn't personal—it's coming to everyone in the room at some point. Tips for making *Cold Call* systematic:

- *Cold Call* students in batches so that it doesn't seem as though you're singling out a particular student.
- Call on students from all around the room.
- Be careful not to *Cold Call* in response to any particular student behavior; for example, don't *Cold Call* students who look as though they might not be listening. In fact, try a few "look-away" *Cold Calls*: call on someone behind your back. This shows that nothing you "saw" in a student's demeanor "caused" the *Cold Call.*

Unbundle It

Maximize the participation ratio by breaking up your question into a series of smaller questions, and pose them to multiple students (technique 2, *Targeted Questioning*). This can increase the pace in your classroom and create the culture of peer-to-peer accountability, as students will have to listen closely to one another.

> Find this blog post at teachlikeachampion.com/blog/recipe-making-cold-call-feel-positive/. It's called "Recipe for Making *Cold Call* Feel Positive." Among other insights, it gives some advice about how you can gradually build up the rigor of questions you ask in *Cold Call.*

ANALYZE A CHAMPION

 Clip FG36. Jon Bogard, Grade 9

What is effective about Jon's *Cold Calling*? In particular, how does he keep it positive?

_____

_____

_____

THE NEXT LEVEL

> **Revisit *Teach Like a Champion 2.0***
>
> When you *Cold Call*, you can still allow students who wish to participate to raise their hands. Strike whatever balance you wish by choosing some hands for certain questions and *Cold Calling* for others. In contrast, you could tell students to keep their hands down. For a more in-depth look at the advantages and limitations of using either, revisit Doug's tables about them under this technique.

Follow-On as Follow-Up

Ask your students to develop one another's answers by asking follow-on and follow-up questions or prompts. ("Therese, expand on Tony's point." "Develop that further, Ashley." "Marco, tell us where you agree or disagree with Kim's account.") This can create a culture in which students listen to their classmates as carefully as they listen to their teacher.

Timing the Name

In a *Cold Call,* it matters when you choose to say the name of the student. The most common and effective approach is to ask the question, pause, and then say the name of the student. When you call on the student and say his or her name *before* you ask your *Cold Call* question, you risk having the rest of the students not following along and answering the question in their heads, thus missing an opportunity to do the cognitive work. (Of course there are sometimes good reasons to do that.)

Place	Effect
"Darren, tell us one cause of World War I, please."	Allows Darren to prepare to hear the question, and may work well at first for a student with less strong command of English, say, but it also lets all others off the hook. They don't even need to catch the question.
"Darren" *(pause),* "tell us one cause of World War I, please."	May allow Darren more time to get set for the question, but does he even know one is coming? Slows down the class and potentially wastes time for everyone else.
"Tell us one cause of World War I, please, Darren."	May catch Darren short and may fail to give other students sufficient time to think and answer internally.
"Tell us one cause of World War I, please" *(pause),* "Darren."	*Best general effect.* During the pause, all begin to answer the question in their heads, in case they might be called. Darren then gets called on to say his answer aloud. Others mentally (or aloud) add their answer to his.

You can also *pre-call*—that is, tell a student to expect to be called on later in the lesson. You can pre-call privately before class or publicly during class:

"Latisha, be ready for when we review the stages of the water cycle!"
"Karen knows I'm coming to her when we get to the subject of Lincoln's goals for the proclamation!"

How might specific approaches we've described here expand what you've generally done in class?

_____

_____

_____

ROLL IT OUT

Revisit *Teach Like a Champion 2.0*

Consider this suggestion from Doug's "Reflection and Practice" in the conclusion of chapter 7.

Take a lesson plan for a class you're getting ready to teach, and mark it up by identifying three places where it would be beneficial to use *Cold Call.* Script your questions and write them into your lesson plan. Make some notes about which students you'll *Cold Call.*

If you haven't yet begun to use *Cold Call*, prepare an introduction for it that you might deliver to your students. In it you might cover:

- What *Cold Calling* is
- Its rationale
- Who will be called on (for example, hands-up vs. hands-down)
- How students should respond if they are called on
- Particular times, if any, students should expect to get *Cold Called*

Also consider the following:

- What do you expect will be challenging about introducing *Cold Call* to your students?
- If you are doing so in the middle of a term, what might you need to say about that?
- What objections, if any, might you need to field from students?
- What ways can you think of to be most effective in introducing its systematic nature? Its predictability? Its positive nature? Possible scaffolding?

Here's the introductory speech Colleen Driggs gave her fifth graders one year.

In some of your classes, your teachers do something called Cold Calling. In fact, I do it. It's when you don't raise your hand and a teacher calls on you, just to see what you know. And it's not like a "gotcha"; it's really just a way to do a quick review. I don't call it Cold Calling, though; I call it "hot calling" because you get a chance to shine and to show that you are on fire. So almost every day when we're talking about genre we're going to do hot calling. It's a great way to review all of these definitions and terms that we've learned.

Here's the hardest part about hot calling: you've got to keep your hands down. Your hands are folded, and I will call on a person. When I call on that person, you track just like you normally do and then you track me when you hear my voice again. Nod if you understand. Nod if you are ready for hot calling. Beautiful. Keep your hands down. Please don't call out. Sit up. Remember SLANT.

What is the definition of genre? Hands down. Robert . . .

Draft your own rollout here:

_____

_____

_____

_____

_____

_____

_____

_____

_____

COLD CALL

ANOTHER CHAMPION

▶ Clip FG37. Beth Verrilli, Grade 12

How does Beth's *Cold Calling* add to what we've discussed so far? How does *Cold Calling* affect her classroom culture?

_____

_____

_____

_____

_____

_____

_____

_____

_____

_____

ACTION PLANNING

Use this action planner to continue your work with *Cold Call*. (Find a printable version of this form at my.teachlikeachampion.com.) You know you're on the right track when . . .

- Your students anticipate being called on and engage accordingly.
- You unbundle questions and involve everyone.
- You keep it upbeat.

HOW AM I DOING?

_____

_____

Design one or more action steps for improvement. Decide on an interval by which you'll revisit this page to assess your progress.

Action Step 1

By when, with whom, and how you will measure your effort

By _____, I will . . .
<small>Date</small>

_____

_____

How Did I Do?

Successes: _____

_____

_____

_____

Challenges: _____

_____

_____

_____

Next steps: _____

_____

_____

Action Step 2

By when, with whom, and how you will measure your effort

By _____, I will . . .

Date

_____

_____

_____

How Did I Do?

Successes: _____

_____

_____

_____

Challenges: _____

_____

_____

_____

Next steps: _____

_____

_____

OUR OBSERVATIONS ON THE CHAMPIONS

 Clip FG36. Jon Bogard

Jon reviews finding the area of a rectangle that has sides that are made up of algebraic equations. It is clear from the beginning that his students are used to being *Cold Called* and are ready to answer his questions.

- Jon keeps things positive. He playfully feigns ignorance so that his students can "turn the tables" by correcting *him*. Then, right after the class says he is wrong, Jon *Cold Calls* on Terry to explain. His playfulness sets the mood for his *Cold Call*. It's not punitive or laborious—it's intended to be fun, game-like, and inviting.
- Notice Jon's positive reinforcement after answers. These contribute to his warm tone: "Good"; "That is exactly right." John seamlessly *Cold Calls* his students after quick empowering compliments.
- Jon has pretaught his kids "snap" to celebrate peers when they get the answers right. Anticipating that things can go wrong for them in *Cold Call,* he's taught them to also snap for someone who's struggling, then send that person some magic.
- Jon *Cold Calls* his first students by simply asking them to provide basic information about the irregular rectangle. (What are the dimensions? What is the other piece of information?) They all know the answer. He's engaging them and helping them feel successful at the outset, Notice how John's questions build on one another from the beginning. This helps ensure students' continued success.
- Unbundling also helps Jon build up to greater rigor. He first begins with questions that are answered directly in the problem, then moves to those that are more challenging. Note the way he gives students longer *Wait Time* for those.

 Clip FG37. Beth Verrilli

As Beth leads a discussion about the text, *Othello,* she takes care to

Time the name. In the clip, she switches back and forth between question-pause-name and name-pause for a couple of reasons:
    To build a *culture of engaged accountability* in her classroom so that all students know they must do the cognitive work—because she may call on them at any time.
    So that her *pacing* throughout this clip feels fast. Her *Cold Calling* is seamlessly inserted into the discussion of this rigorous text.
Be systematic. She calls on many students, all over the classroom.
Be positive and predictable. It's clear that her students are ready for her *Cold Calling* and welcome it, which shows that Beth took time to make sure her students knew that *Cold Calling* is a part of the culture of the classroom.
Unbundle. She uses *Cold Calling* to clarify the larger, more complex themes of the text.

CALL AND RESPONSE

OVERVIEW

Call and Response means using group choral response to build energetic, positive engagement. You ask (call); the students answer (respond) in unison.

There are three uses of *Call and Response* in particular:

- To emphasize and reinforce academic content. After a great comment or correct answer, you can "stamp the learning" by having students repeat it. Or you can show how much you valued a student answer by asking the class to repeat it. *Call and Response* is also effective for reinforcing definitions and pronunciation.
- To invigorate and energize the class with active participation and spirited engagement. It can be fun for students when it's done well.
- To increase engagement by supporting techniques you use to emphasize energetic pacing and build a culture of crisp, timely, positive follow-through.

Call and Response can help your class in a variety of ways. But it's important to remember that it's not a good way to check for understanding and that poor execution can undercut its effectiveness.

Reflection

How much *Call and Response* do you use in class right now? Try to cite at least one recent instance related to each of the three broad purposes.

_____

_____

_____

_____

_____

ANALYZE THE CHAMPIONS

▶ Clip FG38. Janelle Austin, Grade 00

▶ Clip FG39. Jennifer Trapp, Grade 00

View the videos and answer the following questions. Then compare your observations with ours at the end of this technique.

In each clip, which of the three purposes is being served by *Call and Response*?

Janelle Austin:

_____

_____

Jennifer Trapp:

_____

_____

Does each teacher mix *Cold Call* and *Call and Response*? If so, where and possibly why?

Janelle Austin:

_____

_____

_____

Jennifer Trapp:

_____

_____

_____

FUNDAMENTALS

Types of *Call and Response*

Many teachers use only a simplistic form of *Call and Response*—asking students to repeat aphorisms and chants. In fact, there are five levels of *Call and Response* interaction, listed here roughly in order of increasing intellectual rigor.

Repeat

You heard this in clip FG39. Students repeat what their teacher has said or complete a familiar phrase the teacher started. The topic can be behavioral or academic:

"When we see a . . ." "*Preposition!*" "We look for . . ." "*Its object!*"

Report

Students are asked to report the answers to problems or questions they've worked out at their seats. This method lets you more energetically reinforce academic work once it's been completed.

"Tell me your answer to problem number 1 on two. One, two!"

Reinforce

You can reinforce new information or a strong answer by asking the class to repeat it. This method gives everyone additional active interaction with critical new content. And the student who provides the original information sees that his or her answer was so important that you asked the whole class to repeat it.

"Can anyone tell me what this part of the expression is called? Yes, Trayvon, that's the exponent. Class, what's it called?"

Review

Students review answers or information from earlier in the class (or unit).

"What did we say we did to a number when we multiplied it by itself?"
"Who was the first person Theseus met on the road to Athens, class?"
"Who was the second person?"
"And now who's the third?"

Solve

The teacher asks students to solve a problem in real time and call out the answer in unison.

"If the length is ten inches and the width is twelve inches, the area of our rectangle must be how many square inches, class?!"

In-Cues

One of the keys to effective *Call and Response* is having all students respond in unison. An "in-cue" helps make that happen. It signals clearly when to respond and makes it clear you are asking for choral answers rather than taking hands or choosing an individual. In-cues take various forms, each with its own advantages.

Group Name In-Cues

Group name in-cues ("class," "everybody") help foster group identity:

"Who was the first commander in chief of the Continental Army? Everybody!"
"Class! What's pi to the first three digits?"

One benefit of this type of cue is that you can repeat it quickly and simply if all students do not respond: "*Everybody,* please. Who was the first commander in chief of the Continental Army?"

Count-Based In-Cues

A (very) short countdown gives students a second to get ready and can ensure coordination. This can be especially helpful when you are first using *Call and Response*: "Let me hear your answers on two!"

We don't recommend a countdown longer than two. Using more wastes time and loses some of the energy and momentum of *Call and Response*. Instead, count quickly and with positive energy.

Many teachers begin with a count-based in-cue to ensure that *Call and Response* works smoothly from the outset. Then they replace it with a simpler cue.

Gestural In-Cues

Consistent nonverbal in-cues can be quick, even graceful, and noninterruptive: pointing, dropping a raised hand, finger gestures or snaps; finger to ear for "call" and hand extended to class for "response." But keep them and your expression away from "schoolmarmish," by adding a smile, say.

Shift in Tone and Volume

Over the long run, this is often the best and most natural cue for a class that's well accustomed to *Call and Response*. The teacher simply increases the volume in the last few words of a sentence and inflects his tone to imply a question.

Teachers who have mastered *Call and Response* perform this feat seamlessly, effectively, and naturally, but it is the trickiest in-cue and can be prone to error the first times you try it. So consider practicing first or beginning with something simpler and working up to it when you and your class are ready.

Practicing Cues

Here are a few sample questions for which you might use *Call and Response*. Read them through in sequence and practice speaking them aloud as if you were teaching and wanted a choral response.

One challenge to *Call and Response* can be doing it in series—that is, four or five or six times in sequence with pacing and energy—so try to read them all through at once as if you were teaching.

In fact, try this several times. The first time through, cue your students using a group name or count-based cue such as "On two. One, two!" The next time through, try to cue only with voice inflection or a gesture. The third time through, alternate asking a specific student to answer on even-numbered questions and asking for *Call and Response* (in whatever format feels most natural) on odd-numbered questions. If you can, find a partner to answer as if he or she was your student.

1. What do we call it when water changes from a liquid to a gas? [evaporation]
2. OK, so when water evaporates from oceans, lakes, and other bodies of water, where does it go? [into the atmosphere, or just the atmosphere]
3. But remember we also talked about water evaporating from plants. What's that specific form of evaporation called? [transpiration]
4. And remind me, when water is carried in gas form in the air, it is called what? [water vapor]
5. When water vapor reaches the atmosphere, it undergoes what process? [condensation]
6. Yes—and the common name for visible masses of condensed water in the atmosphere is? [clouds]
7. Good, and the term for water when it leaves the atmosphere and returns to the earth is? [precipitation]
8. And when it reaches the earth, we see rainwater washing through the streets and into rivers. That's called? [runoff]

The content of these questions isn't especially critical to this practice, so replace them with something in your content area if you'd prefer.

THE NEXT LEVEL

Sharpen Up

Call and Response reinforces culture in your classroom. You build a habit of students' following through on a request in a coordinated fashion. There's a bit of teamwork, a bit of fun, and a bit of following directions. This can be a helpful combination, but only if your *Call and Response* remains crisp and sharp. If students sense that they can use their responses to test your expectations—by dragging out their answers, answering in a silly or loud manner, or answering out of sync—*Call and Response* can quickly become counterproductive. In that case, make "sharpening up" a priority. Energetically and positively correct with a phrase like "Let's try that again. With all of us, please."

Here are some common sharpen-up challenges and possible responses:

Too loud	"I love the enthusiasm, but let's do it again in our speaking/indoor voice." "Match my voice." Model a quieter response. "Say it as loud as I do." "Try turning it down a notch." Then gesture as if you're turning down the volume to signal you want it quieter.
Not all students respond	"We need the whole team." "I need to hear everyone with us!" "Every voice." "We just need the back row to join us!"
Too fast	"Match my speed." "Slower—so I can hear every number [syllable, and so on]." "Stretch it out now." "Tap the brakes a little."
Nonresponse/low energy	"Let's try again so I can hear your voices." "Match my voice with your voice." "This time, say it loud enough for Ms. Driggs to hear you down the hall." "Again, with a little more [verve, excitement, and so on]." "Column one is bringing it today. Don't let them show you up. Everyone, on two!" Say with a hint of challenge, "I can't hear you!"/"Oh, I know you guys can give me a little more than that."
Out of sync	"On my signal . . ." "Everyone on two. One . . . two!" "On the count of three, tell me . . ." "Gotta make it crisp." "One team [gesturing to class]. One voice."

Stretch and Rigor

> ### Revisit *Teach Like a Champion 2.0*
>
> Doug's lengthy coverage under "Call and Response 2.0" provides examples of how teachers use *Call and Response* in other ways, especially as an extension of *Stretch It* (technique 13) and for increasing rigor. Topics include *Call and Response* for vocabulary, reading, and building culture.

Write wording for and notes to yourself about how you might do the same with at least one of the following.

A *Stretch It*:

_____

_____

_____

An important vocabulary word:

_____

_____

_____

A *Call and Response* moment in reading:

_____

_____

_____

A culture-building *Call and Response* with direct academic application:

_____

_____

_____

ROLL IT OUT

Do this planning with a partner or get feedback if you can.

In a daily lesson plan, find several places where you might use *Call and Response* to increase the level of student engagement and also reinforce academic or behavioral goals. Script each call (what you will say) and the answer you expect from the class. Choose the in-cue you will use (for example, "On two. One, two!"). Label each prompt according to its type: repeat, report, reinforce, review, or solve.

Also find at least one place where you will plan to mix *Cold Call* with *Call and Response.* Keep scaffolding in mind. Plan wording with which you'll signal movement from one to the other as needed.

After class, review your results. Repeat or adjust your approach in future lesson plans. Try to improve your mix of *Cold Call* and *Call and Response,* your script of calls, and your choices of in-cues.

GROUP ROLE PLAY

Consider "A Sharpen-Up Role Play" for this technique, available at my.teachlikeachampion.com.

ACTION PLANNING

Use this action planner to continue your work with *Call and Response.* (Find a printable version of this form at my.teachlikeachampion.com.) You know you're on the right track when . . .

- The class responds crisply with positive energy.
- Participation is usually 100 percent.

HOW AM I DOING?

_____

_____

Design one or more action steps for improvement. Decide on an interval by which you'll revisit this page to assess your progress.

Action Step 1

By when, with whom, and how you will measure your effort

By _____, I will . . .
 Date

_____

_____

How Did I Do?

Successes: _____

_____

_____

_____

Challenges: _____

_____

_____

Next steps: _____

_____

_____

Action Step 2

By when, with whom, and how you will measure your effort

By _____, I will . . .
Date

_____

_____

_____

How Did I Do?

Successes: _____

_____

_____

_____

_____

Challenges: _____

_____

_____

_____

_____

Next steps: _____

_____

_____

_____

OUR OBSERVATIONS ON THE CHAMPIONS

 Clips FG38. Janelle Austin, and FG39. Jennifer Trapp

Janelle uses *Call and Response* here mainly to keep the whole class energized and focused on summarizing the data of the graph on the board. Perhaps she begins with *Call and Response* also as lead-in to *Cold Call,* which may be challenging for some students. When she switches to *Cold Call,* it may also be because she wants to bring weaker students back into focus. Or she may just be doing so to cut off a somewhat boisterous group response. You may have noticed also that at one point she takes a step to sharpen up the group response.

Jennifer's use of *Call and Response* moves back and forth between behavioral and academic uses. On the behavioral side, the technique builds energy and helps her keep the group in a standard routine: "My pencil is about to move, so your pencil needs to . . ." "Move!" Academically, she uses it to increase *At Bats*, reinforcing key bits of information such as the fact that most adverbs end in -*ly*, and she uses it to propagate one student's good answer across the class as a whole. You may have noticed she sometimes uses a gesture that calls on "all" to respond. Like Janelle, she also shifts between *Call and Response* and *Cold Call*, according to ongoing judgments about need.

CALL AND RESPONSE

BREAK IT DOWN

OVERVIEW

Break It Down is a technique you use when students are stuck and you seek to follow up with a question to help them answer. Generally the idea is to give them the smallest possible hint to get them from an incorrect or incomplete response to a correct one. You want students to do the cognitive work rather than just providing them with the answer yourself, but one of the biggest challenges is to also get this to happen in a timely manner. Teachers have to balance the goal of *Breaking It Down* with the necessity of managing time and pacing in a lesson.

Used on the spur of the moment, at one of the more difficult moments during class, *Break It Down* is challenging to master. That said, the likelihood of its success can still be increased by a bit of thoughtful planning.

Reflection

What kinds of things do you currently do when a student gets stuck during verbal questioning? What are the strengths and weaknesses of these various approaches?

_____

_____

_____

FUNDAMENTALS

In *Break It Down,* you are seeking to assess the gap between what the student knows and mastery, while also trying to figure out what the student's actual *misunderstanding* is. This is inherently challenging, but one of the best ways to do it is to anticipate incorrect answers and students' possible sources of misunderstanding in advance, then plan the hints you can use to address those mistakes. Through planning and practice over time, you'll get better at anticipating the kind of things that students get wrong and the responses that help.

Six Ways to *Break It Down*

In response to a student error, *Breaking It Down* means turning the original material into a series of smaller, simpler parts and asking the students to work back to the right answer. There are an infinite number of ways to do that, but it's worth thinking through what some of the consistent approaches are. Here are six especially common and effective methods:

Provide an example. This applies when the question stumping the student was originally based on a category. For example, "Define prime number for us, John. Seven is a prime number . . . so is eleven."

Provide context. "Yesterday we discussed how our government was designed to prevent too much power in any one place."

Provide a rule. Respond to a student misconception by replying with a rule so that your student can correct his or her answer. "What happens when I multiply a negative number by a positive number?"

Provide the missing (or first) step with a simple cue. "What do we always do when the numerator is larger than the denominator?"

Roll back. Repeat a student's answer back to him or her. When you use this approach, carefully manage how much you emphasize erroneous parts of an answer. Saying, "You said evaporation happens when water vapor forms droplets in clouds" without discernible emphasis on any word is a much more challenging prompt than saying, "You said *evaporation* happens when water vapor forms droplets in clouds." The latter phrasing points the student to the error.

Narrow or eliminate false choices. "Let's go through some of the options. If it were a verb, it would be an action or state of being. Is this action? Can you or I *justice*?" "Let me pause you. Your factoring is fine here. What else might have gone wrong?"

> **blog** Find this blog post at teachlikeachampion.com/blog/rollback-can-help-break-tricky-momts/. Check out this post of champion teacher Jessica Bracey: "How the 'Rollback' Can Help You Break It Down in Those Tricky Moments."

Some Champion Planning

As we mentioned earlier, planning can really help. The box here contains a few examples from Maggie Johnson's lessons on *The Diary of Anne Frank*, in which she tried to anticipate a likely error and plan a series of *Break It Down* questions.

PAGES 56–57, *THE DIARY OF A YOUNG GIRL*

Quick Think! (1:30 min writing time)

What does Anne mean when she says, "I thought my days were numbered"?

Target Response:

Anne thought that she was about to die; that she had no days left; that the Nazis would come in and kill her.

Anticipated Misunderstanding:

Anne was counting the days she had been in the Annex.

Anne thought she might be freed from the Annex.

Planned *Break It Down*:

A. How does Anne feel when she says, "I thought my days were numbered"?

B. Why? What might happen if she's discovered?

C. So when she says, "I thought my days were numbered," what is she thinking?

Multiple-Choice Style

Anne's description of her imagination during the scare reveals

A. that she believed the SS soldiers were trying to invade the Secret Annex.
B. that she is relieved that the man pounding on the door was Mr. Kleiman.
C. that she was concerned about the carpenter's inspection of the mysterious-looking bookcase.
D. that she is terrified by the German soldiers and believes that they are ruthless villains.

Target Response:

Choice *D*

Anticipated Misunderstanding:

Choice *a.*—This detail may be true of Anne's thoughts, but her *imagination* reveals something specific (i.e. there is a stronger answer than *a.*). Students who chose this answer would not have gone back to the text, reread the subset of text in which this answer is contained, and accurately identified the purpose of the image. Rather, they made a generalization about how she is feeling during the scare at the Annex.

Planned *Break It Down* **sequence:**

1. Go back, check to make sure you boxed a paragraph and underlined her description of imagination.
2. What did she imagine?
3. How does she describe this?
4. What does this tell you? (. . . about Anne's attitude? . . . about Anne's attitude toward . . . ?)
5. Look back at the answer choices. Which answer is the best match?

How does the author create *more* suspense *after* this conflict seems to be resolved?

Target Response:

The author creates suspense by adding "at least this time," to her statement "everything worked out all right." This makes the reader think about what will happen the next time there is a scare at the Annex and whether or not they will be safe from the SS soldiers or Gestapo.

Anticipated Misunderstanding:

The author creates suspense by leaving the reader feeling scared.

The author creates suspense by describing a scary situation for people in the Annex.

Planned *Break It Down* **sequence:**

1. The question is asking you about suspense created at what point in the text?
2. Identify when the conflict seems resolved. ("everything worked out all right")
3. What else does Anne say? ("at least this time")
4. Why does she say this? How does this make you feel as a reader?

What two or three specific things could you steal from Maggie's approach to planning?

_____

_____

What might you need to do to adapt these ideas to your setting, subject, and grade?

_____

_____

PLAN YOUR OWN

Use this pattern of entries to plan for several *Break It Downs* in an upcoming lesson.
Question to ask student:

_____

_____

Exemplar student response:

_____

_____

Anticipated misunderstanding(s):

_____

_____

Break It Down hints:

_____

_____

ACTION PLANNING

Use this action planner to continue your work with *Break It Down*. (Find a printable version of this form at my.teachlikeachampion.com.) You're on the right track when you're expanding your repertoire of ways to *Break It Down* and . . .

- Keeping it positive
- Managing pacing
- Making the students do the greatest possible amount of cognitive work

BREAK IT DOWN

HOW AM I DOING?

_____

_____

Design one or more action steps for improvement. Decide on an interval by which you'll revisit this page to assess your progress.

Action Step 1

By when, with whom, and how you will measure your effort

By _____, I will . . .
   Date

_____

_____

How Did I Do?

Successes: _____

_____

_____

_____

Challenges: _____

_____

_____

Next steps: _____

_____

_____

Action Step 2

By when, with whom, and how you will measure your effort

By _____, I will . . .
_{Date}

_____

_____

_____

How Did I Do?

Successes: _____

_____

_____

_____

Challenges: _____

_____

_____

Next steps: _____

_____

_____

PEPPER

OVERVIEW

Pepper is a technique that allows you to review content in a way that builds energy and actively engages the whole class. The teacher who uses it "peppers" the class with a rapid series of questions focusing on quick response.

Pepper often involves technique 33, *Cold Call*, but needn't always. And often it starts with *Cold Call* but then proceeds to calling on students whose hands are raised (with increasing eagerness).

Its game-like qualities often set *Pepper* apart from the rest of class and can make it an ideal change of pace. Some of our favorite teachers use it for a few minutes daily or perhaps a few days out of the week, inserting it before or after quiet or more independent work to build energy or change the pace.

Reflection

Do you currently have any experience with asking your students questions in rapid order with quick responses? How well has it worked? What problems have you encountered?

_____

_____

_____

_____

FUNDAMENTALS

What's in *Pepper*?

Pepper's hallmarks are:

Rapidity. It's a fast sequence in which a large number of questions get asked.

Inclusiveness. It's a group activity. It can include *Cold Call* or hands, and often it progresses from one to the other, but it should engage everyone.

Portability. It can be used anywhere (not just the classroom).

Economy. Everyone's language (question or answer) is economical.

Theme and variation. The series of questions focuses on a theme or skill; or one short sequence works one skill, and the next addresses a closely related one.

Constant back-and-forth. Questions and answers are short and rarely discussed; usually an answer is followed by another question (or the same one if the previous answerer got it wrong).

When to *Pepper*

Pepper is a great warm-up activity. You can use it for daily oral drill at the outset of class or as a way to make review fun. *Pepper* can keep the class working while a few students write on the board. It can fill in any stray ten minutes inside or outside the classroom (say, lined up in the hallway) with productive fun.

Mentally review your school day. Identify several short intervals, including those that may occur outside class lesson time, when you might *Pepper* your students. What content could you focus on? What tools (such as a chart or flash cards) might you want to have at hand?

Interval:

_____

Content and useful tools:

_____

_____

_____

Interval:

_____

Content and useful tools:

_____

_____

_____

Pepper and *Cold Call*

At first, it's easy to confuse *Pepper* with technique 33, *Cold Call*, because both can be "hot." These lists compare them.

Pepper	*Cold Call*
Often involves *Cold Call* (and almost always starts with it), but you can ask for hands at times if you wish.	Can happen in a *Pepper* setting, but also in various other settings.

Pepper	Cold Call
Includes quick, fundamental questions, often as review.	Includes any question that furthers thought and learning.
Goes at a fast pace, with high energy and no discussion of answers.	Can be fast or slow.
Uses sequences of approximately ten or more questions. *Pepper* implies volume.	Uses no predetermined number of questions.
Sometimes involves game-like features: students standing, class tracking the number it gets correct, and so on.	Has a wide variety of applications, but employs game-like aspects less often.

You can begin *Cold Calling* at the outset of a session of *Pepper*, then switch to hands as students become more and more engaged and enthusiastic, which is often the case.

THE NEXT LEVEL

Pepper works best if you keep up your game spirit.

1. *Set up boundaries and work the clock.* Compress *Pepper* in time between a clear beginning and end.
2. *Shift.* In reviews, move from unit to unit as part of the game. Ask questions about properties of quadrilaterals for two or three minutes and then move on to a series about coordinate geometry. Or shift between topics that may not seem entirely related: in social studies, for example, spend a few minutes on map skills followed by a few minutes on the original colonies.
3. *Use game gadgets to add novel touches*:
   Start and end with a ding on a bell.
   Ask all students to stand up.
   Call on students in a unique or unpredictable way.
   Point to students if that's something you don't normally do.

Some neat variations that teachers use:

Pick-sticks. Label popsicle sticks with each student's name to pull at random out of a can. Or generate random numbers on a laptop or your smartphone. Your pick can be random, but with the question tailored to the student. And, as one teacher pointed out to me, remember that only you know whose name is really on the popsicle stick! So call whomever you want to. But be aware that a picking process can slow you down a lot.

Head-to-head. Two students stand up to answer a question. The one who gets the correct answer first remains standing to face a new challenger. But don't get sucked into discussing or arbitrating. You're the ump. Next pitch!

Sit-down. At the beginning of class, all students are standing, and the teacher *Peppers* them so that they can "earn their seats" (sit down) by answering correctly. Use no other engagement than a gesture to signal the student to sit.

Stand-up. Pepper to see who's next to join the line for recess.

Reflection

In keeping with *Joy Factor* (technique 62), what other game-like touches could you add? Do your students' favorite sports and games—online, on TV, on the playground—suggest possibly good ideas?

_____

_____

_____

_____

ROLL IT OUT

Pepper takes nerve to try the first time! Enter class with an actual script and notes about how you will respond if students have too much trouble answering. Use the following steps to structure your effort. Practice with a supportive group or partner, and use that experience to identify challenges.

1. Study and mark an upcoming lesson plan for one or two places where *Pepper* might add energy and muscle.
2. Identify the content for each round of *Pepper*.
3. Script the questions you will ask. Keep them specific. Plan scaffolds as needed.
4. Decide how you will choose whom to call on. Consider whether you want a chant to introduce it. (For example, "I say salt, you say pepper! Salt!! [Students: Pepper!!] Salt!! [Students: Pepper!!] What time is it?? [Students: It's pepper time!!]")
5. What format or game context will you use to boost the mojo?
6. How will you keep track of and respond to the overall level of student mastery that the results of the round suggest?
7. After class, assess results. Make notes about how you will continue *Pepper*.
8. How might you vary or reformulate some of the questions from these rounds in a subsequent round of *Pepper* review—perhaps at the start of the next class session?
9. Consider when you might *Pepper* outside your classroom on the same material you covered in this session.

GROUP PRACTICE ACTIVITIES

Peer *Pepper*

Write a script for a two- to three-minute *Pepper* session for your group to review some of the methods of *Pepper*.

Compare Brands

Revisit the individual work you did in the previous section to share and compare your responses and see other options. Also discuss lesson plans. Bring a current or past lesson plan to the group. As a group, identify at least three places in your lessons where a round of *Pepper* could be added:

- What would that round cover?
- What would *Pepper* add at this point?
- What scaffolding might be needed and planned in advance?
- What formats (sit-down, stand-up, game, and so on) might work best for the various rounds?

Mark comments on your own plan, and refer to it later when you plan your next lesson.

Use Your Scripts

With the rest of the group as *Students,* take turns as *Teacher* practicing the script you created in "Roll It Out." Appoint a *Timer* to stop each round at two minutes. After each round, go around the circle of *Students* for them to comment about:

- Ways in which that round reflected a good fundamental of *Pepper*
- Whether it had qualities of a game
- The best moment or question of the round
- Whether any questions could have been improved in some way

Then let the *Teacher* respond by describing something he or she might have done differently.

Brainstorm "Game"

Brainstorm some novelty touches. Then vote on all the suggestions. Each voter awards three points among the suggestions: one point for originality, one point for speed and workability, and one point for being most "over the top."

Reflection

What valuable pointers can you take away from your work with the group?

_____

_____

_____

PEPPER

ACTION PLANNING

Use this action planner to continue your work with *Pepper.* (Find a printable version of this form at my.teachlikeachampion.com.) Use these success points to assess your progress:

- My questions are succinct, and I know what I'll take as an adequate answer.
- The *Pepper* engages everyone.
- I rarely feel compelled to halt the *Pepper* in order to backtrack.

HOW AM I DOING?

_____

_____

Design one or more action steps for improvement. Decide on an interval by which you'll revisit this page to assess your progress.

Action Step 1

By when, with whom, and how you will measure your effort

By _____, I will . . .
     Date

_____

_____

How Did I Do?

Successes: _____

_____

_____

_____

Challenges: _____

_____

_____

_____

Next steps: _____

_____

_____

Action Step 2

By when, with whom, and how you will measure your effort

By _____, I will . . .

<small>Date</small>

_____

_____

_____

How Did I Do?

Successes: _____

_____

_____

_____

Challenges: _____

_____

_____

_____

Next steps: _____

_____

_____

_____

EVERYBODY WRITES

OVERVIEW

Writing is often the ideal preliminary to a discussion. If every student in your class thinks through an answer in writing before you discuss the causes of X or the evidence for Y, a wide array of benefits accrue to both you their teacher and of course to the students themselves.

You can:	Students can:
Choose strategically whom to call on based on what students write.	Remember more of what they think by virtue of writing it out.
Start discussion with answers that are already thought through.	Listen better to their peers because they don't have to try to remember what they were originally thinking.
Enable more students to participate in discussion by letting them take their time to develop ideas before asking for hands.	Rehearse their ideas so they are comfortable talking about them with peers.
	Articulate an answer, whether or not they are called on.

For these reasons, *Everybody Writes* and the other techniques in this chapter are useful in boosting both think ratio and participation ratio.

Revisit *Teach Like a Champion 2.0*

To refresh yourself about ratios, reread Doug's introduction to part 3 in *Teach Like a Champion 2.0*. Meanwhile, here's a brief reminder:

Participation ratio is a measure of who participates and how often. Maximizing it means getting all students involved in speaking, responding to questions, thinking actively, participating on cue, and processing ideas in writing, as often as possible. *Think ratio* refers to the level of rigor in the engagement you foster. What's the quality and depth of thinking in which students are engaged in? Do they revise and improve their thoughts, or leave them in draft version once they've initially thought them through?

Reflection

A teacher could launch a discussion by posing a question and choosing one eager (or not-so-eager) student to start the conversation. In what ways might this tend to steer the ratio downward? Specifically, how might it make the discussion both less rigorous and less widely shared by the class? Feel free to compare your answer with some of our thoughts.

_____

_____

_____

Our reflections (yours might be different): When we drive discussion based on the first answer presented by students or the first hand that goes up, we imply to our students that what we want is the first answer rather than the most thoughtful one. Some students require time to process their thoughts and generate ideas. Others need a few moments to gain the confidence to share them. When you give time to process ideas first through writing, you not only include these more reflective students in your discussion but also increase the quality of the discussion that occurs after the writing.

FUNDAMENTALS

Set your students up for rigorous engagement by giving them the opportunity to reflect on questions in writing before discussion. Ideas that students (both fast and slow processors) produce get better when students are allowed a few moments of reflection. _Everybody Writes_ also promotes think ratio because writing an idea involves locking it down in actual, specific words. This is a rigorous process, and as a result, think ratio tends to be high. In addition, having _Everybody Write_ to a prompt you've given increases participation ratio because all students will be participating.

Asking students to write before engaging in discussion can also give you data on understanding—what your students knew before the discussion began. For more about this, see technique 41, _Front the Writing_.

Hunt (Instead of Fish)

Don't just gather what students write. Hunt _while_ they write by _Circulating_ (technique 24) and reading their answers. This enables you to select effective responses with which to begin your discussion, intentionally shaping and driving the discussion. This is far better than fishing—calling on a student and hoping the comment will add maximum value.

Get the Feel of It

If possible, do the following using actual student writing you've gathered in class, in response to having everyone write in preparation for discussion.

Write out the question you asked, or one you want to ask:

_____

_____

Choose three written responses you got and compare how discussion could have started differently had you begun it with one or more of the three. Or summarize three hypothetical responses and how each might steer the conversation.

1. _____

_____

_____

2. _____

_____

_____

3. _____

_____

_____

ANALYZE A CHAMPION

▶ Clip FG27. Jessica Bracey, Grade 5

Compare your observations with ours at the end of this technique. How does Jessica use writing as a tool to make her reading classroom more rigorous?

_____

_____

_____

PLANNING *EVERYBODY WRITES*

The following items pose different approaches you could take in conducting *Everybody Writes*. For each one, read the possible approaches. Then enter a lesson question you plan to ask students to write about in preparation for discussion in an upcoming lesson. Mark the approach that you would be most likely to use. Then explain your choice.

1. Collected?

a.   Writing in a portion of your lesson handouts that will be collected and graded

b.   Writing on a "reflections" section of your lesson handouts or a "reflections" journal that can be observed and *Show Called* (technique 39) but not collected

c.   Writing on a piece of scratch paper

d.   Other

_____

Lesson question you will ask:

_____

_____

Why you chose a, b, c, or d:

_____

_____

2. Question origin?

a.   Writing in response to teacher-generated questions written on the overhead

b.   Writing in response to a question framed verbally by the teacher at the moment it's assigned

c.   Doing a "free write" in response to a topic students determine to be interesting

d.   Other

_____

Lesson question you will ask:

_____

_____

Why you chose a, b, c, or d:

_____

_____

3. How many?

a.   Writing in response to one question

b.   Writing in response to a series of three or four questions

c.   Choosing from among three or four questions to write about

d.   Other

_____

Lesson question you will ask:

_____

_____

Why you chose a, b, c, or d:

_____

_____

_____

4. Time?
a.   Writing for just long enough to develop initial thoughts
b.   Writing for long enough to cite and discuss evidence
c.   Writing for long enough to develop an idea or argument
d.   Other

Lesson question you will ask:

_____

_____

Why you chose a, b, c, or d:

_____

_____

_____

5. Format?
a.   Writing in complete sentences
b.   Writing in complete sentences with occasional challenges ("Try to use the words _erosion_ and _sedimentation_) or sentence starters ("Try to write a complete sentence beginning with, 'Despite the hardness of the rock, . . .'")
c.   Writing with no format expectations
d.   Other

Lesson question you will ask:

_____

_____

Why you chose a, b, c, or d:

_____

_____

6. Look to start the discussion with:
a. Brilliant answer
b. Student who doesn't always raise hand quickly or participate in discussions
c. A common misunderstanding
d. Other

_____

Lesson question you will ask:

_____

_____

Why you chose a, b, c, or d:

_____

_____

TRY IT OUT

Choose a discussion point in an upcoming lesson and insert an *Everybody Writes* moment. Make sure to include your question, directions for students on where they will write, and notes to yourself about what you will look for as they write and whom you will call on to start. Consider how you want to shape your discussion when choosing student answers.

Success points:

*   Your writing prompts increase think ratio and participation ratio.
*   Students are using writing to develop and refine their ideas.

ACTION PLANNING

Use this action planner to continue your work with *Everybody Writes*. (Find a printable version of this form at my.teachlikeachampion.com.) Consider the aforementioned success points.

HOW AM I DOING?

Design one or more action steps for improvement. Decide on an interval by which you'll revisit this page to assess your progress.

Action Step 1

By when, with whom, and how you will measure your effort

By _____, I will . . .

Date

How Did I Do?

Successes: _____

_____

_____

_____

Challenges: _____

_____

_____

_____

Next steps: _____

_____

_____

Action Step 2

By when, with whom, and how you will measure your effort

By _____, **I will . . .**
     Date

_____

_____

_____

How Did I Do?

Successes: _____

_____

_____

_____

Challenges: _____

_____

_____

_____

Next steps: _____

_____

_____

_____

OUR OBSERVATIONS ON THE CHAMPION

 Clip FG27. Jessica Bracey

Fifth-grade reading teacher Jessica facilitates a stretch of *Everybody Writes* and a brief discussion about *Circle of Gold.* Here are the questions she poses: What is Toni's plan? Why does he create this plan? What does this plan reveal about Toni?

The clip illustrates three important aspects of *Everybody Writes*:

Accountability. At the outset of the clip, we see Jessica transition students out of a sequence of *Control the Game* (technique 23) reading from *Circle of Gold.* She then prompts them to respond to a series of comprehension questions in their reading response journals using evidence from the text. This task holds students accountable to demonstrating and deepening their comprehension of what they just read.

The power of systematizing. Note how quickly students transition out of reading, into writing, and then into discussion. They need few directions before getting started, which means they can spend more time on writing (technique 31, *Every Minute Matters*). From this we can conclude that Jessica has already systematized *Everybody Writes* in her classroom.

Priming the pump for discussion. When time expires, Jessica prompts her students to share their written responses, and we see several shoot their hands up with enthusiasm. It's clear that they're prepared to discuss.

During the discussion, Jessica pushes students to dig deeper and respond directly to one another's comments. Students rise to the challenge, and they're able to do so in large part because they've had a chance to think deeply about her questions. As we see with this example, *Everybody Writes* can be used as a means to a more rigorous end, and not as the end itself.

ART OF THE SENTENCE

OVERVIEW

In *Art of the Sentence,* a teacher asks students to synthesize a conclusion, describe an insight, or summarize a complex idea *in a single, well-crafted sentence.* Just one. Making one sentence do all the work pushes students to use a more extensive array of grammatical forms and vocabulary. This increases the precision with which they can think and write.

Reflection

Write a single sentence of your own that describes your students' writing and a specific skill they would benefit from improving. For example: "My students tend to write wooden, repetitive sentences, and their ideas would be better if they could begin them in a wider variety of ways, including starting with prepositional phrases."

_____

_____

_____

FUNDAMENTALS

Set the stage by emphasizing the importance of quality: "When we write our sentences, our goal is to craft them beautifully and with precision." Consider these two prompts from a history class:

- Write a sentence that describes what Roosevelt did during his first hundred days in office.
- In one artfully written sentence, describe both the problem Roosevelt faced when he took office *and* at least two important resulting actions he took during his first hundred days.

How do they prepare students differently for the task of writing? How do they communicate expectations differently?

_____

_____

_____

The prompts we use to ask students to write communicate a great deal about our expectations for what they produce. Our prompts can also vary in how much they push students to develop proficiency with a variety of formats, engage key ideas, or problem-solve on their own.

Types of Prompts

Consider these different writing prompts:

- In one carefully written sentence, describe Roosevelt's primary actions during his first hundred days in office. Begin with the phrase, "Responding decisively . . ."
- In one carefully written sentence, describe Roosevelt's primary actions during his first hundred days in office. Be sure to use the term *New Deal*.

How are they different in what they do (and do not) require students to do?

_____

_____

_____

In general we distinguish three different categories of prompts for *Art of the Sentence* tasks:

Sentence starter prompts. These provide a specific—and usually challenging—way to start a sentence.
Sentence parameter prompts. These ask students to include certain elements, ideas, or phrases in the sentence.
Nondenominational prompts. These ask students to write a single high-quality sentence about a particular topic, without further guidance.

We don't suggest that any of these is better or worse than the others. As we will discuss, they accomplish different things and develop different skills. We recommend using a mix of all three types.

Sentence Starters

The specific words and phrases of a sentence starter can push students to apply more sophisticated syntactical structures to their own writing, and often to think more critically. A few examples:

- In one sentence, explain Luke's action and motivation in this chapter. Start your sentence with the phrase, "Deciding to investigate . . ."
- Summarize the data from this graph in one complete, well-written sentence that begins with the phrase "Over time, . . ."
- Describe the Mongols' success in establishing a centralized empire in Eurasia. Start your sentence with "To the extent . . ."

Notice the different ways that students are socialized to begin their sentences: with an introductory prepositional phrase or a participial phrase. This sort of practice is among the best ways to help students make a habit of using more complex forms of syntax.

Sentence starters can also challenge students to think in new ways. Starting a sentence about Luke with the phrase, "Unlike his actions in chapter 3" asks students to contrast his actions in two different chapters. That is, it guides them to think about the book in a specific way.

Imagine you have just shown your students this photograph of figures in fog:

Draft two *Art of the Sentence* prompts you might use in asking students to write about the photograph. Each should specify a single sentence using a sentence starter, but try to write two *very different* sentence starters that cause students to think or write differently—either in content or in syntactic structure.

Here are two examples. Notice that the "starter," the phrase students are expected to use and apply, is relatively short.

Describe what's pictured in this photograph in one artful sentence. Begin with, "Emerging from the fog . . ."

Capture the mood of this photograph in one artful sentence. Begin with, "As the sun faded . . ."

_____

_____

_____

_____

Sentence Parameters

Sentence parameters are guidelines students follow to shape the sentences they write. Sentence parameters could ask students to use a specific phrase, engage a certain idea, or work within some other kind of limit. Here are some examples:

- Explain in one well-crafted sentence what Swift says society should do with poor children. Use the word *satiric* or *satire.*
- Explain in one well-crafted sentence that uses a subordinating conjunction what Swift says society should do with poor children.

- Explain in one well-crafted sentence of not more than twelve words what Swift says society should do with poor children.
- Explain in one well-crafted sentence what Swift says society should do with poor children. Use a direct quotation from *A Modest Proposal.*

Imagine you have just shown your students this photograph:

Draft two *Art of the Sentence* writing prompts you might use with students, each containing a sentence parameter. Try to write two *very different* prompts that cause students to think or write differently—either in content or in syntactic structure.

Examples:

Describe what's pictured in this photograph in one artful sentence. Use the word *ironic*.
In one artful sentence, describe what's ironic about this photograph. Use the word *habitat*.

_____

_____

_____

_____

Nondenominational Prompts

Nondenominational prompts give your students more complete latitude in what to write about and how. They merely require a single sentence, though ideally they would do so in a way that explicitly or implicitly stresses quality and craftsmanship.

Imagine you have just shown your students this graph:

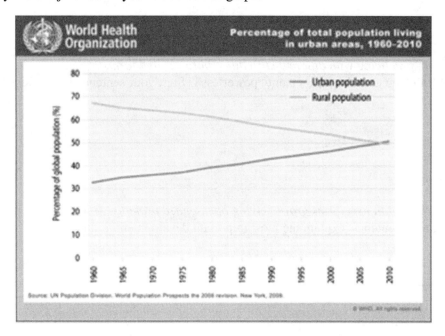

Draft two *Art of the Sentence* writing prompts you might assign that asked students to write about the graph. Each should ask students to respond in a single sentence, and each should require them to use a nondenominational prompt, but try to write two *different* prompts that cause students to think or write differently—either in content or in syntactic structure—in response to the graph.

Examples

In <u>a single</u> carefully constructed sentence, describe <u>two</u> conclusions you might draw from the graph.
In one carefully constructed sentence, describe a question you might want to ask the demographers who
   created this graph.

_____

_____

_____

_____

Gradually Adding Complexity

The following *Art of the Sentence* prompts were used over a series of weeks by seventh-grade reading teacher David Javsicas. Read through them, making notes about what skills David is trying to build at each stage.

First, scaffolded sentences, intentionally taught:
   How did Ralph's actions lead to a "violent swing"? What did he do, and what was the effect of his
     actions? Follow this format:
   Because Ralph _____,
              Ralph's action(s) – cause

_____.
    main effect(s) of Ralph's action(s)

Skill(s):

_____

In a week or two, practicing with different structures, phrases, and forms:
   What did Ralph do to make Jack's taunt "powerless"? Start your sentence with "Despite Jack's . . ."
   Skill(s):

_____

_____

As students' comfort with new forms grows, giving open-ended prompts:
   In one beautiful sentence, explain the most important development in this section of the text.
   Skill(s):

_____

_____

When students have mastered open-ended prompts, asking them to combine multiple ideas in a single sentence:
   Describe in one sentence how Christopher's father was feeling *and* how Christopher's response to the situation is different than his father's.
   Skill(s):

_____

_____

Occasionally having students paraphrase complex sentences written by authors:
   In one sentence, paraphrase Lowry's sentence describing Jonas's feelings at the top of page 108. Be sure to make reference to all of the key ideas in the sentence and the relationships between them.
   Skill(s):

_____

_____

   How might you use or adapt the idea of sequencing prompts from easy to hard in your class?

_____

_____

_____

PLAN *ART OF THE SENTENCE*

Art of the Sentence takes a good deal of time, especially if you revise and edit the sentences students write. For this reason, you may want to choose the *most important idea* from your lesson as the focus of the sentence. Or use *Art of the Sentence* as a closure activity or *Exit Ticket* to summarize the day's lesson. Wherever you use it, be sure to allow plenty of time.

Take a lesson you plan to teach in the next week or so and add the following to plan *Art of the Sentence*, if you think it will serve the lesson objective.

- Note where in the plan.
- Note what aspect of thinking or writing you want to emphasize with your *Art of the Sentence* activity.
- Script the prompt (sentence starter or parameters).
- Note how you will review, assess, and lead students to revise to make sure that students are learning from the experience.

ACTION PLANNING

Use this action planner to continue your work with *Art of the Sentence*. (Find a printable version of this form at my.teachlikeachampion.com.) You're on the right track when . . .

- Your prompts attain the right level of challenge for your students.
- The prompts are leading to richer thinking and use of language.

HOW AM I DOING?

_____

_____

Design one or more action steps for improvement. Decide on an interval by which you'll revisit this page to assess your progress.

Action Step 1

By when, with whom, and how you will measure your effort

By _____, I will . . .

Date

_____

_____

How Did I Do?

Successes: _____

_____

_____

_____

_____

Challenges: _____

_____

_____

_____

Next steps: _____

_____

_____

Action Step 2

By when, with whom, and how you will measure your effort

By _____, I will . . .
<small>Date</small>

_____

_____

_____

How Did I Do?

Successes: _____

_____

_____

_____

_____

Challenges: _____

_____

_____

_____

Next steps: _____

_____

_____

_____

SHOW CALL

OVERVIEW

Holding students accountable for the quality of their written work is one of the most important ways we can help prepare them to succeed. It can also be one of the most challenging, especially if it means having to pore over and comment on every page of student writing. One technique teachers can use to overcome this challenge is *Show Call*, a type of *Cold Call* that involves displaying students' written work (often via a document camera)—and then studying it together with the class. Some benefits of this method:

- It gives students incentive to do their best written work.
- It therefore lets you assign lots of high-ratio in-class writing, knowing it will be done well.
- It teaches students how to study, revise, update, or otherwise improve their work.
- It spotlights outstanding written work, showing what success looks like and how other students can replicate it.

Reflection

How do you typically hold students accountable for the quality of their written work during class? What successes and challenges have you faced with these approaches?

_____

_____

_____

    If you already use *Show Call*, what difficulties have you faced in using this technique that you want to work to overcome?

_____

_____

SHOW CALL

ANALYZE THE CHAMPIONS

▶ Clip FG40. Nicole Willey, Grade 3

▶ Clip FG41. Paul Powell, Grade 6

In clips FG40 and FG41, compare Nicole's and Paul's *Show Calls.* What do they accomplish?

Nicole Willey	Paul Powell

Commonalities:

_____

_____

_____

Compare your observations with ours at the end of this technique. Then continue with Clip FG42.

Clip FG42. Sarah Lord, Grade 5

In Clip FG42, what's effective about how Sarah responds to a student who seems nervous about having his work *Show Called*? How does she keep this *Show Call* positive while upholding high expectations for this student?

_____

_____

_____

What might have been the consequences if she had allowed Jeremiah to opt out of *Show Call*?

_____

_____

FUNDAMENTALS

Follow the Rules of *Cold Call*

Since *Show Call* is essentially a *Cold Call* for written work, it may not surprise you to hear that many of the rules for *Cold Call* still apply. *Show Call* should be

Positive. In many great classrooms, students view a *Show Call* as the opposite of a "gotcha." For them it's a sought-after reward for quality work. To build such a positive culture, teachers routinely use *Show Call* to celebrate success. They're also mindful about how they respond to errors. Saying something like, "This is good work, and now we get to help make it great" makes students feel safe having their written work displayed before their peers and builds a culture in which they learn to embrace the opportunity to improve it. Finally, teachers make sure that students leave a *Show Call* with actionable feedback that empowers them to make their work better.

Systematic. *Show Call* works best when it's universal. That is, every student should feel as though he or she is likely to be on the receiving end at some point and that the process will be both positive ("some nice work here") and constructive ("let's find some ways to make it even better"). Over time, this will ensure that *Show Call* feels like a routine part of how the classroom operates that students welcome.

Predictable. Let students know when a *Show Call* is coming—either now or eventually. We call giving students advance notice a "heads-up." Alternatively, you could announce to the class that you'll be *Show Calling* before you do so. Another way to make *Show Call* predictable is to use it at the same point(s) in every lesson—for example, always after a *Do Now* (technique 20).

Plan Your *Show Call*

The table "Key *Show Call* Questions" summarizes three decisions you'll be making:

- What do I want to focus on during the *Show Call*?
- When should I take the work?
- How many pieces of work should I take?

Key *Show Call* Questions

What to take?	When?	How Many?
Correct work	Midstream	Single participant
Erroneous work (common error)	End point	Multiple participants
Good to great work (include glows and grows)	Post-revision	

For what to take, you have three choices:

Correct work to spotlight writing that is complete, accurate, and possibly exemplary. This builds positive culture around *Show Call* and helps students replicate a rare strength. ("This is a great example of how to 'show' rather than 'tell.'" "Listen to how Alexis uses transitions.")

Erroneous work showing common errors, in order to help the entire class learn. ("What error did he/she make? Convince me.")

Good work, to both highlight strengths in a piece of work and improve on it in order to take the work to "great." This sends a systematic message: good work and work we seek to make better are one and the same.

Likewise, there are three choices for when to "take" student work for a *Show Call*. Managing the timing of your take is one of the most powerful levers you can pull to influence what, when, and how students are accountable for written work.

Midstream—before they finish writing—to "prime the pump" for further discussion or writing, inspire creative thinking, or help students overcome initial hurdles. ("Here's what some people have done so far . . .")

At the end—*after* students have finished drafting and *before* they've revised—to review complete written work. ("Let's read some of your written responses from yesterday's independent practice.")

Post-revision or follow-through—*after* students have revised—in order to verify that students successfully completed the revision and understand its rationale. Highlight work that has been improved to reflect the revision points you emphasized during the initial *Show Call*.

Your last decision is how many pieces to show. Show just one especially when you want to dive deeply into a common error or when you want to highlight a student's unique insight. Show several when you want to compare, sparking students' creative thinking and problem solving with multiple examples. ("There are four different ways to solve this problem. Let's look at an example of each approach together." "Let's compare the way two scholars started their paragraphs.") You can also take a stack, from which you choose a few to show.

Select a configuration of *Show Call* that could strengthen an upcoming lesson plan. Where would it fit? How could it serve your objective?

Two Moments during *Show Call*

What you say and how you frame what you are doing are especially important at these points.

The Take

The "take" is the moment when you take a student's paper off his or her desk intending to project it. You might regard it as a potential source of tension, but the best teachers make it effortless because they implement it with finesse. One way they do this is by maintaining *Emotional Constancy* (technique 61) as they take it. Exuding a calm, easygoing demeanor that says "no big deal" makes it likelier that students will respond in kind. Effective teachers also carefully consider whether they'll give students a heads-up that a take is coming, or simply take their work without saying anything at all.

The Reveal

The "reveal" is the act of showing the chosen piece of writing to the class. How you do this frames how students will interpret the work and sets the tone for the rest of the *Show Call.* Plan whether you will

- Identify whose work you show or keep the student anonymous.
- Show each piece of work you took or just a few from the stack.
- Be more or less directive about what you want students to look for.
- Honor the work by reading it aloud with expression and appreciation, or bestowing ownership and a chance to shine by asking the student to read it.
- Analyze multiple pieces, each deeply and in isolation (vertical analysis), or in quick succession to highlight similarities or differences (horizontal analysis). In the horizontal fashion, you might say, "Check out how these students showed their work. Here's Terry's . . . This is Tamara's . . . Now that's Charlie's. What do they all have in common?"

ANALYZING MORE CHAMPIONS

 Clip FG43. Rick Zadd, Maggie Johnson, Natasha Birch, John Huber, Julia Goldenheim, and Erin Michels

What is effective about how these teachers manage their takes and reveals?

Rick:

Maggie:

Natasha:

_____

_____

John:

_____

_____

Julia:

_____

_____

Erin:

_____

_____

SHOW CALL

Reflection

In which situations might you choose to . . .

Keep the author anonymous or name the author as a reward?

_____

_____

Be more or less specific about what students should look for in the work?

_____

_____

_____

Analyze work vertically?

_____

_____

Horizontally?

_____

_____

Possible reflections: It might help to keep an author anonymous when you're deeply excavating or analyzing an error. The point, of course, is that the error was typical of many students' work. That said, anonymity isn't necessary. Being specific about what students should look for can help if they haven't had much practice evaluating each other's written work or if you're concerned that the discussion could veer off topic. Conversely, you might be less directive if you're confident that students have sufficient background knowledge on the topic at hand or are already versed in analyzing written work. Vertical analysis can be useful when you want to deeply excavate a student's response. Horizontal analysis could be great for priming students for discussion, writing, or further problem solving. Showcasing the different paths students chose to answer a question builds autonomy by tacitly empowering students to choose their own path.

ENGINEER THE FOLLOW-UP

The purpose of *Show Call* is to help students improve the quality of written work, so follow-up is critical. You can follow up in many ways, some better than others.

Two of the most common follow-up tasks are revising and editing. We define editing as the process of marking up and making technical changes to a document (punctuation, capitalization, spelling, subject-verb agreement, and so on). A teacher who asks students to edit might say something like, "Go back to your sentence and make sure you capitalized all of the proper nouns." This is different, and less rigorous, than revision, which we define as the process of improving writing, often by altering or expanding sentence structure and/or word choice to refine or improve ideas. For a revision task, you might say something like, "Go back and revise your sentence so that it starts with the dependent clause *unless.*"

As Judith Hochman, developer of the Writing Revolution framework, once told Doug, if you let students choose, they will often edit, because it is easier to add a missing capital letter than to revise sentence structure. Even many teachers take the easy path of editing, but the real work is revising.

Fostering a "Growth Mindset"

In addition to the academic benefits we've discussed, there are also tremendous cultural benefits to *Show Call.* One of the most powerful of these is that it can help students develop what Dr. Carol Dweck refers to as a "growth mindset." In her book *Mindset,* she defines this as the belief that one's abilities and talents can be grown or developed over time through hard work and persistence. Students with a growth mindset tend to view challenges and constructive feedback as motivating opportunities to get better. They are also more likely to define success in terms of how they stretch themselves beyond their comfort zone and how much effort they devote to a task.

Try drafting some growth mindset language. Adapt one example statement for use in your class. Then come up with a few more.

1. "A lot of us made the same mistake, so we're going to learn a lot from it. Thank you for sharing it with the class."

_____

_____

2. "I love all these bold hands offering feedback for Jayla's writing. I know you're going to help her make it even better. And that's the goal."

_____

_____

3. "I agree that this is good work, but even good work can get better. Let's hear some suggestions."

_____

_____

4. "I see some people _really_ stretching themselves right now as they read this passage from Jamari's response. That's just what I want to see."

_____

_____

5. "Kyla and Kayvon were courageous enough to show us how much they improved their work by revising it just now. Before we take a look, give them two claps!"

_____

_____

_____

6. _____

_____

7. _____

_____

8. _____

_____

Back-Pocket Revision Prompts

Choose two of these examples. Adapt at least one for use in your class. Then come up with a few more examples.

1. "Add an appositive to the sentence you wrote about _____." (Model: "Gandhi had an impact" becomes "Gandhi, a pacifist and important leader, had an impact.")

2. "Now begin this sentence with a subordinating conjunction" (for example, *if, unless, after*).

3. "How can we revise this in the language of a [scientist/historian/writer/A.P. scholar/fifth grader, and so on]?"

4. "Try including a dependent clause" (such as "Until the sun sets . . ." or ". . . unless molecules collide").

5. "What vocabulary can we incorporate from the [text/story problem/scientific article] to make our word choice more precise?"

6. "Underline the pronouns in your response. Replace two with more specific nouns."

7. _____

8. _____

9. _____

10. _____

CASE STUDY: MIDDLE SCHOOL SCIENCE

Read the case and write some glows and grows. Then compare your thoughts with ours.

Ms. Travers prompted the writing with, "In one well-constructed sentence, respond to the following: What happens to air pressure in a cylindrical container as volume increases? Explain why."

Her target response was "As volume increases, air pressure decreases, because there is more space for the air particles to move."

An exemplary response would be, "As volume increases, air pressure decreases, because there is more space for the air particles to move, leading to fewer collisions with the container."

Jeremy's actual response was this: "As volume increases the air pressure would decrease because there is more space for the molecules to go all around and the molecules won't bump into the container and the cylinder as likely as before."

MS. TRAVERS: (Circulating, *stopping to read Jeremy's work*) Can I share the hard work you've done, to make it even better?

JEREMY: Sure.

MS. TRAVERS: (*placing it under the document camera*) Jeremy effectively explained why air pressure would decrease as volume increases. Let's help him take it from good to great by make his writing more concise and precise. Jessica, what's one suggestion for improvement?

JESSICA: He forgot to add a comma after "As volume increases" and before "and molecules won't."

MS. TRAVERS: Thanks, Jessica. We'll make punctuation edits later, but I want us to focus on revising the language. What phrases don't add any new information?

JESSICA: We could cross out "and the cylinder" because the cylinder and the container are the same thing.

MS. TRAVERS: Good. What's a more specific way of saying "molecules" . . . Jace?

JACE: You could replace "molecules" with "air particles."

MS. TRAVERS: Why?

JACE:	Because the prompt says that we're dealing with air pressure, so we can get more specific about what *kind* of molecules.
MS. TRAVERS:	Cole, what's a better way to phrase "won't bump into each other as much"?
COLE:	We could replace that with "fewer collisions."
MS. TRAVERS:	Fewer collisions with what?
COLE:	Fewer collisions *with the container.*
MS. TRAVERS:	What about this last phrase, "as likely as before"?
JEREMY:	We don't need it, so we can cross that out.
MS. TRAVERS:	Good. Now, I want you to do the same thing to your own paper. Go through and cross out unnecessary words and check to make sure your language is scientific.

Glows	Grows
It was effective when Ms. Travers . . .	Next time, she could try . . .

Some Observations on the Case

For the most part, Ms. Travers's targeted questions keep the discussion focused, rigorous, and productive. And when the conversation initially drifts, she reins it in. Instead of "rounding up" students' comments, Ms. Travers holds out for all-the-way right (see technique 12). For example, when a student suggests "fewer collisions," she asks him to clarify that they're "with the container." This crucial addition is what accounts for the change in air pressure.

Rather than opening with a less directive question ("What's one suggestion for improvement?"), which caused students to begin commenting on less relevant aspects of the writing, Ms. Travers could have opened with a targeted question like the second one she asked. Also, she could have selected work that needed less revision, asking students to help her improve just one aspect of their peers' writing. Finally, Ms. Travers could verify whether students are clear about how they're supposed to revise by asking them one or two questions about it. Here's an example:

MS. TRAVERS:	Now, I want you to do the same to your own paper. First, you'll go through and eliminate what . . . Cole?

COLE:	Unnecessary words and phrases.
MS. TRAVERS:	How did we know they were unnecessary, Megan?
MEGAN:	Because they didn't add any new information.
MS. TRAVERS:	And which vocabulary are we going to make sure we go back and include? Jace?
JACE:	"Air particles," "collisions," and "container."
MS. TRAVERS:	Perfect. At my signal, go to work. *(signals)*

ROLL IT OUT

On the lines that follow, plan how you want to roll out *Show Call* to your students. Make sure that your rollout

- Establishes clear expectations for what students should do
- Clearly and positively communicates the purpose for *Show Call*
- Is quick and concise (within two minutes if possible)

_____

_____

_____

_____

_____

_____

If you can, practice your rollout with a partner and ask for feedback.

ROLE-PLAY PRACTICE WITH A COLLEAGUE OR TWO

In this activity, you can use the earlier case study as a role play to practice your *Show Call* skills.

A middle school science teacher asked this of her class: "In one well-constructed sentence, say what happens to air pressure in a container as volume increases—and why."

Her target response was, "As volume increases, air pressure decreases, because there is more space for the air particles to move, which leads to fewer collisions between air particles."

Circulating as the students wrote, she came across samples from students that appear on page 63 of this text or in the downloadable lesson materials packet entitled "Tracking, Not Watching Practice" on my.teachlikeachampion.com.

View those samples and select one for a *Show Call* that you plan here. Then practice implementing your *Show Call* with a colleague, receive feedback, and incorporate it. Exchange roles and repeat.

The take:

Revision focus:

_____

Take pieces that are correct, erroneous, or "good to great"?

The reveal:

Identified or anonymous? Student read aloud?
Questions:

_____

_____

_____

Follow-up task for class:

_____

_____

_____

> **blog**
>
> Find these blog posts at teachlikeachampion.com/blog/kate-butries-show-call-invisible
> -hand-build-culture-guest-post-joaquin-hernandez/ and http://teachlikeachampion.com
> /blog/katie-mcnickles-show-call/.
>   Each includes revealing discussion.
>   In "Kate Butrie's Show Call & the 'Invisible Hand,'" Joaquin explores the culture of
> student ownership that Kate has built around her *Show Calls.*
>   In "Katie McNickle's Show Call," Doug analyzes how Katie skillfully *Show Calls* numerous students in math.

ACTION PLANNING

Use this action planner to continue your work with *Show Call.* (Find a printable version of this form at my.teachlikeachampion.com.) You know you're on the right track when . . .

- Your reveal uses *Positive Framing* (technique 58).
- Your revision task or other follow-up is actionable and effective.

HOW AM I DOING?

_____

_____

Design one or more action steps for improvement. Decide on an interval by which you'll revisit this page to assess your progress.

Action Step 1

By when, with whom, and how you will measure your effort
By _____, I will . . .
   Date

_____

_____

How Did I Do?

Successes: _____

_____

_____

_____

Challenges: _____

_____

_____

_____

Next steps: _____

_____

_____

_____

Action Step 2

By when, with whom, and how you will measure your effort

By _____, I will . . .
　　Date

_____

_____

_____

How Did I Do?

Successes: _____

_____

_____

_____

_____

Challenges: _____

_____

_____

_____

Next steps: _____

_____

_____

OUR OBSERVATIONS ON THE CHAMPIONS

 Clip FG40. Nicole Willey, and Clip FG41. Paul Powell

Differences:

Nicole uses *Show Call* to excavate a deeper conceptual error than Paul needs to address. She maximizes ratio by combining it with a *Turn and Talk* (technique 43) and a *Cold Call*. Nicole doesn't do much *Positive Framing* (technique 58) to set up the *Show Call*. Nevertheless, we recognize that she has established a positive culture around *Show Call* when the second student jumps for joy when Nicole takes his work.

Paul uses *Show Call* to take one piece of work from good to great, but in his case, deep excavation and analysis are unwarranted. He *Positively Frames* his opportunity to "show off" student work, thus making being chosen positive and even desirable. He chooses just one piece of work because he needs to help students fix a small, common mistake. Notice how eager the student whose work he has taken is to participate!

Commonalities:

Both teachers take student work silently, with a neutral expression. Their *Show Call* doesn't cause distraction; it's business as usual. They also leverage *Show Call* to help students improve their work. Notably, at the end of discussion, they ask students to document the right answers and the relevant supportive thinking. Moreover, they use *Precise Praise* (technique 59) to celebrate success and make sure their *Show Calls* feel positive.

 Clip FG42. Sarah Lord

During the take, Sarah communicates civility and warmth when she leans in and asks Jeremiah if she can *Show Call* his work. When he doesn't respond, she lets him know that she's going to take his work once he finishes it; she's showing that she assumes the best about Jeremiah's intentions while maintaining a culture of accountability. When Jeremiah follows Sarah up to the front of the room so that he can finish refining his work, she reassures him and directs him back to his seat. In doing so, she mitigates the anxiety he felt around the take and preserves the timing of the *Show Call*. She continues to keep the culture positive by publicly praising Jeremiah's work. Even better, she does so concretely, with *Precise Praise* (technique 59). This makes it easier for the rest of the class to learn from and apply Jeremiah's strengths to their own work.

Failing to take Jeremiah's work would have

- Signaled that students can opt out of *Show Call*, undermining a culture of accountability
- Communicated that she has low or diminished academic expectations for Jeremiah, and potentially for other students as well
- Legitimized fears that *Show Call* is a "gotcha" that is worth resisting
- Robbed Jeremiah of a chance to shine in front of his peers and for others to learn from the unique strengths of his work

 Clip FG43. Rick Zadd, Maggie Johnson, Natasha Birch, John Huber, Julia Goldenheim, and Erin Michels

Rick: Sensing a bit of possible reticence from the student, Rick leans down and smiles as he asks, "May I? Can I show this?" Rick's words and warm demeanor reassure Ian that this *Show Call* isn't a "gotcha," and within seconds, Ian willingly gives Rick permission to *Show Call* his work.

Maggie: She crouches down to eye level with Romele and whispers her request, framing it as an opportunity to make his good work even better. In doing so, she exudes warmth and compassion and reminds the student that the purpose of the *Show Call* is to help him succeed.

Natasha: Natasha keeps her three takes systematic by picking work up without narration. She treats it as a normal, routine part of her lesson. Her taking *three* pieces of work also underscores the universality of her *Show Call* and will provide a bit of anonymity when she reveals the work—no one will know which of the three she is showing.

John: John reveals the work horizontally, showing students different ideas for how to take notes. This enables him to emphasize accountability for taking notes and autonomy in *how* they take them.

Julia: Julia brings the class together with a simple, efficient prompt, "Pause your writing; track up here." She then lets the class know that she selected one student's work (by name) because she thought it was representative of what she saw many students doing. She then honors the student's work by reading it aloud appreciatively. She reinforces a *Culture of Error* (technique 8) by acknowledging that the writing is "good," while also being clear that it could be "better."

Erin: Erin *Show Calls* a student's work on a whiteboard—a "low-tech *Show Call*—without revealing whether it contains a common error or is an exemplar. This keeps the cognitive burden of analyzing the work on the students, thus keeping think ratio and participation ratio high. Note that Erin preserves the anonymity of the student whose work is being shown, partly because she's asking the class to analyze the error. During the reveal, Erin avoids crowding out student thinking with unnecessary teacher talk.

BUILD STAMINA

OVERVIEW

Building Stamina refers to the practice of gradually increasing students' ability to write for sustained periods of time.

Rigorous independent work in the classroom—and outside of it—should require students to be able to develop ideas in writing for significant blocks of time: five, ten, fifteen, twenty minutes or more. But many students cannot initially sustain quality writing for that long. Five minutes into the in-class essay or extended reflection in journals, and their pens have stopped. They've been asked to run a 10k but can't yet finish a mile. They need a bit of stamina, and the idea is to help them *build* it by framing specific periods that require *nonstop* writing, starting out with as little time as a minute and gradually increasing the span to longer stretches.

The purpose is not so much to teach them to write without stopping. Rather, the goal of *Building Stamina* is to prepare students for tasks in which they're asked to think and write with the highest degree of rigor for longer periods of time.

Reflection

Why is writing for sustained periods of time difficult for students? What sorts of things do they do to avoid it, and how does it affect classroom instruction if students can't think in writing for sustained periods of time?

_____

_____

_____

FUNDAMENTALS

The point of *Building Stamina* is to help students develop the mental disciplines of sustained purposeful thought and steady processing of those thoughts into writing. This of course does not mean that students should always write without pause. Needless to say, good writers often stop to reflect on what they're writing. They, too, sometimes stare out the window. But anyone who writes as part of their vocation knows that writing is hard work and that every time a pen begins to scratch across a page, there are a thousand *nonproductive* reasons even a motivated writer can think of to stop. Learning to keep going is a key unstated skill. Teachers should of course balance the goal of building students' capacity to write productively with the goal of helping them know when and how to slow down or even stop (ideally because an idea requires it, not because they are tired or "sick of writing").

To clarify the *Build Stamina* technique, then, it suggests that you at times *temporarily* set aside the benefits of "slow writing" (captured in technique 38, *Art of the Sentence*, for example) for the sake of training your students to overcome psychological barriers that prevent them from writing productively in quantity. All those novelists gazing out of windows will tell you, in private, that they wish they could have been writing instead. As authors ourselves, we frequently feel as much.

Since a good term paper, say, will require both deep thinking and sustained concentration on writing for long periods of time, a classroom should too. Happily, the more stamina you build, the more you can choose to do other sorts of writing, knowing that any window gazing is due to deep thought, not frustration or passivity.

For this reason, the general rule during stamina writing is for students to write "wire to wire"—straight through the entire allotted period of time. Using *Circulate* and quiet coaching when needed, the teacher helps them sustain it.

Times and Timing

Build Stamina is likely to benefit from steady regular practice: two or three times a week for a minute or two at first, perhaps later five or ten.

Call out the start and insist on prompt response. It can help to remind students that stamina work is drafting. They are not producing finished work. "You can always revise it or reject it if it's not good. The idea is to force yourself to think and write." If you *Show Call* (technique 39) frequently, you could consider making stamina-based work exempt from *Show Calls* at times.

Congratulate students at the finish. Remember they've pushed themselves to run a race. And honor their writing by celebrating it, especially those moments when a student thought that she had "nothing to say," but surprised herself and found that once she began writing, the ideas started to come to her, and not vice versa. Reading aloud is perfect for this.

Giving students interesting prompts and the choice of topic to write about can help, not just because this makes it more likely that everyone can find a starting point, but because providing multiple questions means that those who are "done" always have something else to go on to.

Narrating the Process

Consider outlawing erasers: they are a distraction from writing disguised as a tool of diligence. Crossing out is fine, but even that sometimes can become a distraction. To a student for whom it becomes a distraction, you might say, "I'll give you time later to sort your ideas; try to keep generating them now."

If you're unsure that the class can race into action on the word "Go," prime the pump by questioning them about things they might write about or with a quick, collective brainstorm. Or read from the text in question.

As the clock ticks, *Circulate* to *Be Seen Looking* (technique 51), saying something like "I need to see all pencils moving," and homing in on anyone whose isn't. Motivate the class as a whole with ongoing *Precise Praise* (technique 59) for individuals about their focus and relentless writing.

Now and then alert the class about how much time remains. At the end, congratulate them on their success.

Balkers

Obviously some students will still struggle to sustain their writing. Remember that these are the students who often have the most to gain. Be encouraging but firm. Setting interim goals ("See if you can get to the bottom of the page!") can help. And check out our "Stamina Phrases Scenarios" online resource. It gives phrases you can use to address individual students who struggle with or even resist *Build Stamina* writing. Read through those possibilities, then add another for each of these behaviors or statements:

Doesn't know "what to write."

_____

_____

Says he needs to "take a break."

_____

_____

Is "done" before the end of the interval.

_____

_____

Crosses out or erases, over and over.

_____

_____

Endlessly hunts for the "right" word.

_____

_____

Stops writing to ask an off-topic question.

_____

_____

Stops writing and raises a hand.

_____

_____

> ### Revisit *Teach Like a Champion 2.0*
>
> Under "Valorize Student Writing" in this technique, Doug reflects on his positive feelings when a teacher read a portion of his journal to the class without any actual comments about it. You can do the same with good *Build Stamina* writing, and students will learn by example. Choose writing that you applauded as you first read it, not work that invites criticism or correction. Read it with inflection worthy of its value.
>
> Ask students to read their own work aloud—or a selection from another student's work that you've previously vetted. Doing this will also elevate the value of writing in the minds of the students.

ACTION PLANNING

Use this action planner to continue your work with *Build Stamina.* (Find a printable version of this form at my.teachlikeachampion.com.) Refer to these success points to assess how you're doing:

- Everyone keeps writing the entire time.
- Times are getting longer.

HOW AM I DOING?

_____

_____

Design one or more action steps for improvement. Decide on an interval by which you'll revisit this page to assess your progress.

Action Step 1

By when, with whom, and how you will measure your effort

By _____, I will . . .
   Date

_____

_____

How Did I Do?

Successes: _____

_____

_____

_____

Challenges: _____

_____

_____

_____

Next steps: _____

_____

_____

_____

Action Step 2

By when, with whom, and how you will measure your effort

By _____, I will . . .
Date

_____

_____

_____

How Did I Do?

Successes: _____

_____

_____

_____

_____

Challenges: _____

_____

_____

_____

Next steps: _____

_____

_____

_____

BUILD STAMINA

FRONT THE WRITING

OVERVIEW

Teachers often use writing assignments as a capstone to their lessons. Students might start class by reading a text, hearing a short presentation, or completing a lab. Then they follow it up with discussion that reflects on and amplifies the experience. Then, at the end, they write in response to this sequence of activities. However, "capstone" writing like this, while valuable in many ways, has its drawbacks: one is that it can leave students reliant on discussion with (or overhearing of) their peers to generate meaning from the initial activity. And with no way to assess where apparent understanding came from, you risk not knowing whether your students can derive their understanding directly from the reading, lab, or presentation, or whether they need their classmates to prompt them to understand.

Front the Writing addresses this issue by asking students to write as soon as they experience an activity and before they have discussed it. This means they can still learn from their classmates, but you—and they—also have a record of what they learned on their own. It can help you—and them—recognize how independent they are as thinkers.

Reflection

A skeptic might say that this issue is irrelevant: If students learn the material, who cares how they learn it? Why is this issue important?

_____

_____

_____

Our thoughts: When students depend on discussion, their ideas aren't as independent. Building off the ideas of others is fine some of the time. However, in college, students will have to generate meaning directly from what they read and from their own independent activities—labs, research, and so on. So sometimes students must learn to see things in their own way. And, of course, because you can derive understanding on your own before discussion does not mean you cannot also develop or change your understanding based on discussion.

FUNDAMENTALS

Front the Writing builds on technique 37, *Everybody Writes*, but differs in that the latter is designed to give students time to process their thoughts and rehearse their ideas via writing so that they're comfortable talking about those ideas. It's a way to prime the pump. In contrast, *Front the Writing* is a tool to help you gather data and check for understanding in a more nuanced way.

Front the Writing focuses more on writing immediately after reading or other activities. For simplicity here, we will refer to all of these as "reading" because reading is the most common activity from which we want to ensure that students can directly generate meaning. Of course there are many comparable sources:

- Presentation of important primary documents such as political cartoons
- Analysis of graphs/charts/data
- Labs
- Videos
- Demonstrations
- Dramatic presentations or plays

By having your students first "read," second write about the reading, and only then discuss it, you enable yourself to see whether students truly understood the ideas on their own. In other words, you want to replace a read-discuss-write (R-D-W) cycle with the cycle of read-write-discuss (R-W-D). Even better, run a cycle in which they read-write-discuss and then write *again* (R-W-D-W). This lets you assess what your students learn from the text or activity *and* what they pick up from the discussion that follows the reading.

We especially like this R-W-D-W cycle because it's important to have a final writing exercise that assesses how much your students know at the end and draws their attention to how much they've learned, as judged by changes they make to their second writing.

PLAN IT INTO A LESSON

Mark up a lesson plan you're working on in the following ways:

1. Identify a point at which all your students will write an answer to your question before discussion.
   - What are the questions you want to ask? What do you want to assess and collect data about?
   - Where will students write (in a notebook, graphic organizer, in the margin)?
   - What are your expectations of their writing (quick notes; fully thought out, well-written *AOS* sentences; paragraphs)?
   - Will you collect their work? Will you *Circulate* (technique 24) while *Tracking Not Watching* (technique 4)?
2. Plan your discussion questions. Consider how you want the discussion to support what the student has learned from the text.
3. Plan your final assessment questions. How will you ensure that they assess students' abilities to process and synthesize ideas from the discussion?

ACTION PLANNING

Use this action planner to continue your work with *Front the Writing*. (Find a printable version of this form at my.teachlikeachampion.com.) You'll know you're heading toward success when the writing . . .

- Feels fruitful for you and your students
- Sharpens your (and their) understanding of what they've learned
- Sharpens your students' skill at learning through reading or some other form of "R"

HOW AM I DOING?

_____

_____

Design one or more action steps for improvement. Decide on an interval by which you'll revisit this page to assess your progress.

Action Step 1

By when, with whom, and how you will measure your effort
By _____, I will . . .
   _{Date}

_____

_____

How Did I Do?

Successes: _____

_____

_____

_____

Challenges: _____

_____

_____

_____

Next steps: _____

_____

_____

_____

Action Step 2

By when, with whom, and how you will measure your effort

By _____, I will . . .

Date

_____

_____

_____

How Did I Do?

Successes: _____

_____

_____

_____

Challenges: _____

_____

_____

_____

Next steps: _____

_____

_____

_____

HABITS OF DISCUSSION

OVERVIEW

Productive discussion is usually the result of specific actions participants take. For example, people who make a conversation effective not only listen carefully but also show they are listening by occasionally offering brief summaries of other people's comments or by making an effort to connect a point to what someone else said. Such discussion skills probably won't occur naturally in the classroom unless teachers instill them through deliberate actions that we call *Habits of Discussion*. The goal is to normalize a set of ground rules that make your class discussions more productive, enjoyable, cohesive, and effective.

Revisit *Teach Like a Champion 2.0*

Like the techniques in chapters 7 and 8, our discussion techniques aim at increasing how broadly students participate in class and how much academic thinking they do themselves. As Doug wrote in his introduction to chapter 9, "Building Ratio Through Discussion":

Ratio . . . is the process of making sure there's a mental workout in the classroom and that it belongs to students. The goal is for students to be constantly on their toes, answering questions, drawing on or developing their knowledge base, and refining their ideas. There are two discrete parts of ratio: *participation ratio* and *think ratio*.

Reflection

In your view, what should be the purpose of a classroom discussion?

_____

_____

What do discussions currently look like in your classroom?

_____

_____

Our thoughts (yours might be different): A discussion should be a mutual endeavor by a group of people to develop, refine, or contextualize an idea or set of ideas. This is different from what sometimes gets called a discussion, which is a series of loosely related comments by people in a room.

FUNDAMENTALS

Four ideas can help you build *Habits of Discussion.*

Voice, Tracking, and Names

In order to have productive discussions, you must build a foundation. As simple as it sounds, for example, speakers need to speak loudly enough for others to hear. And when students make a habit of looking at the speaker, they listen better, pick up more information, and demonstrate that they think it's important to listen (see technique 47, *STAR/SLANT*). Responding to speakers by name reminds students that comments are made for and to other class members as much as the teacher. All of these things—easily overlooked—encourage quality discussion.

Follow-On Questions and Prompting

Follow-on questions and follow-on prompts set the expectation during discussion that participants are to listen carefully to others in the discussion. A follow-on question asks a student to respond to what another student has said. (We discuss this in *Cold Call,* technique 33, but follow-ons need not necessarily be *Cold Calls.*) A follow-on prompt is less directive than a follow-on question. It minimizes the disruption to the conversation and lets the student wrestle with an issue independently.

Here are of examples of both. Feel free to add a few of your own.

Follow-on questions	Follow-on prompting
"Alan, do you agree with Kate?" "Ahkilah, build off of what Ben said."	"Develop that . . . Alan?" "Evidence? Ben?" "Build on that . . . D'andre"

In what situations would you choose the question type? In what situations would you prompt?

_____

_____

_____

Sentence Starters

Teach your students to use sentence starters, which are opening phrases used in discussions to frame the relationship between a previous comment and one they are about to make. This helps students learn to talk (and later write) in a more cohesive manner. As you can imagine, sentence-starting frames shape the way people interact, and you can help students build a repertoire of starters they can use to diplomatically agree, disagree, and build on to different ideas. Such frames help students weave their comments into real discussion rather speaking random, disjointed remarks.

Managing the Meta

By "managing the meta" we mean explicitly guiding your students in the dynamics of building conversation, using feedback and modeling to train them how to have productive discussions—ones that are grounded in evidence, say, or that sustain their focus on ideas rather than jumping to a new topic with each comment. While there are times for an "outside-the-box" idea, we think a benefit of managing the meta is that it can help discipline discussions to stay focused on an important topic. We call this staying "inside the box."

Revisit *Teach Like a Champion 2.0*

Doug's discussion "Managing the Meta" tells how history teacher Ryan Miller kept discussion "in the box" when a student tried to take it elsewhere:

> Miller's students were examining primary source documents about President Teddy Roosevelt's intervention in Panama. One student commented that Roosevelt's claims that the United States was not involved were an effort to hide the government's true intentions. The format of class here was a Socratic discussion in which Ryan allowed students to respond directly to one another, while he often stepped back for significant amounts of time. Whereas Ryan was less likely to step in on a point of content (for example, "That's not what the document says; let's read that again"), he was . . . very willing to step in to shape the dynamics of the discussion and to keep the discussion disciplined.
>
> That's what he did in this case. The subsequent student's comment broached a brand-new topic, so Ryan said, "That's interesting, but I'd like to hear someone respond to [the previous student] Sara's comment before we move on to another one." This is what I call *managing the meta*. Ryan recognized that the power was in developing and expanding ideas through a series of connected comments. That sometimes requires keeping a discussion "inside the box."

ROLL IT OUT

Your Introduction

Brainstorm and draft language you would use to speak to your students about the characteristics and benefits of effective discussion, and what shared behaviors make it happen.

Using your brainstorm, plan how you will introduce your students to the fundamentals of voice, tracking, and names: what each involves and why it matters:

Voice: _____

_____

_____

Tracking: _____

_____

_____

Names: _____

_____

_____

Practice rolling this out. If you can, film yourself practicing. Are you compelled by your rationales?

_____

_____

_____

Sentence Starters

Here are some sentence starters you can also model and ask your students to use. Consider and record a use you could make of each example. Then feel free to add a few of your own.

Starter	Purpose it could serve
"I understand why you'd say that, but . . ."	

Starter	Purpose it could serve
"I was thinking of something similar . . ."	
"There was another example of that . . ."	
"The thing that doesn't take into account is . . ."	
"I want to build on what you said . . ."	
"I interpreted that differently . . ."	

Consider how you want to introduce sentence starters to your students. Pick the ones you'd like to introduce first, and practice alone or with a partner.

Follow-Ons, Starters, and Managing the Meta

Plan the following for keeping discussions productive.

What you'll model or say about keeping discussions in the box:

_____

_____

_____

What you'll model or say to encourage students to use sentence starters:

_____

_____

_____

When you'll go with a follow-on question or prompt:

_____

_____

_____

How you'll ensure that students are listening to one another and building off each other's ideas:

_____

_____

_____

How you'll keep it positive (see technique 58, _Positive Framing_):

_____

_____

_____

ACTION PLANNING

Use this action planner to continue your work with _Habits of Discussion_. (Find a printable version of this form at my.teachlikeachampion.com.) Refer to the following success points:

- Students speak up, track, and use names.
- They connect their comments with previous comments.
- More and more, discussion stays on target.

HOW AM I DOING?

_____

_____

Design one or more action steps for improvement. Decide on an interval by which you'll revisit this page to assess your progress.

Action Step 1

By when, with whom, and how you will measure your effort

By _____, I will . . .
<small>Date</small>

_____

_____

How Did I Do?

Successes: _____

_____

_____

_____

Challenges: _____

_____

_____

_____

Next steps: _____

_____

_____

_____

Action Step 2

By when, with whom, and how you will measure your effort

By _____, I will . . .
<small>Date</small>

_____

_____

_____

How Did I Do?

Successes: _____

_____

_____

_____

Challenges: _____

_____

_____

Next steps: _____

_____

_____

TURN AND TALK

OVERVIEW

Turn and Talk—a short discussion between a pair of students—is a common tool used in thousands of classrooms. At its best, it can be a powerful tool for maximizing participation and increasing the depth of student thinking. It can also be used to develop the ideas (and confidence) students need for greater academic independence.

But it takes skill to monitor and manage *Turn and Talk* so that students don't spend the time in unproductive chatter or develop not better ideas but misconceptions, so it's important to design and implement *Turn and Talk* to keep students accountable, maximize rigor, and ensure that it precedes other productive activities.

Reflection

Try to think of an example of a successful *Turn and Talk* you've used or observed and an unsuccessful one. What was the difference?

_____

_____

_____

ANALYZE THE CHAMPIONS

 Clip FG44. Laura Fern, Grade 1

 Clip FG45. Eric Snider, Grade 7

In clips FG44 and FG45, compare Laura's and Eric's *Turn and Talks*. What's similar? Which type of ratio (see pp. 234–235 in *Teach Like a Champion 2.0*) is each emphasizing?

Laura Fern	Eric Snider

Commonalities:

_____

_____

Ratio:

_____

_____

_____

Compare your observations with ours at the end of this technique.

FUNDAMENTALS

We'll begin by exploring the uses of *Turn and Talk*. Then we'll study the tools you can use to make *Turn and Talks* as efficient and productive as possible.

Uses for *Turn and Talk*

Like any other teaching tool, *Turn and Talk* should serve a clear purpose in your lesson and ultimately help students achieve the objective you've defined (with technique 16). Here are some ways it can do that:

Jump-start engagement. Turn and Talk can boost energy and participation by engaging every student in the lesson. This can be especially useful in those moments when you want to build or sustain momentum. *Turn and Talks* give introverted students a chance to shine, along with students who are dying to share their ideas.

Lock in knowledge. Turn and Talk can help students commit essential facts, definitions, or concepts to memory by having them restate them to a partner. This will increase students' ability to apply them during independent practice and beyond. For instance, you might have students repeat the class definition of "theme" before asking students to independently identify the key theme in a short story.

Develop and refine ideas. Turn and Talk can be a low-risk, confidence-building opportunity for students to develop and rehearse their thinking, to turn a notion into an idea, or to revise vague language to make it more precise. This will not only increase the rigor of the immediate task but also improve the depth and quality of whatever task—for example, wider discussion, writing, or revision—that follows.

Look over your lesson plans for one or more days in the coming week. Would a *Turn and Talk* help you achieve your objectives by serving any of the purposes we've listed here?

Efficient and Accountable

The first step to ensuring that students engage productively in a *Turn and Talk* is engineering it for efficiency and accountability (see technique 48, *Engineer Efficiency*). Consider the following:

Setting pairs. Prearrange whom students should be speaking with so that they don't waste time during the *Turn and Talk* trying to sort that out. This eliminates the distracting social anxiety that students might experience about having to find a partner, and negates any excuse for not engaging right away ("But I don't have a partner!" "I didn't know who I was supposed to be talking to"). Stay vigilant about setting pairs throughout the year, especially as seating charts begin to shift or students are predictably absent.

The in-cue. How the *Turn and Talk* starts can set the tone for how it will unfold. If students take a wait-and-see approach, glancing around to check whether their peers will participate, you've already lost momentum. To avoid this, great teachers use crisp, energizing in-cues like "Go" or "Turn and talk" to ensure that students snap into vigorous discussion. You probably noticed Eric Snider's sticky in-cues "long hair to short hair" or "short hair to long hair." Strong facilitators of *Turn and Talk* also "manage turns"; that is, they cue students to start talking while also sometimes signaling who should initiate each pair discussion. This ensures balance in participation levels for students in each pair—some talking and some listening for everyone. Whatever cue you use, strive to be consistent so that students make a habit of responding promptly with quality discussions.

The out-cue. A crisp end to a *Turn and Talk* helps you maximize the time students spend applying the ideas they gleaned from pair discussions to the task that follows. And it helps them share their ideas while those ideas are fresh in their minds. Some common practices include using a countdown ("Bring it back in three . . . two . . . one") or a series of snaps to bring students to a state of quiet readiness. As with the in-cue, the key is to maintain consistency so that students learn to respond automatically to it.

Catching the crest. Cap the *Turn and Talk* at the peak of engagement to ensure that the momentum you established and the ideas students began formulating flow into whatever comes after. Cutting off at the crest of the wave leaves students with both something left to say and more to learn.

Precise time limits. It's often helpful to assign specific, odd increments of time to emphasize the importance and intentionality behind the *Turn and Talk* (see technique 30, *Work the Clock*). Use a timer to track the time, and keep yourself accountable for moving the lesson forward while, amid the creative babble of multiple ongoing discussions, you listen in on conversations. *Working the Clock* can also help students more effectively manage the pace of their conversations.

Here are more ways to make your *Turn and Talk* most efficient and productive:

Use *Cold Call* (technique 33) positively and often transparently to emphasize to students that they should be ready to share whatever insights they gained from the discussions.

Convert *Turn and Talk* into a "Turn and Task" in which each partner writes. For instance, you might say something like, "One minute to list in rank order the three images you think are the most important in the poem. I'll ask a few of you to share your best image. So be ready. Go!" By assigning each partner a piece of a task, you can make them mutually accountable for completing it. We once watched first-grade teacher Hilary Lewis apply this idea during a lesson about lines of symmetry. To kick off the Turn and Task, she asked "partner one" from each pair to first draw a shape on a whiteboard above the line of symmetry, and then to pass it to "partner two" so that he or she could draw that shape below the line of symmetry. By doing so, she made sure that every partner had something unique to contribute and that no one missed out on the chance to learn.

Reflection

What would you need to see and hear from students during a typical *Turn and Talk* to know they were engaging productively in it? Compare your thoughts with ours.

I should see . . .	I should hear . . .

Our thoughts (you've had others): We think it helps to notice students speaking to their assigned partner and getting fairly equal "air time," facing each other and making eye contact, nodding in agreement or shaking heads in disagreement, and jotting down or adding to existing notes. We hope to hear them saying things like, "I understand why you'd say that, but . . . ," "I was just thinking of something similar, that . . . ," "The thing that doesn't take into account is . . . ," "Oh, I hadn't thought of that," "I like that idea!" "Why/how did you . . . ?" and "I want to build on what you said."

ANOTHER CHAMPION

 Clip FG46. Ashley Hinton, Grade 4

What does Ashley do before, during, and after the *Turn and Talk* to increase rigor and participation? What impact do you think her actions will have on the quality of students' writing?

Before:

_____

_____

During:

_____

_____

After:

_____

_____

Impact:

_____

_____

See our observations at the end of this technique.

NEXT LEVEL: PUSHING RIGOR AFTER *TURN AND TALK*

An effective *Turn and Talk* is a way station to greater rigor. It provides students with the opportunity to rehearse, build on, and formulate ideas so that they can synthesize and apply them in a more rigorous task. Arguably, what happens after a *Turn and Talk* is just as important as what happens during. The figure here summarizes ways that teachers manage what happens next to increase rigor and help students make progress toward achieving the objective of the lesson:

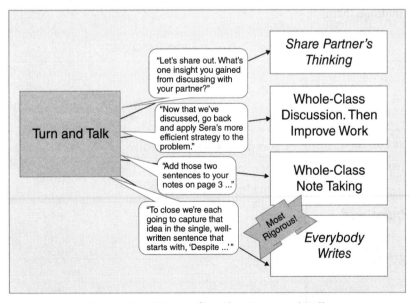

Increasing Rigor after the *Turn and Talk*

Share partner's thinking. Follow up a *Turn and Talk* by having students share their partner's thinking. This signals to students that the purpose of *Turn and Talk* is to learn from others, not just to rehearse or crystallize their own ideas. It's also an easy way to get everyone involved in the whole-class discussion. Nearly all students—regardless of their grasp of the material—can repeat or restate a peer's thinking. This practice also exposes students to the content from other pair conversations, so everyone can learn from the collective wisdom in the room.

Whole-class discussion, followed by improvement. Ask students to discuss their ideas as a whole class, then ask them to improve their work by *Owning and Tracking* (technique 10) the correct answer and the thinking behind it, or to revise their writing to reflect what they've learned. This ensures that students don't just listen to each other but also use what they learn to make their work better. Through repeated use, this may increase students' investment in *Turn and Talk* because they'll see it as a means for helping them do their best work.

Whole-class note taking. Ask students to share the insights they gained from the *Turn and Talk* with the class and then to take notes that capture their classmates' ideas. For example, you might ask students to "add two classmates' observations to your bulleted notes on page 5" or "jot down all the example phrases your classmates identify from pages 34–36 that illustrate the theme of man finding renewal in nature."

Everybody Writes. Facilitate a whole-class discussion in which students share, refine, and build on their peers' ideas. Then ask them to process in writing the most important insights they gleaned from the discussion. For instance, you could follow a discussion about the different forms of energy by saying, "To wrap up this lesson, I want you to describe the differences between kinetic and potential energy in one well-written sentence." Alternatively, you can ask students to write a paragraph that summarizes the factors that caused the decline of the Roman Empire. Following up with *Everybody Writes* not only ensures that students are accountable for carefully tracking the discussion but also requires them to lock down, develop, and, in some cases, transform their ideas through writing.

PLAN A *TURN AND TALK*

Use the template to plan your *Turn and Talk*. (Your library resources at my.teachlikeachampion.com include a printable version.) If possible, share your plan with a colleague who has also prepared one, and look for ways to improve them.

Turn and Talk Planning Template

Lesson Aim	
Primary Purpose for *Turn and Talk*	☐ Jump-start participation? ☐ Lock in knowledge? ☐ Develop/refine ideas?
***Turn and Talk* Question**	

Before	I will . . .	Students will . . .
During	I will . . .	Students will . . .
After: ☐ Share partner's thinking? ☐ Discuss and improve? ☐ Take notes? ☐ *Everybody Writes*?	I will . . .	Students will . . .

Adapt as a "Turn and Task"

On the lines here, describe how you could convert the *Turn and Talk* you planned into a Turn and Task. Share your adaptation with a partner for feedback.

If possible, also practice your Turn and Task with two other colleagues, get feedback, revise, and practice again.

_____

_____

_____

_____

_____

TURN AND TALK

You are on the right track when you . . .

- Establish clear expectations for how students should work with their partner.
- Ask students to generate some type of written product.

 Find this blog post at teachlikeachampion.com/blog/tip-of-the-day-turn-and-task/. This entry suggests a few kinds of tasks: "Tip of the Day: Turn and Task."

ANALYZE A CHAMPION

 Clip FG54. Erin Krafft, Grade 6

If you are already using *Turn and Talk* and want to take it to the next level, watch clip FG54 of Erin Krafft rolling out her system for productive disagreement between students. What ideas could you steal for your own rollout?

_____

_____

_____

ROLL IT OUT

On the lines here, plan how you will introduce *Turn and Talk* to your students. Make sure that your rollout

- Establishes clear expectations for what students should do before, during, and after
- Clearly and positively communicates the purpose for *Turn and Talk*
- Is quick and concise (ideally under two minutes)

_____

_____

_____

_____

TURN AND TALK

If you can, practice your rollout with a partner and ask for feedback.

ROLE-PLAY PRACTICE WITH A GROUP OR COLLEAGUE

Revisit the planning you did for "Plan Your *Turn and Talk*." In role groups of four (one *Teacher*, two *Students*, one *Coach*), plan to facilitate thirty seconds of an "after" task. Or do the same general thing with a partner.

After the *Teacher* practices his or her *Turn and Talk*, *Coach* then gives feedback to the *Teacher* with one glow ("It was effective when . . .") and one grow ("Next time, try . . ."). Using that feedback, the *Teacher* tries again.

Success points:

• The *Turn and Talk* maximizes efficiency and student accountability.
• The "after" task adds greater rigor.

ACTION PLANNING

Use this action planner to continue your work with *Turn and Talk*. (Find a printable version of this form at my.teachlikeachampion.com.) Use the aforementioned criteria for success.

TURN AND TALK

HOW AM I DOING?

_____

_____

Design one or more action steps for improvement. Decide on an interval by which you'll revisit this page to assess your progress.

Action Step 1

By when, with whom, and how you will measure your effort

By _____, I will . . .
    Date

_____

_____

How Did I Do?

Successes: _____

_____

_____

_____

Challenges: _____

_____

_____

_____

Next steps: _____

_____

_____

_____

Action Step 2

By when, with whom, and how you will measure your effort

By _____, I will . . .
_{Date}

_____

_____

_____

How Did I Do?

Successes: _____

_____

_____

_____

_____

Challenges: _____

_____

_____

_____

Next steps: _____

_____

_____

_____

TURN AND TALK

OUR OBSERVATIONS ON THE CHAMPIONS

 Clip FG44. Laura Fern, Grade 1, and Clip FG45. Eric Snider, Grade 7

We spotted these similarities between Laura's and Eric's *Turn and Talks*:

Consistent in-cue and out-cue. Laura's students know that "Turn and talk" is their cue to turn immediately to face their partner and begin talking and that a five-second count is their cue to wrap up their conversation and turn back. Note how she uses the phrase, "On my signal . . ." to set the stage for a crisp start: "On my signal, turn and talk to your partner about the examples of 'show not tell' that you heard. Turn and talk." Eric implements a variation on the same idea. He uses the quick and simple prompt ("long hair to short hair") to initiate the *Turn and Talk*. His in-cue is also a form of managing turns because it lets students know which partner should speak first.

Turn and Talk *nonverbals.* Eric uses a quick nonverbal gesture (moving hand from left to right) to prompt students to face each other. He then snaps to signal the close of the *Turn and Talk*. Similarly, Laura uses a quick clap that the students echo if she needs their attention in the middle of the *Turn and Talk* and a nonverbal to lower the volume of their conversations. Ultimately, Laura's and Eric's cues enable them to transition the class in and out of the *Turn and Talk* with economical language and a sense of urgency.

Engagement you can see. During the *Turn and Talk*, Eric *Circulates* and scans the class for signs of engagement. When Eric notices that a student is slow to comply, he uses a nonverbal gesture to redirect him. This signals to the rest of the class that he cares and notices whether or not they discuss the question. Laura also *Circulates* and listens attentively to conversations, at one point correcting a student who isn't meeting expectations. She also uses a nonverbal to prompt students to lower the volume of their conversations. This enables her to correct without seriously interrupting the flow of their discussions.

We also saw Eric catching the "crest of the wave." He doesn't wait until the conversation sputters to an end, but instead interrupts the students at what seems to be the peak or "crest" of their engagement. In doing so, he ensures that students will have some insights to share and some insights to gain during the whole-class conversation.

What about ratio? Eric maximizes participation ratio by implementing a variety of quick *Turn and Talks* promoting engagement and accountability. Laura uses various systems and subtle moves to emphasize *both* participation ratio and think ratio.

To boost think ratio, Laura poses a *Turn and Talk* question that has multiple correct answers. It requires students to provide evidence from the text and, with follow-up, to explain their evidence. As she *Circulates*, she continues pushing rigor when she asks a student a "How" question. When the first student she calls on struggles to share an answer, she gives him time to think before returning to him. In doing so, she gives him the chance to do the cognitive work instead of prematurely breaking the question down for him.

To increase participation ratio, Laura pulls a bit of a bait-and-switch. First, she asks for hands, but instead sends students into a *Turn and Talk*. This builds positive suspense and tension that is resolved once students begin discussing. When she brings it back, she reduces the transaction costs of calling on different students by taking three hands in advance. This enables her to sustain momentum and engagement coming out of the *Turn and Talk*. Finally, she punches a key understanding with technique 34, *Call and Response*. This gets everyone involved while also making the lesson feel fast and engaging.

Clip FG46. Ashley Hinton, Grade 4

What does Ashley do before, during, and after the *Turn and Talk* to increase rigor and participation?

Before: Before Ashley sends students off to write, she tells them she's going to be looking for work to show off. This sends a few messages: first, that she's going to be carefully tracking work because she cares that they do their best; second, that she's expecting to see great work because she knows they're capable of producing it.

During: She *Circulates* around the classroom to monitor the quality of her students' *Turn and Talk* conversations. While doing so, she uses *Precise Praise* (technique 59)—sharing the impact their writing had on her as a reader: "Yes, I want that one shared out. It definitely helps me picture what you're thinking." She uses a markup system (highlighter) to reward students who come up with especially juicy ideas and her reactions to her students' writing and ideas are genuine and motivating. We can also see that Ashley has established expectations for visible engagement, as students make eye contact, nod in agreement, and jot down notes as their partner shares.

After: Ashley adds another layer of positive accountability by asking students whose papers she marked to stand and read their ideas aloud. She then records these students' ideas on the board, which gives the rest of the class examples to imitate or to add to their list. This system gives a select group of students an opportunity to shine in front of their peers. The *Turn and Talk* and share-out prime the pump for the rigorous writing task that comes next. Thus the *Turn and Talk* is a step toward a more rigorous end (*Everybody Writes,* technique 37), not the end itself.

OVERVIEW

For a variety of reasons, a teacher sometimes needs to guide the conversation by commenting frequently—often after almost every student comment. But when one of your immediate goals is to use discussion to promote student autonomy, say, it's better to avoid mediating after every comment. *Batch Process* is our term for the art of managing a conversation while *not* commenting as frequently. Allowing "batches" of exchanges between students—first in short, direct strings, then in longer and more formal sequences—builds students' ability to engage productively in a discussion without constant teacher support.

Reflection

How often do students talk directly to or respond to other students about their academic work in your class? Is it as often as you'd like?

FUNDAMENTALS: SCAFFOLDING TOWARD OPEN DISCUSSION

In small college classes, professors often step aside, expecting students to be able to discuss some question among themselves, developing the ideas of others and refining or defending their own. But even in college, "fishbowls" and "Socratic discussions" can be unproductive when they lose focus or trade rigor for mere "air time." *Batch Process* begins with numerous scaffolds and repeated short daily practice so that the goal isn't necessarily just for everyone to "talk more." With intentionality even very young students can begin to acquire discussion skills that build toward complex intellectual exchange.

Setting Expectations

To introduce *Batch Process,* briefly tell students how to monitor their own contributions, including considerations based on technique 14, *Format Matters.* In early stages, you may need to assure students that you won't be "scoring" them on the correctness of what they say or asking others to approve or disapprove their comments. At the same time, they can be helped by a reminder to keep thoughts and remarks on topic and on task. You may also set the expectation that each student helps maintain direction by developing previous speakers' ideas.

Launch and Timing

Ideally you'd move to *Batch Processing* as the moment required—whenever a question or a comment seemed worthy of it. Realistically, though, you want your students to know how to discuss without your constant support, before an important question arises. Only if they have practiced the skill can they jump in and execute it at an important moment in class.

When you begin *Batch Processing*, it can also be helpful to think about the end. That is, you might want to set a time limit or decide what would let you know that your goal in the discussion had been accomplished and that it was time to move on. Being explicit about the timing and goal can help students make the most of their discussions. For example, you might say:

"Let's look at this scene. What's Othello thinking when he sees the handkerchief? Two minutes. Mostly you and very little me. Susanna, why don't you start?

Or you could try,

"Let's look at this scene. I want to come out of it agreeing on what Othello is thinking when he sees the handkerchief, or having a very clear picture of why we don't agree. Susanna, why don't you start?"

Choosing Speakers

Often when we decide to let students discuss ideas without comment from us, we step back entirely and let them decide who speaks when. We suggest caution with this approach. It often makes sense to retain control over calling on the next speaker, even if you don't offer comments on what students have said. This avoids a situation where the loudest or fastest are inherently rewarded and where some students are too shy to try to speak. Choosing speakers also gives you the power to draw in reluctant voices and ensure that discussion isn't dominated by a few. Here, you model an inclusiveness that students can learn from as well.

Daily Practice

Students learn discussion skills best through much short practice over time. As you become comfortable with *Batch Process,* try integrating it whenever appropriate, even daily. Brief is best, and even a well-placed minute of practice daily can accrue into serious progress.

Teachers at one school are asked to take one minute during every lesson and say, "OK, it's your turn. You're going to talk to each other about this. Go." Give some thought to planning that into a specific upcoming lesson. In line with technique 16, *Begin with the End,* what "this" might you ask them to discuss?

_____

For your students, how might you phrase such an invitation?

_____

_____

What expectations would you need to set?

_____

_____

_____

Interrupting

Even when students are talking to each other, for the most part it can be beneficial for the teacher to make occasional small interruptions between speakers in order to keep the conversation on topic and productive. A teacher might say, for example, "It seems like we're broaching new topics very quickly but not resolving any. Let's stick with Arturo's question about the Giver's motivation and try to see it all the way through. I'll signal when we're ready for a new topic."

Suggest some other common ways discussions could get off track and what you might say to refocus them.

_____

_____

_____

_____

> ### Revisit *Teach Like a Champion 2.0*
> Much of Doug's discussion of *Batch Process* covers champion teacher Ryan Miller's two-minute application of the technique. It's well worth rereading.

Reflection

Which elements of Ryan Miller's two-minute version might you benefit by trying?

_____

_____

THE NEXT LEVEL

Delegating Questions: Synergy with Writing

You greatly boost students' think ratio when you engage them in deciding what topic and question are most important to discuss. Remember that your students will be asked to do that in writing at least by late high school and certainly in quality college academic programs that require term papers and the like. The process leads students to own and embrace the kinds of questions you want them to be asking. Two possibilities for timed writing:

- Students identify literary passages worthy of analysis, or key passages in nonfiction text.
- Students generate questions for discussion.

What's another you might pursue?

_____

_____

More Complex Forms

Some teachers are immediately drawn to activities like a Socratic discussion or a fishbowl seminar. Their feeling is that activities in which you put all the kids around a table, stand in the background, and say, "Go, now discuss" are the most rigorous, and that this is due to the teacher's absence. Here are a few important caveats to take into consideration. Complex, teacher-free whole-class or panel discussions can often be challenging to set up and costly in time. Not to mention hard to conduct. Conversations among thirty people are difficult and not necessarily productive—in any setting. Can you think of a place where people frequently try to discuss a topic with twenty-nine others that is not a classroom? To address this, you might consider breaking discussions up into multiple rounds to involve everyone, and of course, designing activities for the rest of the class to do while the group discusses.

In short, many of the wisest teachers we know use such large-group activities, infrequently, perhaps to cap off a major unit. They often find that the rareness of this kind of discussion makes it more special and thus highly engaging for students.

GROUP TOPICS FOR DISCUSSION

Before your group of teachers convenes, be sure to complete the reflection on Ryan Miller's use of *Batch Process*. Then you can

- Share your reflections.
- Discuss what each of you is already doing to develop academic discussion skills.
- Discuss what might be your best next step.

Out of the group work, what new intentions do you have for *Batch Process* in your next week's lesson plans?

_____

_____

_____

ACTION PLANNING

Use this action planner to continue your work with *Batch Process*. (Find a printable version of this form at my.teachlikeachampion.com.) Use these success points to gauge how you're doing:

- Students regularly engage in "batches" of unmediated discussion with each other, for longer bursts of time and with greater frequency (approaching daily use).
- Over the course of frequent *Batch Process*, I do get everyone involved.

HOW AM I DOING?

_____

_____

Design one or more action steps for improvement. Decide on an interval by which you'll revisit this page to assess your progress.

Action Step 1

By when, with whom, and how you will measure your effort

By _____, I will . . .
   Date

_____

_____

How Did I Do?

Successes: _____

_____

_____

_____

Challenges: _____

_____

_____

_____

Next steps: _____

_____

_____

_____

Action Step 2

By when, with whom, and how you will measure your effort

By _____, I will . . .
   Date

_____

_____

_____

How Did I Do?

Successes: _____

_____

_____

_____

Challenges: _____

_____

_____

Next steps: _____

_____

_____

THRESHOLD

OVERVIEW

Threshold refers to meeting students at the door, and setting or reinforcing positive expectations before they even enter the room. This is one of the most important moments for building positive culture. It gives you the opportunity to greet each student by name. It's a moment when you can establish a personal connection with students through a brief individual check-in. It's a moment when each student shakes your hand, looks you in the eye, and accepts and returns a civil and cordial greeting. For these reasons, it's beneficial when *Threshold* happens every day.

Reflection

Do you currently stand outside the classroom, and greet each student by name as he or she crosses the threshold of your door? If you do, what do you consider the key ingredients of this activity? If you don't, what reservations might you have about it?

_____

_____

_____

_____

ANALYZE THE CHAMPIONS

▶ Clip FG47. Shadell Purefoy, Kindergarten

▶ Clip FG48. Stephen Chiger, Grade 9

View the clips, ideally more than once, and answer the following questions. Compare your observations with ours at the end of this technique.

What does Shadell do and say in the course of each greeting?

How much do the greetings vary in tone or other respects?

_____

_____

What has Shadell noticed in her greeting with the last student? How does she respond?

_____

_____

What's more sophisticated or high school–appropriate about Stephen's *Threshold* and what he expected students to do upon entering?

_____

_____

_____

FUNDAMENTALS

Basics

See both sides. Stand where you can see the hall and the room, so that you can briefly direct or compliment behavior outside and in. "Thanks, Adele, for going directly to your seat." "Chairs in to let others get by."

Control the flow. Stand where you control movement in and out as much as possible; it's your right and responsibility to control how quickly and when students enter.

Shake hands and initiate eye contact. This builds a tone of civility and should cause each student to pause and make eye contact. The handshake puts you in charge of access to the room. If a student's *Threshold* is a little lacking, gently hold on to the hand until the student does it better.

Use positive chatter. Build positive rapport and connections to students with brief personalized comments: "Looking sharp, Devon!" You won't have time to say something like this to every student, so pick a few each day; over time, connect with everyone as an individual.

Reset expectations. Use *Threshold* as an opportunity to remind and reset students who are in danger of slipping. A gentle reminder of your expectations will go a long way for students struggling to improve.

Consistent on Both Sides

It's best to maintain a consistent positive tone. It can be tempting to greet some students with a smile and positive words and others with subtle verbal or nonverbal corrections, or not greet them at all. Techniques 58 and 60, *Positive Framing* and *Warm/Strict,* can help you address all students with a positive tone that simultaneously communicates high expectations.

Some students may not always respond as you wish without some further instruction, training, and positive encouragement from you. For example, a student may

- Avoid eye contact
- Respond with a silly greeting
- Fail to respond to the greeting
- Offer a greeting that is barely audible
- Offer a limp hand

The basic solution begins with making sure each student knows your *Threshold* expectations. When a student's *Threshold* is out of line, in good spirit you can ask him or her to go back in line and *Do It Again* (technique 50), entering on good terms while also meeting your expectations. The techniques of chapter 12, Building Character and Trust, can also help you address the problem.

Revisit *Teach Like a Champion 2.0*

Find detailed examples of *Threshold* corrections as performed by Dacia Toll and Jamey Verrilli.

Your Current *Threshold* Practice

Have you already incorporated the basics we've described into a *Threshold* routine? For each, briefly note that you do them or that you might improve them. Or identify a possible benefit of ones you don't use now.

See both sides:

_____

Control the flow:

_____

Shake hands/initiate eye contact:

_____

Use positive chatter:

_____

Reset expectations:

_____

Threshold Greetings

Here are some aims your greetings can serve, with examples. Below each one, add other wording you use or could use.

Remind students where they are or where they are going: "Ready for college today?"

_____

Remind students what you expect of them: "I'm ready to see your best!"

_____

Build relationships and rapport with students: "Great shot in yesterday's game!"

_____

Tell students what is coming next: "Are you ready for today's quiz?"

_____

Encourage them: "Oh, you got this quiz!"

_____

Correct behavior: "I know you can give a stronger handshake than that!"

_____

Recognize good behavior: "Excellent patience from you yesterday."

_____

Reinforce academic material: "The Battle of Gettysburg, Marcus. Fought in what year?"

_____

Reinforce academic achievement: "Here he is, the man of thoughtful essays!"

_____

Reflection: What, No Door?

If school policy or logistical reasons prevent meeting students at the door, what other daily ritual might you create to signify the formal start of class? For example, could you walk the rows briefly greeting students during a daily _Do Now_ (technique 20)? Or what other ritual might you do so that students acknowledge they've entered your teaching domain?

_____

_____

THE NEXT LEVEL

With Jamey Verrilli's example in mind (see *TLAC 2.0*), view your *Threshold* as part of a broader routine by which you engage your students and launch the lesson. Do you notice any problem of coordination between *Threshold* and your launch of the actual lesson?

_____

_____

Also, what greeting could you use to reflect your school's team spirit or your classroom's overall climate? Is there a phrase that, if you say it, students will be proud to say back to you?

_____

Exit Ticket (technique 26) is one good routine for closing class sessions with a brief farewell contact. Whatever your current de facto routine that marks the students' departure from class, could you improve it with the use of methods similar to those of *Threshold*?

_____

_____

ROLL IT OUT

In your next lesson plan, incorporate a note about *Threshold* that can strengthen its usefulness as part of your overall opening routine.
Look over your work in "*Threshold* Greetings." Write and mentally rehearse the following:
Two greetings that relate back to your previous session with the class:

_____

_____

Two greetings that connect to some activity or expectation for today:

_____

_____

THRESHOLD

Are any students likely to slip into the room before you've posted yourself at the door? How will you include them in the greeting and make that less likely to happen next time?

_____

_____

WORKING WITH A GROUP OR PARTNER

Observe and notice the behaviors of students entering other classrooms where teachers have or don't have _Threshold_ down.

If you have time for more than the following discussion topics, your group may want to practice with the "_Threshold_ Role Play" from my.teachlikeachampion.com.

To a partner or group, describe a _Threshold_ routine you've used. What purposes does it serve? What do you do? How do students respond?

Tell what's easy or more challenging for you in seeing both sides, controlling the flow, shaking hands, resetting expectations, or using positive chatter. Gather useful comments.

Share your ideas from "_Threshold_ Greetings" and brainstorm others.

ACTION PLANNING

Use this action planner to continue your work with _Threshold_. (Find a printable version of this form at my.teachlikeachampion.com.) You know you're on the right track when you . . .

- Greet and make positive contact with each student.
- Use _Do it Again_ to reset expectations (when necessary).
- Acknowledge student efforts.

HOW AM I DOING?

_____

_____

Design one or more action steps for improvement. Decide on an interval by which you'll revisit this page to assess your progress.

Action Step 1

By when, with whom, and how you will measure your effort

By _____, I will . . .
<small>Date</small>

_____

_____

How Did I Do?

Successes: _____

_____

_____

_____

Challenges: _____

_____

_____

_____

Next steps: _____

_____

_____

_____

Action Step 2

By when, with whom, and how you will measure your effort

By _____, I will . . .

Date

_____

_____

_____

How Did I Do?

Successes: _____

_____

_____

_____

Challenges: _____

_____

_____

_____

Next steps: _____

_____

_____

THRESHOLD

OUR OBSERVATIONS ON THE CHAMPION

 Clip FG48. Stephen Chiger

What stands out about Stephen's *Threshold* and what comes after is the level of ownership students assume for it. Stephen does very little to manage students once they cross the threshold of his door. He barely interrupts to monitor the noise level in the classroom (the expectation is silence). He doesn't distribute any materials. Instead, a "binder helper" distributes binders to classmates as they enter, and students prepare their materials for the lesson once they get it. Even when the binder helper asks Stephen for guidance on what she should do when she can't locate a binder, Stephen encourages her to resolve the issue herself. Once he enters, students are already starting on the *Do Now* without any prompting from Stephen. His acknowledgment that the students know what to do "as always" communicates his trust in them to meet all expectations.

STRONG START

OVERVIEW

As every teacher knows, the opening minutes of class influence the trajectory of a lesson and can often determine whether it succeeds. Lay the groundwork with a *Strong Start*—a sequence of routines that set students up for success from the moment they enter class to when the main lesson begins. Together, these routines build positive momentum and engage students in productive habits from the moment they arrive.

For the purposes of study and analysis, we'll divide *Strong Start* into three stages:

- Door to *Do Now*
- *Do Now*
- Review Now

Reflection

Write and compare your thoughts with ours about these two statements a teacher might make about the start of class.

1. "My lesson starts as soon as I start teaching."
2. "My lesson starts as soon as my students walk through the door."

How are the assumptions behind the two statements different? How might implications for the class also be different?

_____

_____

_____

Possible thoughts (we bet you had others as well): Teachers who ascribe to the second assumption are more likely to build positive momentum from the start by greeting and teaching students with warmth and enthusiasm. They're more likely to set students up for success in the lesson with a purposeful, rigorous *Do Now* and more likely to *Engineer Efficiency* in their procedures (technique 48) from the start so as to maximize the time students spend learning before the main part of the lesson begins. They're less likely to lose valuable instructional time and more likely to maintain effective pacing and momentum throughout the lesson. Structuring your classroom around the second assumption can also cause students to perceive themselves to be "in your class" from the moment they arrive. They are building habits and expectations for that space whether you intentionally shape them or not!

STRONG START

ANALYZE THE CHAMPIONS

 Clip FG48. Stephen Chiger, Grade 9

 Clip FG47. Shadell Purefoy, Kindergarten

What do Stephen's and Shadell's *Strong Starts* accomplish? View the two videos and take a moment to jot down some thoughts. Then see our observations at the end of the technique.

Stephen Chiger	Shadell Purefoy

What are some things Steve's and Shadell's *Strong Starts* have in common? How are they different?

_____

_____

_____

FUNDAMENTALS

As we mentioned earlier, effective *Strong Start* unfolds in three key stages: (1) Door to *Do Now*, (2) *Do Now*, and (3) Review Now.

Door to *Do Now*

The first consideration of *Strong Start* is how students get from the door to the *Do Now*. Unlike *Threshold*, which immediately precedes students' entry into the room and focuses on setting cultural norms and expectations, Door to *Do Now* is about making a habit out of what's efficient, productive, and scholarly as students take their seats.

Listed here are some common procedures that teachers engineer to ensure a smooth and productive transition from the door to the *Do Now*. Although this sequence is not perfect or exhaustive, it contains the bones of an effective Door to *Do Now*:

Threshold: exchange of a handshake and warm greeting between you and students as they cross the threshold of your doorway

Lesson materials pickup: how and where students will pick up important lesson materials, such as handouts, packets, and assignments

Completed work: how and where students will turn in completed work

Transition to seats: how students are expected to make their way to their seats

Desktop setup: which materials students are expected to have on their desks and how they should arrange them

Homework: how and where students will submit their homework or receive sign-off on it from you or the homework monitor

Do Now: where students will find the *Do Now* and how they'll be expected to complete it

Do Now

As you may already know, an effective *Do Now* (technique 20) is a brief academic task that students complete independently and that often requires some type of written product. It's usually found in the same spot every day and is something students can do entirely on their own as soon as they reach their seats.

Review Now

To make the most of every minute of reviewing the *Do Now*, teachers carefully engineer the transition after students complete the *Do Now* so that it's crisp, efficient, and often energetic. The goal is to come out of the *Do Now* as quickly and orderly as possible and with the kind of urgency that signals "we've got a lot of important content to cover today, and I can't wait to get started."

Work the Clock *(technique 30).* Enhance the speed and efficiency of your transition to Review Now by displaying a timer or adding a countdown that gives students *just enough* time ("Pencils in the groove in three . . . two . . . one"). Take your countdown to the next level with a warm smile and upbeat tone that conveys your enthusiasm and excitement about what's to come. This can create a wave of anticipation that builds as the seconds tick by.

Emphasize accountable review. Kick off your review with a series of *Cold Calls* (technique 33), a *Show Me* (technique 5), or *Show Call(s)* (technique 39) to establish a culture of high academic expectations and instantly boost participation ratio. During this review, let the data you gathered via observation inform your decisions about whom to call on and in which format, and which problems you'll review deeply or quickly.

ANALYZE MORE CHAMPIONS

 Clip FG49. Four Champion Teachers

View these teachers transitioning to a review of the *Do Now*. What is effective about their transitions?

Bryan Belanger:

_____

_____

_____

Jennifer Ocello:

_____

_____

_____

Maggie Johnson:

_____

_____

_____

Erin Michels:

_____

_____

_____

▶ Clip FG50. Katie Bellucci, Grade 7

What is effective about what Katie does at each stage of her *Strong Start*?

_____

_____

Postcard from a Champion's Classroom

Pay special attention to what you see at the numbered arrows in the photo "Maggie Johnson's Door to *Do Now*." What evidence do you see of procedures for efficient entry and a *Strong Start*? After you write, compare your observations with ours.

Maggie Johnson's Door to *Do Now*

Our Observations on the Arrows

(1) Maggie warmly greets each student at the door with a handshake. (2) Students know that the expectations are to enter silently and in a single-file line. (3) Lesson packets are located on a desk near the entry to ensure that students have everything they need for the lesson by the time they reach their seat. (4) One student is already sitting and copying the objective before she starts the *Do Now*. She's able to get right to work, in part because she knows exactly where to look for both the objective and the *Do Now*. They're posted in the same place every day (on the board). (5) Students who have backpacks or jackets hang them up on hangers in the back of the classroom. This ensures that the aisles stay clear and clutter-free for a smooth entry.

THE NEXT LEVEL

Standardize the Field

Consider these questions as you develop a plan for how you'll standardize the field (see technique 3) in your classroom *Strong Start*. After you respond, exchange and discuss your plan with a partner. Incorporate at least one piece of feedback.

Threshold. How will you and your individual students greet each other as they cross the doorway of your classroom (handshake, single-file line, silently or with light chatter, and so forth)?

Lesson materials. Where will students pick them up?

_____

Prior work and notes. Where will students retrieve binders or folders with completed work?

_____

Transition to seats. How will students be expected to transition to their seats (silently or light chatter allowed, one or more single-file lines, and so on)?

_____

_____

Personal belongings. Where will they place belongings (jackets, backpacks, and so forth)?

_____

Desktop setup. What should students have on their desks, and where, once they begin the *Do Now*?

_____

Homework. How and where will students submit their homework or have you check it off? (in a bin by the door, pass in to teacher, stamped by homework monitor)?

_____

_____

Do Now. Where will students find the *Do Now* every day (at their desks, on the board, on a table by the door)?

_____

Look and you shall receive. What one or two most important productive behaviors do you want to look for and narrate back to students? Script the language you'd use to reinforce them.

_____

_____

_____

Plan data-driven review. How will the data you gather inform your review? (whom to call on, which questions to review more or less deeply)?

_____

_____

_____

Transition to review. What will you typically say to transition students out of the *Do Now* and into review?

_____

_____

Rolling Out an Entry Procedure

Technique 49 (*Strategic Investment: From Procedure to Routine*) includes a Rollout Template to plan the rollout for any procedure. Print it out from the "Useful Tools" section at my.teachlikeachampion.com. Use it to plan the rollout for one of your entry procedures. If possible, share your plan with a colleague who has also prepared one, and look for ways to improve them.

Script Your Transition to Review

In the space provided, draft the standard language you'd like to use to transition to review. Here is some language you can adapt from montage clip FG49:

Cut 1. Bryan. "All right. Here we go. Pencils down. Three . . . two . . . one. *[Scans.]* Good morning, Williams! [the class name]. Rock-paper-scissors your answer on two. One, two! *[Hands shoot up.]* How can I defend my answer, whether it be increase or decrease?"

Cut 2. Jennifer. "Three . . . two . . . one. Thank you. Let's look at this person's work." (*Begins* Show Call.)

Cut 3. Maggie. (*Timer beeps.*) "Pencils down when you're ready. Make it quick. Need two [students]. Thank you. On question one: who is Scout talking about when she says 'some members of the family'? Be ready to defend your answer with analysis."

Cut 4. Erin. (*Students are solving a rigorous problem on whiteboards.*) "Finishing up in ten . . . nine . . . eight . . . seven . . . six . . . five . . . four . . . three . . . two . . . Markers down. Show! *[Students raise whiteboards.]* Boards down. *[Holds up a student's board.]* Talk to me . . ."

Strive to include the following:

- *Observable directions and countdown.* "Pens down, books over, eyes up in three . . . two . . . one."
- *Acknowledgment of readiness.* "Now we're ready to go." "Thank you."
- *A signal to start the review.* "What did you get for question one, Janice?" "Hands down for question one. Be ready for my Cold Call."

_____

_____

_____

If you can, practice your script with a colleague, get feedback, and incorporate it.

STRONG START CASE STUDIES

For each case, share some constructive feedback you might give to help improve the *Strong Start*.

Case 1. Door to *Do Now*, Grade 8 History

Students are entering class in late November.

MR. RICKS: I like how Lana is showing me urgency. Remember to pick up your primary source documents from the back table as you come in. The objective and *Do Now* are up on the board as usual.

(*Some students begin to chat.*) I'm hearing way too much talking from the back. I know we're just coming from lunch, but that's not going to fly.

(*After Mr. Ricks has spent a few minutes stapling packets.*) Jeremy's pencil is already moving. He's getting right to work. Kayla is already on number two. OK, class, your *Do Now* time starts . . . *now*! Five minutes, on the clock."

Glows	Grows
It was effective when Mr. Ricks . . .	Next time, he could try . . .

Case 2. Transition to Review, Grade 3 Math

Ms. McCrady is beginning a transition out of the *Do Now* and into review. Her timer beeps, signaling the end of a writing task.

MS. MCCRADY: "Your pencils need to be down . . . and your hands need to be in the air in five . . . four . . . three . . . two . . . one . . . zeeeroooo. Just waiting on a few in the back to join us. (*A few seconds later, all students are with her.*)

Show me hands on two. One . . . two! (*Several hands shoot up.*) Wow. I've got so many hands. Now I have ten. Look at you guys! You're making it hard for me to choose. Let's go with . . . Shanice! What'd you get for number one?"

Glows	Grows
It was effective when the teacher . . .	Next time, the teacher could try . . .

Our Case Glows and Grows

Case 1. Door to *Do Now*

One glow is that students pick up their packets at a predetermined location, which helps Mr. Ricks eliminate the need to distribute materials and ensures that the start to the lesson stays efficient. The *Do Now* and objective are located in the same place every day ("The objective and *Do Now* are up on the board as usual"). As students stream in, Mr. Ricks builds momentum by narrating students who are meeting expectations ("Jeremy's pencil is already moving. He's getting right to work. Kayla is already on number two").

Mr. Ricks could make his language more concise and preserve momentum by eliminating redundant and counterproductive narration. For instance, he could stop reminding students about his expectations for routines that they already have down pat, such as where to find the *Do Now*. He could avoid describing what students *are* doing that they *shouldn't* be. Mr. Ricks could keep urgency higher by establishing the expectation that students begin the *Do Now* as soon as possible, rather than wait for his signal.

Case 2. Transition to Review

Ms. McCrady *Works the Clock* and effectively *Brightens Lines* between the *Do Now* and the review. Specifically, she uses a timer, countdown, and prompts for hands to go up on cue. When a few students don't follow through, she uses a nice anonymous individual correction you'll see described in technique 53, *Least Invasive Intervention*, which enables her to correct the last two students while preserving their privacy.

As improvements, she could strip down the language by eliminating redundant positive narration: saying "Wow. I've got so many hands" conveys a message similar to "You guys are making it hard for me to choose." Although she uses a countdown, she gives students more time than they need to follow her directions (five seconds instead of three) and stretches it out (". . . three . . . two . . . one . . . zeeeroooo"). This undermines the sense of urgency and momentum she's trying to build.

GROUP ROLLOUT ROLE PLAY

Revisit the planning you did in "Rolling Out an Entry Procedure." In role groups of four (*Teacher*, *Coach,* and two *Students*), plan to facilitate thirty seconds of *Student* practice.

After the *Teacher* practices the rollout, the *Coach* gives feedback (one glow, one grow—for example, "One thing I liked about your rollout was . . . Next time, try . . ."). The *Teacher* tries again, implementing the feedback.

You know you're on the right track when you . . .

- Explain the purpose in a way that cultivates student buy-in.
- Clearly model and describe the procedure.
- Are economical with words.

ACTION PLANNING

Find a printable version of this form at my.teachlikeachampion.com. Evaluate where you are in terms of applying of *Strong Start.* You're on the right path when . . .

- Your lessons begin as soon as your students walk through the door.
- Your *Strong Starts* run energetically and efficiently through the key stages.

HOW AM I DOING?

_____

_____

Design one or more action steps for improvement. Decide on an interval by which you'll revisit this page to assess your progress.

Action Step 1

By when, with whom, and how you will measure your effort
By _____, I will . . .
    Date

_____

_____

How Did I Do?

Successes: _____

_____

_____

_____

Challenges: _____

_____

_____

_____

Next steps: _____

_____

_____

_____

Action Step 2

By when, with whom, and how you will measure your effort

By _____, I will . . .
_{Date}

_____

_____

_____

How Did I Do?

Successes: _____

_____

_____

_____

_____

Challenges: _____

_____

_____

_____

Next steps: _____

_____

_____

_____

STRONG START

OUR OBSERVATIONS ON THE CHAMPIONS

 Clip FG48. Stephen Chiger, and Clip FG47. Shadell Purefoy

Stephen

Stephen assigns a *Do Now* that gives students practice engaging with important content that will help them master the lesson objective.

He goes out of his way to highlight the autonomy he gives students. For instance, as he enters, he thanks students for knowing "as always" what to do, which draws attention to the fact that students know how to start each lesson and that they chose to follow suit. This is particularly important given just how much autonomy high school–age students crave.

Shadell

Shadell does not assign a *Do Now*. She primarily uses her *Strong Start* to strengthen classroom culture and get kids excited for the learning they're about to do on the reading carpet. This is arguably grade-level appropriate, since her students are still learning how to write and might not be entirely able to complete written work without direct support and supervision.

Even though her students also operate with some autonomy, she's not as obvious or explicit about it.

Commonalities

Both use their *Strong Starts* to kick their lessons off on a positive and productive note. Whether they're warmly greeting students with a firm handshake at the door, gently reminding students of their expectations, or doing everything they can to ensure that students get to work as soon as possible, they send the message, "I'm glad you're here because we've got a lot of important learning to do today. Let's get started."

These teachers get their lessons off to a brisk and urgent (but not frenetic) start and then do everything they can to maintain the pace. Specifically, they use words sparingly, narrate the productive urgency they see, and keep transitions tight.

 Clip FG49. Four Teachers

Cut 1. Bryan Belanger

Bryan builds urgency with a three-second countdown that gives students *just enough* time to wrap up what they're doing. Once students reveal their answers using hand signals, he slowly swivels his head, almost as if he's eyeing the finish line for the *Do Now* as the class crosses it. Within seconds, students are analyzing their peers' responses to the *Do Now*.

Cut 2. Jennifer Ocello

Jennifer calls students to attention with a countdown to signal urgency. She *Works the Clock* (technique 30) with an odd increment of time (four seconds). This makes the timing of the transition seem deliberate and important. She then *Brightens Lines* (technique 28) with a brief pause and scan before shifting into the more casual register she assumes during her *Show Calls* (technique 39). Her *Show Call* "take" and "reveal" are quick, efficient, and concise, in part because *Show Call* is such a routine practice in her classroom. As soon as she achieves 100 percent, she dives right into this class discussion of student work.

Cut 3. Maggie Johnson

At the beep of the timer, Maggie signals to students that she's not going to give them the usual countdown because she wants to wean them off it so that they can learn to be ready for the Review Now without it.

The trust she conveys motivates students to transition with urgency to prove they're worthy of it. Once all are with her, she acknowledges: "Now we're ready." This marks the finish to the *Do Now* and the start of the review. Maggie's concision helps her efficiently transition students into the rigorous lesson on *To Kill a Mockingbird.*

Cut 4. Erin Michels

Erin's start with a ten-second countdown gives students just enough time to wrap up their whiteboard work. She gives a longer countdown than usual, in part because the *Do Now* task is so rigorous and the whiteboard task is more complex than a typical pencil-and-paper *Do Now.* At her cue, whiteboards go up in unison, which *Brightens Lines* between the *Do Now* and the Review Now. She facilitates this transition with just a handful of directions. Within seconds of ending the *Do Now,* students are engaging in a rigorous discussion of student work.

 Clip FG50. Katie Bellucci, Grade 7

In her Door to *Do Now,* Katie begins each student's day with a handshake greeting at the door. This routine instantly brightens their affect and helps Katie set a positive tone for the lesson. Upon entering, students pick up their own lesson materials, which frees Katie of the burden of distributing them and enables students to start working right away. When the last student enters, Katie "shows the clock" to build urgency, and her students get right to work.

For the *Do Now,* Katie sweats the small stuff, prompting students to do everything from adjusting their desks to fixing their headings. She lets students know when half the time has expired, to maintain urgency and help students manage their time more effectively. As she *Circulates,* she checks in with individual students to make sure they catch up on what they've missed or to break down trickier problems.

At the beep of the timer, Katie transitions students out of the *Do Now* and into the review with a three-second countdown. The transition unfolds smoothly and without interruption, in part because she avoids detours such as unsolicited questions ("Tiana, we'll get you in just a second"). Within seconds, the class is already excavating student responses to the *Do Now.* This efficiency ensures that students get to the heart of the matter—important academic content—as quickly as possible.

STAR/SLANT

OVERVIEW

STAR and *SLANT* are acronyms that summarize "base expectations"—default behaviors conducive to learning in class that we want students to demonstrate as a matter of habit. One example is sitting up rather than slumping over or putting your head down in class; another is tracking the speaker—that is, looking at the person who is talking.

By *STAR/SLANT* we mean those acronyms, others like them, or some other handy, easy-to-use tool that sets the parameters for what it means to be present and involved in class.

Here's what STAR and SLANT often stand for:

Sit up **T**rack the speaker **A**sk and answer questions **R**espect those around you	**S**it up **L**isten **A**sk and answer questions **N**od your head **T**rack the speaker

While you can depart from these exact phrases—and many classrooms and schools have replaced them with their own distinctive phrases or acronyms—STAR and SLANT are useful in at least two ways. First, they are "sticky," or easy to remember; second, as acronyms, they can be broken apart when necessary to emphasize each component part. For example, a teacher who uses STAR can ask students to "check your T" if they forget to track.

Reflection

Do you promote and reinforce basic expectations like those captured in *STAR/SLANT* in your classroom? What tools and methods do you use, and how effective are they?

_____

_____

_____

_____

ANALYZE THE CHAMPIONS

Clip FG52. Janelle Austin, Alex Bronson, Maura Faulkner, and Denarius Frazier

In this montage of teachers reinforcing *STAR/SLANT*, what themes do you notice? What moments appeal to you most?

_____

_____

_____

We share brief observations about them at the end of this technique.

FUNDAMENTALS

Embed It Deeply

When something like SLANT becomes an expectation it's easy to remind students of it quickly and simply, especially when it has a simple name. The more familiar it is to students, the more you can ensure that it happens with the smallest intervention.

To support your being able to remind students seamlessly, consider placing a poster at the front of the classroom with phrases that describe each letter of the acronym. You can call attention to it now and then just by pointing, or possibly even glancing.

In the best classrooms, the acronym is deeply embedded in the vocabulary of learning, as a noun (for example, "Where's my STAR?") and as a verb ("Make sure to SLANT"). Components combine into other punchy routine phrasing like "Turn and track." "Track me" is a great way to ask for eye contact from a student. If students know the acronym well, teachers can simply remind them about, for example, "your S [or T]" in SLANT.

Using the acronym of your choice, write and try out three or four phrases you could use to call it to the class's attention.

_____

_____

_____

Consider various contexts in which you might want to call upon a specific component of the acronym. Write and try out several phrases in which you embed some component.

_____

_____

_____

_____

_____

Nonverbal Signals

Use the space here to invent some nonverbal signals to reinforce *STAR/SLANT* without interrupting your teaching. For example, folding your hands in front of you while straightening your back can mean "Sit up straight"; pointing to your eyes with two fingers can mean "Track the speaker."

Component:

_____

Signal:

_____

Component:

_____

Signal:

_____

Component:

_____

Signal:

_____

Component:

_____

STAR/SLANT

Signal:

_____

_____

THE NEXT LEVEL: NEED BETTER FIT?

STAR/SLANT is effective even as students get older. In response to one of our blogs, high school teacher Chris Bostock told us about using a "Minds on" posture reminder: "We struggled for a while to find a phrase that allowed for more collegiate variation, and we landed on that. It allows for furrowed brows, cocked heads, hands on foreheads, and deep paper-tracking. Our non-example to make it uber clear is 'face smush.'"

If your "kids" seem too grown up for *STAR/SLANT,* try isolating a particular component of *STAR/SLANT* that you'd like your students to focus on, and make it applicable to the professional world that they are about to enter—for example, "Professional Posture" or "engage the speaker." To increase buy-in, make sure that you ground the direction in a way that emphasizes purpose, rather than power.

ANOTHER CHAMPION

 Clip FG51. Caitlin Reilly, Grade 6

To prepare for the section on rollout, watch Caitlin's inspirational rollout and steal a few ideas. Caitlin is welcoming her students back to school at the beginning of the year. They are almost all returning students and therefore know the expectation and how it works, so she doesn't have to do a lot of modeling and practice. But she still wants them to understand her rationale.

I could steal:

_____

THE ROLLOUT

Students deserve to understand *why* you are asking them to *STAR/SLANT,* which is to help them learn and to build a culture that honors their ideas. The older the students, the more they'll need to believe in your rationale in order for it to work. In short, *STAR/SLANT* requires a rollout and maybe even some periodic explanation.

To teach your class to *STAR/SLANT,* also see the general methods of creating any strong routine that are discussed in technique 49, *Strategic Investment: From Procedure to Routine.*

Plan the talking points for your rollout and practice it with a colleague. On the day you roll out, install your poster about *STAR/SLANT* at the front of the room. In the spirit of technique 58, *Positive Framing,* use language and an upbeat (but not canned) tone that motivates students to execute *STAR/SLANT* with energy and enthusiasm.

Explain the value of *STAR/SLANT* to your students—and yourself—always in terms of purpose, not power: "We do this so you can be STARS," rather than ". . . because when I ask you to do something I want it done."

Also explain how it improves your students' ability to learn by attending to the words of others—yours as well as those of classmates.

Just as you may practice other routines, plan to lead your class in learning and practicing each part of *STAR/SLANT* before you begin to require it. Model what you mean by *S* or *T* and check each student's attempt. Also ask students to show you what good tracking looks like, practicing it a few times. This will help make students aware of what to do and that it applies to everyone.

Occasionally, when you may need to take the class back to practicing some part of *STAR/SLANT*, use suggestions from technique 50, *Do It Again.*

PRACTICE WITH A GROUP OR COLLEAGUE

If you plan to cover more than one technique in the practice session, start with this one.

1. Tell the group which version or variation of STAR, SLANT, or other acronym you've chosen. If it's other than STAR or SLANT, say what's different about it and how it suits you.
2. Compare experiences of using it in class so far.
3. Share and compare your earlier phrasing work in "Fundamentals."
4. Remind the group which version you are using. Then run through your hand signals, with the rest of the group repeating them back.
5. If the session continues to another technique, direct some part of your *STAR/SLANT* toward others in the group at appropriate moments.

ACTION PLANNING

Find a printable version of this form at my.teachlikeachampion.com. Using feedback from your study group or other peers, and reviewing your own lesson notes and observations, monitor your progress on *STAR/SLANT.* You know you're on the right track when . . .

- The students in your class respond appropriately to your *STAR/SLANT.*
- Your *STAR/SLANT* is unobtrusive, rarely requiring a pause in the basic rhythm of the lesson.

HOW AM I DOING?

_____

_____

Design one or more action steps for improvement. Decide on an interval by which you'll revisit this page to assess your progress.

Action Step 1

By when, with whom, and how you will measure your effort

By _____, I will . . .
    Date

_____

_____

How Did I Do?

Successes: _____

_____

_____

_____

_____

Challenges: _____

_____

_____

_____

Next steps: _____

_____

_____

Action Step 2

By when, with whom, and how you will measure your effort

By _____, I will . . .
_{Date}

_____

_____

_____

How Did I Do?

Successes: _____

_____

_____

_____

_____

Challenges: _____

_____

_____

_____

Next steps: _____

_____

_____

_____

STAR/SLANT

OUR OBSERVATIONS ON THE CHAMPIONS

 Clip FG52. Janelle Austin, Alex Bronson, Maura Faulkner, and Denarius Frazier

Because SLANT is a defined expectation in this montage, teachers can reinforce quickly and gently. But it's important to note in the montage that you also see teachers reinforce ("glad to see you doing it"), enforce ("please make sure to do it"), and remind ("check yourself to make sure you are . . ."). Also important is that these teachers have adapted the technique to their grade level, setting, and own individual styles.

ENGINEER EFFICIENCY

OVERVIEW

As teachers, we want to maximize learning by minimizing time spent on mundane but often necessary tasks like submitting homework or moving from place to place. Moreover, outstanding teachers recognize that students can also become more efficient and productive at valuable academic procedures like taking notes and participating in discussion. *Engineer Efficiency* involves creating procedures by which students can perform both mundane and academic tasks in ways that yield more time for learning. Three types of procedures can be engineered efficiently: behavioral, cultural, and academic. The same design criteria work for all of them:

- Simplicity
- Quick is king
- Little narration required
- Planned in detail

Reflection

From recent classroom sessions, isolate some moments when you found yourself idling while students took too long at the academic or procedural business of the classroom, such as passing materials from one to another. Also identify slow-down points at which you had to verbally walk them through some routine you wish they could complete on their own.

_____

_____

_____

_____

ANALYZE THE CHAMPIONS

 Clip FG53. Julia Goldenheim, Grade 7

View the clip more than once and answer the following questions. See the end of the technique for some possible answers.

Julia uses numerous procedures that her students have already learned as routines. Isolate at least three separate routines and identify them here with a short phrase. What is the purpose of each? How many seconds does it take?

Procedure	Purpose	Length
1. _____	_____	_____
2. _____	_____	_____
3. _____	_____	_____
4. _____	_____	_____

What else do you notice in this rich clip?

_____

_____

FUNDAMENTALS

If you've implemented the techniques in this chapter, you've already established a few efficient classroom procedures. We hope you're noticing that procedures work for a great many tasks beyond the behavioral and logistical ones. To help you think of others you might work on, we've started a list for you:

Behavioral	Academic	Cultural
Hand raising	Complete-sentence answers	Verbal props to celebrate peers
Sitting in "learner's position" (*STAR/SLANT*)	*No Opt Out*	Hands down when a peer speaks
Moving students in the classroom	*Habits of Discussion*	Correcting a peer's mistake
Passing papers in	Note taking	Placing eyes on the speaker
	Turn and Talk	Nonverbally showing support (snapping fingers to express agreement with a peer's comment)
	Text markup/reading interactively	

Criteria: Simple, Quick, Largely Silent, Closely Planned

Simplicity

Break every procedure into a handful of specific, discrete steps that you and your students can remember.

Don't be tempted to embellish or extend a procedure with steps that seem fun and lively at first but soon become gimmicky and take time away from what's more important. For every step in your procedure, ask yourself:

- Does it help my students accomplish the task?
- Do I want them to do it every time for the rest of the year?
- For what it costs in time, is it giving back more in terms of productivity?

Quick Is King

How quickly your students can master—and then routinely and correctly carry out—a procedure (see technique 49, *Strategic Investment*) depends first on how well you've crafted and honed it. Unneeded steps will make it longer, but so will missing steps that allow confusion or turbulence to disrupt students' execution of it. You can draw students into faster performance by counting out steps and announcing how long you expect the procedure to take.

Reflection

Continuing from the previous reflection, how much actual teaching time might you add to your students' school year by creating quicker routines at particular points in your lesson?

_____

_____

_____

Little Narration Required

Plan a procedure so that it requires as few words from you as possible. Focus your few spoken words or counts on helping students act in unison at the pace you choose. Plan the procedure to avoid any need to micromanage it routinely. In the end, it should be something the students can do autonomously, without your explaining details. The fewer hints or reminders you need to provide, the prouder students can be of their own performance.

Plan the phrases you will use at each step so that they are clear, efficient, and consistent. Avoid adding other comments. Over time, begin replacing verbal reminders with nonverbal signals that students can rely on if they need them. Then gradually remove those reminders as well.

Review some routines you are already using. Is there narration you tend to provide that you could reduce?

_____

_____

_____

Planned to the Detail

Teachers with the tightest procedures get them that way by planning what they and the class will do at every step. Such teachers often walk through it themselves (or with peers) to make sure that it works. They plan and practice all key phrases.

> ### Revisit *Teach Like a Champion 2.0*
> "Planned to the Detail" in this technique provides two great examples.

Case Studies

Here are some common classroom procedures practiced by five teachers. Judge each one in terms of the four criteria. In the table below each, check off the criteria that this procedure satisfies ("glows") and what could be improved ("grows") before you move on to ours.

Case 1. Mr. McCormick

Before they begin the daily "Mad Minute" drill, Mr. McCormick

- Holds up his index finger to nonverbally prompt students to clear their desks.
- Raises a second finger, reminding them to hold their pencils out in front of their desks with a fist.
- Raises a third finger, prompting students to raise their pencils up.
- Holds up a fourth finger, prompting students to flip their papers.
- Releases students to begin their Mad Minute drill with the prompt "Five . . . four . . . three . . . two . . . one . . . *go!*"

Glows	Grows
☐ Simple?	
☐ Quick?	
☐ Minimal narration?	
☐ Planned in detail?	

Case 2. Ms. Marker

At the start of class, Ms. Marker

- Gives each "row captain" a stack of handouts for note taking.
- Answers two unsolicited questions about the upcoming unit exam.
- Scans the class as each student takes a handout and passes it down.
- Hands each row captain a second stack of handouts (tonight's homework). She gives her students seventy-five seconds to pass it down and file it.
- Hands each row captain a third stack of handouts (*Exit Tickets*). She gives her students another seventy-five seconds to pass it down.

Most rows finish with plenty of time left, while others finish much later.

Glows	Grows
☐ Simple?	
☐ Quick?	
☐ Minimal narration?	
☐ Planned in detail?	

Case 3. Mr. Murray

To check for understanding (per part 1), Mr. Murray routinely calls on students to report their answers to multiple-choice questions (A through D) from a *Do Now*. He then tallies the number of students who selected A, B, C, and D for each question so that he knows which answer choices to discuss.

Glows	Grows
☐ Simple?	
☐ Quick?	
☐ Minimal narration?	
☐ Planned in detail?	

Case 4. Ms. Mendes

As soon as all five of Ms. Mendes's students sit down at a U-shaped table for a reading lesson, she

- Reaches for her bookshelf and grabs multiple copies of the reading book.
- Hands a copy of the shared text to each student.
- Gives students ten seconds to flip to page 5. A few students have trouble finding it, so she helps them.
- Thirty seconds later, Ms. Mendes starts her lesson.

Glows	Grows
☐ Simple?	
☐ Quick?	
☐ Minimal narration?	
☐ Planned in detail?	

Case 5. Ms. Michelson

Ms. Michelson asks students to record their answers to a math question on their whiteboards. Here's how it unfolds:

- Immediately before the whiteboard exercise, Ms. Michelson answers a few unsolicited questions about the upcoming unit project.
- She then prompts students to raise their whiteboards up to show her when they're done.
- Several students raise their boards up right away, while the rest take longer. She has to remind some students to keep their boards in the air.

Glows	Grows
☐ Simple?	
☐ Quick?	
☐ Minimal narration?	
☐ Planned in detail?	

Our Observations on the Cases

Case 1. Mr. McCormick

☐ Simple? ☐ Quick? ☑ Minimal narration? ☑ Planned in detail?

Possible grows: Asking students to hold their pencils out in front of their desks with a fist adds unnecessary complexity. Mr. McCormick could also shorten his countdown from five seconds to three seconds.

Case 2. Ms. Marker

☐ Simple? ☐ Quick? ☑ Minimal narration? ☑ Planned in detail?

Possible grows: Ms. Marker could table the questions about the unit exam for a more appropriate time. She could also shorten the amount of time she allows students to spend passing papers.

Case 3. Mr. Murray

☐ Simple? ☐ Quick? ☑ Minimal narration? ☑ Planned in detail?

Possible grows: Instead of asking students to reveal answers one at a time and tallying them up, Mr. Murray could ask students to use hand signals to reveal their answers in unison. For instance, he could ask students to each raise the number of fingers that corresponds with their answers (for example, A = 1 finger, B = 2 fingers, C = 3 fingers, D = 4 fingers).

Case 4. Ms. Mendes

☐ Simple? ☐ Quick? ☑ Minimal narration? ☑ Planned in detail?

Possible grows: Instead of spending time distributing books, Ms. Mendes could leave them out for students at the U-table with the page they need to flip to marked with a sticky note.

Case 5. Ms. Michelson

☐ Simple? ☐ Quick? ☑ Minimal narration? ☑ Planned in detail?

Possible grows: Ms. Michelson could refrain from answering the unsolicited questions until a later time. She could also develop a procedure to ensure that students reveal their answers on cue, such as telling students to raise their boards by the time she counts up to the number three.

Design a Routine

Take a look at the Design Your Own Routine template for designing a routine procedure. You can use it as a model or download and print a page-size version at my.teachlikeachampion.com.

Directions: Using the template, plan out a simple, multistep routine for your classroom.

Design Your Own Routine

Multistep Routine
Examples: passing in homework; correcting a peer's mistake; cleaning off one's desk; completing a header, etc.
Vision of Success
Once students master this routine, they will be able to . . .

Goal Time (if applicable):
Upon mastery, this should take . . .

Materials Needed	Preparation Needed

Step-by-Step Expectations

Step	Teacher Will . . .	Students Will . . .
1		
2		
3		
4		
5		

By yourself or with a partner, use the template to design a routine that would often be useful to you in class to move in simple, quick, order through some business of the class. Or design a routine that would be useful to your students in performing some oft-repeated academic task. Critique with your partner or bring your work to a group session for comparison.

THE NEXT LEVEL

Improve on What You've Done

In this chapter, *Threshold, Strong Start,* and *STAR/SLANT* involve creating efficient procedures. So did many earlier techniques, such as *Format Matters, Do Now,* and *Exit Ticket.* Think about exactly what happens now when your students perform one or two of them. Rate and critique each one in terms of *Engineer Efficiency.* Use the "Action Planning" section to plan desired changes.

Technique: _____
Could be better: ☐ Simple ☐ Quick ☐ Minimal narration ☐ Planned in detail

Technique: _____
Could be better: ☐ Simple ☐ Quick ☐ Minimal narration ☐ Planned in detail

Technique: _____
Could be better: ☐ Simple ☐ Quick ☐ Minimal narration ☐ Planned in detail

Enriching Behavioral Routines with Academic Practice

When procedures unavoidably take up valuable amounts of time, enrich that time with oral academic practice.

> Access this blog post from my.teachlikeachampion.com/clip-week-megan-broome-makes-routines-academic/.
>   Check out the post "Megan Broome Makes Her Routines Academic" to see how one champion first-grade teacher enriches routine classroom process.

PRACTICE WITH A GROUP OR COLLEAGUE

There's advice about group participation, "Giving Feedback in Group Practice Activities," at my.teachlikeachampion.com. With one or more colleagues,

- Discuss your responses to your earlier reflections.
- Also compare thoughts about the case study work you did.
- Distribute copies of your earlier work for "Design a Routine." Together, note some positive similarities. Share at least one round of "glows" about the designs in terms of *Engineered Efficiency.* Share one or more rounds of "grows" as well.

For a Similar Grade and Subject Group or Partner

1. Thinking about your lesson plan objectives and supporting activities, together brainstorm a list of procedures you currently teach or might want to create. Choose a mutually interesting item from the list.
2. Separately or in pairs, line or crease a sheet of paper down the middle. With the four criteria in mind:
   On the left side, write down the procedure as your students should perform it.
   Spaced across the left bottom line of the page, abbreviate the first, second, and fourth criteria as S, Q, and P.
3. Pass your sheets around. On each sheet, each member reads, then chooses to place congratulating check marks by the three abbreviations.
4. Return the pages to their owners. Compare differences in the basic steps. Also allow each member to comment on his or her own sheet and to invite discussion or helpful advice.
5. Separately or in pairs again, with the four criteria in mind:
   On the left side, write down the procedure as your students should perform it.
   On the right side, write down the spoken or signaled directions you would be giving routinely as the students move through the steps.
   Spaced across the right bottom portion of the page, abbreviate all four criteria as S, Q, M, and P.
6. Again, pass your sheets around for each member to read and check-mark.
7. Return the pages to their owners. Allow each individual or pair the opportunity to comment or invite discussion.

Reflection

What future use might you make of the Design Your Own Routine template, as-is or with some modification?

_____

_____

_____

_____

ACTION PLANNING

Use this action planner to continue your work with *Engineer Efficiency*. (Find a printable version of this form at my.teachlikeachampion.com.) Use these success points to assess how you're doing at creating a procedure:

- Simplicity
- Quick is king
- Little narration required
- Planned in detail

HOW AM I DOING?

_____

_____

Design one or more action steps for improvement. Decide on an interval by which you'll revisit this page to assess your progress.

Action Step 1

By when, with whom, and how you will measure your effort

By _____, I will . . .

Date

_____

_____

How Did I Do?

Successes: _____

_____

_____

_____

_____

Challenges: _____

_____

_____

_____

Next steps: _____

_____

_____

Action Step 2

By when, with whom, and how you will measure your effort

By _____, I will . . .
<u>Date</u>

_____

_____

_____

How Did I Do?

Successes: _____

_____

_____

_____

Challenges: _____

_____

_____

_____

Next steps: _____

_____

_____

_____

OUR OBSERVATIONS ON THE CHAMPION

 Clip FG53. Julia Goldenheim

Julia is managing a number of procedures as she moves from one activity to another: passing in free-edits, passing down and filing homework, passing down notes and completing a heading, and starting the main lesson. Without students' having practiced these routines, these necessary housekeeping tasks could have eaten up a lot more time, but Julia is speedy and efficient. That means more learning time!

ENGINEER EFFICIENCY

STRATEGIC INVESTMENT: FROM PROCEDURE TO ROUTINE

OVERVIEW

After you've *Engineered Efficiency* with procedures and systems that are simple, efficient, and carefully planned, your next step is to teach students how to execute them consistently. This involves rolling out systems and procedures, having students practice them to a point of habitual routine, and then upholding high performance standards. Ideally, you also take them to the level at which the students "own" them genuinely enough to do them largely on their own.

From the start of the school year, strategic teachers invest heavily in foundations for strong systems and routines. We call this technique *Strategic Investment: From Procedure to Routine.* We use this name for it because we think of the initial time you spend installing routines as an investment, one you make at the outset to reap ongoing benefits.

Reflection

What factors might hold teachers back from making the early investment in time and energy that's required for effectively installing systems and procedures? Do not read on until you have answered.

_____

_____

_____

What are the potential consequences of this?

_____

_____

Possible reflections (all right, you've thought of others!): Common barriers include a teacher's overriding sense of urgency to begin covering academic content as quickly as possible; a belief that spending time teaching systems and procedures inevitably comes at the expense of time for academic instruction; lack of knowledge about how to effectively teach procedures or what it should look like when students master them; underestimating the time needed to teach them; not incorporating time for teaching systems and procedures into short- and/or long-term planning. Potential consequences are unproductive behavior; less time for academic instruction; student lack of urgency and engagement; and student frustration with misunderstanding your expectations.

ANALYZE THE CHAMPIONS

 Clip FG54. Erin Krafft, Grade 6

 Clip FG55. Nikki Bowen, Grade 3

View clip FG54 with question 1 in mind, and write your response. Then proceed to just the first, end-of-year cut of clip FG55 and answer question 2. Then continue clip FG55 to the second, start-of-year cut, and answer question 3. Compare your answers with our observations at the end of this technique.

1. In clip FG54, what is effective about how Erin installs procedures for agreeing and disagreeing with a partner during *Turn and Talk* (technique 43)?

_____

_____

_____

2. In the first, end-of-year cut of clip FG55, what's effective about this transition? What do you think Nikki had to do on day 1 to make such a smooth transition possible?

_____

_____

_____

3. In the second, start-of-year cut of clip FG55, what's similar to and different from what you expected to see from Nikki's day 1 rollout?

_____

_____

_____

Reflection

Teachers know that teaching students how to correctly execute a system or procedure is much harder than it sounds. Identify a key classroom procedure or system that you have struggled to help them master. What aspects of it were problematic for them? For you in teaching it?

_____

_____

_____

_____

FUNDAMENTALS: INSTALLATION

Like great teaching, effective installation of procedures often requires careful modeling, explanation, and practice. We'll divide discussion here into rollouts and pretend practice.

Rolling Out

The rollout is a first and crucial step toward routinizing any system or procedure. In it you publicly explain what the system or procedure is, what it entails, and why it matters. Nail your rollouts, and you're well on your way to building a productive and orderly classroom. Three principles apply:

Lead with the "why." [1] Cultivate student buy-in by briefly explaining how a system or procedure will help them learn and succeed.

Break into steps. [2] Chunk the task into a small number of discrete steps. Number them if you want students to implement them sequentially: "When I say 'one,' we'll stand and push in our chairs. At 'two,' we'll turn to face the door . . ."

Model and describe. Efficiently teach procedures and systems by describing them at the same time as you model them in action. The description becomes a common language for talking about the procedure.

Here's the transcript of a strong rollout of _Cold Call_ led by former fifth-grade reading teacher and current Teach Like a Champion team member Colleen Driggs. Read it through several times with the principles in mind.

> In some of your classes, your teachers do something called Cold Calling. In fact, I do it. It's when you don't raise your hand and a teacher calls on you, just to see what you know. And it's not like a "gotcha"; it's really just a way to do a quick review. I don't call it Cold Calling, though; I call it "hot calling" because you get a chance to shine and to show that you are on fire. So almost every day when we're talking about genre we're going to do hot calling. It's a great way to review all of these definitions and terms that we've learned.
>
> Here's the hardest part about hot calling: you've got to keep your hands down. Your hands are folded, and I will call on a person. When I call on that person, you track just like you normally do and then you track me when you hear my voice again. Nod if you understand. Nod if you are ready for hot calling. Beautiful. Keep your hands down. Please don't call out. Sit up. Remember SLANT.
>
> What is the definition of genre? Hands down. Robert . . .

_____

[1] You might notice that we've added this subtechnique, which wasn't included in _TLAC 2.0_. Like you, we're constantly trying to update our thinking. We believe that sharing the "why" is important for buy-in.

[2] We changed this from "Number the Steps" so that it applies to systems and procedures that don't require numbered steps (e.g., "vertical hands").

In the language of the principles we named earlier, what's effective about how Colleen rolls out *Cold Call* to her students? Don't read on until you've written your own observations.

_____

_____

_____

_____

What's effective and why

Colleen leads with the "why" when she explains to students that she will *Cold Call* (or "hot call") to give them a chance to "shine" and to show that they're "on fire." By clarifying her positive intentions for using *Cold Call*, she assuages students' anxieties about it and increases their buy-in. She then chunks *Cold Call* into a sequence of specific steps that students can expect to follow every time.

Case Studies of Rollouts

In these rollout case studies, use the principles to spot what each teacher does that's effective and what could be improved. Record your observations in the "Glows and Grows" tables. Then see our thoughts.

Case 1. *Cold Call* in Grade 1 Math

TEACHER: Scholars, whenever we share our thinking, it is important that we hear from as many different voices as possible, so we're going to use Cold Call. I also know you all have so much to share with the group, and that we miss an opportunity to learn when we don't hear from you. Cold Call allows us all to show what we KNOW, show what we . . . [students respond "KNOW"]. During Cold Call, I'll ask a question, and you will wait for me to call on you. Show me you are ready for a Cold Call by sitting in STAR! Just like I see Janiya doing, like Sarah's doing! All right, scholars, time to turn your brains on. What number do I need to add to three to get to TEN? To get to . . . [students respond "TEN"]? I see Adam has his hands in STAR. We're still thinking . . . Kiara?

Glows	Grows
It was effective when the teacher . . .	Next time, the teacher could try . . .

Case 2. AIR in Grade 8 Reading

TEACHER: In high school and college, your teachers are going to ask you to do a lot of reading on your own outside of class. And you won't just be expected to do the reading, but to really dig into it and come prepared to discuss it on a deeper level. To get ready for this kind of rigor, we're going to practice these skills of being a good independent reader with an activity we'll call AIR [accountable independent reading]. The way it works is that you're going to read a short chunk of text with a specific focus in mind. We'll start small, and then as the year progresses, you'll have the opportunity to read more on your own.

For this first independent reading task, I want you to do the following: put a box around the first two paragraphs on page 35 and take three minutes to read independently. Then take two minutes to write your response to this focus question: "How does the author use setting to develop mood?"

Glows	Grows
It was effective when the teacher . . .	Next time, the teacher could try . . .

Our Observations on Case 1

The teacher was effective in leading with the "why." She also explained what will happen during the *Cold Call*. Next time, she might explain her purposes for *Cold Calling* more succinctly. For instance, she could combine both "why" sentences into one by saying, "Scholars, whenever we share our thinking, it is important that we hear and learn from as different voices as possible, so we're going to use Cold Call." She could also be more specific about what she wants students to be doing during *Cold Call* besides waiting to be called. Should they stay seated in *STAR/SLANT* (technique 47)?

Our Observations on Case 2

The teacher cultivates buy-in with a compelling "why." He's specific about what AIR will entail, with clear directions for each step. He is also mindful about starting small, so students can succeed on their first attempt. However, before releasing students to begin reading independently, he could have checked for understanding (chapters 1 and 2) to make sure they understood his expectations and directions. For example, he could have asked, "Before I release you to do X, tell me: What part of the text are you reading on your own? What will you underline? How much time will you have to read?" Also, he might be more deliberate about giving students a clear annotation task that prepares them to answer the focus question, saying perhaps, "Take three minutes to read this excerpt and underline words or phrases that the author uses to convey mood."

STRATEGIC INVESTMENT

Pretend Practice

Repeated pretend practice is the most often overlooked essential in teaching students how to execute procedures. Without it, students will falter and ultimately get better at doing it wrong. To make pretend practice more effective, savvy teachers often deliberately distort it in useful ways like these:

Isolate steps. Practice one aspect of a procedure repeatedly and more slowly so that students get it.

Simplify portions. Remove potential distractions to make practice more effective. For example, you might have students practice a transition from one part of the classroom to another without carrying their folders the first few times. That way, students can focus solely on moving with excellence, without materials rolling all over the floor.

Explore common errors. Present students with common errors or pitfalls and ask them to role-play their responses—for example, "What do you do if you went to the left when everyone was going to the right? Let's try it, and work it out."

Combining Rollouts and Practice

Use the Rollout Template to plan the rollout for a simple procedure. (Find a printable version at my.teachlikeachampion.com.) Use the procedure that you drafted as part of *Engineer Efficiency,* or create a new one. If you are designing a new one, make sure it meets the four criteria of *Engineer Efficiency.* If possible, share your template with a colleague who has also prepared one, and look for ways to improve them.

Rollout Template

Procedure: The "why":	
The specific steps	**How I'll model and describe them**
My plan for pretend practice:	

Rebooting Systems and Procedures

Despite our best efforts to install strong systems and routines in August or September, inevitably some things won't go as planned. Come midyear, you may notice that students are no longer performing them at a satisfactory level, or you may see the need for some new routine. In either case, a "reboot" is in order. Here are some tips for framing the reboot to make your intentions clear and cultivate student buy-in:

Invent a "news peg." Connect the reboot to an inspiring, headline-grabbing goal—for example, "We have only sixty-eight days left until we rock our state test!"

Reboot after an extended break. Take advantage of vacations; they provide you with a natural excuse to reintroduce old procedures or to make a clean break from the past and get a "fresh start."

Be transparent. Briefly explain *why* you're rebooting. Not doing so risks confusing students and losing their buy-in.

Let students model and describe. Reward outstanding students with an opportunity to model a procedure that you want to reintroduce.

Reinforce with technique 59, Precise Praise. Acknowledge progress, and praise students who exceed your expectations. If students pick up the procedures with less practice than they did at the beginning of the year, recognize their growth.

Do the following now or when you see the need to reboot. Identify one system or procedure that needs rebooting. It could be a brand-new one or an old one that's gone awry. Following these two example rationales, draft one of your own.

"In September, we never talked about the right way to do a Turn and Talk. And as a result, we're not getting the most out of our pair discussions. Starting today, we're going to work together to change that by . . ."

"In the beginning of the year, you guys were coming in and out of your Turn and Talks quickly and crisply. But as the months have gone by, our transitions have been getting rusty, which means our Turn and Talks are taking longer, and we're getting less out of them. To get back on track, let's refresh ourselves on what it looks like to do an A-plus Turn and Talk."

Rationale:

_____

_____

_____

_____

If you can, try out your rationale with a partner and exchange feedback.

ANALYZE ANOTHER CHAMPION

▶ Clip FG48. Stephen Chiger, Grade 9

Comment on to what degree these students "own" this transition into the classroom and the benefits of this level of ownership. Then see our observations.

_____

_____

_____

_____

THE NEXT LEVEL: TRANSFERRING OWNERSHIP AND STUDENT AUTONOMY

As students master a procedure, great teachers often allow them to execute more of it on their own. This simple act of transferring ownership is a powerful way to instill in students a greater sense of accomplishment, independence, and ownership over the classroom and its culture.

One of the most effective ways to transfer ownership is to grant "earned autonomy," by which we mean giving students more autonomy in completing a task once they have mastered it. This is how eighth-grade teacher Maggie Johnson prepares her students to transition out of independent work with less supervision on her part: "Pencils down when you hear the beep. No countdown today. Here it comes. Be quick. Be silent." She scans the classroom. "Now we're ready."

By announcing that she is removing the countdown, Maggie tells her students that she trusts them to own the rate at which they come to attention because they have proven that they can do so quickly and consistently. This reward of autonomy motivates them to also master other classroom structures.

ANOTHER CHAMPION

 Clip FG56. Sari Fromson, Grade 5

In this video, compare a transition at two different points in the school year. What evidence do you see that students are assuming more ownership for it over time? Compare your thoughts with ours.

_____

_____

_____

Reflection

Some teachers frame autonomy differently. Imagine that a teacher says this on the first day of school:

> I'm going to start off by giving you all a lot of autonomy. But to keep it, you have to show me that you can handle it. If not, I'll have to be a lot stricter about exactly how things get done. And I know you guys don't want that!

What is the risk of offering autonomy and ownership in such a way?

_____

_____

Possible reflections (we're sure you've thought of others as well): Unless you've clearly outlined your expectations for what it looks like to execute class routines, students may not understand how to show you that they can "handle" the autonomy you give them. Inevitably, you will have to remove this autonomy, which will only confuse and frustrate your students even more. Also, students won't truly value the autonomy you give them because they'll come to expect it as opposed to viewing it as a reward. And they may resent or even resist your later attempts to install classroom structures because they'll interpret them as punishments.

GROUP ROLE PLAY: ROLLING OUT A SIMPLE PROCEDURE

Revisit the planning you did with the Rollout Template. In role groups of four (one *Teacher*, two *Students,* one *Coach*), practice your rollout of a simple procedure and then plan to facilitate thirty seconds of *Student* practice to go with it.

After the *Teacher* practices his or her rollout, *Coach* then gives feedback to the *Teacher* (one glow, one grow—for example, "One thing I liked about your rollout was . . . Next time, try . . ."). *Teacher* tries again, implementing the feedback.

You know you're on the right track when you . . .

• Explain the purpose in a way that cultivates student buy-in
• Clearly model and describe the procedure
• Maintain economy of language

ACTION PLANNING

Use this action planner to continue your work with *Strategic Investment: From Procedure to Routine.* (Find a printable version of this form at my.teachlikeachampion.com.) Use the aforementioned three success points to evaluate your ability to effectively roll out and practice a simple procedure to the point of routine.

STRATEGIC INVESTMENT

HOW AM I DOING?

_____

_____

Design one or more action steps for improvement. Decide on an interval by which you'll revisit this page to assess your progress.

Action Step 1

By when, with whom, and how you will measure your effort

By _____, I will . . .
   Date

_____

_____

How Did I Do?

Successes: _____

_____

_____

_____

_____

Challenges: _____

_____

_____

_____

_____

Next steps: _____

_____

_____

_____

_____

Action Step 2

By when, with whom, and how you will measure your effort

By _____, I will . . .

_{Date}

_____

_____

_____

How Did I Do?

Successes: _____

_____

_____

_____

_____

Challenges: _____

_____

_____

_____

Next steps: _____

_____

_____

_____

STRATEGIC INVESTMENT

STRATEGIC INVESTMENT

OUR OBSERVATIONS ON THE CHAMPIONS

 Clip FG54. Erin Krafft

Erin installs a system that students will use to express agreement or disagreement with their partner during the *Turn and Talk*. This not only supports a productive *Turn and Talk* but also helps her establish a *Culture of Error* (technique 8) in which students come to expect disagreement among their classmates as a normal by-product of smart people tackling the same question.

Erin's *Turn and Talk* procedure starts with clearly managed turns. "Door partners" were instructed to speak first, and Erin checked with a show of hands to be sure that students were clear on which partner was "door partner." Then it would be the "window partner's turn." This ensures that everyone has the opportunity to talk. To clarify how the first partner should start, Erin provides a sentence starter: "My answer is _____ because . . ." This steers students toward reporting not just their answers but also their reasoning.

Despite the clarity of her directions, before starting the *Turn and Talk,* Erin checks to make sure that students are truly clear on what they're supposed to do. This set students up to engage in productive practice of her *Turn and Talk* procedures on their first attempt.

 Clip FG55. Nikki Bowen

As we can see in this first cut from the end of the year, students are able to complete the transition with the smallest amount of instruction. Nikki simply says, "Stand up" and "Switch," and within seconds it is done. The students also truly own the process. Nikki is so "hands-off" that she has a moment to take a sip of coffee while students carry it out.

In the second cut of this clip, we catch a glimpse of what Nikki did on day one to install this transition. First, she assigned roles by dividing the class into groups A and B, and she checked for understanding to make sure everyone knew which group he or she was in. Nikki chunked the transition into a small number of discrete steps and then tagged each step with a verbal prompt. ("Stand up" tells students to stand behind their chairs without their materials.) She used "point-to-point" instruction, which helped her show students from each group exactly where they need to go at each phase of the transition.

As Nikki described each step, she modeled it as well, thus marrying some shareable "common language" to each part of the process. She also asked the students to practice the transition as she described each step, imbuing it with several bits of friendly competition between the groups. Right after students practiced, she gave them feedback on how well they did.

This second cut also shows Nikki already beginning to transfer ownership during practice, reducing the amount of guidance she was giving, narrating what's happening rather than saying what comes next.

 Clip FG48. Stephen Chiger

We can tell students have already assumed ownership of much of their entry routine because

- Stephen does very little to manage students once they cross the threshold of his door. He doesn't even distribute materials; a binder distributor does this for him.
- Stephen positively acknowledges their mastery of his system for entering class. ("Thank you guys as always for knowing what to do.")
- Students know where to find the *Do Now* and begin right away without a single prompt from Stephen.

We can tell that students don't fully own this transition yet because

- Stephen still has to give students a few *What to Do* reminders. For instance, he responds to potential chatter by reinforcing his expectations for silent entry ("I thought I heard whispering, but I don't.").

- At one point, the binder helper still tries to ask Stephen for guidance on what she should do when she can't locate a binder. In response, Stephen encourages the student to resolve the issue herself—and she does.

This level of student ownership enables students to start working right away, without interruption or outside intervention. It also gives Stephen the freedom to focus on other things, such as preparing for the main lesson or *Circulating* to read student work. Finally, it gives students a greater sense of achievement and ownership over the classroom and its culture.

 Clip FG56. Sari Fromson

In cut 1, filmed in spring 2015, students know exactly how to do their independent work. Sari's transition from that work to discussion takes a fraction of a second, and every student is attentive, ready to answer. Time is honored and diligence is universal, with no effort at all from Sari. She has transferred ownership, as her phrase "You know what to do" intimates. She turns off the music, and everything falls into place.

In cut 2 of Sari's classroom from fall 2014, we see *how* she built and reinforced expectations for this transition (which hadn't yet become routine). She stopped the music and gave students a full twenty seconds to prepare for the transition. She then provided a series of reminders, followed by two self-interruptions that helped build expectations. Throughout, her tone was positive but persistent.

Ultimately, when we compare both cuts (spring versus fall) side by side, what stands out is how much more structure she gave students early in the school year. Over time, and with success, she then eliminated parts of the procedure to simplify it and give students more ownership.

STRATEGIC INVESTMENT

DO IT AGAIN

OVERVIEW

Do It Again is an ideal tool for times when students do something passably but could—or need to—do it better. It's a simple and low-impact intervention for nonproductive moments, and best of all it requires no follow-up, no filling out of forms, no keeping a student from joining the class for recess. When it's not right, we do it over again as well as we can. This gives students more practice when they're not up to speed—not just doing something again but, framed positively, doing their best at even the small things, which helps build a culture of "always better."

Reflection

Have you tried *Do It Again* with students? If not, what keeps you from trying it? If you have, note one aspect that's worked well and one aspect that you feel could go better.

_____

_____

_____

_____

ANALYZE THE CHAMPIONS

 Clip FG57. Six Champion Teachers

In this montage of six teachers using *Do It Again,* each part really flies by! See if you can identify the moment of the *Do It Again*, its purpose, and how the teacher frames or triggers it. Also, how many of them say, "Do it again"?

Linda McGriff:

_____

_____

_____

Evan Stoudt:

_____

_____

_____

Denarius Frazier:

_____

_____

_____

Sarah Ott:

_____

_____

_____

Lauren Moyle:

_____

_____

_____

Jennifer Townsend:

_____

_____

_____

FUNDAMENTALS

Key Points

Try not to think of *Do It Again* as punishment but rather as practice, refinement, a chance to nail the details. If you think your students regard it as a punishment, double down on being attentive to your own language and demeanor. How you frame it is how it will feel to students.

Star three of these statements or actions that you could apply or adapt in your classroom to keep your *Do It Again* positive and constructive.

Saying, "One more time. Let's see if we can nail that."
Smiling warmly before asking for a *Do It Again.*
Saying, "This is not the beautiful [transition, hand raising, consideration for others, etc.] I've come to expect from this class. Let's try again, but this time, show me Harvard [class name]."
Signaling a *Do It Again* without words and only with a hand gesture.
Saying, "Show me your best [transition, hand raising, etc.]"
When it's been completed, saying: "Ah, much better. Thank you for that [insert desired behavior]."
Saying, "That was good, but let's try again and shoot for great!"

Do It Again is recyclable. You can request it twice in a row or even more and still be positive: "I still think we can do this even better. Let's give it one more shot!"

Use it for individuals and for the class as a whole, promoting group culture and accountability to you and to each other.

Also remember that *Do It Again* has a very low transaction cost. This lets you address behaviors you might otherwise not have the means to address. Recently we observed the high school math class of Denarius Frazier. One student, getting up during independent work time to get something from across the room, took the opportunity to touch a classmate on the head while she was working, thereby distracting and slightly annoying her. Mostly it was a plea for attention at exactly the wrong time—the kind of thing teachers often let go. But Denarius said, very calmly and quietly, "Let's try that again please." Then the student walked back to his desk and came across the room again without disturbing anyone. A tiny consequence to make sure a small inconsiderate act didn't become a habit.

Reflection

Are there any small incivilities in your classroom you might address similarly to Denarius? Which ones, and how?

Four Pointers

Cut the task short. Don't wait for the entire task to be completed. Restart once you know you're going to *Do It Again.* Begin the redo as close as you can to the part of the task that didn't measure up.
Think good, better, best. Set a powerfully positive tone (technique 58, *Positive Framing*): "That was good. But I want great."
Manage affect as well as behavior. Students often change from the outside in. In *Do It Again*, if you tell them you want to see something done with more spirit or enthusiasm, you are using an effective tool for managing their affect. If you model enthusiasm yourself, asking a low-energy class to repeat something with enthusiasm can start a self-fulfilling cycle.
Give specific feedback. Look for opportunities to provide specific feedback on how to do something better: "I want to see those eyes up so you look like scholars. Let's do it one more time."

Wording

One of the best ways to word a *Do It Again* is to offer it as a challenge (though the word "challenge" need not appear):

Which of these is likely to be more effective as a *Do It Again*? Why?

"Oooh, let's line up again and prove why we're the best reading group in the school."
"Class, that was very sloppy. We're going to do it again until we get it exactly right."

_____

_____

Now pick up from the opening reflection. Recall some other moments or tasks. Name what behaviors could have been better. Phrase a *Do It Again* for each that takes off from the point when you did halt or should have halted the task. Use the four pointers.

Moment:

_____

Improvable behavior(s):

_____

_____

Do It Again:

_____

_____

Moment:

_____

Improvable behavior(s):

_____

_____

Do It Again:

_____

_____

Moment:

_____

Improvable behavior(s):

_____

_____

Do It Again:

_____

_____

_____

PLAN *DO IT AGAIN*

Here is a sample of class situations in which *Do It Again* could apply: transitioning from math to lunch, from writing in journals to reading aloud, from gym to reading class, or from desks to a small-group reading area; or a class that doesn't track the teacher well or gives a halfhearted *Call and Response* (technique 34).

In a lesson plan or general routines, identify several procedures that your class does not yet do acceptably or could do better. Prepare for one or more of those moments by anticipating how you will cut off a task if it's not up to snuff and by scripting and rehearsing your *Do It Again* in advance.

Your script should anticipate that one *Do It Again* may not be enough. Also script and practice any explanation of *Do It Again* that you think will benefit the class.

THE NEXT LEVEL

Adding a stopwatch to some routines will strengthen the challenge of *Do It Again*, adding to its excitement and power. You can also sometimes turn *Do It Again* into a friendly competition between different sections of the class.

Do It Again is also useful as an intervention when follow-through or errant behavior are the issue. See the techniques of chapter 11, High Behavioral Expectations, in which *Do It Again* can feature as a simple and low-impact "consequence" for nonproductive individual behavior.

> **blog**
>
> Access this blog entry at my.teachlikeachampion.com/blog/first-week-advice-verbal-and -non-verbal-feedback-with-do-it-again/.
>
> "First Week Advice: Verbal and Non-Verbal Feedback with Do It Again" describes why and how, in *Do It Again,* champion teachers *verbally* reward students who follow through, but communicate with *nonverbal* cues to those who do not.

WITH A GROUP OR COLLEAGUE

From your individual work, share in writing or orally several phrasings of *Do It Again.* Together, come up with possible rephrasing. From there, expand to other situations and possible statements of *Do It Again.*

ACTION PLANNING

Use this action planner to continue your work with *Do It Again*. (Find a printable version of this form at my.teachlikeachampion.com.) You know you're on the right track when you . . .

- Cut the task short.
- Think good, better, best.
- Manage affect (and with affect) as well as behavior.
- Give specific feedback.

HOW AM I DOING?

_____

_____

Design one or more action steps for improvement. Decide on an interval by which you'll revisit this page to assess your progress.

Action Step 1

By when, with whom, and how you will measure your effort
By _____, I will . . .
<small>Date</small>

_____

_____

How Did I Do?

Successes: _____

_____

_____

_____

_____

Challenges: _____

_____

_____

_____

Next steps: _____

_____

_____

_____

DO IT AGAIN

Action Step 2

By when, with whom, and how you will measure your effort

By _____, I will . . .

Date

_____

_____

_____

How Did I Do?

Successes: _____

_____

_____

_____

Challenges: _____

_____

_____

_____

Next steps: _____

_____

_____

OUR OBSERVATIONS ON THE CHAMPIONS

 Clip FG57. Six Teachers

Cut 1. Linda McGriff

When all but one student participates during the *Call and Response*, Linda uses the correction "one boy" to quickly and anonymously remind him to join the class when they *Do It Again*. Her feedback to this student is so concise and minimally invasive that she's able to quickly get him back on track without having to interrupt the flow of her instruction. Her tone, which is both upbeat and enthusiastic, makes the *Do It Again* feel like a positive reminder to participate—and to do so with gusto.

Cut 2. Evan Stoudt

Once Evan Stoudt, a math teacher at Sci Collegiate Academies, hears students *Turn and Talk* to answer a question in incomplete sentences, he cuts the *Turn and Talk* short. The immediacy of his response helps him minimize the transaction cost of it. He then reminds students to answer in complete sentence format (*Format Matters*, technique 14) and reformats the response so that they can practice success when they *Do It Again* ("The rate of the change of the table is two"). In explaining to them *why* his version is better, he also reinforces his expectations for how students should format their responses to future questions in his class.

Cut 3. Denarius Frazier

When some of Denarius's students don't track a peer while she speaks, Denarius pauses the discussion and expresses concern that some students are going to miss a student's valuable insight. In doing so, he frames the purpose of the *Do It Again* in academic and cultural terms. It's not about power; he's making sure students learn as much as possible and uphold a culture of mutual respect toward their peers. When they try again, he actively scans the class to *Be Seen Looking* (technique 51). He then adds a "thank you" to publicly acknowledge that students did it again—and just as he asked.

Cut 4. Sarah Ott

By providing some quick *What to Do* ("go faster"), Sarah gives students specific feedback about how they can do it better on their next try and beyond. The combination of Sarah's positive tone and the language of "gotta go faster" helps her frame the *Do It Again* as a motivating challenge rather than a punishment. It also signals to students how quickly and crisply Sarah would like them to snap to attention at her signal so that they can return to the business of discussing math content together as soon as possible.

Cut 5. Lauren Moyle

Lauren's nonverbal (for each step as well as her *Do It Again*) allows her to instantly isolate the step that students need to do again, help students fix it without interrupting instruction, and then move on.

Cut 6. Jennifer Townsend

When Jennifer's students don't transition correctly from the *Do Now* to their Words of Inspiration routine on the first day of school, she asks them to *Do It Again* and again until they get it right. More specifically, after student's first attempt to transition, Jennifer warmly and patiently restates her expectations. When they *Do It Again* passably well, but not quickly enough, she positively challenges them to pick up speed. On their third attempt, they complete the transition with seamless urgency. By taking the time to teach students how to do things correctly from the start and then holding out for that—repeatedly if necessary—Jennifer sets students up for success and fosters a culture in which they do *everything* with excellence (*Strategic Investment*, technique 49).

RADAR/BE SEEN LOOKING

OVERVIEW

Being able to see your classroom clearly and accurately is the first step to ensuring that student behavior stays positive and productive. As every teacher knows, the simplicity of this idea belies the challenges of doing it well. With so many factors competing for your time, energy, and attention, it can be easy to miss the student who launches a rubber band or the one who doodles during instruction instead of taking notes. Not to mention the student whose eyes widen with insight.

Teachers who seem to have "eyes in the back of their head" position themselves to clearly monitor student behavior, and they emphasize that they're observing the classroom so that students know it matters to them.

Reflection

What sorts of student behaviors do you sometimes fail to see in class and wish you were better able to notice? Why is it so easy to miss them? Write your response before you read on.

_____

_____

_____

Possible reflections (among many others): We're not always clear on what it should look like for students to follow through correctly on our directions. Therefore, it can be difficult to see what we're not intentionally looking for. As teachers, we're constantly multitasking—for example, trying to monitor others' behaviors while checking in privately with one student. Overfocusing on one thing—such as off-task behavior—causes us to lose sight of others. And it can be hard to see everything clearly from certain locations in the classroom.

ANALYZE THE CHAMPIONS

 Clip FG58. Kerri Rizzolo, Grade 6

At first glance, Kerri may not seem to be doing anything especially noteworthy, but in fact her actions are helping ensure that her students are meeting her expectations. Can you identify the moves that enable her to maintain positive culture in the classroom? Write your response before you view the next clip.

_____

_____

Save the following lines for later!

_____

_____

_____

▶ **Clip FG59. Patrick Pastore and Rodolpho Loureiro**

In this clip, note Patrick's and Rodolpho's physical position in the classroom. Why is it effective? What else do they do to build *Radar*?

_____

_____

_____

Compare your observations on clip FG59 with ours at the end of this technique.

FUNDAMENTALS

In the course of studying great classrooms, we learned a few simple moves that top teachers use to make sure they see their room accurately *and* ensure that students know they do. We call those moves *Radar/Being Seen Looking.*

To differentiate these terms: *Radar* is the ability to see what happens in your classroom; *Be Seen Looking* is your ability to let students know you see what happens. When you see events in the classroom accurately and students know that you do, off-task behaviors disappear.

Reposition Your Antennae

Many teachers with strong *Radar* routinely move to a front corner of the room to check whether students follow their directions. Doug first observed this champion move while watching footage of master teacher Patrick Pastore, hence why we call that corner "Pastore's Perch." As shown in the figures, moving to that vantage point widens and deepens your scan. Second, standing there can help you eliminate blind spots at the far ends of the room that commonly plague teachers.

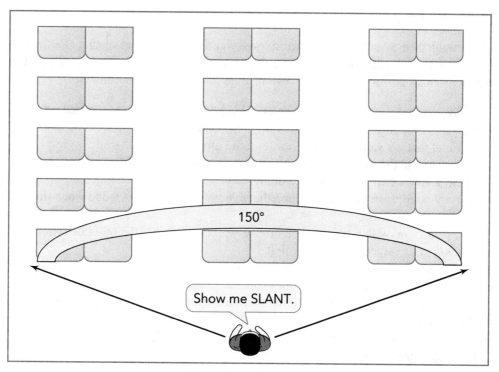

Typical Positioning

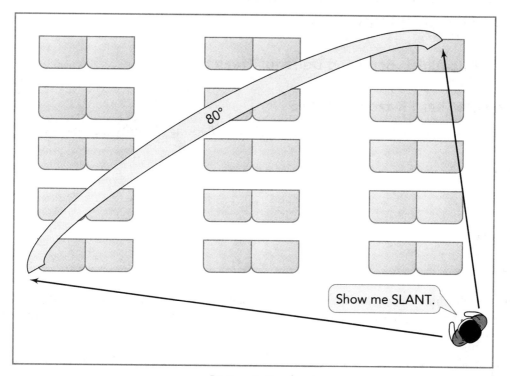

Pastore's Perch

Use Your Dance Moves

Once you've established a vantage point that allows you to see the room clearly, *Be Seen Looking* to remind students that you care whether they meet your expectations, and check to see that they do so. "Dance moves"—small gestures that subtly demonstrate careful looking—can help.

Swivel. The swivel is the foundation for *Be Seen Looking.* Simply scan the room methodically, from one side to the other, making sure to see everything, especially your common blind spots. The swivel is so fundamental that it's worth trying to master first before you add other moves to your repertoire.

Invisible column. Lean to the side as if trying to look around an invisible pillar to show it's important that you get a clear view of what students are doing.

Politician. Warmly point to students in an unpredictable pattern to acknowledge when they are complying with your expectations.

Sprinkler. Scan your room with a swivel, then briefly snap back a bit in the other direction once or twice as if to quickly verify student follow-through.

Tiptoe. Stand on your tiptoes as if you're trying to see over something that's obstructing your view and to show students that whatever is going on in the back is important.

Quarterback. When you crouch down during instruction—to conference with a student at his or her desk or the like—glance up and use your swivel to monitor the rest of the class.

Disco finger. As you swivel, extend your finger and trace the arc of your scan with it to emphasize that you're looking. (Channeling John Travolta in *Saturday Night Fever* may help.)

Effective classroom managers routinely use these moves and others to ensure that students are learning from start to finish. When students say things like, "She has eyes in the back of her head," it's not an accident.

MORE CHAMPIONS

 Clip FG60, Akilah Bond and Denarius Frazier

Clip FG58, Kerri Rizzolo, Grade 5

In Clip FG60, what do Akilah and Denarius do to *Be Seen Looking*? Identify their moves.

Akilah:

_____

Denarius:

_____

Now watch Clip FG58 again. How does Kerri make sure that students meet her expectations? Go back and revise your earlier response to incorporate what you've learned. Then compare it with our observations at the end.

THE NEXT LEVEL: WARMTH AND POSITIVITY

Your affect communicates a lot about what you're seeing and what you expect to see. In *Being Seen Looking,* some teachers think that a firmer expression is always better, and even cast a look of heightened suspicion in hopes of discouraging nonproductive behavior. Although a firm scan has its place, it's not always best. There's a difference between appearing firm and serious and looking around as if you're expecting trouble. Not only is the latter ineffective; it can become a counterproductive, self-fulfilling prophecy.

Try *Be Seen Looking* with a warm and genuine smile. This positivity shows students that you value their presence, appreciate their follow-through, and expect to see even greater things from them. Some teachers, like Patrick Pastore, even add positive nonverbals to their scanning, such as an approving thumbs-up or subtle head nod. Gestures like these normalize follow-through and encourage other students to follow suit.

PRACTICE WITH A FRIEND OR TWO

With a partner, role-play as a *Teacher* giving one of the following observable directions to a *Student*:

- "Eyes up here."
- "I should see you annotating the text."
- "Novels out and open to chapter 2, please."

After saying it, scan while using a dance move to *Be Seen Looking*.
Take turns trying out various moves. For each move, run through three rounds:

1. Try it out.
2. Add subtlety: make your moves twice, back-to-back—obvious the first time, more subtly the second time.
3. Add warmth: scan with a smile or other positive nonverbals (head nod, thumbs up, and so on).

Success points:

- Make consistent eye contact with students.
- Execute and adapt dance moves so that they feel natural to you.
- Scan with a warm, genuine smile.

> **blog**
>
> Access this blog post at teachlikeachampion.com/blog/kathryn-orfuss-using-radar-every -thing-going-well-video/.
>   Check out the blog post "Kathryn Orfuss: Using Radar When Everything Is Going Well" on how champion fifth-grade teacher Kathryn Orfuss scans systematically throughout a lesson.

ACTION PLANNING

Find a printable version of this form at my.teachlikeachampion.com. Use the aforementioned success points to evaluate where you are in mastering *Radar/Be Seen Looking*.

HOW AM I DOING?

_____

_____

Design one or more action steps for improvement. Decide on an interval by which you'll revisit this page to assess your progress.

Action Step 1

By when, with whom, and how you will measure your effort

By _____, I will . . .
   Date

_____

_____

How Did I Do?

Successes: _____

_____

_____

_____

_____

Challenges: _____

_____

_____

_____

Next steps: _____

_____

_____

_____

Action Step 2

By when, with whom, and how you will measure your effort
By _____, I will . . .
<small>Date</small>

_____

_____

_____

How Did I Do?

Successes: _____

_____

_____

_____

_____

Challenges: _____

_____

_____

_____

Next steps: _____

_____

_____

OUR OBSERVATIONS ON THE CHAMPIONS

 Clip FG58. Kerri Rizzolo

Kerri calls the class to attention after some independent work with concrete directions ("Pencils down in three . . . two . . . one") that tell students precisely what she expects them to do and by when. Her direction is especially effective because it's so observable—and therefore easier to monitor and enforce. Kerri then intentionally moves to Pastore's Perch. This not only helps her see more accurately but also maximizes the efficiency of her scan. She then stands on her tiptoes and swivels her head back and forth to draw attention to the fact that she's looking to see if students are doing as she asked. Finally, Kerri backs up her observable directions by smiling as she "narrates the positive" (technique 58, *Positive Framing*), which signals confidence and normalizes follow-through: "Ooh, Bella's already there. Thank you, Bella." When she realizes that one student isn't with her, she corrects him—anonymously at first and then publicly when he doesn't follow her direction. Within seconds, she achieves 100 percent, and her students are off and running with a *Turn and Talk* (technique 43).

 Clip FG59. Patrick Pastore and Rodolpho Loureiro

After delivering observable directions, Patrick and Rodolpho move to a front corner (Pastore's Perch) to verify whether students follow through. From this angle, each can readily see and reinforce desired behaviors. Later, Rodolpho's shift to the other front corner gives him a new perspective and therefore an even more comprehensive read on the room.

At one point, Patrick presumably has difficulty seeing a student, so he exaggeratedly cranes his neck to the side as if he is trying to see past an invisible pillar. His rendition of what we call the "invisible column" dance move strengthens his *Radar* while subtly reminding students that he sees them.

 Clip FG60. Akilah Bond and Denarius Frazier

It can be easy to appreciate the importance of *Being Seen Looking* when you're standing in front of a classroom of thirty students. But as Akilah's first-grade clip demonstrates, this technique is just as important and effective during small-group instruction. In particular, she uses her swivel during a guided reading lesson to make sure students track and therefore learn from each other's remarks.

Denarius's application of the dance moves is equally subtle, but he uses a broader variety of moves to ensure that his thirty high school students can see him looking. For instance, he opens the clip with a swivel and a subtle invisible column after calling his class to attention. He also uses an adaptation of the quarterback when he lifts his head after jotting notes at the projector and scans to check if students are tracking their peers during discussion.

Neither Akilah nor Denarius use the dance moves just to reinforce their expectations for behavior; they do so also to uphold a culture in which students routinely show respect for and learn from their peers.

MAKE COMPLIANCE VISIBLE

OVERVIEW

As much as possible, and certainly when ensuring follow-through may be tricky, strive to give directions that are "visible"—that is, that can be easily observed when completed—so that you can more easily ensure follow through.

Reflection

Are there moments during class when you're uncertain whether or not students are following your directions? One example might be that you can't tell for sure who has finished a task and who is just sitting there without having completed it. What other examples can you add?

_____

_____

_____

FUNDAMENTALS

Revisit *Teach Like a Champion 2.0*

Doug summed this one up concisely:

> As a rule of thumb, the more visible the action you ask students to execute, the easier it is for you to see what students do, and the more that students implicitly recognize that you can clearly see what they do. This makes them more likely to do what you've asked and makes it easier for you to hold them accountable. Some of the most clever teachers I've watched have a way of making "observable directions" fun and tactile, increasing both the incentive to follow through and their ability to manage.

ANALYZE THE CHAMPIONS

▶ **Clip FG61. Amy Youngman, Grade 6**

▶ **Clip FG62. Patrick Pastore, Grade 6**

In clip FG61, which of Amy's directions are especially visible? How does she make them engaging for students?

_____

_____

_____

In clip FG62, how does Patrick *Make Compliance Visible*? What other elements of 100% (techniques 51–55) do you see in this clip?

_____

_____

_____

Compare your observations with ours at the end.

PRACTICE

Here are some common classroom instructions. Rewrite them to *Make Compliance Visible*. Then practice incorporating them in an upcoming lesson. Be sure that you are asking your students to do something visible, and that it's manageable, not too complex. Also plan to *Circulate* so that you'll be able to clearly scan the room to see that your directions have been followed.

"Pencils down."	*"Pencils in the tray."*
"Books out."	
"Pay attention."	
"Be quiet."	

"Walk properly."	
"You're working."	
"Stop."	

ACTION PLANNING

Use this action planner to continue your work with *Make Compliance Visible.* (Find a printable version of this form at my.teachlikeachampion.com.) You know you're on the right track when you can see quickly whether or not students are following your directions.

HOW AM I DOING?

_____

_____

Design one or more action steps for improvement. Decide on an interval by which you'll revisit this page to assess your progress.

Action Step 1

By when, with whom, and how you will measure your effort

By _____, I will . . .
<small>Date</small>

_____

_____

How Did I Do?

Successes: _____

_____

_____

_____

_____

Challenges: _____

_____

_____

_____

Next steps: _____

_____

_____

_____

MAKE COMPLIANCE VISIBLE

Action Step 2

By when, with whom, and how you will measure your effort

By _____, I will . . .

Date

_____

_____

_____

How Did I Do?

Successes: _____

_____

_____

_____

_____

Challenges: _____

_____

_____

_____

Next steps: _____

_____

_____

OUR OBSERVATIONS ON THE CHAMPIONS

 Clip FG61. Amy Youngman

We noticed three visible directions from Amy:

- "When I say go, and not before I say go, I want you to get out your whiteboard, whiteboard marker, and your whiteboard eraser. Go . . . I can tell that 100 percent of students are ready."
- "Three, two, one, marker cap on . . . marker cap on . . . show what you know."
- "Show me your marker when you're ready for it."

 Clip FG62, Patrick Pastore

Patrick efficiently transitions his class from individual writing to whole-class instruction by emphasizing compliance you can see. In doing so, he also uses elements of technique 51, *Radar/Be Seen Looking,* and upcoming 53, *Least Invasive Intervention,* and 54, *Firm Calm Finesse.*

Patrick counts down when he wants his students to begin the transition. When the count is done, he gives a universal positive group correction (technique 53) that maximizes visibility: "I need all pencils in the tray at this time."

He is then *Seen Looking* across the room as he narrates the number of students who continue to write ("I still have one, two, three, oh good, I spoke too soon"). This gesture builds momentum while reminding the remaining student that the class is still waiting for him.

Patrick continues in a positive tone with an anonymous individual correction (technique 53), "Now I only have one person writing." Patrick then looks at the student. The student puts his pencil down on his desk, but Patrick avoids marginal compliance when he smiles and says, "And his pencil should be in the tray." The interaction is firm, but friendly.

Patrick ends the sequence with some *Firm Calm Finesse,* smiling as he announces, "Now we're ready to go." This is effective because it

- Reinforces the universality of the expectation and makes 100% a normal part of his class
- Emphasizes the fact that Patrick values purpose (for example, that the whole class needs to be ready for what comes next) over power
- Helps Patrick build positive momentum at the start of class

LEAST INVASIVE INTERVENTION

OVERVIEW

One of the most important goals for any teacher when managing behavior is to use the least invasive form of intervention possible to correct off-task students. Using the *Least Invasive Intervention* means keeping corrections nearly invisible and thereby private (or as private as possible). This honors their right to struggle toward high expectations with a bit of privacy, and makes it far less likely that they (or their classmates) will respond to a correction publicly. It also allows you to keep teaching and students positively on task. When you interrupt your teaching to discuss a student's behavior with him or her, no one is on task. Of course you won't always be able to be whisper smoothly and without disruption, but it's important to make minimal invasiveness the goal.

Reflection

What tools do you and your colleagues currently use to address off-task students? To what degree are they invasive or noninvasive? With what results?

_____

_____

_____

_____

FUNDAMENTALS

One key to using the least invasive form of intervention is to combine it with the idea of "catching it early" (see *Firm Calm Finesse,* technique 54). Act sooner rather than later when you realize a student is beginning to become off task. This allows you to step in with a smaller correction. Once a behavior is "major," it is very hard to correct it invisibly. Here is a list of potential interventions, from least to most invasive. The goal is simply to be as high on the list as you can, as often as you can.

1. Nonverbal Intervention

The ideal correction involves a nonverbal intervention (NVI) made while you are still teaching. This ensures that the task of learning continues for the class. A visible NVI can include a gesture (remind a student to take notes by mimicking "writing" with one hand) or a form of modeling (asking a student to sit up by modeling sharp posture yourself). You can also use the self-interrupt discussed in *Strong Voice* (technique 56) as a form of nonverbal intervention. Self-interrupt is a brief break in your speech, which commands a student's attention.

Students respond to consistency. Consider using the same gesture every time for the most common low-level classroom distractions (perhaps related to *STAR/SLANT*), so that processing and responding to the cue becomes a simple habit for students.

If you don't normally make intentional eye contact with students, write several reminders in your next lesson plan to make an eye contact intervention with three to five students in the course of the lesson. During the next lesson, make eye contact several times again, now having in mind a particular message you want the student to absorb.

2. Positive Group Correction

Another, slightly more invasive tool for bringing students back into the fold as soon as they begin to stray off task is a positive group correction (PGC): a quick verbal reminder given to the entire group that describes the solution. As in technique 57, *What to Do*, positively describe what students *should* be doing rather than what they shouldn't be doing. Be brief:

"Scholars, make sure to be following along in your books."
"Check yourself to make sure you're tracking."
"Show me SLANT."

This general description of the correct positive behavior reminds everyone in class of the expectation, which can help you correct students you don't see as well as those you do. If you're concerned that the student you had in mind might not respond, you can add a little bit of eye contact or perhaps a brief nod to him or her to make it clear you'd like to see a correction. Try to avoid calling anyone out by name.

As you may have read in *Strong Voice*, quieter is often stronger, so a whisper (or a stage whisper) can fortify a PGC.

3. Anonymous Individual Correction

As with the PGC, the anonymous individual correction (AIC) involves describing behavior you'd like, *quickly*, to all students, but it adds a statement that makes it clear that not everyone is meeting expectations:

"I'm waiting for two more pairs of eyes."
"Just a minute. We need one more person with his pencil ready."

You can also tag an AIC on to the end of a PGC, as in, "We need everyone open to page 3 [PGC]. Waiting for two [AIC]. Thank you."

Consider for a moment the difference between the three interventions we've discussed so far, NVI, PGC, and AIC. Note some situations in which you might use (or avoid) one or another. What are their strengths and limitations?

Script an effective PGC or AIC for each of these situations. The first one is done for you.

1. Student slouching in his chair

   Intervention: *PGC.* Script: "*Class, check your SLANT!*" _____

2. Student with her head down on her desk (eyes up)

   Intervention: _____ Script: "_____

   _____"

3. Student with her head down on her desk (eyes hidden)

   Intervention: _____ Script: "_____

   _____ "

4. Student gazing out window while peer is talking

   Intervention: _____ Script: "_____

   _____ "

5. Student engaged in sustained looking under desk for "something"

   Intervention: _____ Script: "_____

   _____ "

6. Student persistently raising hand (for reasons unrelated to your questions)

   Intervention: _____ Script: "_____

   _____ "

7. Student writing when it's "pencils down"

   Intervention: _____ Script: "_____

   _____ "

8. Student sending the bathroom signal at critical time during lesson

   Intervention: _____ Script: "_____

   _____ "

9. Frequent struggler doing well and working hard today

   Intervention: _____ Script: "_____

   _____ "

4. Private Individual Correction

When you use a private individual correction—a PIC—you speak to a student directly about his or her behavior, but do so as privately and quietly as possible. You might, for example, walk by the off-task Johnna's desk, lean down and in as private a voice as possible, quickly and calmly say, "Johnna, answering the reading questions is important. And an expectation. I need to see your pencil moving and you hard at work." You could of course say the exact same thing from the front of the room and be heard by your student's classmates, but private is usually better.

When you need to make a PIC, you can make it less invasive by issuing a "task for the class"—something for them to do while you are addressing the behavior. As always, stress purpose over power: "This will help you in high school" rather than "You need to do what I say." Finally, be short and to the point. Get the student's attention. Describe the solution and perhaps very briefly why it matters. Express (verbally or through tone and body language) your concern for your student, then get back to the class. A PIC that lasts more than ten or fifteen seconds is no longer private and probably taking time away from teaching.

Suppose you've told your students to read to the bottom of the page on their own. For a student who is doing one of the following things, plan a PIC and practice it, preferably with a partner. Exchange glows and grows.

- Consistently staring out the window
- Has head down because of an earlier consequence
- Consistently raises a hand at an inappropriate time

Example:

Paul, eyes on me. I noticed that you haven't been following along in the text. If you aren't looking at the book, you aren't reading, and that's too important for me to let go. When we pick up next, I expect your eyes on the page and for you to be ready when I call on you to read.

Your PIC:

_____

_____

_____

5. Private Individual *Precise Praise*

The intervention we call PIPP is a natural counterpart to PIC but relies on technique 59, *Precise Praise,* and makes you less predictable. Walk over to a student and whisper positive feedback instead of criticism. By balancing criticisms with praises, you earn greater trust and condition students away from expecting that a private intervention will be negative. This weakens the tendency of other students to delight in anticipating the misfortune of others and creates more privacy around interventions in general.

For a student who is doing one of the following things, plan a PIPP and practice it, preferably with a partner. Exchange glows and grows.

- Student whose comments drove discussion to a higher level of rigor; his or her homework was really good, too
- A sometimes struggling student who is engaged and diligent in taking notes
- Student who helps a peer who came in late to catch up and join activity

Your PIPP:

_____

_____

_____

6. Lightning-Quick Public Correction

Private or anonymous corrections are not always possible. Sometimes (ideally not often) you are forced to correct individual students during public moments. Train yourself to do the following confidently and quickly, without hesitation:

- Minimize the time a student whose behavior has been negative is "onstage."
- Tell him what to do right rather than scolding or saying what he did wrong.

- Divert class attention to a student whose behavior is worthy of attention: "Joaquin, I need your eyes. Just like Corales and just like Paula" or "Joaquin, I need your eyes. Looking sharp, Corales. Thank you, Paula."

Another way to make a public correction work is to model it on a PIC. That is, just by dropping your voice into a stage whisper—"Danny, I need to see you writing"—you can gain a modicum of privacy, and intimate to Danny that you are striving to maintain his privacy even while you correct. We call this a "whisper correction" and think it's often the best way to correct an individual student when there's no opportunity to be entirely private.

ANALYZE THE CHAMPIONS

▶ **Clip FG63. Ashley Hinton, Alexandra Bronson, Bob Zimmerli, Ijeoma Duru, Jaimie Brillante, and Jason Armstrong**

In cut 1, how does Ashley Hinton enable herself to keep her tone so positive as she makes corrections nonverbally? What other techniques support her success at intervention?

_____

_____

Cut 2 is of Alexandra Bronson's positive group corrections (PGC). What does she say and do that makes these corrections effective?

_____

_____

Cuts 3 and 4 are anonymous individual corrections (AICs) by Bob Zimmerli and Ijeoma Duru. What differences do you see?

_____

_____

_____

Cut 5 is Jaimie Brillante's private individual correction (PIC). How does Jaimie maintain "privacy"?

_____

_____

_____

Cut 6 shows two whispered lightning-quick public corrections by Jason Armstrong. How does he imbue these corrections with "privacy" despite their public nature?

_____

_____

LEAST INVASIVE INTERVENTION

Find this blog post at teachlikeachampion.com/blog/110-upgrades/.
blog   "100% Upgrades" is another clip and discussion whose theme is how to use *Least Invasive Intervention* to ensure that 100% of students are with you for teaching and learning.

LEAST INVASIVE INTERVENTION

GROUP WHISPER-CORRECTION SPEED PLAY

Because intervening starts out as a substantial social challenge for many of us, it may be worth your while to discuss it with a colleague or group as you practice it.

This simple "Whisper-Correction Speed Play" lets you practice dropping into a whisper to correct "students" while maintaining anonymity and the pace of the lesson. However many you are, sit around a table. One person stands as *Teacher* and teaches from a lesson of his or her choosing, slipping at some point into a whisper saying, "Need you taking notes." Everyone else is a *Student*.

Take turns so that everyone is *Teacher* at least once. In a second round, *Teachers* can replace "Need you taking notes" with any other statement they choose.

Then discuss the experience.

Revisit *Teach Like a Champion 2.0*

Even if you've already worked on it alone, the "Reflection and Practice" at the end of chapter 11 is a good set of summary activities to practice with a partner or small group.

Reflection

How could using *Least Invasive Intervention* affect your relationships with your students?

_____

_____

_____

ACTION PLANNING

Use this action planner to continue your work with *Least Invasive Intervention*. (Find a printable version of this form at my.teachlikeachampion.com.) You know you're on the right track when you are . . .

- Intervening early
- Using the least invasive option possible
- Losing less and less time for interventions

HOW AM I DOING?

_____

_____

Design one or more action steps for improvement. Decide on an interval by which you'll revisit this page to assess your progress.

Action Step 1

By when, with whom, and how you will measure your effort

By _____, I will . . .
      Date

_____

_____

How Did I Do?

Successes: _____

_____

_____

_____

Challenges: _____

_____

_____

Next steps: _____

_____

_____

Action Step 2

By when, with whom, and how you will measure your effort

By _____, I will . . .
Date

_____

_____

_____

How Did I Do?

Successes: _____

_____

_____

_____

Challenges: _____

_____

_____

_____

Next steps: _____

_____

_____

FIRM CALM FINESSE

OVERVIEW

Students are more likely to follow through when you are calm and steady at the helm—especially when you are managing behavior. When your anxiety, tension, or frustrated emotions become visible, they can create a distraction or even an incentive not to do as you've asked. In contrast, when your demeanor suggests that it's hard for you to imagine a world in which students wouldn't want to follow your directions, that expectation often becomes a self-fulfilling prophecy.

Seeing their actions cause their teacher to get upset can tempt a small number of students to want to further explore the empowering feeling they get by having a perverse control over the classroom. Take that option off the table. Manage your emotions and stay steady at the helm to keep your students focused on what makes them successful.

Reflection

Are there times when you struggle to remain "steady at the helm"? If so, what are the things that get you upset? Why do you think they affect you?

_____

_____

_____

FUNDAMENTALS

Catch It Early

One important action to help ensure *Firm Calm Finesse* is to address off-task behaviors early. This might sound counterintuitive, but addressing something very early when it is a small issue and not reflective of persistent behavior allows you to fix it with a small correction. And we often get upset because a behavior has persisted. So rather than letting small problems escalate to disruptive ones that require a major intervention, fix them early with a tiny adjustment. Doing so will make your corrections more likely to feel gentle. You can make them noninvasively and often with a smile. For this reason, one of our favorite phrases is, if you're mad, there's a good chance you've waited too long.

Value Purpose over Power

Consistently emphasize that the goal is to help students learn and succeed rather than to reinforce your power as the head of the classroom. Such statements as "We track each other [we look at the speaker] to show respect" make the point more subtly than "When I ask you to track, I need you looking at the speaker." The more you call attention to purpose rather than power, the more your students will invest in your expectations.

The Strength of "Thank You"

Saying "thank you" to students who follow a direction is one of the most subtly powerful things you can do. First, saying "thank you" when students follow your directions shows that civility and courtesy reign. Modeling saying "thank you" and "please" reinforces this notion. Second, saying "thank you" shows and reminds everyone very subtly that students whom you have addressed with a correction have now followed your directions. This reinforces expectations and normalizes the idea that students in your classroom follow through on their teacher's requests. That might sound like this: "We need to all be writing out our thoughts. All of us, please [looking at Daniel]. Thank you."

Use Universal Language

Remind students that expectations in your classroom are universal and not personal. Convey a sense of community. For example, replace "I" with "we" as often as possible. Or you can remind students that there are classwide expectations. Notice the language in this example. We've italicized a few words for extra emphasis: "Just a quick reminder about *our* Habits of Discussion. *Let's* make sure *we're* all using them."

Show Your Bright Face

A calm and peaceful countenance is one of a teacher's most powerful tools. It shows warmth and caring, not to mention a belief that everything's going to be OK, especially when some might think otherwise. It shows your students that you are calm and in control, that all is well, that you are happy when you are teaching and students are learning. We call that your "bright face," but it doesn't have to be a beaming smile, just a pleasant expression that communicates positivity and confidence in whatever way matches your style and the age group of your students– from a subtle, wry smile to a beaming grin.

Find this blog post at teachlikeachampion.com/blog/erin-krafft-uses-just-enough-correction-smile-keep-students-task/.

For inspiration, watch Erin Krafft's bright face in the post "Erin Krafft Uses Just Enough Correction—& a Smile—to Keep Students On-Task." Read the commentary, too.

Deploy Your Confirmation Glance

Sometimes a student needs just a bit of space to decide if he or she wants to do the right thing. A confirming glance can provide it. Sometimes after giving a direction, the best move is to walk away (as if you are certain the direction will be followed) and then glance back to ensure follow-through. This signals that you trust a student to make the right decision but allows you to follow up—varying the delay between request and confirmation as appropriate—with degrees of subtlety to make sure. Of course, you will need to follow up if you glance and see that someone hasn't followed through, but using the glance can intimate a potent, calm self-assuredness to your class.

Stay Steady at the Helm

Sometimes we think a raised voice can really drive a point home. But getting louder can distract students from reflecting on and adjusting their own behaviors. Instead of thinking about what they need to do, they are wondering why you are shouting at them, whether you shout equally at everyone, how it feels to be shouted at, and perhaps how you look when you are shouting. None of these things help them concentrate on their own behaviors and take accountability for them. Keep your students focused on what they need to do, by staying calm and steady. For more guidance, see technique 61, *Emotional Constancy*.

ANALYZE A CHAMPION

▶ Clip FG62. Patrick Pastore, Grade 6

What's effective about Patrick's *Firm Calm Finesse*? Compare your observations with ours at the end of this technique.

PRACTICING ALONE OR WITH OTHERS

If you do this as a group, start out by formulating a few success points that observers should use to focus their feedback.

Valuing Purpose over Power

To practice valuing purpose over power, take a few minutes to rewrite some of these prompts or to script some prompts that you can use frequently in class.

"I want you to track [look at] the speaker."	*"When we track the speaker, we show that we are listening and care about what they have to say . . . thank you."*
"I need you to sit up."	

"Voices off."	
"I need you working."	
"Pay attention."	

Bright Face

Practice your bright face by practice-teaching the interrupted sentence in the script or some other short sentence that you enjoy teaching. The script includes beginning the phrase, halting to make a correction, returning to your bright face, and continuing to teach. Do this in the mirror or while being filmed. Keep at it to find your best, most natural teacher bright face and a smile intended to instill a sense of optimism in your students.

Sample script:

"What is the rule of—book open in front of you [bright face]—What is the rule of the conch?"

Or your own:

Confirmation Glance

In three rounds, practice your confirmation glance with the scenario and prompt we've provided or ones of your own. Give your correction, and practice walking away and giving your confirmation glance. The rounds vary the amount of time in between your direction and confirmation glance so that you can practice what you are messaging to your students. (The faster you give your confirmation glance, the more cautious you are being with your student.)

Scenario: What you'll say to a student who's not starting the assignment that you've just asked him/her to work on	*Prompt:* "Make sure you're writing."
Scenario:	Prompt:

Round 1. Give your prompt, walk away, give your confirmation glance immediately.
Round 2. Give your prompt, walk away, give your confirmation glance after a three-second pause.
Round 3. Give your prompt, walk away, give your confirmation glance after a five-second pause.
Round 4. Give your direction, walk away, give your confirmation glance after more than five seconds, then go back to your student and give him or her a reminder.

ACTION PLANNING

Use this action planner to continue your work with *Firm Calm Finesse.* (Find a printable version of this form at my.teachlikeachampion.com.) Refer to the following success points:

- Catch it early; keep corrections small.
- Remain steady at the helm with *Emotional Constancy* and show bright face.
- Use universal language and show purpose, not power.

HOW AM I DOING?

_____

_____

Design one or more action steps for improvement. Decide on an interval by which you'll revisit this page to assess your progress.

Action Step 1

By when, with whom, and how you will measure your effort

By _____, I will . . .
Date

_____

_____

How Did I Do?

Successes: _____

_____

_____

_____

_____

Challenges: _____

_____

_____

_____

Next steps: _____

_____

_____

_____

Action Step 2

By when, with whom, and how you will measure your effort

By _____, I will . . .

Date

_____

_____

_____

How Did I Do?

Successes: _____

_____

_____

_____

_____

Challenges: _____

_____

_____

_____

Next steps: _____

_____

_____

_____

OUR OBSERVATIONS ON THE CHAMPION

 Clip FG62, Patrick Pastore

Patrick shows some *Firm Calm Finesse* by smiling as he announces, "Now we're ready to go." This is effective because it reinforces the universality of the expectation and normalizes full compliance; emphasizes the fact that Patrick values purpose over power—the purpose here being that the whole class is ready for what comes next; and helps Patrick build positive momentum at the start of class.

ART OF THE CONSEQUENCE

OVERVIEW

A consequence should not just be a euphemism for a punishment. Its goal should be to teach—to help students reflect on and learn from mistakes. At the same time, it should make the fairness and universality of rules visible to all students. And it should reinforce positive and orderly classrooms and protect the sanctity of the important work that on-task students are doing. When students struggle to meet expectations, a consequence should protect their dignity, provide clarity about how to improve, and express the urgency of their doing better.

Consequences should, in short, reduce negative behavior over time. But as many teachers know, consequences do not always do that. Sometimes they fail to help. Other times, they escalate unproductive behavior. To avoid this, we outline a handful of simple and powerful principles for designing and delivering effective consequences, which we call the *Art of the Consequence.*

In general, strive to keep consequences

Quick and quiet. Deliver them quickly and often quietly, with the least disruption and time away from instruction possible so that you preserve privacy and allow students to get back on track right away.

Incremental. Give consequences that start small and scale up in increments as necessary. This allows students to learn from mistakes at a limited cost and reinforces expectations consistently. It also helps you avoid the trickiest situation of all: a student who has lost all of his or her privileges and has little left at stake.

Consistent. Predictably stand by your expectations. This reduces the temptation for a student to "test" them. It's also important to be consistent across students—they should know that the rules are the same for one and all.

Depersonalized. Deliver consequences *as privately as possible* while remaining *calm and in control* of your emotions. Use language that judges actions instead of people. Reengage a student positively in the lesson soon after a consequence if you possibly can.

Reflection

Write down what you typically say in situations where you are delivering a consequence to a student.

_____

_____

_____

My revision: (Skip this for now. We'll come back to it later.)

_____

_____

_____

ANALYZE THE CHAMPIONS

▶ **Clip FG64. Sarah Ott, Kindergarten**

View this clip. What evidence do you see that the consequence Sarah delivers is quick, incremental, consistent, and depersonalized? After you respond, note our observations at the end of the technique.

_____

_____

_____

_____

_____

_____

FUNDAMENTALS

How to Give a Consequence

How you give a consequence matters just as much as the consequence itself. Here are four principles that can help you ensure that consequences end in success.

1. *Tag the behavior.* Quickly and efficiently tell the student which behavior resulted in the consequence so that they know and can learn from it. For example, "Damian. Check. Please track your classmates" or even, "Damian. Check. Tracking, please" lets him know what behavior he needs to fix.
2. *Use a bounce-back statement.* Encouraging students to demonstrate their resilience after receiving a consequence reminds them to view it as a small obstacle, not a major setback. For example, "Damian. Check. Please don't shout out your answers. Raise a silent hand. Now, show me your best."
3. *Maintain the pace.* To minimize the interruption to your lesson and keep the consequence as private as possible, make it as quick and concise as you can.
4. *Get back on track.* Immediately after you give a consequence, resume the lesson with warmth and energy, to show students that it's over and that you're still calm and in control.

Of course, it won't always be possible to do all of these things for every consequence. The idea is to apply them as consistently as you can.

Revise Some Consequences

Your Opening Reflection
Go back to what you wrote in the opening reflection about what you typically say when giving a consequence, and revise it to reflect or further emphasize some or all of the four principles. See if you can tag the behavior and include a bounce-back statement.

More Practice at Revision
Read the example here. Then rewrite the numbered originals to reflect what you've learned so far about effective consequences. You may revise the words the teacher says or the consequence itself.

Example: "Pencils should be moving. Tiara, did you not hear what I just said? When I ask you to be writing, I expect to see you writing. Move your card to yellow for not following directions."
Revised: "Tiara, check. Our pencils are moving. Let me see you with us." (Three checks equal a color change.)

1. "Jack, that's a check. We're not talking with our lab partners right now."
   Revised:

   _____

   _____

2. "David, I asked for voices off. That's the third time. Next time it'll be two scholar dollars."
   Revised:

   _____

   _____

3. "Maurice. We don't sleep in Geometry class. Pick your head up off your desk. You know better. That's a detention for you."
   Revised:

   _____

   _____

4. "Pause, Cassandra. We're still waiting for a few scholars to listen while you are speaking. Michael, Jennifer, if I have to talk to you about that again, it will be a phone call to your parents. Continue please, Cassandra."
   Revised:

   _____

   _____

5. "Carly, you're not writing. I know you can do better than that. When I come back, I expect to see the whole first page completed."
Revised:

_____

_____

ANALYZE A CHAMPION

 Clip FG65. Bridget McElduff, Grade 5

View this clip. Respond in writing and compare your observations with ours at the end of the technique. Here's what Bridget says:

> Track me. It's important that when other [classmates] are working through something, that you're respectful and compassionate. You know this. You need to do it. Track me. Laughing is ten dollars, but I know you're going to fix it and bounce right back. Go ahead.

What's effective about how Bridget delivers a consequence in this clip? Use the language of the principles we named earlier.

_____

_____

_____

What factors do you think played a role in Bridget's decision to deliver a larger consequence as opposed to a mere correction?

_____

_____

_____

Consequence versus Correction

One of the most challenging aspects of managing behavior is deciding whether to give a student a consequence or just a correction. It's not always an either-or decision. In some cases, it may be prudent to give both at the same time. The next time you're faced with this challenge, consider following these rules of thumb for consequences.

Motivation. If the student knowingly and or willfully defies your expectations, go with a consequence. If the motivation seems benign or is unclear, consider correcting instead.

Persistence and repetition. If a student persistently engages in off-task behavior, a consequence is more likely to be required. If it's happening over and over, the student is telling you that correction isn't quite enough and that a stronger reminder may be warranted.

Degree of disruption. If the behavior interferes with other students' learning, a consequence is probably best. If not, it may be wiser to respond with a correction.

Read each scenario here and indicate whether you would give the student(s) a consequence or a correction. State your rationale. Then script the consequence or correction you would use.

1. During a mini-lecture and discussion, you notice that Jamie and Alex aren't taking notes as expected. While teaching, you quietly approach them and use a nonverbal writing gesture to prompt them to take notes. Jamie picks up her pencil to take notes, but Alex turns around to talk to a peer. When you pause to address Alex, he says, "I'm only asking for a pencil!"
   I would give Alex a (consequence/correction) because . . .

   _____

   _____

   My consequence/correction:

   _____

   _____

2. Alfred has been slouching repeatedly during the lesson. First, you used a nonverbal gesture to correct him, and he sat up. A few minutes later, you corrected him privately during independent work, and he corrected his posture. Five minutes later, he is slouched over, this time with his head down.
   I would give Alfred a (consequence/correction) because . . .

   _____

   _____

   My consequence/correction:

   _____

   _____

3a. To call the class back to attention after a *Do Now*, you deliver the following direction: "Pencils down, hands folded, and eyes on me in five . . . four . . ." Everyone except Casey follows all of your directions by the time you say "one." Casey continues writing.
   I would give a (consequence/correction) because . . .

   _____

   _____

My consequence/correction:

_____

_____

3b. To call the class back to attention after a *Do Now*, you deliver the following direction: "Pencils down, hands folded, and eyes on me in five . . . four . . ." Everyone except Casey follows all of your directions by the time you say "one." But Casey is looking out the window and has not completed his *Do Now*. I would give a (consequence/correction) because . . .

_____

_____

My consequence/correction:

_____

_____

4. You notice that Charlie, who almost always follows directions, is whispering to the girl next to him during independent practice. When you walk over to address Charlie, he slides something into his desk and says, "I was helping her with number 3!" I would give a (consequence/correction) because . . .

_____

_____

My consequence/correction:

_____

_____

5. During whole-class instruction, Miguel, a naturally energetic student, begins to do a little dance in his seat. When you look in his direction, he immediately stops. But once you look away, he continues. I would give a (consequence/correction) because . . .

_____

_____

My consequence/correction:

_____

_____

6. One of your more challenging students, Katie, has been actively participating throughout your lesson. But as soon as you send her into a *Turn and Talk,* she starts laughing as if she's engaging in off-topic conversation. As you walk over to address this, she stops talking altogether.
   I would give a (consequence/correction) because . . .

_____

_____

My consequence/correction:

_____

_____

ANALYZE THE CHAMPIONS

▶ Clip FG66. Hilary Lewis and Jacobi Clifton

In this clip, Hilary Lewis and Jacobi Clifton are practicing giving a consequence to a student who then reacts negatively. Try to steal one effective move you see them use in responding to their student.

_____

_____

_____

THE NEXT LEVEL: ENCOUNTERING PUSHBACK

In spite of our best efforts, there will be times when a consequence causes a student's behavior to worsen. Students can respond with anything from open defiance ("Whatever!") to a passive shrug to attempts at changing topics ("How come you're always getting on my case?!") to a temper tantrum.

Calm, Controlled, and Quiet

As you may have gathered from the video, one of the best ways to respond to pushback is to calmly, coolly, and firmly uphold your expectations without becoming entangled in a debate or standoff. To accomplish this, try to exude calm and stay in control of your emotions by using the principles of "exude quiet power" and "do not engage," which we preview here from technique 56, *Strong Voice*.

Do not engage. Resist students' attempts to engage you in a debate or discussion about the consequence. You can remind him or her that there is a time and a place to discuss concerns about consequences. Otherwise maintain focus on making sure the student does what you asked.
Teacher: Please put your feet under your desk.
Student: But *she's* in my space.
Teacher: Please put your feet under your desk. You may bring that to my attention at lunch. Right now, I need to see your feet under your desk.
Student: (follows through)

Exude quiet power. Speak lower and slower to draw attention to your words and show students that you're calm, poised, and in control of your emotions.

Keep it as private as possible. In line with depersonalizing the consequence, preserve the student's privacy by whispering the consequence or, when appropriate, by giving the consequence in a one-on-one setting.

Advise a Colleague

Imagine that a colleague in his or her first year of teaching approaches you with the following concerns:

I feel really torn about giving consequences. On the one hand, I know I have to use them to manage my classroom. But on the other hand, I think they make things worse, causing students either to "blow up" or shut down. They also make it hard for me to build relationships with students. If I'm always giving consequences, I'm afraid I'll turn into the kind of teacher who's always trying to show kids "who's boss." What should I do?

Respond to your colleague in light of what you've learned about consequences so far. Complete your entries before proceeding to the possible replies we've given.

Teacher's Statement	My Response/Advice
"I think [consequences] make things worse, either causing students to 'blow up' or shut down."	
"They also make it hard for me to build relationships with students."	

Teacher's Statement	My Response/Advice
"If I'm always giving consequences, I'm afraid I'll turn into the kind of teacher who's always trying to show kids 'who's boss.'"	

Some possible replies:

[Consequences] just make things worse: "Students sometimes get upset when they receive a consequence because they feel blindsided by it and/or think it was unfair. The best way to combat this perception is to be consistent about using consequences to manage your classroom."

They also make it hard for me to build relationships with students: "As you build strong relationships with students, you also must earn their respect and show them that you have their best interests at heart and are able to set limits. This includes their right to a safe, orderly learning environment where they know what's expected and know how they can be successful."

I'm afraid I'll become the [bossy] teacher: "I agree that consequences should never be used with the intent of showing students 'who is boss.' That's why I try to use language that shows students that my goal isn't to assert my authority but to help them succeed. For example, if I catch a student trying to speak with his neighbor, I might say, 'Sam. That's two. Voices off. *I don't want you to miss this.*' I also make sure my consequences tell students what *to do* ('Voices off') as opposed to what *not to do* ('Stop talking!')."

Planning for a "Blow-Up"

Following the example, read and complete the two "blow-up" scenarios.

Example:

Teacher: Scholars, your pencils are down, and your eyes are on me in three . . . two . . . one.
Tyrell: *(continues whispering to a classmate)*
Teacher: *(whispering)* Tyrell, I need your eyes up here and all voices off.
Tyrell: But I wasn't doing anything!
Teacher: *(lower, slower, still whispering)* I asked for your eyes up here, please.
Tyrell: *(tracks teacher)*
Teacher: *(nods briefly to acknowledge)*

1. Blow-up

Teacher: Scholars, I need your books out and binders out and ready to go in ten seconds. Nine . . .
Justin: *(continues writing on a piece of paper)*
Teacher:

_____

Justin: But I was just trying to finish my work!

Teacher:

_____

Justin: *(follows directions)*

2. Double blow-up

Teacher: *(during a class discussion)* Scholars, eyes on Kenisha.
Drew: *(tries to talk to the student sitting behind him)*
Teacher:

_____

Drew: But I wasn't doing anything!
Teacher:

_____

Drew: *(slams pencil down on desk and sulks)*
Teacher:

_____

Drew: *(complies)*

ROLL IT OUT

Plan here how you want to roll out your consequences management system to students. Make sure that your rollout

- Establishes clear expectations for how students should respond to consequences
- Clearly frames why you give consequences
- Uses language economically

_____

_____

_____

_____

_____

_____

_____

If you can, practice your rollout with a partner and ask for feedback.

"BLOW-UP" ROLE-PLAY PRACTICE WITH A COLLEAGUE

Watch clip FG66 (Hilary Lewis and Jacobi Clifton) again as preparation for this activity, this time considering what's effective about how they practice together.

With a colleague or by pairs in a group, revisit what you did in "Planning for a 'Blow-Up.'" Taking turns in the roles of *Teacher* and *Student/Coach*, practice scenario 1. Get feedback from your colleague, reteach, and then switch roles. Repeat for scenario 2.

You know you're on the right track when you . . .

- Deliver the consequence quickly and efficiently.
- Remain poised, calm, and in control.
- Resume teaching with warmth and enthusiasm.

ACTION PLANNING

Use this action planner to continue your work with *Art of the Consequence*. (Find a printable version of this form at my.teachlikeachampion.com.) Use the three aforementioned success points to evaluate where you are in using the technique.

HOW AM I DOING?

_____

_____

Design one or more action steps for improvement. Decide on an interval by which you'll revisit this page to assess your progress.

Action Step 1

By when, with whom, and how you will measure your effort
By _____, I will . . .
Date

_____

_____

How Did I Do?

Successes: _____

_____

_____

_____

Challenges: _____

_____

_____

_____

Next steps: _____

_____

_____

_____

Action Step 2

By when, with whom, and how you will measure your effort

By _____, I will . . .

Date

_____

_____

_____

How Did I Do?

Successes: _____

_____

_____

_____

_____

Challenges: _____

_____

_____

_____

Next steps: _____

_____

_____

OUR OBSERVATIONS ON THE CHAMPIONS

 Clip FG64. Sarah Ott

Tag the behavior. Sarah follows a consistent pattern whenever she gives a consequence: say student's name, give consequence, give direction for how to fix behavior. She says, "Janiah. Check. Head up." By sticking with this standard approach, she efficiently lets her students know what the consequence was and which behavior caused it.

Maintain the pace. Sarah keeps her consequence so quick and concise that it avoids disrupting the flow of her instruction and minimizes the amount of time her student Janiah is left "onstage."

Get back on track. After Sarah gives her consequence, she gets right back to teaching with warmth and energy. This shows her student that the interaction is over and that the teacher isn't rattled by it. It also refocuses everyone's attention on what's most important: the content of the lesson.

 Clip FG65. Bridget McElduff

These aspects of Bridget's consequence make it especially effective.

Tag the behavior. She tells the student what his consequence is and the behavior that caused it. This teaches the student to avoid laughing at his peers when they struggle academically. The size of the deduction ($10) also helps Bridget emphasize the seriousness of the student's breach of classroom culture.

Give a bounce-back statement. Bridget uses language that shows the student that she has faith in his ability to fix his behavior and models the compassion that she'd like him to show his classmates.

Get back on track. Bridget gets in, gets out, and continues monitoring and supporting students as they complete their independent work. Bridget's shift in focus also reminds the student that the most important thing he can be doing is getting back to work right away.

These factors may have contributed to Bridget's decision to deliver a consequence and not merely a correction:

Motivation. Given the context and the student's action, there doesn't appear to be any other reasonable cause or motivation for his behavior besides the fact that he intended to make light of his peer's academic struggles. His laughter was in no way innocent, benign, or due in some way to an honest misunderstanding. It was deliberate and ill conceived.

And, not or. Given the seriousness of the student's actions, Bridget knows she can't afford to merely correct. Instead, she chooses to add the consequence. In doing so, she maintains a strong classroom culture and preserves the integrity of her relationship with both students.

Clip FG66. Hilary Lewis and Jacobi Clifton

This is how Hillary and Jacobi respond effectively to pushback:

Do not engage. They avoid engaging students on topics other than the correction they initiated. This helps them avoid spiraling into a potentially costly public debate.

Exude quiet power. Both drop their tone and speak lower and slower as they deliver the consequences. This draws the student's attention to their directions and helps them emphasize the importance of follow-through. Their quiet, calm, and cool demeanor also helps them de-escalate an emotionally charged situation.

Keep it as private as possible. Both teachers enhance privacy by increasing their proximity to the student and then leaning over slightly as they whisper the consequence.

Firm Calm Finesse. Both work to use *Firm Calm Finesse* during this interaction. Both remain calm and steady at the helm.

We noticed these other things about their practice:

At Bats *(technique 25).* Both Hilary and Jacobi move swiftly back and forth between practice rounds to ensure that they have the most time to practice and get feedback.

Fast feedback. Feedback is focused on one "glow" ("It was effective when . . .") and one "grow" ("Next time try . . .") so that the "teacher" knows what's working and what he can build on. They deliver the feedback quickly to maximize the time they spend together.

Culture of practice. The culture of practice is positive—both participants are eager to practice and to receive and give feedback. As soon as they receive it, they're off and running to implement it.

State-dependent learning. Practice is held in the same or similar location where this type of interaction may occur. This provides *real* practice so that muscle memory can be built.

STRONG VOICE

OVERVIEW

Some teachers have an "it" factor. They can walk into a hectic room full of the giddiest students (gym, cafeteria, class room) and immediately ensure that students listen and respond to their instructions. Even if such teachers have a presence that can at times seem mysterious, having spent time studying them, we've distilled six *Strong Voice* principles that characterize how they ensure that students listen to them carefully:

- Formal register
- Square Up, Stand Still
- Quiet power
- Economy of language
- Do not talk over
- Do not engage

Reflection

Have you encountered any "it" teachers? If so, what was your impression? What actions, attitudes, or skills helped them command a room?

_____

_____

_____

ANALYZE A CHAMPION

▶ **Clip FG67. Ijeoma Duru, Grade 9**

In clip FG67, what does Ijeoma Duru do to "command the room"?

_____

_____

_____

Compare your observations to ours at the end.

SIX FUNDAMENTALS

Use Formal Register

We use the word *register* to describe the general tenor expressed by a person in a conversation or interaction. Register encompasses eye contact, body position, gestures, facial expression, and rhythm of language. In any conversation, we shift in and out of three such registers: casual, formal, and urgent. In moments when follow-through is critical, *Strong Voice* teachers tend to use formal register and to shift visibly from casual to formal. They also tend to avoid urgent register, as it increases tension and signals panic. The table here differentiates the three.

Three Registers

Register	Voice/Words	Body Language
Casual	Words may run together (pitter-patter rhythm) Wide range of inflection and tone Language itself is colloquial	Asymmetrical/relaxed body posture (e.g., leaning more on one foot, or leaning on a wall) Inconsistent eye contact Repetitive/sweeping hand gestures
Formal	Clear, slower articulation of syllables and distinction between words Words chosen carefully	Symmetrical body posture Standing up straight Steady eye contact Chin up Hands clasped or behind back; simple, controlled hand gestures
Urgent	Heightened tone and volume Words run together Increased tension in voice	Wide eyes Leaning in vs. standing straight up Sharp gestures

Reflection

Why might the urgent register be counterproductive for ensuring follow-through?

_____

_____

_____

When would the casual register be beneficial? When would it not?

_____

_____

_____

When you want to ensure listening and follow-through, we recommend using some version of the formal register. It underscores the clarity of the message and stresses its importance.

When you're teaching and discussing academic content, you'll likely use a register that is more casual—either fully casual or a more conversational and relaxed version of formal, depending on your personal style.

This provides a useful juxtaposition to the full formal register you use to ensure attentiveness to directions. Making visible the shift into (and out of) this more formal register can help you gain more attention from students.

Square Up, Stand Still

You can often convey the importance of something you are saying by pausing as you say it—move too much and it looks like you have something else on your mind. You can often ensure better follow-through by squaring up your body—holding your posture erect and facing the students you are addressing.

Exude Quiet Power

When you want control of the room and you sense that control is slipping away, your immediate instinct may be to talk louder and faster. However, we find that students often match the teacher's louder voice with increased volume of their own and, what's more, your getting loud may suggest that you're becoming a bit frazzled. This can result in students perceiving less order in the room and becoming less inclined to follow your directions. So go against your initial instinct: get quieter and slower. Drop your voice and exude poise and calm.

> **blog** Find this blog post at teachlikeachampion.com/blog/managing-emotions-dan-cotton
> -strong-voice/.
>   Read "Managing Emotions (Yours): Dan Cotton on Strong Voice" for three practical tips about how to stay in quiet power as you navigate an emotional challenge.

Use Economy of Language

Brevity is your ally. Communicate not only what you want students to do but your confidence in and clarity about the directions by using the fewest words possible. This lets students focus only on what is most important and emphasizes your own composure.

Do Not Talk Over

When you need your students to listen, demonstrate that your words are critical by ensuring that they aren't competing with talking, humming, rustling, and so forth. Pause briefly midstatement—or even midword—if you don't have full attention. We call this a "self-interrupt," and it's the quickest way to remind students that listening to you comes first.

Do Not Engage

When discussing behavior with students, avoid engaging in other topics until you have satisfactorily resolved the topic you initiated.

STRONG VOICE

STRONG VOICE

MORE CHAMPION ANALYSIS

▶ **Clip FG67. Ijeoma Duru, Grade 9 (revisited)**

Rewatch Ijeoma Duru in clip FG67. What's effective about her *Strong Voice*?

_____

_____

▶ **Clip FG68. Laura Fern, Grade 2**

In clip FG68, note some details about Laura's use of self-interrupt and Square Up, Stand Still to quickly bring her student back to full attention.

_____

_____

Note details also about how she shifts her register during the self-interrupt from the more casual mode she uses for teaching content to the more formal mode in which she uses her *Strong Voice*.

_____

_____

▶ **Clip FG69. Christy Lundy, Grade 6**

In clip FG69 we watch Christy Lundy, a former reading teacher. How does she avoid engaging?

_____

_____

Compare your insights with ours.

INDIVIDUAL, PARTNER, OR GROUP PRACTICE

You'll get the most out of these activities if you do them with a colleague or a group. We frame them here for groups, but you should have no trouble adapting them for individual or partner work.

Practice the Registers

In a group, take turns as *Teacher.* Listeners, respond with these success points in mind:

* *Teacher* demonstrates a clear difference between instructional tone and formal register.
* *Teacher* is able to naturally shift between instructional tone and formal register.

Round 1. First practice each register (casual, formal, urgent) in order using the direction "Pencils down and eyes on me."

Round 2. Teach in energetic instructional tone (using or adapting one of the scripts here—feel free to use an excerpt from your own classroom or lesson instead). Drop into formal register, paying special attention to your voice and posture, as you say "Pencils down." Then resume teaching in a more casual instructional tone. Receive feedback from the group. Repeat, incorporating the feedback.

Register Scripts

Math. "Nice; six times six does give us thirty-six square centimeters. What happens to the area if I increase the length of the two sides?"

Science. "Yesterday we discussed the three states of matter. Solid is one and liquid is another. What is the third?"

ELA. "I'm excited to share today's vocabulary words. The first word is *resilient*. Repeat after me, 'Resilient.'"

Copy-Cat Practice for "Do Not Talk Over"

Practice your self-interrupt using one of these scripts or content from an upcoming lesson.

Self-Interrupt Scripts

Math. "Nice; six times six times six does give us 216 cubic centimeters. What's another way to write this?"

Science. "Today, we are going to learn about the properties of the second state of matter: liquids. Your job is to compare and contrast properties of liquids to properties of solids."

ELA. "*Resilient* means tough, or able to experience hardship successfully. Let's start with the literal meaning. These flowers are 'resilient' because they're growing out of a rock in a sunny hot desert, and they are still alive and beautiful. In your own words, what makes them resilient?"

Success points during the self-interrupt:

1. Teacher squares up and stands still.
2. Teacher uses formal body language and facial expression.
3. Teacher exaggerates the pause used to self-interrupt.

Scenarios and Practice for Do Not Engage

Brainstorm scenarios in which you would need to use *do not engage.* Following the example, list several more, including what you would say and do. Plan more than one reaction per situation.

STRONG VOICE

STRONG VOICE

Potential Moment	What I Will Say	What I Will Do
Students kicking each other under the desk	*"Inappropriate time . . . three, two, one [pause] answer my question please . . ."*	*I will square up my body, keep a neutral face, and articulate my instructions.*

If you can, practice in front of a group, partner, or mirror. Get feedback about these success points:

- Is able to use body language and tone to convey the importance of the do-not-engage moment
- Redirects student's behavior to what teacher wants the student to be doing
- Uses quiet power

ACTION PLANNING

Use this action planner to continue your work with *Strong Voice*. (Find a printable version of this form at my.teachlikeachampion.com.) You know you're on the right track when you . . .

- Stay mainly in your instructional version of formal registers.
- Shift deliberately as needed in and out of formal, casual, and urgent registers.

HOW AM I DOING?

_____

_____

Design one or more action steps for improvement. Decide on an interval by which you'll revisit this page to assess your progress.

Action Step 1

By when, with whom, and how you will measure your effort

By _____, I will . . .
<small>Date</small>

_____

_____

How Did I Do?

Successes: _____

_____

_____

_____

Challenges: _____

_____

_____

Next steps: _____

_____

_____

Action Step 2

By when, with whom, and how you will measure your effort

By _____, I will . . .
<small>Date</small>

_____

_____

_____

How Did I Do?

Successes: _____

_____

_____

_____

Challenges: _____

_____

_____

_____

Next steps: _____

_____

_____

_____

OUR OBSERVATIONS ON THE CHAMPIONS

 Clip FG67. Ijeoma Duru

Ijeoma exudes confidence and poise by standing stock-still and facing the class directly while she gives her directions. After she sends students off to independent work, she conducts a thorough scan of the room to show students that she's looking to make sure they're working. Her calm expression and slow, controlled movements help emphasize her formality. Other pointers:

Economy of language. Ijeoma gives clear, concise, instructions that set students up for success during independent work. She uses familiar, standardized language to explain tasks, which helps her communicate with a minimum of words (for example, telling students they will be working "solo"). Ijeoma is also precise with her language, pointing out that students have "exactly five minutes," which underscores the intentionality with which she's planned this important exercise.

Tone drop. Once Ijeoma finishes answering a student's question, she drops her tone to give directions, and becomes slightly more formal. This tone drop signals authority and confidence and draws students' attention to her words.

Quiet power. She speaks with a slower cadence and enunciates each word more clearly to emphasize the importance of what she's saying.

 Clip FG68 Laura Fern

During and shortly after her self-interrupt, Laura illustrates these principles of *Strong Voice*:

Square Up, Stand Still. She draws attention to her self-interrupt by stopping midword, standing still, and pausing her gestures. In fact, the self-interrupt is so noticeable that the distracted student instantly turns around and gets back into STAR.

Formal register. During the self-interrupt, Laura makes strong, direct eye contact with the student and freezes her facial expression. Once the student responds, she smiles and continues teaching with palpable warmth and enthusiasm.

 Clip FG69. Christy Lundy

Christy leads a reading lesson with seven students. Seconds into the clip, two of those students begin to kick each other from underneath the table. Rather than go down the rabbit hole of determining who kicked whom first, Christy refuses to engage: "Inappropriate time. I need you to answer my question."

Even from the camera's vantage point, it is nearly impossible to determine which student first kicked the other. It would therefore be impossible for Christy to effectively resolve this situation in the moment. This is why her decision not to engage is especially effective.

Christy uses the phrase "inappropriate time" to sideline any debate or discussion about which student started the altercation, and shifts students' focus back to the question at hand ("You need to answer my question"). It also implies that there may be a more appropriate time to discuss what just happened, which gives students some hope for resolution.

In terms of other *Strong Voice* elements, Christy smoothly transitions between registers and is able to use quiet power to avoid engaging in this debate with students.

Her countdown adds urgency to her request (which is for students to answer her question) while giving them a bit of time to manage their frustration. By the end of the clip, we see the fruits of Christy's refusal to engage pay off when the students who were involved in the altercation raise their hands to participate in the academic discussion.

WHAT TO DO

OVERVIEW

Often students want to follow your instructions, but find it hard to do so because those instructions aren't as clear as they could be. In some situations, they can take advantage of ambiguity and choose to interpret directions in the version most appealing to them at the time. In other words, clarity matters. So set your students—and your classroom—up for success by giving *What to Do* directions that say clearly and simply *What to Do* next.

Reflection

Here are two phrases we overheard on a school visit: "Ricky, stop fooling around" and "Talia, pull it together!" Neither worked. Why?

Our thoughts on why they didn't work (you may have had others): These directions were ineffective because they are vague, confusing, and tell the student what *not* to do. What should Ricky be doing instead of fooling around, for example? How should Talia pull it together? Both students remained unsure of what the teacher wanted them to do. Unclear directions force students to guess.

FUNDAMENTALS

Effective Directions

Effective directions—those that are likely to be understood and followed, even under duress—are

Specific. They set students up for success by describing precise actions they should take. Rather than "Get to work!" for example, try "Pencils moving" or "Begin answering question number 1, please."

Concrete. Good directions involve clear, actionable tasks that students can execute. They eliminate gray areas wherein a student might not know *What to Do* (or plausibly claim not to).

Sequential. Try to break complex tasks into a series of simple actions. For a student who appears unwilling to begin a writing task, you might try "Pencil in your hand, please. Thank you. Point to prompt number 1. Now: begin."

Observable. To help you check for accountability, strive to make what you ask a student to do easy for you to observe. Then you'll know when it's been done (see technique 52, *Make Compliance Visible*).

In addition, students will *know* you can easily see whether it's been done, and this makes them less likely to be tempted to exploit any gray area. Try substituting "Eyes up here" for "Pay attention" or "Pencils down and eyes on me" for simply "Eyes on me."

Causes of Off-Task Behaviors

What to Do also has diagnostic value. Effective directions help you identify the potential root of the off-task behavior. Directions that are specific enough to be all-but-impossible to misinterpret can help you understand whether a student doesn't understand or is trying to avoid doing as you've asked. If we give consequences or censures to students before we know whether they understand, we risk eroding our relationships with them and their faith in us. But if a direction is utterly unambiguous and a student still does not follow through, it is far easier and much fairer to hold that student accountable.

ANALYZE THE CHAMPIONS

 Clip FG70. Teacher Art Worrell, Grade 12

Why are Art's directions effective? Compare you observations with ours at the end of this technique.

_____

_____

_____

PRACTICE

Remembering that directions to students should be specific, concrete, sequential, and observable, read these scenarios and rewrite the teacher's direction. Then pick some to practice by yourself or with a partner. Use these success points to evaluate your work:

- The teacher describes the solution by telling students what they should be doing (instead of explaining what they should *not* be doing).
- The directions are concise.

1. It is September in your kindergarten. You notice that Denise and Elise have been talking to each other on the carpet during your read-aloud.
    Direction: "Elise, please stop talking to Denise."
    Revised with What to Do:

_____

_____

2. You are trying to distribute social studies materials to your second graders. The first students in the row are playing with materials from the previous lesson in their desks.
   "Please take a packet and pass it."
   Revised:

   _____

   _____

3. Your fourth-grade students have just finished their math assignment. You are late for lunch, and half of your class still has their materials out on their desks.
   "Line up for lunch."
   Revised:

   _____

   _____

4. You are walking with your fifth graders to PE and hear several students talking in line.
   "Shhhhhh."
   Revised:

   _____

   _____

5. Your sixth graders are taking a practice state exam. There are three eighth graders whom you do not know who are talking loudly and goofing off outside your classroom.
   "Stop fooling around."
   Revised:

   _____

   _____

6. You have outlined the major characters in *To Kill a Mockingbird* for your ninth graders, and you notice that only half of the class is taking notes.
   "You should be writing this down."
   Revised:

   _____

   _____

7. You are about to begin your second-period eleventh-grade chemistry class. Several students are talking to each other (turned around in their seats and across the aisles), and one student is playing with his pencil.
   "I'd like to begin. Please get ready for class."
   Revised:

   _____

   _____

8. You're teaching an algebra lesson on adding and subtracting polynomials. During independent work, you notice that Sherene isn't showing her work and is just writing down her answers.
(Teacher pauses in front of Sherene's desk.) "What am I going to say about your work?"
Revised:

9. You asked students to complete one page of Cornell notes for section 3 of chapter 3. Some students forget to include their summaries, while others are forgetting to note keywords.
(Teacher points to a copy of exemplar Cornell notes on the wall.) "Remember to follow this format when writing your Cornell notes!"
Revised:

10. You just asked your first graders to write two sentences in response to the prompt, "What did you do last weekend?" You check in with a student who seems overwhelmed and reluctant to start. Here are the expectations you've already expressed to the class:
   - Read the prompt, "What did you do last weekend?"
   - Before you write words down, whisper them five times to yourself.
   - Write *two* complete sentences in response to the prompt.
"Get started on your writing assignment, Marshon!"
Revised:

11. After finishing a stretch of oral reading of *Call of the Wild* as a class, you ask students to finish the last page of the chapter on their own while using their interactive reading skills. You notice that approximately half of the class is finishing the chapter but not reading interactively.
"Pencils in hand, please!"
Revised:

12. You instruct your students to *Turn and Talk* (technique 43), but notice that some pairs are slow to start, some students are dominating their pair conversations, and others are discussing the wrong question.
"You should be discussing your answer to the question we just discussed."
Revised:

13. During a lesson on the French Revolution, you ask students to read a paragraph-long excerpt from "Declaration of the Rights of Man" by following the steps you've taught them for analyzing a primary source document. Instead, students skip the analysis and begin writing answers to the comprehension questions.

"Remember to analyze the document before you answer the questions."

Revised:

_____

_____

THE NEXT LEVEL

Here are more tips about *What to Do* that we pass on from observing and talking with masterful teachers.

Consistent What to Do. Standardize the language of your directions, or at least seek to make the language for frequent directions consistent. Using the same direction in the same words over time will make it a habit and maximizes the efficiency of your directions.

Adding a gesture. Add a nonverbal gesture to your direction to increase understanding and follow-through. Over time, you can also make the nonverbal gesture itself a consistent *What to Do.*

What to Do *and checking for understanding.* If students do not appear to respond, check that they understand your directions with a *What to Do.* "So, before I send you off, which pages are you going to read independently? Terry? What are you going to underline for as you read, Janean? What are you going to do next, Simone?" This can also help you check yourself and ensure that your directions were clear and not confusing.

Simplified What to Do. If you are in a tricky situation where a student appears not to want to follow a direction, try breaking down your *What to Do* into an even more specific task. "I asked you to begin writing. Let me see you pick up your pencil. Good. Now begin, please."

What to Do *out front.* Give the *What to Do* direction in advance of cueing a routine, in order to build autonomy. "When you hear the timer, please have pencils in your trays and show me you're ready to review."

Assuming the best. Whenever the root cause of a student's noncompliance is unclear, assume the best by showing students that you believe they are making a good-faith effort and will comply once they understand what you're asking them to do. "Hmm. I must not have been clear enough! When I said pause your writing, I also meant your pencils should be down as well."

Use the table to practice some of these variations. Write down three directions you commonly give as *What to Do* in your classroom. For each, also write ways in which students might demonstrate marginal compliance and a *What to Do* correction that would address these anticipated mistakes.

With a partner or by yourself, practice delivering the corrections. The following are success points:

- You describe the solution or what students should be doing.
- Your language is precise but brief.

What to Do Direction	Potential Marginal Follow-Through	What to Do Correction Using a "Next Level" Variation
Example: *"Meet me at the top of page 8 and follow along with your finger as I read aloud."*	*Student flips to page 8 but doesn't point to words on the page.*	*"Finger to page." Add a gesture/ simplified What to Do.*

ACTION PLANNING

Use this action planner to continue your work with *What to Do*. (Find a printable version of this form at my.teachlikeachampion.com.) You know you're on the right track when you . . .

- Describe the solution or what students should be doing.
- Phrase it precisely but briefly.

WHAT TO DO

HOW AM I DOING?

_____

_____

Design one or more action steps for improvement. Decide on an interval by which you'll revisit this page to assess your progress.

Action Step 1

By when, with whom, and how you will measure your effort

By _____, I will . . .

Date

_____

_____

How Did I Do?

Successes: _____

_____

_____

_____

Challenges: _____

_____

_____

Next steps: _____

_____

_____

_____

Action Step 2

By when, with whom, and how you will measure your effort

By _____, I will . . .

Date

_____

_____

_____

How Did I Do?

Successes: _____

_____

_____

_____

Challenges: _____

_____

_____

Next steps: _____

_____

_____

OUR OBSERVATIONS ON THE CHAMPION

 Clip FG70. Art Worrell

In his twelfth grade US History class, Art gives a clear *What to Do* to facilitate a transition between a stretch of whole-class review and his introduction to a new unit of study. His directions are effective because they're

Specific. He tells kids precisely where to put the resource they just reviewed in the *Do Now* section of their binders. He then lets students know exactly how they'll show him they're ready to move ahead and precisely where they can then find the divider for their next unit (on their desks). He makes this last direction even more unmistakable by projecting a copy of the divider that shows what he's referring to.

Concrete and observable. His directions are actionable ("You can click this into your binder," "Track me") because he tells students to perform concrete, physical tasks that he can plainly see them do. This concreteness makes it easier for students to follow his directions and for Art to enforce them.

Sequential. He tells students *What to Do* in the order they need to do it. For instance, instead of skipping ahead into the next unit, he begins by telling students *What to Do* with the resource they just finished reviewing. *Then* he asks them to track so that he knows when they're ready to move on. Finally, once students have put everything away and track him, he then gives directions for his transition into the next unit, telling them where to find the new unit divider.

Art facilitates this transition using just a handful of verbal directions. His economy of language makes it easier for his students to keep track of what he wants them to do and to then follow through.

WHAT TO DO

POSITIVE FRAMING

OVERVIEW

Positive Framing means using positive language to motivate and inspire students when you are making corrections or encouraging them to sustain effort. *Teach Like a Champion 2.0* describes some of the ways to do that:

- Live in the now, and focus on what should happen next.
- Assume the best.
- Allow plausible anonymity.
- Build momentum (by narrating the positive).
- Challenge!
- Talk expectations and aspirations.

Positive Framing takes time to perfect, but the payoff is often great.

Reflection

Do your colleagues consider you a positive teacher? Do your students? What makes them think so, and to what degree is their perception accurate?

If you already feel that you set a positive tone in class, working on all six approaches offers the opportunity to broaden and develop the skills you can use to create a positive climate so that you can respond to different types of students and in different types of situations. Of the six types of *Positive Framing* we've described, which comes most naturally to you? Are any of them harder to use?

_____

_____

_____

_____

ANALYZE A CHAMPION

 Clip FG71. Emily Bisso, Grade 5

What phrases of *Positive Framing* do you hear in this montage from Emily's classroom? How was the way she framed these phrases beneficial to her?

How might it have sounded different in a less positive teacher's words? What would the impact be on her students?

_____

_____

_____

_____

FUNDAMENTALS

Using *Positive Framing* means intervening to correct student behavior in a positive and constructive way. It's based on the idea that people are motivated by a vision of a positive outcome more than by a wish to avoid a negative one.

Positive Framing does not mean avoiding interventions or talking only about the positive behaviors you see. It means improving what needs improving, but doing so in a positive way.

Positive Framing is often confused with *Precise Praise* (technique 59). Certainly there's a lot of overlap, but whereas *Precise Praise* helps you reinforce in an effective way behaviors that are already correct or positive, *Positive Framing* helps you make corrections in a way that still motivates students and builds your relationship with them. This is important. Corrections are not necessarily a bad thing. Most often we give them because we are teaching; corrections they tell students: this is the change you need to make to write a better sentence, or this is the change you need to make to be more successful in school. The goal, then, isn't to stop correcting students. This is obvious to coaches—they know that when they are doing their jobs well, they are constantly telling players, "Less wrist," "More energy," "Bend your knees," and so on. The same goes for teachers.

Live in the Now

Positive Framing can help you avoid nagging. You talk about what should happen next (technique 57, *What to Do*) rather than what went wrong. There's a time and place for processing what went wrong—but it's usually not in the midst of a lesson. Give instructions describing the next move on the path to success.

"Keira, I want to see that pencil working away."	Not "~~Keira, stop looking back at Tanya.~~"
"Show me your eyes, fifth grade."	Not "~~Fifth grade, some of us are looking out the window.~~"
"Third grade, Tina is describing the setting. Show me your best tracking while she's talking."	Not "~~Third grade, you're eyes are not on the speaker.~~"

Assume the Best

We sometimes assume that a mistake was intentional when in fact we don't know the cause. Or our language can imply to a student that we think he or she did something on purpose or, worse, imply a broader judgment of character: that the student was selfish, disrespectful, or lazy, say. We must strive to remember how many garden-variety causes for mistakes there are: distraction, fatigue, genuine misunderstanding, and so on. Unless you have clear evidence that a behavior was intentional, it's better to assume that your students are trying to do as you've asked, and subtle differences in word choice are critical to that end. Two of our favorite words are *forgot* and *confused,* as in:

"It seems like some people forgot to write in complete sentences."
"It seems like some people might be confused. This should be a silent activity, please."

Phrases like these assume the best. Attributing a behavior to an excess of enthusiasm can also be effective:

"I'm glad to see so much enthusiasm for getting started, but please wait until Samia has finished her question."

Versions of the phrase, "I must not have been clear" are also helpful:

"Whoops, I must not have been clear that I wanted you to find *all* the verbs in the passage. Please continue working."

Framing positively costs you nothing, because following that framing, you can still set whatever standard or even deliver any consequence you choose. In fact, even while you deliver a consequence, you can and should still assume the best. By removing from the discussion any assumption about intentions, you also remove much emotion from the consequence. The message isn't "You did this on purpose, and you have to take the consequences." Rather, it's "We do things a certain way, and we fix it when we fail to do that."

Assuming the worst—the opposite of assuming the best—makes you appear as though you're waiting for misbehavior to happen, that you expect it. In contrast, showing that you assume your students are always trying to comply with your wishes demonstrates that you're in charge.

"Thank you" can be strong language. Show that you assume the best by thanking students as you give them a command: "Thank you for taking your seats in three, two, one . . ." You can still apply a consequence if needed.

Allow Plausible Anonymity

When students are working toward meeting your expectations consistently, allow them to do so in private. When possible, begin by correcting without using names; for example:

"Check yourself to make sure you've done exactly what I've asked." (Not "Rhondesia, make sure you did what I said.")
"Fourth grade, make sure you've got your pencil out and your notes in front of you." (Not: "Jason, I want to see you in SLANT with your notes page in front of you.")

In most cases, this approach will yield fast results and a bit of appreciation from your students.

Build Momentum (by Narrating the Positive)

Narrate the positive with momentum in mind. Narrate the evidence of your own command, students doing as they're asked, and things getting better.

"Charles is looking sharp and Mahogany is ready to go. Jason has his bright eyes right here . . ."	PLUS	"They can't wait to get going on their math facts."
(After instructing students to draft a thesis statement) "I see those pencils moving" *(pause to let students work, then a whisper)* . . .	PLUS	"Those ideas are rolling out . . ." *(pause several seconds)* "Nice. Angela, Marcus, can't wait to read 'em!"

This can resonate with students who want to feel "normal" or to "fit in." When you call students' attention to how normal it is for their classmates to do as you asked, they will want to follow. It's especially important to narrate the positive for something you see that's worthy of recognition.

Notice that this means always narrating your strength, never your weakness:

Narrating Strength	Narrating Weakness
"I see some brave hands going up to try to answer. Now a few more. Love the risk-taking I'm starting to see."	~~"I'm seeing the same few hands. A lot of you are not participating, and it's going to show up in your participation grades."~~
"Thank you for being very attentive to my directions. Just like Jabali and Camela. And to those of you who are now fixing it. Now we're looking sharp."	~~Class, I gave a very clear direction, and a lot of you are not doing it. Some of you seem to think the rules do not apply to you.~~

But narrate the positive only when you truly see behavior that meets your standards. Don't try to pretend that mediocre follow-through is the ideal—you'll only reinforce it. Narrate to motivate group behavior as students are deciding whether or not to make the effort to meet your expectations. When they aren't, use another approach.

Also, don't narrate to correct individual students who clearly have not met expectations, by praising students around them who are on task. Show you're not afraid to address the problem directly—just do so positively: "Susan, show me your best, with your notebook out. We've got lots to do."

For momentum during a countdown, narrate behaviors when they appear before the time has elapsed: "Five, four. Jason is ready. Three. Two Jessica. Looking sharp. One." This is better than narrating follow-through *after* the countdown, which makes it sound as though you are pleading for students to do as you asked.

Supply this scene with a narration that is positive and builds momentum:

You've just told your class of twenty-five to put away their books. About half the class does so quickly and is ready to go. Another handful are slower. One sighs as she does it. Several poke around in their packs before straightening up. One is slower than all the rest because he is still looking at a picture in the book. The person next to him asks him a quiet question.

Example: *"I love how many of us I see putting our books away quickly."*

_____

_____

_____

_____

Challenge!

Challenge students. They love to show you that they can do more than you think they can (or more than they *think* you think they can). In a classroom, challenging them as groups is usually better than challenging them as individuals. Ask them to compete against others within or outside the class, abstract standards, new circumstances, or impersonal foes like the clock:

"You guys have been doing a great job this week. Let's see if you can take it up a notch today."
"You've got the idea, but let me hear you use the word *elusive* in your answer. Can you do it?!"

"The sixth-grade girls are killing it, boys. Can you keep the pace?"

"Let's show we can write for six minutes without stopping. Go."

"Three minutes left, but let's see who can beat that!"

"These sentences are good. Can you make them even better?"

"This is going to be a really tough question—let's see if you scholars can answer it."

Talk Expectations and Aspirations

Talk about who your students are becoming, who they aspire to be, where they can be going; and work that into your challenges. When you ask them to do something differently or better, remind them that doing so will help them fulfill these aspirations: moving from third grade to fourth, from middle to high school, for example. When tempted to praise them by saying they look "great," say they look like "college students," "scientists," or some similar term. Connect them to the goal.

"If you finish early, great; check your work. Make sure you get 100 percent today. Every week, college gets closer."

(To a fourth grader) "Good, Juan. Now let me hear you make it a fifth-grade answer by using the word *product*."

"Can you answer that in the words of a scientist [historian, editor, manager]?"

"When you get to college, your thesis statements are going to blow your professors away. Let's see if we can do this one more time so you really take the campus by storm."

What aspirations do you most want to foster in your students? Follow these examples by identifying some aspirations and writing phrases that will connect them to your students.

Aspiration: *Independent thinkers*

Phrase: *"These answers are good. But I want to hear some new and daring ideas. Can you wow me?"*

Aspiration: *Great writers*

Phrase: *"These are solid sentences. But now I want to hear some sentences that sound like they're from your first novel."*

Aspiration: *College*

Phrase: *"The Titans always track. Who has a college-level answer?"*

Aspiration: _____

_____

Phrase:

_____

_____

_____

Aspiration: _____

_____

POSITIVE FRAMING

Phrase:

_____

_____

_____

More Reframing

Use these examples for support in some reframing of your own:

Live in the now: *Keena, I need your eyes forward. James, put your pencil down.*

_____

_____

Assume the best: *Oops, it looks like we forgot to push in our chairs; let's go back and try that again.*

_____

_____

Allow plausible anonymity: *Check yourself to make sure you did exactly what I asked.* [or] *Tigers, let's raise our hands again with no calling out.*

_____

_____

Build momentum (with positive narration): *I need four people to put their pencils down, now I'm missing only one, and now we're ready to start our oral drill.*

_____

_____

Challenge: *Let's see if we can get our homework out silently in ten seconds. Ready, set, go!*

_____

_____

> **Revisit *Teach Like a Champion 2.0***
>
> If you haven't done so already, view *Teach Like a Champion 2.0* clip 70 and see if you can spot at least fourteen examples of Janelle Austin's *Positive Framing.* Then revisit Doug's notes about it.

CASE STUDIES

Evaluate the following classroom cases. In each table, jot down your observations on what was effective about the teacher's *Positive Framing* ("glows") and what could be improved ("grows") before you move on to ours. If possible, discuss the cases with one or more colleagues.

Case 1. Grade 8 Science

You walk into this classroom during independent practice. About half the students are on task, working at writing up a lab. The other half seems to be either disengaged (staring out the window or at the clock) or mildly disruptive. In four minutes of observing, you hear the teacher say:

1. *To a daydreamer.* "What should you be doing right now?"
2. *To two students whispering.* "Carla and Maria, I'm tired of telling you two to stop chatting."
3. *To one who taps his pencil while thinking.* "Jason, stop!"
4. *To all.* "As usual, it looks like only about half of us are getting anything done."
5. *To the back row.* "Come on guys; get it together."
6. *To a student out of her seat.* "Why do I always have to remind you to be in your seat?!"
7. *To a sometimes challenging student who is on task.* "Oh, look who's working today!"

Glows	Grows
It was effective when the teacher . . .	Next time, the teacher could try . . .

Case 2. Grade 5 Reading

As you walk into the classroom, the students are answering written questions about a text, in preparation for whole-class discussion. They are hard at work and clearly engaged in the content. They seem very invested in the classroom and good about following the teacher's instructions. Then discussion begins. In your ten minutes of observation, you hear the teacher say:

During work time:

1. *To a student not writing.* "John, that's a demerit; you need to have your eyes down and should be working all the time."

While Circulating and checking student work:

2. "Keep working. Pick up your pencil and write, Steven."
3. "Alaysia is ready to go. Thank you, Alaysia. Terrence is also writing quickly. Excited to see their urgency and wish that the rest of you could move as quickly as they are. I'm still waiting on about half the class to be writing."
4. "That's not a complete sentence."
5. "Why is your text not annotated?"
6. "Where's that whispering coming from? Shh. This is not partner work time."
7. *To two students off pace.* "I see that we don't have question number four answered; this means you need to hustle."
8. "Point to where you are. Yikes . . . I need to see at least three-quarters of the way done by now."

During discussion:

9. *To a student not tracking.* "This is the second time I have to remind you to start tracking; it's a de-merit—track."
10. "Jahari, pause please. No one in columns three or four is tracking you. I shouldn't have to remind you that *all* eyes need to be on Jahari to show him respect. We're waiting . . . OK, go ahead Jahari."
11. *To a student reading the passage in a quiet voice.* "I'm going to have to stop you right there. We can't hear you. It's the same problem we always have when you read. You're going to need to read more loudly."

Glows	Grows
It was effective when the teacher . . .	Next time, the teacher could try . . .

Reflection

What specific things do you hear the teachers in your building say when they struggle with remaining positive?

THE NEXT LEVEL

> **blog** Find these blog posts at teachlikeachampion.com/blog/coaching-and-practice/annals-coaching -positive-motivating-critical-feedback-video/ and teachlikeachampion.com/blog/coaching -and-practice/tale-two-affirmations/.
>
> If you like to envision teaching as a form of coaching, watch a soccer coach's *Positive Framing* at "Annals of Coaching: More on Positive, Motivating Critical Feedback."
>
> For an insight about addressing the student in *Positive Framing*, visit Doug's entry "A Tale of Two Affirmations."

Where in your next lesson plan do you need to be most ready to keep things positively framed? Prepare what you can say to frame and narrate the positive.

PARTNER WORK

Compare your responses to the activities in this chapter with a partner. Make revisions based on your discussion. Ask the partner to watch you teach and to transcribe some of your phrases. Note some you like and revise some you don't.

ACTION PLANNING

Use this action planner to continue your work with *Positive Framing*. (Find a printable version of this form at my.teachlikeachampion.com.) You know you're on the right track when you are using the technique . . .

- In a range of ways
- With a positive or upbeat tone

HOW AM I DOING?

_____

_____

Design one or more action steps for improvement. Decide on an interval by which you'll revisit this page to assess your progress.

Action Step 1

By when, with whom, and how you will measure your effort

By _____, I will . . .
   Date

_____

_____

How Did I Do?

Successes: _____

_____

_____

_____

_____

Challenges: _____

_____

_____

_____

Next steps: _____

_____

_____

Action Step 2

By when, with whom, and how you will measure your effort

By _____, I will . . .

<small>Date</small>

_____

_____

_____

How Did I Do?

Successes: _____

_____

_____

_____

_____

Challenges: _____

_____

_____

_____

Next steps: _____

_____

_____

_____

OUR OBSERVATIONS ON THE CHAMPION

 Clip FG71. Emily Bisso

Cut 1

Emily calls attention to the enthusiastic participation she sees ("Lots of hands") and even adds a wink to acknowledge a student who gets back on task. The way she narrates the positive normalizes engagement and inspires other students to participate as well.

Cut 2

Emily effectively delivers a correction that lives in the now and allows plausible anonymity ("Make sure that you're writing with me"). She then adds *Firm Calm Finesse* (technique 54) to her correction by providing a clear rationale for it ("otherwise you won't be able to finish on time"). This shows students that the correction isn't about her. It's about helping them succeed.

Cut 3

When Emily notices that she doesn't have all students' eyes, she gives an anonymous correction ("I'm waiting for some eyes"). She then smiles subtly to acknowledge the students who get back on task while assuming the best about their intentions ("You'll have more time to write in a second").

Cut 4

Emily ascribes positive intentions to the behavior she sees—even while she's correcting it. For example, she responds to a few students who are slow to give her their attention by saying, "I know you guys want to get your thoughts down." Emily also preserves students' privacy by allowing plausible anonymity ("waiting on a couple pairs of eyes"). Her corrections—both verbal and nonverbal—are so firm, positive, and discreet that students do what she asks them to quickly and willingly. Within seconds, they return to the business of learning.

PRECISE PRAISE

OVERVIEW

Skilled teachers are strategic about the positive reinforcement they give to students in the classroom. They are aware of the immense power of positive reinforcement, but also the degree to which its power can be squandered and even unintentionally made counterproductive. Aware that positive reinforcement is the subject of some of the most interesting and intensive research in the education sector—Dr. Carol Dweck's *Mindset* is a prime example—these teachers seek to be specific, genuine, real, encouraging, and motivating. And they reflect on ways to make the praise (and other kinds of reinforcement) best support their students' success. When they do this, they are using the technique we call *Precise Praise*.

Reflection

What are your goals when you give positive reinforcement in the classroom? That is, what are you trying to accomplish when you give it?

_____

_____

What's one way your goals inform your practice? That is, if your goal for positive reinforcement is to make students feel good about themselves, do you perhaps deliver praise liberally in a bright, sunny voice?

_____

_____

ANALYZE A CHAMPION

 Clip FG72. Stephen Chiger, Grade 11

In this clip, you'll see Steve give a student some positive reinforcement and then start to walk away before doubling back to say a few more things. What's the difference between his first and his second round of feedback? Why is it important?

_____

_____

_____

_____

FUNDAMENTALS

We begin by arguing that teachers should divide positive reinforcement into two types as often as they can: acknowledgment and praise.

Acknowledgment is recognizing—or perhaps thanking—students for doing what's expected of them. It does not heap praise on the students in question, describing their behavior as "awesome," "outstanding," or "incredible." It merely makes note of the fact and expresses appreciation. "I see you have your homework ready today" and "I appreciate your having your homework done every day" are examples of acknowledgment. They say to a student, I see that you are doing the things you need to do. They matter.

But, unlike praise, acknowledgment doesn't suggest that doing what's expected is exceptional. To praise would be to say, "It's fantastic that you have your homework today." The word "fantastic" suggests that doing your homework is over and above what's expected, and worthy of exceptional notice. That can be problematic, because in this case, your praise may make it seem as though you are surprised that the student has done his or her homework, and tacitly that doing so is over and above.

This doesn't mean you can't praise. "Awesome job on your homework last night" is a great thing to say—when the homework was truly exceptional and showed special insight or effort. Or if a student did her homework every single night for an entire semester, maybe that would be "great." But a big part of making positive reinforcement work lies in distinguishing that which is truly outstanding from that which merely deserves appreciation.

Acknowledgment is best to use when students meet expectations, and praise is best when they exceed them. If you mix the two, you risk suggesting that your stated expectations were not in fact expectations at all, as in: "Awesome—you brought a pencil to class today!" A teacher would say that only if the presence of the pencil were a surprise.

Reinforce Actions, Not Traits

When possible, reinforce behaviors and actions that students can choose to repeat rather than attributing their work to traits like being "smart."

Praising students for being "smart," Carol Dweck has pointed out in her important book *Mindset*, can incline them to take fewer risks because they may believe they will risk no longer being "smart" if they get something wrong.

If we want students to love challenge, to be diligent and not cut corners, to take their time and think a question through before answering, we should try to reinforce those things specifically by replacing reinforcement of a trait, such as "Wow, what a smart answer," with "You really wrestled with this and took a risk" or "Love that insight . . . it really helped that you went back and reread the passage. Nice."

Align Praise with the Lesson Objective

We've noticed that some of the best teachers deliberately align their praise to learning objectives:

"Scholars, look at Melanie's paper. In this paragraph, she went back and revised her transition to make it capture the contrast between the paragraphs more clearly. Now her paper really holds together. Great work, Melanie."

In other words, the teacher in this sequence is reinforcing not just replicable actions but specific academic actions that support her class's learning objective—in this case, revising. And not just revising but thinking intentionally about transitions in writing.

Take a moment to brainstorm some actions specific to your subject or grade level that you'd like to see students do more of. These are things you might specifically reinforce. We've given you a few examples:

In a math class: checking your work.
In a history class: referring to specific evidence
In an English class: using quotations from the text

_____

_____

_____

_____

Keep It Real

One common mistake by new teachers in particular is overpraising: in an effort to keep the classroom positive, they praise (rather than acknowledge) as much as they can. But excessive or insincere praise can be counterproductive.

Too much praise can trivialize its value. When we use praise to bolster self-esteem, students often stop listening. When everything is "awesome," the word becomes commonplace, and nothing is truly awesome.

Other research suggests that students learn to discount excessive praise as cheap and, further, to hear it as an indication that their work is inferior. Here's a passage from an article on praise by the writer Po Bronson that appeared in *New York Magazine* in 2007.

Only young children—under the age of 7—take praise at face value: Older children are just as suspicious of it as adults.

Psychologist Wulf-Uwe Meyer, a pioneer in the field, conducted a series of studies where children watched other students receive praise. According to Meyer's findings, by the age of 12, children believe that earning praise from a teacher is not a sign you did well—it's actually a sign you lack ability and the teacher thinks you need extra encouragement. And teens, Meyer found, discounted praise to such an extent that they believed it's a teacher's criticism—not praise at all—that really conveys a positive belief in a student's aptitude.

New York University professor of psychiatry Judith Brook explains that the issue for parents is one of credibility. "Praise is important, but not vacuous praise," she says. "It has to be based on a real thing—some skill or talent they have." Once children hear praise they interpret as meritless, they discount not just the insincere praise, but sincere praise as well.

Substituting acknowledgment for praise—"You did it just as I asked, Shayna. Thank you"—can help, but say it only if Shayna really did do it, not as a roundabout message to Sally, sitting next to Shayna, who has gotten sidetracked. Correct Sally more directly so that you jeopardize neither your relationship with each student nor the relationship between them.

And consider making your positive reinforcement feel more real by varying the tone and format—sometimes loud, sometimes quiet, using different words and tone of voice. If it's the same every time, it can seem canned and therefore disingenuous.

When you deliver praise, be sure to do so with a positive tone. Otherwise, you run the risk that students will misinterpret your well-intentioned praise as sarcasm.

Reflection

Do you suspect you overpraise? If you're not sure, listen to a recording of yourself in the classroom. How often do you praise? Does it seem real and scarce enough to retain its value? Why or why not?

_____

_____

_____

Thinking a bit more about varying your praise, what's one way you could change up your positive reinforcement to make it sound less canned?

_____

_____

_____

Champions' Words

Read these transcriptions of first-grade teacher Hilary Lewis and seventh-grade teacher David Javsicas. Then come back here and respond to these questions. (You can also revisit their work in video clips 71 and 72 in *Teach Like a Champion 2.0.*)

How many times does Hilary acknowledge? Does she also praise? When?

_____

_____

Is David acknowledging or praising? What strikes you about how he delivers his message?

> ### Transcript: Hilary Lewis, Grade 1
>
> #### Teach Like a Champion 2.0, *Clip 71*
>
> HILARY: Which table group is ready? All right, you may begin. Did you notice that they didn't make a lot of noise when they were choosing their first shape? They made sure that everyone had an opportunity. So I see Darnell and Jala and Olivia and Chinuray—they've already gotten their first shape, and they put it right up against that line of symmetry and began to trace it.
>
> I already see Sean, he has already flipped his shape over to make the mirror image; that's awesome. Let's see it, scholars, I want to see at least four. That means you could do five, you could do six, and you can do seven, whatever you can fit on that line.

> ### Transcript: David Javsicas, Grade 7
>
> #### Teach Like a Champion 2.0, *Clip 72*
>
> DAVID: Oh, I see what you're doing. OK. I'll get you in a minute; I can only read one thing at a time. Goodness gracious, you have been very industrious today. Can you use context to figure out what *industrious* means? Use context. If I just said, "Wow, you've been very industrious today," what do you think *industrious* means?
>
> STUDENT: Um, productive?
>
> DAVID: Ah, good. That's a nice synonym. Excellent. Keep it up, scholar dollar coming your way. I like that. You know what else, I like how actively you participated in discussions. Your hand is up all the time. That's probably part of the reason why your ideas are so good. Keep that up; you help everybody learn when you do that.

Acknowledge, Praise, or Criticize?

These common classroom occurrences warrant a response. Following the example in the first, write what type of response is called for (acknowledge, praise, or criticize) and what you would say.

1. A student who struggles to track catches herself looking out the window, and tracks the speaker.
   Response: *Acknowledgment*
   You say: *"Thank you for tracking, Mahogany. You're really getting it now."*
2. A chronically unprepared student brings in her pencil and begins class correctly.
   Response:

PRECISE PRAISE

You say:

_____

_____

3. A student answers your question with a complete sentence, as you expect.
    Response:

    _____

    You say:

    _____

    _____

4. Students get to work immediately at the beginning of class.
    Response:

    _____

    You say:

    _____

    _____

5. Students are enthusiastically participating in class, raising hands, smiling, and tracking.
    Response:

    _____

    You say:

    _____

    _____

6. A student delivers a well-thought-out complete answer of unusually high quality.
    Response:

    _____

    You say:

    _____

    _____

7. A student turns a negative attitude around since the morning.
   Response:

   _____

   You say:

   _____

   _____

8. A student who sometimes shouts out the answer raises her hand.
   Response:

   _____

   You say:

   _____

   _____

   Get used to saying these things by practicing them out loud—ideally with a partner or a small group acting as students.

Loudly, Quietly, Publicly, Privately?

> **Revisit** *Teach Like a Champion 2.0*
> Review Doug's extended technique 59 thoughts at "Modulate and Vary Your Delivery."

As we explained in chapter 11, generally, privacy is best for critical feedback, but balance private criticism with instances of private reinforcement, complement private praise with brief bits of public praise. For example, you might stop the class to read Shanice's sentence aloud and say to the class, "Now that is how a strong, active verb can give muscles to a sentence!"

With some exceptions, positive reinforcement is often most powerful when public. Public reinforcement motivates others to strive and gives the recipient attention that can make him or her feel proud and honored. To your mix add touches of loud praise and semiprivate praise that you deliberately intend for others to overhear.

Positive reinforcement works best when it is memorable. To make it so, you'll want it to stand out a bit, keeping its format a bit unpredictable. For example, you might say in a formal tone, "Mr. Ramirez, may I speak with you please?" followed by a quiet, "Your essay was truly outstanding. You should be very proud of your work."

How might you make your acknowledgments memorable?

_____

_____

What genuine, deserved praise could you give that might surprise the class or individual students?

_____

_____

How could you deliver genuine, deserved praise in a surprising way?

_____

_____

_____

> **blog** Find this blog post at teachlikeachampion.com/blog/teaching-and-schools/how-positive
> -framing-and-precise-praise-fit-together/.
>   *Positive Framing* (technique 58) goes hand in hand with *Precise Praise*. Doug talks
> about how in his post "How Positive Framing and Precise Praise Fit Together."

THE NEXT LEVEL

Planning Positive Reinforcement

This exercise could be useful for planning praise in an upcoming lesson. As you praise routines, be thoughtful about praising the right behaviors for the right reasons. For each item here, identify one or two behaviors or actions as specifically as you can that you'd love to see from every student. For example:

1. As students enter the classroom
    Behaviors you want: *Entering the classroom and moving swiftly and professionally to their seats.*
    Why you want them: *Reflects a sense of urgency about getting started learning.*
    Phrasing: *"I love seeing how [Sayvion, for example] is moving quickly to his seat showing me he is eager and ready to learn!"*
2. As you introduce new material to the class (or other routine: _____)
    Behaviors you want:

    _____

    _____

    Why you want them:

    _____

    _____

Phrasing:

_____

_____

3. Independent practice (or other routine: _____)
   Behaviors you want:

_____

_____

   Why you want them:

_____

_____

   Phrasing:

_____

_____

4. A lesson wrap-up (or other routine: _____)
   Behaviors you want:

_____

_____

   Why you want them:

_____

_____

   Phrasing:

_____

_____

To take this further, from your stash of tools at my.teachlikeachampion.com, print out "Planning Positive Reinforcement with *Precise Praise*." Use it for deeper and additional planning for common routines.

Printable Praise

Here are some ideas for fortifying spoken praise. Adapt or adopt them for use in your classroom and think of others.

Posting praiseworthy (not merely expected) behaviors on the board, and writing the names of students who do them.

_____

_____

Writing into lesson plans or student materials the kinds of behaviors you are most eager to praise on that day ("Today I'm looking to see who can even . . ."). Then devote a part of your bulletin board to naming students in praise.

_____

_____

Prewriting notes to pass out to students every day commending or encouraging them.

_____

_____

ACTION PLANNING

Use this action planner to continue your work with *Precise Praise*. (Find a printable version of this form at my.teachlikeachampion.com.) You know you're on the right track when you . . .

- Name precise behaviors when you reinforce.
- Acknowledge readily and praise selectively.
- Vary public and private delivery in keeping with your purpose.

HOW AM I DOING?

_____

_____

Design one or more action steps for improvement. Decide on an interval by which you'll revisit this page to assess your progress.

Action Step 1

By when, with whom, and how you will measure your effort

By _____, I will . . .
   _{Date}

_____

_____

How Did I Do?

Successes: _____

_____

_____

_____

Challenges: _____

_____

_____

_____

Next steps: _____

_____

_____

Action Step 2

By when, with whom, and how you will measure your effort

By _____, I will . . .
 _{Date}

_____

_____

_____

How Did I Do?

Successes: _____

_____

_____

_____

_____

Challenges: _____

_____

_____

_____

Next steps: _____

_____

_____

_____

WARM/STRICT

OVERVIEW

Many of us are inclined to think of warm and strict as opposites: to be more of one is to be less of the other. But being both warm and strict at the same moment can communicate not only high expectations but caring and respect.

When you are simultaneously clear, consistent, firm, and unrelenting *and* positive, enthusiastic, caring, and thoughtful, you send the powerful message that having high expectations is part of caring for and respecting someone. To make *Warm/Strict* effective,

- Explain to students why you're doing what you're doing—that setting limits is part of caring about someone.
- Distinguish between criticizing behavior and criticizing people. In fact, remember to emphasize your caring for people exactly when you are discussing a poor choice.
- Demonstrate that consequences are temporary. Get over it quickly yourself and show your warmth and caring in your first interaction after a correction.
- Use warm nonverbal behavior.

Reflection: How You Come Across

Would your students describe you as warm, strict, both, or neither? What evidence would they cite to support their view? Is there evidence they might overlook?

_____

_____

_____

Could students' sentiments possibly be divided—one group seeing you in one way and another in a different way? Who are the groups? Why might they differ? Is that a problem you need to address?

_____

_____

ANALYZE A CHAMPION

Clip FG73. Kesete Thompkins

How is Kesete both warm and strict in his interactions with students? What messages does he convey through his words, body language, and actions?

_____

_____

_____

Compare your observations with ours at the end of this technique.

FUNDAMENTALS

Warm	Strict
Positive, enthusiastic, caring, thoughtful	Clear, consistent, firm, unrelenting

Many people are socialized to the false conviction that warmth and strictness are opposites. This outlook will undercut your teaching. The degree to which you are warm has no bearing on the degree to which you are strict, and vice versa. Here's how to make them work together.

Explain what you do. Tell students why you're doing what you're doing and how it will help them:

"Sweetheart, we don't do that in this classroom because it keeps us from making the most of our learning time. I'm going to have to try to help you remember that."

"Priya, we don't do that in this classroom because it keeps us from making the most of our learning time."

Use warm nonverbal behavior. Put your arm on a student's shoulder and use facial expression to convey your sympathy that he'll have to redo the homework and that you know he's capable of better. Bend down to a third grader's eye level and explain firmly that she won't be allowed to talk to her classmates that way. But don't apologize because you care.

Show that consequences are temporary. Once you give a consequence, your next task is to forgive. You use a consequence so that you won't have to hold a grudge. Get over it quickly. *Without Apology* (technique 15), model for students that when they've fulfilled the consequences of a mistake, it is immediately in the past. Be sincere, but try to make your modeling include smiling and greeting them naturally. Show that the slate is clean.

"After you're done, I can't wait to have you come back and show us your best."

Overcome "the tyranny of the 'or.'" In balanced combination, *Warm/Strict* can even help students resolve apparent contradictions and realize that many of the either-or choices in their lives are false constructs. It helps students realize that they can be hip and successful, have fun and work hard, be happy and say no to self-indulgence.

As with Precise Praise, *call out problematic behavior, not supposed traits.*

Behavior: "Your talking over was inconsiderate."

Trait: "You're inconsiderate."

Observations on Behavior

Translate the following into observations about behavior:

1. "Who's the troublemaker right now?"

_____

2. "You're in one of your hyperactive states."

_____

3. "Why are you so mean to everyone?"

_____

4. "You're not very generous."

_____

5. "You're stubborn today, aren't you!"

_____

Compose *Warm/Strict*

Read through these situations. Compose a *Warm/Strict* response for at least three of them. Responses can include verbal and nonverbal elements.

1. The student is a gifted, amiable comic, but you've just had to issue a light consequence because a one-liner that you, too, found funny has caused a distraction.

_____

_____

2. A six-year-old with a seriously ill parent balks and complains about arithmetic.

_____

_____

3. You've just had to issue a consequence to a sensitive student who tries hard but burst out in frustrated anger when it looked as though someone had stolen his eraser.

_____

_____

4. As you begin to instruct, three athletes at the back of the room begin to muse together quietly over a moment in which their team lost last night's game.

_____

_____

5. You've just had to separate two genuine friends because, sitting together, they can't refrain from talking and giggling.

_____

_____

6. A student is persistently humming during independent work, inciting annoyed glances and complaints from classmates even after reminders from you. You're not sure she's aware of it, but you think you need to give her a consequence at this point.

_____

_____

7. A tired student in a funk slumps at a desk and puts his head down. You suspect he's not getting much sleep these days.

_____

_____

8. A struggling student in a funk harmlessly tosses a pencil, probably in part because she has no idea how to tackle a *Do Now.*

_____

_____

Reflection

Of people you have known, who has best exemplified *Warm/Strict*? Is there something of theirs that you can apply in the classroom?

_____

_____

_____

ROLL IT OUT

There's no need to try to do all these at once. Plan and try one in your next session of teaching. Retry and expand from there.

1. Is there any class routine or activity in which you are almost entirely strict, without some outward sign of warmth? Would you gain anything by changing that? What *Warm/Strict* language can you prepare?
2. Is there any extended moment in class when you are almost exclusively warm? Would you gain anything by changing that? What *Warm/Strict* language can you prepare?
3. Look at an upcoming lesson plan. Note any points in the lesson where you may feel cornered into being just plain strict. Even if strictness must rule right then, how can you liberate yourself from feeling forced?
4. Are there any individuals in the class toward whom you feel compelled to be consistently either warm or strict? With those individuals in mind, prepare and practice some *Warm/Strict* language.

PRACTICE WITH A GROUP OR COLLEAGUE

Sharpen participation with "Giving Feedback in Group Practice Activities" at my.teachlikeachampion .com.

Take a Stand

For a group, here's what a *Facilitator* needs to do:

1. Before the group meets, become familiar with the script.
2. With the group standing in a circle, read the script, adding touches of *Precise Praise* if needed:
   FACILITATOR: Please close your eyes. *(Pause to see that eyes are closed.)* I'm going to offer two choices. Raise one hand as soon as I finish—right hand for the first choice, left hand for the second. Eyes closed. Show me you can do right for the first. *(Pause for show.)* Good. Hands down. Show me left for the second. *(Pause for show.)* Good. Hands down. You must choose without thinking and raise only one hand. Here goes: In the classroom, if you could only be one, would you be warm? . . . or strict? Up and keep them up, sweethearts! *(Pause.)* Open your eyes and count. *(Group members open their eyes and count.)* Thank you. Let's all sit.
3. After everyone sits, lead a thoughtful discussion of what just happened. In any order as opportunities arise, try to solicit thoughts on all of these challenges members may face:
   Distinguishing between behavior and person
   Conveying to students that there is no either-or
   Showing students that consequences are temporary
   Themselves putting classroom incidents behind
   Using warm nonverbal behavior
4. Solicit a summary from several members of the group.
5. If members have not already done so, invite them to say how they go about being *Warm/Strict*.

Discussion Ideas

1. In a group with other colleagues, compare your thoughts in response to "How You Come Across." Is it a problem if different segments of the class see you differently in terms of *Warm/Strict*? If so, what are some solutions?
2. From the student's point of view, evaluate the message in the *Warm/Strict* responses you created under "Compose *Warm/Strict*."

Your takeaways from collaborative work:

_____

_____

_____

ACTION PLANNING

Use this action planner to continue your work with *Warm/Strict*. (Find a printable version of this form at my.teachlikeachampion.com.) You know you're on the right track when you . . .

- Combine verbal warmth with strict instruction.
- Combine warm nonverbal signs with straightforward instruction, correction, or consequence.
- Quickly return yourself and the classroom atmosphere to normal, getting over a challenging moment.

HOW AM I DOING?

_____

_____

Design one or more action steps for improvement. Decide on an interval by which you'll revisit this page to assess your progress.

Action Step 1

By when, with whom, and how you will measure your effort

By _____, I will . . .
    Date

_____

_____

How Did I Do?

Successes: _____

_____

_____

_____

Challenges: _____

_____

_____

Next steps: _____

_____

_____

Action Step 2

By when, with whom, and how you will measure your effort

By _____, I will . . .

_{Date}

_____

_____

_____

How Did I Do?

Successes: _____

_____

_____

_____

Challenges: _____

_____

_____

Next steps: _____

_____

_____

_____

OUR OBSERVATIONS ON THE CHAMPION

 Clip FG73. Kesete Thompkins

Kesete strikes a balance between setting and maintaining expectations while also communicating warmth. To signal high expectations, he encourages students to bring their best selves to class. He promises to come and check to make sure. He asks them to look sharp. But to convey warmth, he personalizes his greetings: ("How's it going, Christina?" "You all right?"). His body language is sometimes formal, but also punctuated by moments when he leans in warmly for a high-five or a gentle touch on the shoulder. He is clearly connecting with students as they walk by.

EMOTIONAL CONSTANCY

OVERVIEW

A teacher who can maintain *Emotional Constancy* is able to steer students through the emotions of growing up, and to help mitigate those emotions rather than making them more intense. This often means a more productive environment and a calmer one, with students learning over time to rely on their teacher to be a source of calm and consistency. Conversely, getting angry with students distracts them from thinking about their own behaviors and actions, and it can provide a perverse incentive: seeing their teacher upset, frustrated, or volatile may be gratifying or even funny for some students.

This is not to say you will not or should not have strong emotions in the classroom. Of course you will, and those emotions will sometimes be clear to students. The goal is to manage them as often as possible. These reminders may help:

- When you criticize, focus on behaviors ("Charles, that's rude") rather than people ("Charles, you are rude").
- Discuss student actions ("Responding to a teacher's comments on your paper is part of being a student. You need to do that now"), not your feelings ("I worked really hard to give you detailed instructions about what parts of your essay require revision, and you didn't make any of those changes").
- Avoid globalizing ("You don't seem to think you have to take other people's feelings into account").
- Try to speak (and often walk) steady—slower than you are inclined to—if you feel your frustration mounting. This makes you appear calm and buys you time to process your emotions before acting.

Reflection

What student behaviors—academic or otherwise—tend to frustrate you? Do you ever feel sucked into defending yourself or chastising students with a negative tone? What's been the effect on the student, the behavior, and the flow of classroom learning?

_____

_____

_____

_____

EMOTIONAL CONSTANCY

ANALYZE THE CHAMPIONS

▶ Clip FG65. Bridget McElduff, Grade 5

▶ Clip FG69. Christy Lundy, Grade 6

Consider the following questions as you view these clips of potentially disruptive emotional moments. How do these teachers avoid being pulled into an emotional encounter themselves?

Bridget McElduff:

_____

_____

_____

_____

Christy Lundy:

_____

_____

_____

_____

What other *Emotional Constancy* do they provide?
Bridget McElduff:

_____

_____

_____

Christy Lundy:

_____

_____

_____

_____

FUNDAMENTALS

An Emotional Laboratory—for Students

School is a laboratory for some students. It is a setting in which they figure out how to behave in a variety of situations that are challenging, public, and often unique to school. Some students have grown up with home lives that provide lots of guidance and support; some have not. Some want to see if their parents' high expectations are equaled by the rest of the world. Some may have learned nonproductive approaches to getting their way outside of school that they have now begun to apply in school.

What should a person do when he is frustrated, angry, tired, and eager to win the approval of peers? These aspects of learning, too, are often part of a school's mandate. Strive to keep a clear head and not personalize things too much.

In the long run, success is about a student's consistent relationship with productive behaviors. She will benefit if she knows that when emotions run hot, the teacher will de-escalate them. She needs to be able to trust your hand on the rudder that steers her back to calm and productivity by the shortest route.

Think about a difficult behavior you faced recently from a student. Make a list of all of the possible reasons the student might exhibit that behavior. Assume it's the last day of school for the year and the student has come to you for advice.

What are some pieces of productive long-term guidance you could give him or her to follow to make effective decisions in similar situations in the future? If you could deliver this advice with absolute calmness and describe clear *What to Do* actions, what would you say?

_____

_____

_____

_____

The goal, of course, is to be able to provide this guidance to your students during the year. What could you do to help you be able to accomplish that?

_____

_____

_____

_____

Maintaining your *Emotional Constancy*

As you respond to the prompts in this section, also keep in mind techniques 47 (*STAR/SLANT*), 56 (*Strong Voice* "quiet power"), 57 (*What to Do*), 58 (*Positive Framing*), and 60 (*Warm/Strict*).

EMOTIONAL CONSTANCY

Approach the Student Slowly

Approaching the student who behaves improperly is a strong first step of intervention. Walking slowly displays your calm control and gives you precious time to compose yourself and choose your words carefully.

In clip FG65, you may have noticed Bridget McElduff embodying the power of *Circulating* to students with a slow, stately pace. This signaled to the student whom she was correcting that she was confident and in control of her emotions. It also modeled the calmness and civility she'd like him to respond to her correction with.

Criticize Behaviors Rather Than People

In clip FG65, Bridget McElduff doesn't tell the boy what he "is" in any manner. Rather, with *Positive Framing*, she identifies his behavior by telling him what behavior she expects and why: "it's important" for everyone to show respect. By saying this, she requires and expresses faith that he can behave better.

In clip FG69, Christy Lundy was already equipped with the understood phrase "inappropriate time" to call attention to the feud, whether or not she knew who started it or exactly what is going on. She criticizes the behavior as inappropriate rather than attempting to assign uncertain blame. She's saying, "I'm not blaming anyone for now. Just see that this fighting stops here and now."

Edit or replace these feeling statements with words that avoid judging people, and connect instead to expectations that underlie future achievement.

1. "Why are you so lazy?"

_____

2. "Why aren't you even willing to try?"

_____

3. "There's no excuse for disrespect."

_____

4. "Calvin, why are you being mean to Wendy?"

_____

5. "I can see you're not excited about math class today, but . . ."

_____

Take Your Relationship out of It

Control your own emotions rather than letting students experiment with controlling you. At times, that's what they're after. Deflect the effort and defuse emotions by framing things impersonally and focusing on expectations. Edit or replace these statements about oneself with wording based on behavioral expectations, such as "You can do better, and I expect that."

1. "This behavior makes me sad."

_____

2. "You have no idea what teaching is like."

_____

3. "Why can't I count on you?"

_____

4. "You've really let me down."

_____

Avoid Globalizing

Students learn how to succeed behaviorally by trial and error. Leave past behaviors out of the moment. Leave out saying that a student "always" does something wrong or is heading in a bad direction. Leave out whether the student may show a pattern of testing limits. Don't issue "gotchas." Issue feedback as correction. Focus on what needs to be done right now because that's what's immediately under the student's control. If it's necessary to discuss a serious pattern with the student, plan to do that at a separate, private time.

Edit or replace these feeling statements with words that avoid globalizing:

1. "You need to control your emotions!"

_____

2. "After all I've said, none of you seem to think you have to listen."

_____

3. "You two could talk all day, couldn't you?"

_____

_____

Prepare by Scripting

Look back at your earlier comments, including those under "An Emotional Laboratory—for Students." Then make a list of situations in which you are most vulnerable to losing your _Emotional Constancy_. For several, script a comment you might make to the other people involved that communicates calmness and poise and also reminds you to remain constant.

Situation: _____

_____

What I could do and say:

_____

_____

Situation: _____

_____

What I could do and say:

_____

_____

Situation: _____

_____

What I could do and say:

_____

_____

Constancy in Academic "Right and Wrong"

Emotional Constancy has applications beyond problematic student behaviors. Many teachers feel a need to label every student academic answer as either right or wrong. In our experience, that's often unnecessary. Just get on with moving students from wrong to right answers, or with building on correct ones. Show your students it isn't a huge deal if students give right or wrong answers, since you expect both when students are engaging with challenging work.

Wrong Answers: Don't Chasten or Excuse

If wrong answers are truly a normal and healthy part of the learning process, they don't require reproof or excuses. If all students are getting all questions right, the work you're giving them isn't hard enough.

Each of these teacher responses contains some element of chastening or excuse. Revise the wording to leave it out. Revise each in two possible ways that assist while also adding challenge, interest, and maybe even suspense for "Larry" and the rest of the class. In your second version, don't actually reveal whether his answer was right or wrong.

"No, Larry, we already talked about this. You have to flip the sign."

_____

_____

"That was a toughie, wasn't it, Larry. Sorry. I should have suggested you look at the sign."

_____

_____

"The first step, Larry! How can you miss it?"

_____

_____

"Class, Larry's struggling here with remembering about what we can do with signs. Are others of you in the same boat?"

_____

_____

Right Answers: Don't Flatter or Fuss

Too often, over-praising a correct answer can suggest to students that you doubted they could get it right in the first place. Too much fuss suggests surprise. And praising students for being "smart" perversely gives them an incentive *not* to take risks. By contrast, praising them for working hard motivates them to take risks and take on challenges.

Generally, when a student gets an answer correct, acknowledge that the student has done the work correctly or has worked hard, then move on: "That's right, Noah. Nice work." Of course, there will be times when you want to sprinkle in stronger praise ("Such an insightful answer, Carla. Awesome"). Just do so carefully, so that such praise isn't diluted by overuse.

Keep Moving

Think of the job of your outward emotion as keeping the learning moving forward.

View the end of a consequence (technique 55) as a fresh start. After all, you chose that consequence because you considered it a sufficient disincentive. Once the student has acquiesced, the consequence has done its job and the cycle is over. Go back to teaching in a positive manner. If the consequence wasn't sufficient, use a stronger one rather than getting angry.

Reflection

Recall some recent moment when your *Emotional Constancy* lapsed or seemed in serious peril of doing so. What student behaviors were in play? How did you respond? How might you have responded better?

_____

_____

_____

_____

THE NEXT LEVEL

1. Consider how *Threshold* might help you assess and address students' emotional states. What reminders of your *Emotional Constancy* might students appreciate hearing from you?

_____

_____

_____

EMOTIONAL CONSTANCY

2. Similar to Christy Lundy's phrase "inappropriate time," what short, *Emotionally Constant* phrases might you introduce and train your students to recognize as signals to regain their emotional equilibrium?

_____

_____

_____

3. Check and possibly improve the strength of your routines for orderly behavior when students must be out of their seats (for example, when moving to another room) or are following some instruction that requires them to interact directly with each other.

WORK WITH GROUPS AND COLLEAGUES

Indoors or outdoors, do you share responsibility for student behaviors with a co-teacher or other school staff? Arrange to talk with them about ways that you can work together to consistently run class in a calming and *Emotionally Constant* manner.

With a partner or group, take notes as you compare the following:

1. Your responses to the opening reflection. How do your challenges and responses compare with those of others in the group?
2. Your rewrites in the "*Emotional Constancy* in Academic Interactions" section. When teachers free themselves from a need to chastise, what other more productive considerations do they come up with instead?
3. Experiences with student-teacher mutual "trust" and "mistrust."
4. How you manage to park your own emotional challenges outside the classroom door.

Or, also with a partner or group, take notes as you explore along these lines:

1. Have you ever been angry or frightened as a student in the classroom? Was the teacher aware of that? What emotional steadying or control was the teacher able to give? What would have benefited you most?
2. What student behaviors push your buttons? To what extent can you change their behaviors? What helps you reestablish your own calm?
3. What consequences have you used or witnessed that give students space to cool down and regain self-control?
4. How do *Strong Voice* techniques tie in with *Emotional Constancy*?
5. Does a current class of yours pose particular challenges to *Emotional Constancy*? Invite others to describe what they might do.

Reflection

Distill some useful takeaways from your discussion with the group.

_____

_____

_____

_____

ACTION PLANNING

Use this action planner to continue your work with *Emotional Constancy*. (Find a printable version of this form at my.teachlikeachampion.com.) You know you're on the right track when you can . . .

- Collect your thoughts as you approach an intervention.
- Criticize specific behaviors, rather than globalizing, characterizing people, or calling attention to yourself.
- Use your *Emotional Constancy* to help students weather their own emotionally driven missteps.

HOW AM I DOING?

_____

_____

Design one or more action steps for improvement. Decide on an interval by which you'll revisit this page to assess your progress.

Action Step 1

By when, with whom, and how you will measure your effort

By _____, I will . . .
  <small>Date</small>

_____

_____

How Did I Do?

Successes: _____

_____

_____

_____

_____

Challenges: _____

_____

_____

_____

Next steps: _____

_____

_____

_____

Action Step 2

By when, with whom, and how you will measure your effort

By _____, I will . . .

<small>Date</small>

_____

_____

_____

How Did I Do?

Successes: _____

_____

_____

_____

Challenges: _____

_____

_____

Next steps: _____

_____

_____

OUR OBSERVATIONS ON THE CHAMPIONS

 ### Clip FG65. Bridget McElduff

Emotional Constancy is key in this clip of Bridget using a private, individual correction to address a culture breach. After approaching the boy slowly under the guise of a calm, routine *Circulate* (and using that time to plan her strategy), Bridget uses a bit of familiar *SLANT* to establish eye-to-eye contact as she steers him back into line. She avoids upping the emotional ante, escalating his snicker into frustration from herself or from the offended Precious or one of Precious's friends. Bridget is also reassuring Precious that she's in a safe, calm place where no one gets away with teasing her.

One wonders about the boy's current emotional state and how in charge of his emotions he is right now. Is he anxious about his own reading ability? Was his snickering a play for attention or approval from others in the class? Bridget may not know exactly, but she's focusing on behaviors over which she believes he has some control and reassuring him that he, too, has some space and ample ability here to govern his emotions and bring his behavior back in line.

We note overall how Bridget's *language* illustrates *Emotional Constancy,* especially her reference to a boy's behaviors, not his traits as a person and not her own feelings. She also frames the correction in terms of the cultural norms of the class, helping the student understand *why* his actions were inappropriate as well as how to show compassion to his peers in the future:

> Track me. It's important that when other [classmates] are working through something, that you're respectful and compassionate. You know this. You need to do it. Track me. Laughing is ten dollars, but I know you're going to fix it and bounce right back. Go ahead.

She doesn't make this about *her,* but about upholding a culture of respect in the classroom.

 ### Clip FG69. Christy Lundy

As Christy leads seven students in a reading lesson, two of them begin to kick each other under the table. Rather than go down the rabbit hole of determining who kicked who first, Christy refuses to engage: "Inappropriate time," she says of the behavior, followed by a quick countdown to the phrase, "You need to answer my question." Good call—not only because it tells them what to do next but also because she couldn't possibly resolve things in the moment without wrecking the lesson. Her words do not dismiss the behavior or suggest that either boy overlook it or accept a presumed attack. "Inappropriate time" suggests they'll likely have to talk about the root of the conflict later in private.

JOY FACTOR

OVERVIEW

Joy Factor is a technique that helps teachers bring more productive fun and playfulness to their class-room. It celebrates the work of learning, not by offering an antidote to academic work—that is, by saying "If we work hard, we'll get to do X as a reward"—but on the contrary, by bringing joy to the work of learning itself.

At their best, activities that are both fun and demonstrate *Joy Factor* reinforce the lesson objective and draw students into the content. *Joy Factor* also has the benefit of building students' sense of belonging to a unique school or classroom culture.

Reflection

In what ways (small, large, planned, and unplanned) do you currently try to bring joy to your classroom? What are the strengths and limitations of what you presently do?

_____

_____

_____

_____

ANALYZE THE CHAMPIONS

▶ Clip FG74. Julie Jackson, Grade 3

▶ Clip FG75. Roberto de Léon, Grade 3

View each video clip, ideally more than once, and answer the following questions. Compare your own written observations with our thoughts at the end of this technique.

How do both Julie and Roberto make academic work joyful?

_____

_____

What's different about what they do?

_____

_____

What do the two teachers say and do to build anticipation?

_____

_____

_____

FUNDAMENTALS

Finding joy in the work of learning—the *Joy Factor*—is a key driver not just of a happy classroom but of a high-achieving one. People work harder when they enjoy working on something and punctuate the work with moments of joy ("whistling," metaphorically, as they work like Disney's Snow White).

For most teachers, it's best not to try to conceive of or pull off *Joy Factor* without some planning. The idea can be impromptu, but it's often wise to jot it down when it comes to you, then take it home and plan the details, rehearse a few lines, and sharpen the plan before you open on Broadway.

Beyond the fun itself, there are three main hallmarks of a great *Joy Factor* activity:

- Like a faucet, you need to be able to quickly turn it on and off.
- We whistle while we work, making the fun part of the work, not a break from it.
- The best *Joy Factor* serves the lesson objective.

> Find this blog post at teachlikeachampion.com/blog/teaching-and-schools/tlac-clips-eric-snider-and-the-joy-of-practice/.
>
> See "Eric Snider's Joy Factor." In what ways does Eric Snider's activity meet the three characteristics of a strong *Joy Factor*?

FIVE TYPES OF *JOY FACTOR*

Fun and Games

Games draw on students' love of competition and play. You might take advantage of this by designing a contest or competition in which students solve math problems quickly or identify the speaker of a series of quotations from the novel you've just read. Your games could be individual (geography bee) or team activities (such as a relay race) and could require verbal or written participation.

If they are team based, they could pit groups of students against each other, against a clock, against an abstract standard, or, even as kindergarten teacher George Davis showed us, against the teacher. In fact, George uses games tacitly to teach his students how to win and lose: narrating relevant thoughts, such as, "I can't believe I lost—I'm so upset—no, I shouldn't be upset—I had fun playing, and I should be happy for my friends who won." This lets him develop future competitions in the confidence that students will know how to participate positively.

See if you can come up with two other game scenarios; think about how they might be adapted to make them true *Joy Factors* in your classroom:

1. _____

_____

_____

2. _____

_____

_____

Us (and Them)

There's great power in students feeling that they belong to something important, are members in a group that is distinctive and special—an "us." You can build this sense of belonging through the use of unique language, names, rituals, traditions, imaginary presences, songs, and so forth. In many cases, the more inscrutable these rituals are to outsiders, the better. Some examples:

Nicknames. Who gives you a nickname? The people who care about you and are close to you. So giving kids nicknames can show you care, notice individualities, and believe that everyone belongs. And it shows these things every time you use a nickname. If you use them, be sure to have one for every student in your class, keep them positive and fun, and make sure kids can tell you if they don't like their nickname.

Secret signals and special words. Mr. Lee's class has a "No-Lee" discussion at the end of every unit when they discuss the key ideas with "No Mr. Lee." He jokes, "If I ask can I please join you, you say: No, Mr. Lee, it's a No-Lee discussion." The secret code makes it a bit silly, but also makes the discussion belong to the class—which is the idea.

Class songs. Related to academics or culture, you take the popular song of the moment and give it new words to reflect your class culture, and all of a sudden everyone wants to sing it.

A shared myth or story. For example, before every test, refer back to a funny story you told them about your cousin Martha: "Remember my cousin Martha, who gives up when the going gets tough. Don't pull a Martha! Keep going."

Drama, Song, Chant, Movement, and Dance

"Let's all stand up and . . ." is often a good way to begin *Joy Factor*. Group song, chants, dramatic play, and movement raise spirits and also reinforce belonging. Acting things out and singing about them are great ways to remember information.

On a more or less ambitious scale, students can take part in short, scripted enactment. You see evidence of that in clip FG75, in which Roberto de Léon adds dramatic touches while teaching *Phantom of the Opera*.

Songs have many applications. For example, a song (and added gestures) in a foreign language that students are learning can let them practice, enjoy, and remember vocabulary and expressions for the rest of their lives. Other songs can help students master sequences or processes, as with the "Do-Re-Mi" song from *The Sound of Music*.

To teach chant or song:

Posterize. Write the lyrics large on poster-size paper for the class to read.

Teach a phrase at a time. Use *Call and Response.* As you call out the phrase or a line of a song, point to your ear or collar bones to signal students to listen. Then point to them to repeat. Gradually combine phrases.

Cue words or melody with gestures. In teaching a song, you can cue students that the next note goes up or down (and about how far) by holding your hand in front of you flat and parallel to the floor, raising or lowering the hand sharply as the pitch goes up or down. At the same time, slide the same hand a small distance sharply front to mark the beat.

Get tips and coaching. Ask a nearby cheer or song leader.

As the blog post shows, chants can be elevated further academically by containing changeable elements that the student must supply.

> **blog** Find this blog post at teachlikeachampion.com/blog/joy-factor-christina-fritz-skip-counting-pep-rally/.
> Watch grade 2 teacher Christina Fritz lead academic joy at "Joy Factor: Christina Fritz and the 'Skip Counting Pep Rally.'"

Reflection

What simple chants or songs do you want to try? Record a few ideas right here. Expand them on separate paper or a computer. Then practice teaching one to a mirror.

Idea:

_____

Idea:

_____

Idea:

_____

Humor

Shared laughter can strengthen and spread an environment in which happy and fulfilled students and teachers can thrive. It should always be positive. It's often especially disarming when it involves teacher stories that are slightly self-deprecating.

Here are ideas for few starting points.

Math problems and sentences for editing or correction always need protagonists. They can be stock characters (for example, "Tom Foolery") who are always doing foolish things. They can be characters from the class who do triumphant (or good-naturedly silly) things.

They can involve stories with stock characters. "I really, really don't like to talk about my cat," says Ms. Tolbert, "But she's very bright." Her students groan when she says this. Ms. Tolbert is always telling stories about how her cat mistook one vocabulary word for another—"hostility" for "hospitality," say—and thanked Ms. Tolbert's friends for their hostility after being a house guest.

"Special guests" are always a fun and funny surprise. Ms. Bellucci routinely showed up in Mr. Kramer's math classes dressed as "Aunt Sally" (as in Please Excuse My Dear Aunt Sally, a common mnemonic for order of operations). When she came, she usually left a few things behind, such as an awkward picture of Mr. Kramer as a child taped to the whiteboard, which appeared when Mr. Kramer raised the projection screen. "Oh, my," Aunt Sally said. "Now how did *that* get there?"

Suspense and Surprise

Having strong classroom routines makes occasional variations from the usual all the more fun, surprising, and memorable. Some examples:

- Occasionally hand out material (such as vocabulary words) to individual students in sealed envelopes, as you saw Julie Jackson do in clip FG74. Whisper, "Don't open them yet! Not till I say."
- Wrap something you plan to show the class (art, a map, a specimen for study) as a gift. Then build anticipation by playing at "deciding" when to open it.
- Keep referring to some future event: "Oh, man, you're gonna love the last verse of this addition song. It's really funny. If we keep working, we'll be there soon."
- One teacher we know has a "word of the week." It's always a bit of advanced technical vocabulary from her subject. If someone uses it unprompted in conversation, she rings a bell and the student wins a small prize.

Take a few minutes now to summon some ideas:

Idea(s) for surprise or suspense:

_____

_____

_____

How to extend or intensify further:

_____

_____

_____

Precisely how it or they will end:

_____

_____

_____

Sharing and Managing Joy

Shared joy needs also to be managed by teachers and by students themselves so that it can end to everyone's satisfaction rather than a chiding about coming back to order. Recognize that your job is not only to share joy but also to teach students to manage it well.

Start small. While you're still learning what works, try for little lively moments rather than massive fun-fests.

Keep *Joy Factor* activities short and embedded in the instruction. In your planning, know how you'll mindfully prepare students' expectations for the *Joy Factor* moment and how they will come back when you end it. For older children, a gentle "SLANT" can be a good way to come down quietly from a high.

Sometimes your own doubts can be self-fulfilling prophecies. If your students don't warm to your joy ideas, try selling them a little more. Also ask your peers what *they* do.

For more about managing joy, see "Case Studies in Joy" at my.teachlikeachampion.com.

THE NEXT LEVEL

Identify some version of *Joy Factor* with which currently you feel a little uncomfortable. If you can, watch others as they pull it off, live or on video. If possible, talk with them about how they prepared to do it. Push yourself to try it.

Joy Factor Case Studies

In order to perfect *Joy Factor*, it's important to continually think about how to do so. For each case here, come up with several "glows and grows." Then see our thoughts at the end of the cases.

Case 1. Ms. Green

The students are focused and working on their grammar lesson for the day—the difference between the subject and object of a sentence. Students turn in their desk work, and Ms. Green says, "That was great diligence you displayed today, University of Chicago. Let's all stand up and sing one of our favorite songs before moving on to math."

The students are all smiling, and stand up quickly and silently. They sing "I Like Big Books," a song based on a popular one whose lyrics Ms. Green modified to make it about how much students love reading. They sing in unison, loud and proud, and it goes on for a couple minutes. When they finish the song, Ms. Green silently counts to three with her fingers, and the students sit down, still grinning, and immediately get started on their math.

Glows	Grows

Case 2. Miss Violet

Miss Violet created an incentive that seemed to make her students happier and more focused. She knew they loved to compete against each other, so with good behavior, they could earn minutes at the end of class for playing Heads Up, Seven Up, or a math facts game.

JOY FACTOR

Glows	Grows

Case 3. Mr. Gold

Mr. Gold welcomes his students one by one at the *Threshold*. With some, he bumps fists; with others, he gives high-fives and back slaps. He asks one about a recent track-meet success. He gives one a serious stare-down until the student laughs and then smiles. He asks a student who is visibly upset, "What's up?" They talk for a minute and then he continues. As one student approaches, he tips his head and says, "Yo." The student smiles and enters the class.

Glows	Grows

Case 4. Mrs. Rose

In Mrs. Rose's class, a student is expected to answer her questions thoroughly and with a complete sentence. When Josh does so today, she tells the students, "We are going to give Josh a 'Roller Coaster Cheer'—ready?" They do the cheer with big smiles and giggles, not in unison, but they generally finish around the same time. They are laughing and giggling, and some students sitting next to Josh also give him a high-five or a pat on the back. Mrs. Rose begins the next part of the lesson while some students are giggling, or talking quietly. She stops and says, "If we can't handle celebrating in this class, we won't be able to do it anymore. We will just work, work, work."

Glows	Grows

Some Possible Glows and Grows

Case 1. Ms. Green

The students' behavior before and after in this case shows that singing creative Ms. Green's song inspires pride and joy, and "The faucet whistles and waters" (our mnemonic for achieving the three hallmarks of successful *Joy Factor*). A possible grow: although the song relates to language arts, the lesson may have had more to do with mastering writing and *Art of the Sentence*. If that was the case, perhaps she might tailor a song that had more academic content for that line of skills, rather than generally liking "big books."

Case 2. Miss Violet

One advantage of Miss Violet's system is that it builds in time for review and reinforcement of students' fluency with arithmetic. This ensures that review doesn't get "squeezed out" of lessons. A possible grow: this system might suggest to students that the overarching goal of a good scholar is to be well behaved as opposed to learning and engaging productively in academic work. Also, the most crucial part of the lesson (independent practice) often occurs toward the end of the lesson—so rewarding students at the end with a game (math facts or otherwise) means you shortchange students on this valuable practice.

Case 3. Mr. Gold

Mr. Gold seems to be creating positive social bonds with all the students in various ways and is personably "inviting" them in. However, the style may not really fit efficient *Threshold* if it means other students must wait as one student receives more individual time. Others may begin to behave in ways that require him to stop for them as well. Also, he may be inviting students to continue socializing with him and each other in class rather than focusing on learning. What's lost here is any connection with student performance yesterday or their readiness for today's objective. Another grow could be that his informal greetings may convey to students that it's acceptable to greet the teacher informally, as if they were speaking to a peer ("Yo").

Case 4. Mrs. Rose

Mrs. Rose is lavishing a joyful reward on a student for simply complying with her *Format Matters* expectations, thereby setting a low standard and possibly making other students think they too should be rewarded for the same. She's taking focus away from content, and her response to students' restlessness may signal that she's concerned that she's losing control, thereby reinforcing it. Her implicit threat sets up a possible dynamic of students finding other ways also to "get her goat" in an ongoing power struggle. Mrs. Rose needs to reevaluate the value of and purpose to which she's putting the cheer. One step might be to go back to much shorter, simpler forms of joy that she can control, rather than threatening no joy at all.

WORK WITH A GROUP OR COLLEAGUE

For discussion, share and compare your case study work. For any needed improvement on which the group agrees, brainstorm more solutions. Share and compare (or even try out) your ideas from "Suspense and Surprise."

Perhaps give volunteers the chance to practice teaching a chant or song that they bring to the group. Someone among you may already have methods he or she can share, or there may be a music teacher, cheerleading coach, or other individual whom volunteers can consult with ahead of time or invite to the group. Simple songs will work best here and in the classroom. An early-grade teacher might use "Rockin' Readers!" based on Chuck Berry's "Rockin' Robin." (Find printable lyrics among the online resources in your school library.)

Or plan some joy together:

1. With one member writing the ideas down, group members each announce a *Joy Factor* he or she came up with in his or her independent work, then brainstorm as a group to add more ideas.
2. As a group (or in subgroups), choose a popular one and flesh it out together as follows:
   - Name of activity
   - Purpose
   - Step-by-step instructions for

   What the activity looks and sounds like; if a song, write out the song; if a game, script the rules of the game; and so on

   How you will present the activity or teach it to students, and when you will use it
   - Estimated time
   - Materials needed
3. Try it out.
4. Collectively critique the work, allowing praise and constructive criticism. For example, you might ask:

   How well does this activity serve the purposes of *Joy Factor*?

   How would this activity best be used?

ACTION PLANNING

Use this action planner to continue your work with *Joy Factor*. (Find a printable version of this form at my.teachlikeachampion.com.) Ask yourself, Does the faucet whistle and water? (That is, are you able to quickly turn it on and off, make the fun part of the work, serve the lesson objective?)

JOY FACTOR

HOW AM I DOING?

_____

_____

Design one or more action steps for improvement. Decide on an interval by which you'll revisit this page to assess your progress.

Action Step 1

By when, with whom, and how you will measure your effort

By _____, I will . . .

Date

_____

_____

How Did I Do?

Successes: _____

_____

_____

_____

_____

Challenges: _____

_____

_____

_____

Next steps: _____

_____

_____

Action Step 2

By when, with whom, and how you will measure your effort

By _____, I will . . .
<small>Date</small>

_____

_____

_____

How Did I Do?

Successes: _____

_____

_____

_____

_____

Challenges: _____

_____

_____

_____

Next steps: _____

_____

_____

_____

OUR OBSERVATIONS ON THE CHAMPIONS

 Clip FG74. Julie Jackson, and Clip FG75, Roberto de Léon

In small-group reading, Julie creates suspense and surprise when she conceals vocabulary words in envelopes. Notice how her voice drops and a smile creeps over her face as she prepares to pass them out. As she passes them out, she asks, "Who wants the first word?" This enhances the allure of receiving a vocabulary word and creates a faux-competitive moment for them (notice that they all want to be the first to get their word). While passing them out, she warns her boys, "Don't open it, though," which further heightens their suspense as they wait.

Roberto de Léon uses physical drama and stage props to add some academically relevant joy to the lesson. He uses the Phantom's mask to draw his youngsters right into the role and get them thoroughly involved in the character's sad story.

Both teachers have put serious planning into their *Joy Factor,* then milk it for all it's worth.

Index

Page numbers in italics refer to illustrative material.

A

Academic ethos: briefly described, with list of techniques, *8*; and lesson structure, 245–301; and pacing, 303–338; and planning for success, 211–244; and setting high academic expectations, 139–210. *See also specific techniques*

Academic expectations: culture of, shifting the, the quickest and the most, technique for, 2; low or diminished, what communicates, 419; reinforcing, 281, 525. *See also* High academic expectations

Academic procedures: design criteria for, 492–493; list of, *492*

Accountability: checking for, directions that help with, 583, 584; communicating, 60; culture of, building a, 56, 80, 120, 121, 129, 139, 183, 261, 275, 279, 281, 286, 347, 349, 357, 393, 419, 420, 519; and efficiency, engineering *Turn and Talk* for, 441–442; emphasizing, for Review Now, 471; engineering lesson materials for, 237–238; mutual, 87, 441; nonverbal and verbal tools for, *281*; student peer-to-peer, 351; teacher peer-to-peer, 7; for written work, importance of, 405

Accountable independent reading (AIR) exercise: double planning, *241*; as a reading activity, 240; rollout of, case study involving, 507

Achievement, mistaking activity for, avoiding, 54

Acknowledgment: comparing, to praise, 606; determining whether or not to respond with, and what to say, 609–611; in

holding out for all-the-way right, 158; providing, 197, *281*, 347, 420, 467, 482, 509, 514, 525, 604, 633; substituting, for praise, 608

Acronyms, use of, 259, 483. *See also STAR/SLANT*

"Action Planning" framework, generic form for, accessing online, 4

Actions/behaviors: calling out, that are problematic, instead of traits, 618, 619; criticizing, rather than traits, 630, 638; reinforcing, instead of traits, 606, 633; that are visible, giving directions for, 535. *See also Behavioral entries; specific behaviors and actions*

Activity, mistaking, for achievement, avoiding, 54

Adaptability, embedding, into lesson materials, 239, 244

Addeo, Julia, 279, 286

Administrators/coaches, guidance for, 7

Affect and behavior, modeling, 519

Affirmations: blog post on, 601; offering, during *Circulate*, 281, 286; responding to right answers with questions instead of, 169. *See also Positive Framing; Precise Praise*

Affirmative Checking: analyzing the champions' use of, 81–82; and comments on the champions, 87; continuing to work with, action planner for, 84–86; fundamentals of, 82–83; next level of, 83–84; overview of, 81; planning for and rolling out, 83; reflecting on, 81; success points for, 84; video clips of, 81–82

Affirmative Checking, combining, with *Standardize the Format*, 82, 87

Alcala, Leah, 129

All Hands: analyzing the champions' use of, 322–323; continuing to work with, action planner for, 325–327; fundamentals of, 322; observations on the champions' use of, 328; overview of, 321; reflecting on, 321; scripting and practicing, 323–325; success points for, 324, 325; video clips of, 322, 328

All Hands, combining: with *Call and Response*, 322, 328; with *Change the Pace*, 322; with *Cold Call*, 322, 328; with *Wait Time*, 322, 328

All-the-way right, holding out for: by asking students to clarify during *Show Call*, 414; planning for, 159, 244; striving for, importance of, 155

Alternative activities, coming up with, 213

Alternative answers, asking for, and comparing, 116

Alternatives to apologizing: models of, 205; practicing, 205–206; rehearsing, 200–201

Ambiguity, 583

Anonymity, 71, 409, 411, 420, 525, 534, 540, 595, 604. *See also* Privacy

Anonymous individual correction (AIC), 477, 542–543, 604

Answer rollbacks, 90, 370

Answers: "almost-right," confusing, with "right" answers, avoiding, 155, 159; alternative, asking for, and comparing, 116; analyzing wrong, involving students in, 116; asking for another way of arriving at, 170; constancy in approach to both "right" and "wrong," 632–633; format of, establishing expectations for, 193; formats

HOW TO ACCESS THE ONLINE CONTENTS

To access the video clips and a collection of downloadable material, please visit:

my.teachlikeachampion.com

You will need to answer a verification question. If this is your first time visiting the site, please follow the instructions to create an account. If you experience any issues please contact us at:

teachlikeachampion@wiley.com

HOW TO USE THE DVD

SYSTEM REQUIREMENTS

PC or Mac with a DVD drive running any operating system with an HTML-compatible web browser

USING THE DVD WITH WINDOWS

To view the content on the DVD, follow these steps:

1. Insert the DVD into your computer's DVD drive.
2. Select Home.html from the list of files.
3. Read through the license agreement by clicking the License link near the top right of the interface.
4. The interface appears. Simply select the material you want to view.

IN CASE OF TROUBLE

If you experience difficulty using the DVD, please follow these steps:

1. Make sure your hardware and systems configurations conform to the systems requirements noted under "System Requirements" above.
2. Review the installation procedure for your type of hardware and operating system. It is possible to reinstall the software if necessary.

CUSTOMER CARE

If you have trouble with the DVD, please call the Wiley Product Technical Support phone number at (800) 762-2974. Outside the United States, call 1 (317) 572-3994. You can also contact Wiley Product Technical Support at http://support.wiley.com. John Wiley & Sons will provide technical support only for installation and other general quality-control items. For technical support of the applications themselves, consult the program's vendor or author.

Before calling or writing, please have the following information available:

- Type of computer and operating system
- Any error messages displayed
- Complete description of the problem

It is best if you are sitting at your computer when making the call.

MORE WAYS TO ENGAGE
AND LEARN WITH TEACH LIKE
A CHAMPION

COMPANION WEBSITE

We invite you to join the Teach Like a Champion team on our website, www
.teachlikeachampion.com, to continue the conversation through Doug's blog, free
downloadable resources, and our community forum.

TRAIN-THE-TRAINER WORKSHOPS

Uncommon School's train-the-trainer workshops prepare instructional leaders to
deliver high-quality training on *Teach Like a Champion, Reading Reconsidered,* and
Practice Perfect techniques. Participants learn both the fundamentals and subtleties
of various techniques through analysis of video clips, case studies, and live demonstrations, then apply their emerging understanding immediately in carefully designed
practice.

PLUG AND PLAYS

Designed specifically for busy instructional leaders, Uncommon Schools' Plug and
Plays provide all needed materials for two- to three-hour teacher training sessions on
specific *Teach Like a Champion* and *Reading Reconsidered* techniques. Each Plug
and Play provides leaders with ready-made PowerPoint presentations with embedded
videos of the technique in action, facilitator notes, practice activities, and handouts.
View a sample on teachlikeachampion.com.

teachlikeachampion.com